T0375331

SONGS *of* JOSEPH

SONGS of
JOSEPH

A Bible Devotional

Sing a New Song Everyday

OLABODE OSOSAMI

authorHOUSE®

AuthorHouse™
1663 Liberty Drive
Bloomington, IN 47403
www.authorhouse.com
Phone: 1-800-839-8640

© 2012 by Olabode Ososami. All rights reserved.

No part of this book may be reproduced, stored in a retrieval system, or transmitted by any means without the written permission of the author.

Published by AuthorHouse   11/20/2012

ISBN: 978-1-4772-4618-4 (sc)
ISBN: 978-1-4772-4619-1 (e)

Library of Congress Control Number: 2012922026

Any people depicted in stock imagery provided by Thinkstock are models, and such images are being used for illustrative purposes only.
Certain stock imagery © Thinkstock.

This book is printed on acid-free paper.

Because of the dynamic nature of the Internet, any web addresses or links contained in this book may have changed since publication and may no longer be valid. The views expressed in this work are solely those of the author and do not necessarily reflect the views of the publisher, and the publisher hereby disclaims any responsibility for them.

All Holy Scriptures quotations are taken from the King James version unless otherwise stated. Songs, Choruses and Hymns are in the Public Domain and authors/ composers not always recognized.

There's within my Heart a melody

There's within my heart a melody
Jesus whispers sweet and low,
Fear not, I am with thee, peace, be still,
In all of life's ebb and flow.

Refrain
Jesus, Jesus, Jesus,
Sweetest Name I know,
Fills my every longing,
Keeps me singing as I go.

All my life was wrecked by sin and strife,
Discord filled my heart with pain,
Jesus swept across the broken strings,
Stirred the slumbering chords again.

Feasting on the riches of His grace,
Resting 'neath His sheltering wing,
Always looking on His smiling face,
That is why I shout and sing.

Though sometimes He leads through waters deep,
Trials fall across the way,
Though sometimes the path seems rough and steep,
See His footprints all the way.

Soon He's coming back to welcome me,
Far beyond the starry sky;
I shall wing my flight to worlds unknown,
I shall reign with Him on high.

Words & Music: *Luther B. Bridgers, 1910. Bridgers wrote this song after a tragic fire killed his wife and three sons.*

CONTENTS

PREFACE

The life of Joseph in the wisdom of God shows how God can take a life from behind to the front . . . from nothing to something. From about the youngest in the family to the point of making all the elders bow to such a fellow. Joseph was born a son to Jacob who was a man of God of a high prophetic anointing . . . Jacob's anointing as a high level Prophet is evident in his pronouncements over his sons who became the 12 tribes of Israel. But the story of Joseph is more than just a story with a happy ending. It includes insights on the ways of God and Jesus Christ, the son of God . . . our New Testament Joseph. The story is also about a tribe that blossomed in different directions to form a great nation.

Joseph who was almost the last born of Jacob and a child of Jacob's old age grew up under such heavy unction of his father while the elder brothers went in charge of family business rearing cattle, he stayed at home with the father learning so much wisdom. Joseph grew up as a young boy under his father's open Heavens . . . and that meant a lot in structuring his life and destiny. Such preparation was so solid that he does not stagger in his integrity despite temptations hurled at him. A normal person would have fallen in Egypt and been changed by Egypt, but not Joseph. Rather he changed Egypt and started introducing change in a nation to which he was sold as a common servant. Rather than give in to temptations of immorality or unrighteousness, he called such acts wickedness in the sight of God. He brought integrity and sanity into the prison as the master in the prison entrusted into his hands the other prisoners until God now saw that he was fit to appear before the Pharaoh of Egypt. He had gone through the painful pressure of hatred from his own blood brothers to the pressure of a promiscuous mistress that was His master's wife . . . but always standing his ground in righteousness. He had dreamt that the sun, the moon and indeed his brothers would bow to him but he had to bow to others first.

He started his spiritual journey by dreaming dreams from his father's house and God graduated him into interpreting dreams in the prison as the time to meet Pharaoh came. He would not be relevant to Pharaoh as a dreamer but as an interpreter of dreams. God similarly takes us through processes to make us eventually relevant to the situations of peoples and nations we must be brought to. By the time Joseph stood before Pharaoh, he had gone through the fire of processing and came out refined enough for God to use in the destiny of Egypt - well positioned to feed other nations in the time of famine. The famine that brought the brothers of Joseph to Egypt was a global phenomenon requiring a uniquely prepared vessel. There are many similar situations in present times requiring God's uniquely prepared vessels.

Scriptures refer to God as the God of Abraham, Isaac and Jacob. There were many in the time of Abraham but still God singled him out. Abraham had two sons, Ishmael and Isaac - but God was the God of Isaac. Isaac had two sons, Jacob and Esau and God became the God of Jacob. Jacob however had twelve sons . . . who will next be next in line . . . a struggle ensues that rippled through generations. Judah according to I Chronicles 5 is to prevail over his brethren but Joseph stood out first to become a spiritual prophet that ruled over Egypt after the Pharaoh. He could prophesy and see ahead that God was still going to visit and bring them out of Egypt. Joseph initially stood out spiritually until Judah came to prevail later. Joseph began to lose ground spiritually when he brought his two sons Manasseh and Ephraim to his father Jacob for blessing and his father crossed his hand laying the right hand on the younger and the left on the elder. The Bible says Joseph was displeased and went to remove his father's hand. Perhaps, he should have asked his father why he did as he did instead of attempting to remove his father's hand. That singular act of removing his father's hand meant a lot in the spirit realm - he should have humbled himself and inquired from his father. By the time you go to Matthew Chapter 1 and Verse 2, where we saw the genealogy of Jesus, Judah prevails as the leader that will produce the Messiah. We should be careful how we deal with fathers as this could affect our future positioning.

Joseph forgave his brothers and Christ has forgiven you. But even in spite of superior blessings on Ephraim, the younger, over Manasseh—Ephraim becomes a model of carelessness in consecration and is left to join himself to idols. There are several lessons on the birthright struggles in the family and destiny of the different brothers. In the story of Joseph we see a shadow of Christ. In Goshen, we see a shadow of God's provision. In the Exodus of Egypt, Joseph's bones are eventually carried to be buried in Canaan, a shadow of God's eternity in the Heavenly Jerusalem.

This devotional has been written to augment others in encouraging and supporting the saint in the middle of God's processes to fulfill divine destiny. There are hard lessons but there are also wonderful promises to keep us holding on. The imagery of song is selected and hymns, psalms and spiritual songs—some contemporary are added to adorn meditations. You do not need to know all the tunes . . . but you can still enjoy the sublime poetry and benefit from the inspiration of matured writers who through varied spiritual experiences birthed hymns with truths that remain unforgettable.

The *Songs of Joseph* is a new song . . . a fresh integration of scriptural devotions, prayers and a compendium of songs of mercy, salvation, new beginnings, spiritual fulfillment and victory albeit as the reader goes through deep formative divine processes to make what God originally intended. We can expect as we trust and obey that our end will indeed be ultimately glorious no matter what we face because God is working His marvelous agenda. It also contains lessons that warn that rebellion comes at a heavy cost and that repentance must not be delayed any further. Be blessed as you read and sing along, daily.

INTRODUCTION

SONGS OF JOSEPH

ᴧ

A Bible Devotional

Psa 81:1 Sing aloud unto God our strength: make a joyful noise unto the God of Jacob. 2 Take a psalm, and bring hither the timbrel, the pleasant harp with the psaltery. 3 Blow up the trumpet in the new moon, in the time appointed, on our solemn feast day. 4 For this was a statute for Israel, and a law of the God of Jacob. 5 This he ordained in Joseph for a testimony, when he went out through the land of Egypt: where I heard a language that I understood not.

Joseph in the Bible stands out not only as a type of revelation of Christ but is an example with rich details of a life in which we witness different turns until God's glorious plan is fully revealed. In the study of Joseph, we do not see God advocate a quick path to bypass the processes God has preordained. Nor do we imagine we will escape the important milestones needed for our preparation. Instead we see a real man in a real world with like passions but also a glimpse into a truth that victorious living is indeed possible. If Joseph did it in the worst of circumstances and without any Mordecai to daily guide him, we are encouraged that God alone is more than sufficient.

Joseph did not compose any psalms or songs that we know . . . but I discern he had in his heart a melody that sustained him in his spirit. At the most trying periods of his life, all that men gave and could be taken away was taken from him . . . but not his song.

Excerpt from "The Glory yet to be"

While Joseph's brothers made a pile,
Young Joseph suffered for a while
That "while" did seem a lengthy season,
with no design nor rhyme, or reason.

The brothers didn't care a bit
That Joseph languished in a pit.
They showed no sorrow for his plight,
They cared not for the wrong or right.
But God was there behind the cloud!
(He does not shout His plan aloud)
The path through pit and prison led
For Joseph to the nation's head.
Not then did Joseph weep or groan,
Each step was leading to a throne!
The starving brothers soon behold
A ruler with a chain of gold.
They wept and each his breast did smite
Before one sold to Ishmaelite.
Their brother! with the power of death!
Each man fell down with bated breath.

Forgiving, Joseph understood
"Ye meant for evil God meant for good !
He did not leave me or forsake,
He knew each step I had to take.
My Shepherd led by pastures green.
No other way could there have been.
For me I proved that He is God.
Endured the dark and kissed the rod!"

Take this example from His Word!
And follow on to know the Lord.
Now through a darksome glass we see,
But oh! The glory yet to be!

Leonard Ravenhill (1907-1994)

JANUARY 1

Child of Destiny

Bible Text: Genesis 30:22-24

Gen 30:22 And God remembered Rachel, and God hearkened to her, and opened her womb 23 And she conceived, and bare a son; and said, God hath taken away my reproach: 24 And she called his name Joseph; and said, The LORD shall add to me another son.

Can God forget? Certainly not. The Bible says He has even our hair numbered and remembers the number of each. God can decide in His wisdom to turn His attention away from us . . . not just because of sin but because of His plans and great purposes that are larger than all our issues. Rachel is a woman forgotten. A woman who was not perfect—but destined to bear a very important child of destiny.

At the appointed time. At the time when Joseph was to be born . . . in the order that he was to be born into the tribe of Jacob . . . at the exact moment, God looks upon Rachel. God hearkened to her not because she prayed louder but the appointed time had come. Remember, it really did not matter what anyone thought of her cries and issues, it was time for Rachel to deliver. Joseph had to emerge.

I do not know the project you must deliver - but I sense the time has come for you to be what God has ordained even before time. It is no coincidence that you have bought this devotional to read. Your delivery will provoke changes that you cannot imagine and the devil will not be able to spoil your future.

God dismantled all the locks to the womb of Rachel and scattered all obstructions to her fertility. She conceived after many had pronounced that she could not. The impossible has become possible. Soon you will deliver a child that will be a sign and a wonder to your generation . . . a world changer. The angels and all of creation were waiting for Joseph. Instructions had been given concerning him in eternity. Indeed, this child was to be a child of destiny. God is starting something new in your life. Glory be to God.

Song

Child of destiny. Born to reign
Child of destiny. Born to rule
Fearfully made . . . wonderfully conceived
Child of destiny. Unstoppable
Child of destiny. Tried and true

All the locks are opened
The doors are opened wide
Come alive . . . the young baby cries
If only Rachel knew it was worth the wait
To have a child of destiny.

Child of destiny. Born to reign
Child of destiny. Born to rule

Prayer: O Lord bring forth your children of destiny—all over the world. Amen

JANUARY 2

Mercy said No

Bible Text: Genesis 30:22-24

Gen 30:22 And God remembered Rachel, and God hearkened to her, and opened her womb 23 And she conceived, and bare a son; and said, God hath taken away my reproach: 24 And she called his name Joseph; and said, The LORD shall add to me another son.

Joseph emerged from a situation of barrenness, delay and many hurts. The home of Laban was controversial, a place of deceit and Jacob dwells under the shadow of stolen blessings. Still the mercy of God could not be obstructed from visiting Rachel despite all misgivings. God opened that which seemed will never open. When God opens - none can close and He does not seek the permission of any to work His mercy. God will have mercy on you. As the reproach of Rachel was taken away so will yours. It was a great beginning because God was at work and had stepped in. When God steps in fully, mercy steps in and shame must step out. God is the architect of all great beginnings. Man is full of inventions and plots. You recall the plots of Jacob and his mother Rebekah. Not once in those verses is the name of God mentioned in Genesis 27:1-26. But here, God remembers, God hearkens, God opens, God takes away and then God shall add. May God master all our beginnings. I prophesy concerning someone. God remembers you. God has heard your prayers and cries. God has opened that which was considered permanently closed and God is going to give you double for all your troubles for another shall be added. What an awesome God we serve.

God adds to His work and not to the good intentions of another. His works are known to Him. There are many things God cannot add to. These must be allowed to fade away on their own. God builds on the Rock and never on sand. He is the wisest of men. Christ is the Rock of Ages. Whatever is of Christ is the best foundation ... all other ground is sinking sand. Have you given your life to Jesus Christ? If not God can add nothing to your wandering and drifting. Today as you begin afresh, remember God must build or labors are in vain. God builds on His word. Therefore be committed to start every day by reading and studying the word to get aligned with the master architect. God cannot add to that which the newspapers say or the entertainment on the screen. Tune to the frequency of God and see His divine additions manifest again and again. Remember it was mercy that initiated the story of Joseph. All agreed that Rachel deserves her barrenness given all the unfair favoritism that preferred her to the unloved Leah but mercy said NO.

Song.

A debtor to mercy alone,
Of covenant mercy I sing;
Nor fear, with Thy righteousness on,
My person and off'ring to bring.
The terrors of law and of God
With me can have nothing to do;
My Savior's obedience and blood
Hide all my transgressions from view.

The work which His goodness began
The arm of His strength will complete;
His promise is yea and amen,
And never was forfeited yet.
Things future, nor things that are now,
Not all things below or above,
Can make Him His purpose forgo,
Or sever my soul from His love.

Prayer: O Lord begin your wonderful works as your mercy touches my situation afresh. Amen

JANUARY 3

New Beginning

Bible Text: Genesis 30:25-27

Gen 30:25 And it came to pass, when Rachel had born Joseph, that Jacob said unto Laban, Send me away, that I may go unto mine own place, and to my country. 26 Give me my wives and my children, for whom I have served thee, and let me go: for thou knowest my service which I have done thee. 27 And Laban said unto him, I pray thee, if I have found favour in thine eyes, tarry: for I have learned by experience that the LORD hath blessed me for thy sake.

Every new beginning seems to have certain characteristics. You have a child of destiny . . . a new work of the Holy Spirit seeking expression. You also have the parents and midwives of the new baby—Rachel and her nurses as well as Jacob. Then you have the resistance - Laban. This is the agent of hell that says 'no' in vain to the work of God. Then there is God who blesses His own. In this new beginning all these elements were all present to play their part. It is good to recognize these forces at work.

How do you push through? We can learn from Jacob. First, there must be a challenge to the resistance of Laban. Nothing new starts without a push . . . even a new plant shoots out of the soil through stones - with a force. God must be on your side as you move with a new expression of His grace. Even Laban knew that God was with Jacob. Do not attempt anything - if you are uncertain of God's support. It is better to wait on God. Soon it will be so clear, that even the heathen see God upon you.

There is someone reading this devotional. You have prayed and found no support but God is going to send you midwives and helpers. You sense the help of God - move forward against all the wiles of Laban . . . challenge him boldly and enter where you were meant to be. God is with you . . . even Laban can see it - so what are you waiting for? It is time to move forward. The Lord of all life has come to make you free of every Laban and remove all resistance. Joseph cannot be exposed to the household of Laban. It is time for you to relocate.

Song

Lord of all being, thronèd afar, Thy glory flames from sun and star;
Center and soul of every sphere, Yet to each loving heart how near!

Sun of our life, Thy quickening ray, Sheds on our path the glow of day;
Star of our hope, Thy softened light cheers the long watches of the night.

Our midnight is Thy smile withdrawn; Our noontide is Thy gracious dawn;
Our rainbow arch, Thy mercy's sign; All, save the clouds of sin, are Thine.

Lord of all life, below, above, Whose light is truth, Whose warmth is love,
Before Thy ever blazing throne - We ask no luster of our own.

Grant us Thy truth to make us free, and kindling hearts that burn for Thee,
Till all Thy living altars claim - One holy light, one Heavenly flame.

Prayer: O Lord look upon the nations and populations in bondage . . . let there be new beginnings of freedom and change for good. Amen

JANUARY 4

Who are You Serving?

Bible Text: Genesis 30:25-27

Gen 30:25 And it came to pass, when Rachel had born Joseph, that Jacob said unto Laban, Send me away, that I may go unto mine own place, and to my country. 26 Give me my wives and my children, for whom I have served thee, and let me go: for thou knowest my service which I have done thee. 27 And Laban said unto him, I pray thee, if I have found favour in thine eyes, tarry: for I have learned by experience that the LORD hath blessed me for thy sake.

This is the time to move forward, to go on and win. Start afresh. But not without a fight. Your new song begins when you realize you must change who you are serving. Do you know everyone is serving a lord. What you serve is what you bow to, what you slave for and what you are addicted to do. Many serve sin thinking they are free. There is no one who is really free for we serve either God or Satan. Remember the children of Israel under the bondage of Pharaoh. God was going to free them to worship and serve Him . . . not to serve themselves wandering in the wilderness as most eventually did. You cannot serve two masters. Consider your life and discover what you are serving. This is important for your future glory. Again consider a lady getting married or a bachelor bidding farewell to the single life. In marriage they happily serve each other - they are not free. Nor is the man deceived into divorce free as he soon finds himself serving his lusts, passions or money or a dream that he seeks to attain. We all serve . . . none is free.

The birth of Joseph signified a time to move forward. It begins with changing your master. Christ wants to be Lord of your life and not a prop or helper. He promises that His yoke is easy and His burden is light. Freedom from Laban means higher ground and new doors. Come up. Leave sin and bondage. Today, you must decide whom to serve and who will be your Lord. Not making a choice for higher ground is to remain tied to old frustrations. Deciding to serve yourself is to commit to help the enemy of your soul. How did Jacob begin to serve Laban? He was lured by his lust to satisfy his passions . . . today the devil still uses the same baits. He knows what we want and thirst for and fashions the appropriate bait to trap whosoever he targets—but it needs not be you. Like Laban was challenged, you can challenge the place of the enemy in your life.

Christ taught us that the way to worship Him was in spirit and in truth. Jesus Christ said He is the truth. Give your life to Christ and see your destiny change from that of destruction and shame to new glory. Remember that when we worship but not according to God's pattern i.e. anyhow or anything . . . we are really worshipping the devil. Be free, today. Arise . . . put on your armor. Fight for your freedom and those of others trapped in sin.

Song.

Soldiers of Christ, arise
And put you armor,
Strong in the strength which God supplies
Thru His eternal Son.
Strong in the Lord of hosts
and in His mighty pow'r;
Who in the strength of Jesus trusts
Is more than conqueror.

Prayer: O Lord my life is full of unbearable burdens. Today I make a new choice to serve Christ. Amen

JANUARY 5

Why am I thus

Bible Text: Genesis 30:28-30

Gen 30:28 And he said, Appoint me thy wages, and I will give it.29 And he said unto him, Thou knowest how I have served thee, and how thy cattle was with me. 30 For it was little which thou hadst before I came, and it is now increased unto a multitude; and the LORD hath blessed thee since my coming: and now when shall I provide for mine own house also?

Have you noticed that whatsoever you touch seems to blossom for others - but not for you? Have you noticed that those you help to move forward seem to thrive - but you are frustrated?. Have you seen Laban grow fat and benefit from your labors? Have you asked yourself . . . am I cursed to be manipulated and dominated by others ?

Do not despair. Laban must soon release you. Not just because of you, but because of Joseph . . . the promise that you carry with you. The dreamer cannot thrive in the house of Laban. Joseph must not be influenced by Laban. It is time for your location to change. Indeed you have an anointing to excel . . . somehow you have not been permitted to benefit from it and everyone else has. But the story is about to change. Stop mourning concerning the past. If you were worthless . . . how is it that many have been blessed by your gift?

You carry a gift—a seed that causes increase and expansion for others while you are not expanded. Your beginning is tough, but it will not remain so. Things are soon going to change for you. Stop weeping. Get up and move forward. Keep challenging Laban. Ask the devil to leave you alone. Be prepared to separate from all God has appointed you to be separated from.

Song.

'Tis a point I long to know, oft it causes anxious thought;
do I love the Lord, or no? am I His, or am I not?

If I am, why am I thus? Why this dull and lifeless frame?
Hardly, sure, can they be worse, who have never heard His name!

Could my heart so hard remain, pray'r a task and burden prove;
ev'ry trifle give me pain, if I knew a Savior's love?

When I turn my eyes within, all is dark, and vain, and wild;
fill'd with unbelief and sin, can I deem myself a child?

If I pray, or hear, or read, sin is mix'd with all I do;
you that love the Lord indeed, tell me, Is it so with you?

Yet I mourn my stubborn will, find my sin, a grief, and thrall;
should I grieve for what I feel, if I did not love at all?

Could I joy His saints to meet, choose the ways I once abhorr'd,
find, at times, the promise sweet, if I did not love the Lord?

Let me love Thee more and more, if I love at all, I pray;
if I have not lov'd before, help me to begin today.

Prayer: O Lord open the eyes of and free millions dominated by Laban (i.e. sin and evil). Free many carriers of great dreams and futures living under demonic oppression and control. Amen

January 6

Night or Light

Bible Text: Genesis 30:28-30

Gen 30:28 And he said, Appoint me thy wages, and I will give it.29 And he said unto him, Thou knowest how I have served thee, and how thy cattle was with me. 30 For it was little which thou hadst before I came, and it is now increased unto a multitude; and the LORD hath blessed thee since my coming: and now when shall I provide for mine own house also?

Laban is a wicked trickster even as all he offers albeit disguised is eternal night. Do you know his tricks are still the same. His lies are still being used today. The devil asks you to name your wages but he knows you will pay a heavy cost. He changes his word and is full of craftiness pretending to want to help you. But, from the beginning he has always been a wicked slave master. Have you been lured to serve an agent of hell who has promised you great wages without describing full details of the cost? The true cost of serving Laban is to terminate the mission of Joseph. The real cost of serving agents of hell is to forgo a glorious destiny.

What will you have to show your creator on the appointed day of accounting? When will you begin to be what God has ordained you to be? Alas you have no answer - because you were occupied with serving for the wages of Laban. Do you not see how the fruits and cattle of Laban thrive? Is it not evident to you that the wicked continue to gain more ground and revival tarries. You are too busy serving Laban. See how increased are the trappings of worldliness. You have many assets purchased to maintain a high standard of living but all on credit. You contribute little to God's work—while your father's house is not cared for. You were ordained to be God's steward and not Laban's pawn.

Joseph is born into a controversy. Laban's contract must be challenged and terminated because our destiny is not eternal night and Laban cannot pay enough to compensate us to forgo God's light. Revival tarries because Laban is busy recruiting many by his baits. In this text do you notice that Laban did not pay Jacob even fair wages? Why is Jacob's house not provided for?

Today is a day for fresh discernment. Consider every contract and commitment. Is there anything you are involved in that will cost you your destiny. If there is, know that Christ is born and He has paid the price for the cancellation and annulment of that evil covenant. Come out of every secret society, strange club or fraternity. Come out of every deal in which salvation through Christ and Christ alone is denied. It's only a trap.

Song

I was born to fight devils and factions. It is my business to remove obstructions,
to cut down thorns, to fill up quagmires, and to open and make straight paths.
But if I must have some failing, let me rather speak the truth with too great severity
than once to act the hypocrite and conceal the truth.

Martin Luther

Prayer: O Lord expose all the lies of Laban fashioned to trap targets into an eternal night. Amen

JANUARY 7

What Shall I Give Thee?

Bible Text: Genesis 30:31-35

Gen 30:31 And he said, What shall I give thee? And Jacob said, Thou shalt not give me any thing: if thou wilt do this thing for me, I will again feed and keep thy flock. 32 I will pass through all thy flock to day, removing from thence all the speckled and spotted cattle, and all the brown cattle among the sheep, and the spotted and speckled among the goats: and of such shall be my hire. 33 So shall my righteousness answer for me in time to come, when it shall come for my hire before thy face: every one that is not speckled and spotted among the goats, and brown among the sheep, that shall be counted stolen with me. 34 And Laban said, Behold, I would it might be according to thy word. 35 And he removed that day the he goats that were ringstraked and spotted, and all the she goats that were speckled and spotted, and every one that had some white in it, and all the brown among the sheep, and gave them into the hand of his sons.

Laban plots an alternative destiny and asks "What shall I give thee?" This is a bribe from hell to derail your destiny. Do not receive it. Do not be tricked. Laban seeks to stop Jacob . . . even as the baby Joseph grows. God hides Joseph amidst all these games and Laban's plots to hold on to Jacob. Laban is always seeking to hold on to you—to pin you down. What is at stake is the child of destiny? Do not be deceived.

Why has Laban not offered relief until Jacob resists the oppression? Jacob answers right . . . *you shall not give me anything.* In the end, the wealth that was built on the flock of Laban was completely wiped off by a future famine. Jacob should have just got up and asked for nothing but his family. With Christ you have all things . . . everything the enemy can give you is cursed. There is no point holding on to his gifts. In the end, you will wish you said like Abram said . . . Laban devices a bait—do not fall for it.

Gen 14:22 And Abram said to the king of Sodom, I have lift up mine hand unto the LORD, the most high God, the possessor of Heaven and earth, 23 That I will not take from a thread even to a shoelatchet, and that I will not take any thing that is thine, lest thou shouldest say, I have made Abram rich:

Song

*My hope is built on nothing less
Than Jesus' blood and righteousness.
I dare not trust the sweetest frame,
But wholly trust in Jesus' Name.*

On Christ the solid Rock I stand. All other ground is sinking sand; 2ce.

*When darkness seems to hide His face,
I rest on His unchanging grace
In every high and stormy gale,
My anchor holds within the veil.*

*His oath, His covenant, His blood,
Support me in the whelming flood.
When all around my soul gives way,
He then is all my Hope and Stay.*

*When He shall come with trumpet sound,
Oh may I then in Him be found.
Dressed in His righteousness alone,
Faultless to stand before the throne.*

Prayer: O Lord destroy all the baits of Satan used to trap and deceive millions of people. Amen

JANUARY 8

Watch your Vision

Bible Text: Genesis 30:31-35

Gen 30:31 And he said, What shall I give thee? And Jacob said, Thou shalt not give me any thing: if thou wilt do this thing for me, I will again feed and keep thy flock. 32 I will pass through all thy flock to day, removing from thence all the speckled and spotted cattle, and all the brown cattle among the sheep, and the spotted and speckled among the goats: and of such shall be my hire. 33 So shall my righteousness answer for me in time to come, when it shall come for my hire before thy face: every one that is not speckled and spotted among the goats, and brown among the sheep, that shall be counted stolen with me. 34 And Laban said, Behold, I would it might be according to thy word. 35 And he removed that day the he goats that were ringstraked and spotted, and all the she goats that were speckled and spotted, and every one that had some white in it, and all the brown among the sheep, and gave them into the hand of his sons.

As Josephs grows from a baby in the cradle to a little boy, Laban continues his plots to see Jacob remain enslaved. He removes from sight that which will result in the freedom of Jacob. Let us pause to examine an important principle. The Bible says my perish for lack of vision. If we see a future glory, and catch a vision of God's revival then we will eventually be part of these events. If we envision vanity, lusts and filth often enough . . . soon we will be drawn into paths that bring these ills into our lives. What are you seeing ? What has been removed from your sight.

In future verses, Jacob counters this plot by ensuring his own cattle see what they need to see so they will produce in kind. We produce not what we wish but what we see. That is why media is an extremely powerful tool for good or for bad. Youths are glued to media, internet and mobile devices, androids and a convergence of telephony, visual and digital media to bring visions in a twenty four by seven mode. The future is being created by the creators of content which all will see and the removal of content that will lead to our freedoms from the chains of the culture. Pornography, violence and angst are disguised as harmless entertainment, innocent cartoons and TV games. As more view, the destiny of many are also altered accordingly.

Today know that you have a responsibility to watch what you see, for it will be your future. The power of media to keep billions enslaved in vanity must be fought by having more Godly content to flood the networks and shunning the viewing of that which does not glorify. If Laban's plan was not countered by Jacob's, slavery would have continued.

What is Christ urging us to see. In John 19:14 He says "Behold your King" . . . look up . . . look to Jesus. We shall eventually be like Him. We look to Jesus by looking at His word as He is the word made flesh. Jacob countered with a different strategy involving vision. You must make up your mind to start every day with the right vision founded on the word of God. Do you have a plan to complete reading the Bible in a year. Get one. Soon you will birth that which is Christ-like—a character with a renewed mind.

Song.

I see the Lord(4ce)
He is high and lifted up and His train fills the temple (2ce)
The angels cry holy (3ce)
He is the Lord.

Prayer: O Lord shut down every transmission of Laban and strengthen me to behold more of your word that I may be released into a glorious destiny. Amen

JANUARY 9

The Blessings of Esau

Bible Text: Genesis 33:1-2

Gen 33:1 And Jacob lifted up his eyes, and looked, and, behold, Esau came, and with him four hundred men. And he divided the children unto Leah, and unto Rachel, and unto the two handmaids. 2 And he put the handmaids and their children foremost, and Leah and her children after, and Rachel and Joseph hindermost.

Are we not amazed how rich Esau has become, how expanded . . . It seems something has gone wrong here. It was Jacob who stole the birthright. Jacob was told Esau would serve him. But watch this scene . . . it is Jacob that bows to Esau. Esau is so far richer and wealthier in his profanity and idolatry as Jacob wanders around frightened and uncertain of the future. It seems nothing is going to happen good to Jacob. But God has not even yet started with Jacob and Esau already thrives.

First, a blessing obtained by tricks yields the wind. The seed was craftiness, the harvest can only be a whirlwind . . . but Jacob will still be blessed . . . but from Isaac, all he has obtained is a delusion. Esau eventually reaps the fruit of his profanity and becomes Edom a tribe destined for only desolation. Jacob meets Esau—Jacob is frightened, confused and nervous. But he should have lifted up his eyes to God who loved him even from the womb. Eventually Jacob moves beyond the profane Esau and is blessed by God . . . many years later at Bethel.

Gen 35:3 And let us arise, and go up to Bethel; and I will make there an altar unto God, who answered me in the day of my distress, and was with me in the way which I went. 4 And they gave unto Jacob all the strange gods which were in their hand, and all their earrings which were in their ears; and Jacob hid them under the oak which was by Shechem. 5 And they journeyed: and the terror of God was upon the cities that were round about them, and they did not pursue after the sons of Jacob. 6 So Jacob came to Luz, which is in the land of Canaan, that is, Bethel, he and all the people that were with him. 7 And he built there an altar, and called the place Elbethel: because there God appeared unto him, when he fled from the face of his brother. 8 But Deborah Rebekah's nurse died, and she was buried beneath Bethel under an oak: and the name of it was called Allonbachuth. 9 And God appeared unto Jacob again, when he came out of Padanaram, and blessed him. 10 And God said unto him, Thy name is Jacob: thy name shall not be called any more Jacob, but Israel shall be thy name: and he called his name Israel. 11 And God said unto him, I am God Almighty: be fruitful and multiply; a nation and a company of nations shall be of thee, and kings shall come out of thy loins; 12 And the land which I gave Abraham and Isaac, to thee I will give it, and to thy seed after thee will I give the land.

Jacob does not know that the profane Esau and his 400 men are irrelevant to his future blessing. Quickly move beyond and far from Esau. Let Esau prosper quickly if it must be so - ahead of you while you wait for your Bethel. Bethel is the place of meeting with God in truth. Hold on to the sweet name of Jesus . . . while you wait on Him. Soon . . . Bethel.

Song

How sweet the Name of Jesus sounds in a believer's ear!
It soothes his sorrows, heals his wounds, and drives away his fear.

It makes the wounded spirit whole, and calms the troubled breast;
'Tis manna to the hungry soul, and to the weary, rest.

Dear Name, the Rock on which I build, my Shield and Hiding Place,
My never failing treasury, filled - with boundless stores of grace!

Prayer: Lord give us grace to wait on you and to wait for your blessing and increase. Amen

JANUARY 10

God who protects Destiny

Bible Text: Genesis 33:1-2

Gen 33:1 And Jacob lifted up his eyes, and looked, and, behold, Esau came, and with him four hundred men. And he divided the children unto Leah, and unto Rachel, and unto the two handmaids. 2 And he put the handmaids and their children foremost, and Leah and her children after, and Rachel and Joseph hindermost.

Jacob escapes from Laban but must still face Esau. How many past action stand to haunt our future. Jacob prepares for the worst and puts Joseph behind to protect his safety. Jacob means well but he may not know that the destiny of Joseph is already secure in God. No harm can come to you because of your destiny. If they knew why Jacob came up with this arrangement, all these actions would surely have annoyed the brothers of Jacob and inflamed resentment in the family against Joseph.

Do you know that God can arrange to have you at the back only to protect you and His destiny for your life? Do you not see that a glorious destiny needs time and care. It needs to be protected when it glows in uncertain embers and is yet to blaze as a sure flame. When old hurts and errors rage against the flame of God, God must conceal His chosen ones. Even as Jesus in infancy was hidden in Egypt from a murderous Herod . . . consider that your delayed emergence and times of being kept at the back could be part of God's plan. Joseph was special and so are you. God must make you ready and prepare you to be what He has ordained. You cannot be put in situations of early risky battles and unpredictable circumstances.

Reflect on the truth that God is the ultimate sponsor and guardian of His glorious destiny in your life. A life that is not prepared and protected by God is useless to God. Joseph is a young vulnerable lad. If Esau needed a target to avenge Jacob's deceit, Joseph would have been ideal to aim for. Those who do great things for God know that the glory must return to the one who kept them, helped them, hid them. There are no self-made Generals of God only prepared servants. Today is a day to thank God for so many unseen mercies to protect and hide you from harm. Many were sacrificed so that you would be still intact to be what God has promised you. Many are pushed ahead of you only to shield you from devastation. The one who carries Christ cannot be conquered even when He is not yet ready for certain battles - destroying temptations are kept away from him. Thank God and praise Him. Appreciate His process. Remember that when you find yourself still standing ages after others failed - it was God's protective hand at work to preserve you. Thank Him again and again. Remember when you reign with Him. It was Him that did it all. On your own you would not have stood a chance. Joseph was preserved by God.

Song

Praise to the Lord, who doth prosper thy work and defend thee,
Surely His goodness and mercy here daily attend thee;
Ponder anew what the Almighty can do,
If with His love He befriend thee.

Prayer: I praise you the Almighty God who defends me and causes my work to prosper. Help me never to stop praising you especially when I do not understand your strange preservations. Amen

JANUARY 11

A Different Upbringing

Bible Text: Genesis 37:1-3

Gen 37:1 And Jacob dwelt in the land wherein his father was a stranger, in the land of Canaan. 2 These are the generations of Jacob. Joseph, being seventeen years old, was feeding the flock with his brethren; and the lad was with the sons of Bilhah, and with the sons of Zilpah, his father's wives: and Joseph brought unto his father their evil report. 3 Now Israel loved Joseph more than all his children, because he was the son of his old age: and he made him a coat of many colors.

Joseph and Jacob become inseparable. While others are on the fields—Joseph has a different upbringing. Jacob is a deeply spiritual man who has learnt a lot of bitter lessons. He teaches Joseph the old truths. He explains the deep and narrow way of Jehovah, the jealous God. Joseph has a lot to learn in a very short time and is immersed at home. What Joseph knows is not the same as what his brothers know. His understanding is made different. His perspective is made completely different. Joseph was always with their father, occasionally going out but only to bring back evil reports. His brothers see him as definitely unfairly favored.

Perhaps your early upbringing is peculiar and different. Your way of looking at things is very different from others. Joseph will need his different upbringing in the pit. Joseph will need his different outlook in the house of Potiphar. Joseph will need the lessons of Jacob when forgotten in jail for two full years. The wisdom and friendship to an old man is not in vain . . . it will yield something different. Joseph did not have an ordinary upbringing. He was the best friend of a deeply spiritual old man. Joseph was only seventeen but had a mind that was decades ahead of the others who preferred to be in the fields than listen to an old man. But it had a reason . . . it all had a reason. There is a purpose to everything you have gone through. It is no coincidence that you did not fit in to play with your colleagues. Rejoice in your uniqueness. God has a special purpose for your life. Teach me to love to be with you JESUS . . . to love your company . . . to learn from you. Teach me to enjoy and appreciate my uniqueness. There were times when Joseph must have preferred to play around with others. The company of Jacob is boring but it was required for His destiny. Be drawn closer to Jesus. Come apart and spend more time with Him for present and future strength.

Song

I come to the garden alone
While the dew is still on the roses
And the voice I hear falling on my ear
The Son of God discloses.

And He walks with me, and He talks with me,
And He tells me I am His own;
And the joy we share as we tarry there,
None other has ever known.

He speaks, and the sound of His voice,
Is so sweet the birds hush their singing,
And the melody that He gave to me
Within my heart is ringing.

I'd stay in the garden with Him
Though the night around me be falling,
But He bids me go; through the voice of woe
His voice to me is calling.

Prayer: O Lord draw your saints all over the world to you . . . to learn of you . . . to love you. Amen

JANUARY 12

Uncommon Favor

Bible Text: Genesis 37:1-3

Gen 37:1 And Jacob dwelt in the land wherein his father was a stranger, in the land of Canaan. 2 These are the generations of Jacob. Joseph, being seventeen years old, was feeding the flock with his brethren; and the lad was with the sons of Bilhah, and with the sons of Zilpah, his father's wives: and Joseph brought unto his father their evil report. 3 Now Israel loved Joseph more than all his children, because he was the son of his old age: and he made him a coat of many colors.

Joseph is now seventeen and he walked in uncommon favor. He was not the youngest, and Benjamin was born after him. Still he enjoyed an uncommon favor even from the beginning. He saw the evil that his brothers did and brought back the plots of his elder brethren. He was given a coat of many colors by his father Jacob. Though uncommonly favored no one had an idea of the glory ahead for Joseph. It seemed to his brothers that Joseph may inherit the wealth of their clever father or the blessings of the first son. Jacob would find some way to give him an advantage. But God knew all the wealth and substance of Jacob will be exhausted in the famine that was coming.

Be encouraged. What God has prepared ahead is far ahead of what your enemies are incensed about. There is an untouchable destiny and position that men cannot in any way pull down. The future glory that will be yours has not been exposed to your brothers. Do you see that everything man can give other men can be and will be taken away? Joseph had a preferred position given to him by Jacob in the household. He lost that to become a slave in Egypt. Joseph had a coat of many colors given to him by his doting father. He also lost that and the coat ended up torn and stained with blood to deceive his father. But there are gifts that men did not give Joseph. Joseph could see the unseen . . . he had an access to the secrets and wisdom of God . . . God gave him answers when others had questions. These were not taken from him because they could not be taken.

Rejoice if men have taken anything from you. It only reveals that men gave them to you. Instead there are gifts of faith, discernment, wisdom . . . talents from God for His favored servants. Even the earthy life of Jesus that came through Mary was released to be taken by the other men who crucified Him. But none could take from Jesus the position next to the father that was always His even from the beginning.

A life with Christ is a favored life not because we have no trials and we do not lose things. But because we are gifted from Heaven. If earthly fathers know how to spoil their favored sons with gifts, imagine what God who has no limitation in resources is able to do for His beloved ones. To be a Christian is to enjoy unfair advantages. Anything men have offered you pales into insignificance and one day will be taken by other men. To be a Christian is to be positioned to receive many things from God that others will not be given and that cannot be taken by men. But ponder today, what does God want in return for showering you with so many undeserved gifts? He asks us to go and share the good news. Have you gone?

Song

And I have brought to thee, Down from my home above,
Salvation full and free, My pardon and my love.
I bring rich gifts to thee;
What has thou brought to me?

Prayer: O Lord help me realize the need for me to serve you even more. Amen

JANUARY 13

Alone with God

Bible Text: Genesis 37:4-5

Gen 37:4 And when his brethren saw that their father loved him more than all his brethren they hated him, and could not speak peaceably unto him. Gen 37:5 And Joseph dreamed a dream, and he told it his brethren: and they hated him yet the more.

Communication is very important and the ability to interact peaceably with others is a great blessing. Joseph and his brothers could not communicate . . . this was perhaps because he thought and spoke like his father. It was clear that Joseph thought differently from his brothers. He shared little in common with his brothers. There was always a tension when Joseph was around but this was preordained to be so. Joseph had to be different because of his different destiny.

There was no one to speak peace to Joseph but his father. Joseph did not hate his brothers. But what Joseph missed in camaraderie with his brothers was made up by long and late evening conversations with a father that loved him dearly. There is someone reading this devotional . . . you have spent so much time with God and become so much like God . . . and that has cost you the friendship and understanding of men. You have learnt to live alone. God comforted Joseph. You have no one to talk to . . . but you have God . . . He will listen. He is waiting. He will also cause even your enemies to be at peace with you. Joseph did not have this grace. But it was part of his training and preparation. It was needful that Joseph would be hated and thrown into a pit that would move him to where he would rule and save his brothers from a famine. Meanwhile, there were to be no peaceable words for Joseph. Joseph was prepared to be forgotten in an Egyptian prison. He was accustomed to rejection and being ignored and learnt to receive harsh words without speaking back. Be still. Let God finish shaping you to be his masterpiece. Jesus was also alone in his toughest moments . . . and was later glorified above all of creation. Jesus was scorned, derided and denied of peaceable words for us . . . for our salvation. Go and talk to Jesus—He does not scorn or make fun of you, instead He waits for you.

Song

My song is love unknown, my Savior's love to me;
Love to the loveless shown, that they might lovely be.
O who am I, that for my sake my Lord should take, frail flesh and die?

He came from His blest throne salvation to bestow;
But men made strange, and none the longed for Christ would know:
But O! my Friend, my Friend indeed, who at my need His life did spend.

Sometimes they strew His way, and His sweet praises sing;
Resounding all the day hosannas to their King:
Then "Crucify!" is all their breath, and for His death they thirst and cry.

Why, what hath my Lord done? what makes this rage and spite?
He made the lame to run, He gave the blind their sight,
Sweet injuries! Yet they at these - themselves displease, and 'gainst Him rise.

Prayer: Lord release the grace to obey and love you in unfriendly situations. Grant this grace to your missionaries in strange lands. More grace to laborers who must serve amongst hostile brethren. Amen

JANUARY 14

Hated with a Passion

Bible Text: Genesis 37:4-5

Gen 37:4 And when his brethren saw that their father loved him more than all his brethren they hated him, and could not speak peaceably unto him. Gen 37:5 And Joseph dreamed a dream, and he told it his brethren: and they hated him yet the more.

The hatred for the Christian is motivated by the special love and protections available only to God's chosen. There is good reason for it. From the beginning, the Bible says the Devil led a mutiny to protest against the authority of God resulting in being banished with an army of fallen angels. A place without any opportunity for repentance in eternal damnation now awaits them. This appears unfair. Why have ordinary men been given the opportunity to fail, rebel repetitively and then the chance to repent? Why is man so favored by God? This is a deep mystery that none has been able to unravel ? Why does God fuss so much over man ? Angels are mystified at the mercies reserved for man.

Job_7:17 What is man, that thou shouldest magnify him? and that thou shouldest set thine heart upon him? Psa_8:4 What is man, that thou art mindful of him? and the son of man, that thou visitest him? Psa_144:3 LORD, what is man, that thou takest knowledge of him! or the son of man, that thou makest account of him!

Legions of demons, fallen hosts and wicked trinity of the devil, antichrist and false prophet also ask these questions but with unbridled hatred. Instructions are given from hell that man must be continually attacked to bring shame to the creator. The favored ones in Christ are to be specially hated because of the favor they enjoy.

Today, let your thoughts reflect on this hatred and what it means. The Bible says we should rejoice when we are targeted wickedly for the truth we bear as this gives testimony to our identity in Christ. The story of Joseph reveals that this hatred had value as God used it to cause the brothers of Joseph to release him into a far more glorious destiny than would have been achieved even if he inherited all the cattle and lands of Jacob. If they knew they were helping Joseph by selling him to Ishmaelites they would not have done so. If they knew they were moving Christ forward into His glorious destiny to defeat principalities and powers and be with God in glory, they would have left Him alone. We need help to react well to hatred so as not to miss the realization of great blessings especially reserved for the hated.

Instead, we must pray for our enemies to do what God has empowered them to do . . . and do it quickly. Thank God that all things including things done in hatred must all work together for the good of those in Christ. If you are not in Christ, what are you still waiting for ? Come to Him today.

Song.

'Tis mystery all the immortal dies! Who can explore His strange designs?
In vain the first born seraph tries to sound the depth of love divine!

'Tis mercy all! Let earth adore
Let angel minds inquire no more.

Prayer: In an environment of hostility, Joseph receives dreams of glory. Lord may I remain positioned not to miss the dreams you are giving me. Amen

JANUARY 15

Born to Reign

Bible Text: Genesis 37:10-11

Gen 37:10 And he told it to his father, and to his brethren: and his father rebuked him, and said unto him, What is this dream that thou hast dreamed? Shall I and thy mother and thy brethren indeed come to bow down ourselves to thee to the earth? 11 And his brethren envied him; but his father observed the saying.

Is there a day coming when every knee shall bow to Jesus. That is what the Bible says. It does sound somewhat unrealistic . . . every man that has ever existed. Every Chinese, Indian, American, Africa, white or black, good or bad, every monarch, every prime minister, every dictator, every criminal, every pope, every pastor, every servant or master. Everyone will one day realize that Jesus and no one else is Lord.

We are in times when there is a dangerous teaching that says without Christ, God will grant salvation by other means. Even Jacob wonders how all the older brethren and parents of Joseph will bow to him.

Indeed, the earthly parents will bow . . . all the older prophets—good and evil - that came before will bow. Jezebel will bow, Mohammed will bow, Ahab will bow . . . there will be no exceptions. We can ether bow now or bow later. This revelation was not welcomed and it may have been unwise for Joseph to share it.

But it is an important truth for us as we are joint-heirs with Christ. One day we shall reign with Him. How then are we to prepare if one day we shall be co-rulers sometime in God's eternity.

The attitude of a future King will irritate those who do not understand this destiny. Have you watched all the fuss and attention that is given to future kings even when this is uncertain. Have you seen the great care in conduct not to bring the throne to shame? May God equip us to see our destiny as co-heirs with Christ then we will pay the price in self-discipline and sacrifice. Reflect this day on how your ways do not reflect well on the throne and adjustments you need to make to prepare you for monarchy in Christ. You could have the martyr's crown and your name in the book of kings . . . Christ being the King of kings. Will you make yourself ready?.

Song

The saints of old were beaten, tried. Condemned and even crucified.
These martyr men beat no retreat when flames were licking at their feet.
They saw the tyrant's brandished steel, But still they offered no appeal.
They struck no bargain for their lives; For their children or their wives.
All slowly roasted in the flames while angels wrote each of their names
Within a book God calls His own to be proclaimed before His throne.
Then we shall know of these renown when each receives his martyr's crown,
When God shall say to these "Well done" You ran the race, pressed on and won.
When in that race men said "Insane" but now I gladly own your name
Now you are home! Come dwell with Me - in my joy through all eternity.
                                   Leonard Ravenhill

Prayer: O Lord, may I not miss my place in the throne room. Let me not miss my crown. Amen

JANUARY 16

Rebuked

Bible Text: Genesis 37:10-11

Gen 37:10 And he told it to his father, and to his brethren: and his father rebuked him, and said unto him, What is this dream that thou hast dreamed? Shall I and thy mother and thy brethren indeed come to bow down ourselves to thee to the earth? 11 And his brethren envied him; but his father observed the saying.

Joseph was rebuked by his father. Many times we must be rebuked for going ahead of our timing. We must be rebuked for saying things we have not been told to say. Many things that are true are not yet to be said. And for many messages the timing is not right. May God help us to have seasoned speech that will not create unnecessary tensions. Joseph was rebuked by a father that loved him deeply. There are many times that God must rebuke His beloved children. When last did you sense the rebuke of your father? We are not told that Jacob rebuked his other children . . . not even once. It seems that they were all fine . . . but there is a record of Jacob rebuking Joseph. We are not even told that when Joseph reported his brothers that Jacob rebuked them. Indeed, it is strange that there is no other reported instance of Jacob rebuking any of his other sons.

Heb 12:6 For whom the Lord loveth he chasteneth, and scourgeth every son whom he receiveth. 7 If ye endure chastening, God dealeth with you as with sons; for what son is he whom the father chasteneth not? 8 But if ye be without chastisement, whereof all are partakers, then are ye bastards, and not sons.

Joseph endured the rebuke of his father. Rebuke and chastening is a sign of love. When it is mentioned in this remarkable way . . . it only indicates a greater love that Jacob has for Joseph. It is not always so easy to endure chastening . . . and scourging is painful. But this is the evidence of son-ship. You cannot be allowed to stray out of destiny. You are different and must be sternly rebuked when you miss your timing . . . your tongue must indeed first and foremost be trained. We must learn silence until God by His Spirit tells us to speak. Jacob knew Joseph had a lot to learn. He knew his words were too unguarded. Jacob saw the reaction to Joseph's words and pretended to be very tough - silencing Joseph very sternly. But the Bible says he observed the words. He did not dismiss the words of Joseph as nonsense although he spoke harshly to Joseph in the presence of his brothers. May God give us wisdom. When were you rebuked last? Did you take it well? It was wise that you were strongly and openly rebuked while others are not. You are different.

Song

Nearer, my God, to Thee, nearer to Thee!
E'en though it be a cross that raiseth me,
Still all my song shall be, nearer, my God, to Thee.

Though like the wanderer, the sun gone down,
Darkness be over me, my rest a stone.
Yet in my dreams I'd be nearer, my God to Thee.

There let the way appear, steps unto Heav'n;
All that Thou sendest me, in mercy given;
Angels to beckon me nearer, my God, to Thee.

Then, with my waking thoughts bright with Thy praise,
Out of my stony griefs Bethel I'll raise;
So by my woes to be nearer, my God, to Thee.

Prayer: O Lord, strengthen your saints at times when the Lord ordains rebuke and chastening. Amen

JANUARY 17

Is it well?

Bible Text: Genesis 37:12-14

Gen 37:12 And his brethren went to feed their father's flock in Shechem. 13 And Israel said unto Joseph, Do not thy brethren feed the flock in Shechem? come, and I will send thee unto them. And he said to him, Here am I. 14 And he said to him, Go, I pray thee, see whether it be well with thy brethren, and well with the flocks; and bring me word again. So he sent him out of the vale of Hebron, and he came to Shechem.

Is it well with you? Does God really care? Is God some distant super being that is not touched by our failings? David wrote so many poems to express his great surprise on how and why God cares so much for mankind. David knew how wicked all of humanity was. Still, God misses our company and is saddened by our wanderings. He is grieved by our disobedience and scandals. God forgives us when he has all the evidence of our misdeeds while men hate us just out of speculations.

Is it well with you? How will you answer that question. Perhaps you will answer based on your memories and disappointments or you will answer based on the present challenges you face or you will answer thinking about a bill that cannot be paid or you will let someone answer for you. In this story, from the perspective of God . . . everything was ok. All His plans were about to happen as He had planned it would be. As far as God was concerned all was well . . . it will soon be time for Joseph to be sent to Egypt . . . as a slave . . . to be sold to the house of Potiphar. Has your destiny been tampered with? Is it well?

Is it well with you? How is your faith? How is your prayer life? How is your family life? How is your marriage? How is your ministry? Is it well with your nation? How do you know when it is well? It seems when God's purpose is intact and the child of destiny is exactly where he should be . . . then it is well. God dwells in eternity and declares it is well with the righteous but not to the wicked. If you are not on the way to Heaven then it is not well. Let the word of God search your heart.

Isa 3:10 Say ye to the righteous, that it shall be well with him: for they shall eat the fruit of their doings. 11 Woe unto the wicked! it shall be ill with him: for the reward of his hands shall be given him.

Song

Through the love of God our Savior, All will be well,
Free and changeless is His favour; All, all is well.
Precious is the blood that healed us, Perfect is the grace that sealed us,
Strong the hand stretched forth to shield us, All must be well.

Though we pass through tribulation. All will be well.
Ours is such a full salvation; All, all is well.
Happy, still in God confiding, Fruitful, if in Christ abiding,
Holy, through the Spirit's guiding, All must be well.

We expect a bright to-morrow; All will be well,
Faith can sing through days of sorrow, All, all is well.
On our Father's love relying, Christ our every need supplying,
Whether living now, or dying, All must be well.

Prayer: Lord, controller of the universe—as we dwell in Jesus - our righteousness, let all be well with us. Amen

JANUARY 18

Who shall I send?

Bible Text: Genesis 37:12-14

Gen 37:12 And his brethren went to feed their father's flock in Shechem. 13 And Israel said unto Joseph, Do not thy brethren feed the flock in Shechem? come, and I will send thee unto them. And he said to him, Here am I. 14 And he said to him, Go, I pray thee, see whether it be well with thy brethren, and well with the flocks; and bring me word again. So he sent him out of the vale of Hebron, and he came to Shechem.

Jacob still missed his sons - as mischievous as they may be. Like the father of the prodigal son, God awaits and pines for reconciliation with His own. Do not for a minute imagine that God has adjusted to the fact that we are in sin. He is not. Rather, He wants us back home with Him. Jacob sent Joseph to find out the situation and confirm that all was well with his sons. They must have delayed in their return and he wondered if they were fine. God loves you even in your wanderings and misses you. He sent Christ His only begotten son to be crucified for us, to seek us out and save us. Christ was not welcomed by the Jews just as Joseph was despised. Concerning Christ, the Bible says He was despised and rejected, a man of sorrows and acquainted with grief. Joseph was accustomed to the poor treatment constantly received in the hands of his brothers. Yet, he says . . . yes . . . here I am. Father, send me.

God seeks who He will send to troubled situations, to the people He misses and needs to return home. But the journey of spreading the gospel is also the journey that links to destiny. Refusing to respond to the call to go and remain in places we are not welcome does not permit other important events that must happen. If Joseph had presented an excuse claiming the distance was far and dangerous, saying he was unsure of their location etc., Joseph may have died in Israel as a nobody. Ponder over these thoughts and you will understand the true cost of disobedience.

Jeremiah, Isaiah, Ezekiel and others heard this call and went. David was sent with provisions for his brother in battle . . . he was taunted and abused as he arrived. But this errand introduced him to his famous encounter with Goliath the gatemen at his destiny to be king. The pattern is repeated over and over again. The entrance to destiny is disguised as a tough call that most will normally decline. How will you respond? Do not judge the call of God only by prevailing circumstance for you do not know what the next moment brings.

The words "Here am I—send me" will push you farther in the right direction and deliver you from more wanderings and bondage than a billion other prayers. Remember David said "Is there not a cause?". Although he had already obeyed Jesse to go to his brothers before he eventually perceived the cause. There is a reason, there is a cause attached to your destiny. Soon you will discover it. Go first . . . the cause comes later.

Song

Lead me Lord, I will follow. Lead me Lord I will go
You have called me. I will answer. Lead me Lord, I will go.

Prayer: Lord, help me to hear and respond appropriately and obediently to your call. Indeed, obedience is the key that unlocks my future destiny. Amen

JANUARY 19

Wandering

Bible Text: Genesis 37:15-17

Gen 37:15 And a certain man found him, and, behold, he was wandering in the field: and the man asked him, saying, What seekest thou? 16 And he said, I seek my brethren: tell me, I pray thee, where they feed their flocks. 17 And the man said, They are departed hence; for I heard them say, Let us go to Dothan. And Joseph went after his brethren, and found them in Dothan.

To wander is to lose your way and be heading not in the direction you intended. How many of us wander? In ministry we can wander? We can wander in our business pursuits? Our so called walk with God can in reality be nothing but wanderings? May God help us. We mean well . . . but alas we only wander. Joseph was anointed . . . a child of destiny sent and who went obediently but soon found himself wandering. But do not despair, just as God did not leave Joseph to continue in his wanderings . . . you will not be left alone to just wander aimlessly. But it is better than to be disobedient in refusing to go the long distance uncertain of the journey. God will lead you, God will help you. God will guide you. God will locate you.

Joseph was not used to the field . . . he was a man of the home . . . he understood the depths, valleys and mountains of his father's thoughts but did not know the way to the fields . . . nor was he accustomed with the route and ways of his brethren. Do you know that you cannot have it all? The one who is close to God and buried in His word will sacrifice familiarity with other things. He is powerful and yet so vulnerable. He is strong and yet so weak. He is a man who must depend on the helper—the Holy Spirit. He cannot depend on the Holy Spirit for certain things and for others lean on his understanding. On the field without help from the God he knows . . . he is often found wandering. Many children of God are said to be earthly useless. This is not so, but they are not self-made they are God made and God dependent. They do not go without help from God . . . they must be helped by the Holy Spirit or they will be drifting foolishly of no use to God or men. Holy Spirit, help my wanderings.

Song.

Spirit divine, attend our prayer,
And make our heart Thy home;
Descend with all Thy gracious power;
Come, Holy Spirit, come.

Come as the light! to us reveal
The truth we long to know;
Reveal the narrow path of right,
The way of duty show.

Come as the fire and purge our hearts
Like sacrificial flame,
Till our whole souls an offering be
In love's redeeming name.

Come as the dew, and sweetly bless
This consecrated hour;
May barrenness rejoice to own
Thy fertilizing power.

Prayer: O Lord, help us to depend always on you. Amen.

A Certain Helper

Bible Text: Genesis 37:15-17

Gen 37:15 And a certain man found him, and, behold, he was wandering in the field: and the man asked him, saying, What seekest thou? 16 And he said, I seek my brethren: tell me, I pray thee, where they feed their flocks. 17 And the man said, They are departed hence; for I heard them say, Let us go to Dothan. And Joseph went after his brethren, and found them in Dothan.

A certain man found Joseph and not vice versa. Help has been sent ahead to assist every decision to honor and obey God. His name was not mentioned, but the Bible gives the impression that this man was also sent to locate Joseph to help him. Who is this man in our walk of faith?

Joh_14:26 But the Comforter, which is the Holy Ghost, whom the Father will send in my name, he shall teach you all things, and bring all things to your remembrance, whatsoever I have said unto you.

The Holy Ghost is sent by the Father in the name of Jesus Christ. He knows all the ways and paths and must be sent and He finds His poor wanderer in need of comfort. The Holy Ghost knows the path of obedience and will be there to locate you and give you all the comfort and help that you require to come back. Like Joseph, you may be full of doubts concerning the awkward assignment you suddenly find yourself in and wonder where help and comfort will come. The Omniscience of God is revealed through the counsel of the Holy Ghost. No wonder, Christ warns His disciples to go and wait in the upper chamber until the day of visitation of the Holy Ghost fully.

Many things are done without the Holy Ghost but they are not just often fruitless but do not lead to the glory prepared ahead. We must praise and thank God, because the glorious destiny designed for our life is also fully helped by God Himself. No one will achieve anything close to the preplanned glory - without the certain man. Did you notice that it seemed that this man only ushered Joseph into more troubles and indeed many suggest Joseph may have been delivered from the pit if he had missed the certain man. It would have been a wrong deliverance to be rescued from the help of the Holy Ghost to die to self and our schemes. Still many have embraced this deliverance and rejoice in their folly.

Reflect on this devotional to establish that you walk with the direction of the Holy Ghost. You need to be more than familiar with scripture to know that the Holy Ghost will not deny the word of God which asks us to also test the spirits if they be of God. Also, when the Holy Ghost asks "what seekest thou?" . . . the answer will not be that you seek your selfish wants and desires but first and foremost, the salvation of your brothers. Help did not come to Joseph to be connected to the path of his destiny until he got this answer right. The Holy Ghost is still asking before repositioning you for greatness. "*What seekest thou?*".

Song.

Once it was the blessing, Now it is the Lord; Once it was the feeling, Now it is His Word;
Once His gift I wanted, Now, the Giver own; Once I sought for healing, Now Himself alone.
Once it was my working, His it hence shall be; Once I tried to use Him, Now He uses me;
Once the pow'r I wanted, Now the Mighty One; Once for self I labored, Now for Him alone.

Prayer: O Lord, as I refocus on lost souls and my divine assignments. Send help to comfort and guide me. Amen

JANUARY 21

Divine Conspiracy

Bible Text: Genesis 37:18-24

Gen 37:18 And when they saw him afar off, even before he came near unto them, they conspired against him to slay him. 19 And they said one to another, Behold, this dreamer cometh. 20 Come now therefore, and let us slay him, and cast him into some pit, and we will say, Some evil beast hath devoured him: and we shall see what will become of his dreams. 21 And Reuben heard it, and he delivered him out of their hands; and said, Let us not kill him. 22 And Reuben said unto them, Shed no blood, but cast him into this pit that is in the wilderness, and lay no hand upon him; that he might rid him out of their hands, to deliver him to his father again. 23 And it came to pass, when Joseph was come unto his brethren, that they stript Joseph out of his coat, his coat of many colours that was on him; 24 And they took him, and cast him into a pit: and the pit was empty, there was no water in it

Reuben stands out to speak out that Joseph's life be spared. Even from afar they conspired for his destruction. What kind of hatred could this be that wanted Joseph dead. But this was a supernatural situation . . . . God wanted Joseph in a pit and prepared to be sent to Egypt. Jacob would not have released Joseph into Egypt even if a thousand angels appeared to him. God knows what to do. He would use the hatred of Joseph's brothers to achieve His purpose.

To conspire against brethren is evil. Envy and bitterness are horrible vices before God. But this time, the conspiracy to send Joseph to the pit was needed. This scene is so much like the stripping of our Lord Jesus as our Lord is put on the cross. Again a conspiracy that God required for the salvation of all mankind. So similar to Joseph who also must suffer a wicked conspiracy that he may be used to save the entire tribe from a future famine. This is one of the earliest pictures of the passion of Christ. The helpless Joseph is not said to resist . . . indeed he was like a lamb that went to the slaughter . . . on a mission to seek after their welfare only to be attacked and thrown into a pit.

The Bible says blessed are you when you are innocent in conspiracy because of your faith. It is a rare privilege to suffer in this form for Christ. Be encouraged. God will see you through. He knows all about your struggles. But do not suffer for your own foolishness and wickedness.

Mat 5:11 Blessed are ye, when men shall revile you, and persecute you, and shall say all manner of evil against you falsely, for my sake. 12 Rejoice, and be exceeding glad: for great is your reward in Heaven: for so persecuted they the prophets which were before you.

Song

My Lord knows the way in the wilderness,
all I have to do is to follow

Prayer: O Lord, bless your missionaries in nations where Christians are brutally persecuted. Lord watch over them. Lord help us all not to abandon our posts. Amen

JANUARY 22

The Pit is Dry

Bible Text: Genesis 37:18-24

Gen 37:18 And when they saw him afar off, even before he came near unto them, they conspired against him to slay him. 19 And they said one to another, Behold, this dreamer cometh. 20 Come now therefore, and let us slay him, and cast him into some pit, and we will say, Some evil beast hath devoured him: and we shall see what will become of his dreams. 21 And Reuben heard it, and he delivered him out of their hands; and said, Let us not kill him. 22 And Reuben said unto them, Shed no blood, but cast him into this pit that is in the wilderness, and lay no hand upon him; that he might rid him out of their hands, to deliver him to his father again. 23 And it came to pass, when Joseph was come unto his brethren, that they stript Joseph out of his coat, his coat of many colors that was on him; 24 And they took him, and cast him into a pit: and the pit was empty, there was no water in it

In this devotional, reflect on the truth that God goes ahead to remove everything in the pit that could harm or drown you. A plan is hatched against Joseph and death hovers around to terminate the story. But nay. Death is not permitted to stop God's plan. The pit is a temporary location, but God has made it a safe abode. Like Daniel in the Lion's Den, the lions have been transformed to kittens ... the viper that coiled round the arms of the Apostle Paul has been transformed to a woolen rope. The flames are not able to burn Shedrach, Meshach and Abednego. God often times will permit us to be thrown into environments of great danger because that aspect of our process is required for us, but He will not permit any harm to come to us.

Psa_34:19 Many are the afflictions of the righteous: but the LORD delivereth him out of them all.

The psalmist says all - without exception. But this is a promise for the righteous not for all. The righteous are in Christ. The righteous are obedient. The righteous have received grace to please God ... the evidence of their righteousness and obedience is their present location ... the pit. God goes ahead to make an oasis in the deserts. He makes rivers in the wilderness - the rough places plain and exalts the valleys.

A raven was once sent to feed Elijah in the barren desert, then a widow was used to preserve him. You may not know how God will preserve you through your challenges, but you are assured that He will not leave or forsake you in the pit He has led you into. Sing in the pit. Soon you will come out launched into the next stage of destiny.

Song

I am rejoicing my name has ben written
I am rejoicing for I am born again - Hallelujah

Prayer: O Lord, thank you for always being ahead of every plan that seems set for my destruction and instead you turned them to steps for my elevation. Amen

JANUARY 23

Unholy Communion

Bible Text: Genesis 37:25-28

Gen 37:25 And they sat down to eat bread: and they lifted up their eyes and looked, and, behold, a company of Ishmeelites came from Gilead with their camels bearing spicery and balm and myrrh, going to carry it down to Egypt. 26 And Judah said unto his brethren, What profit is it if we slay our brother, and conceal his blood? 27 Come, and let us sell him to the Ishmeelites, and let not our hand be upon him; for he is our brother and our flesh. And his brethren were content. 28 Then there passed by Midianites merchantmen; and they drew and lifted up Joseph out of the pit, and sold Joseph to the Ishmeelites for twenty pieces of silver: and they brought Joseph into Egypt.

How would you describe this communion? Brothers are eating bread and drinking wine . . . while Joseph is in the pit. What kind of communion can we have when we have our fellow brethren in trouble? Can God be pleased with this bread breaking? Yet do we not often sit down to break bread in communion unmindful of the troubles we have devised for others. Such wickedness.

The brothers lift up their eyes and their eyes catch the rich spices, balm and myrrh and they have a better idea - to cash in on the sorrows of their brothers. Greed revises an already horrible intent to murder . . . but God was moving Joseph into his destiny even amidst these wicked and poisonous emotions. How wicked are the hearts of men . . . brothers wicked to brothers . . . sisters wicked to sisters . . . but God observes all . . . his plans are not disturbed in the least. Judah is the one who speaks this time . . . generations later, the Lion of Judah will speak for us, intercede for us before the throne of Heaven.

The Bible says the brothers are content . . . they are satisfied. How many have peace in evil? How many consciences are completely hardened by lust for power and position or hatred for their fellow men . . . even being at peace, undisturbed in the least at the harvest that such an evil seed will surely one day yield.

The most evil aspect of this communion is their disregard for the feelings of their father. They knew their father would mourn till the end of his days . . . but they did not care. They were completely uncaring for the feelings of their father . . . but again it was all the working of God's Holy Spirit to achieve His purpose.

Song

Beneath the cross of Jesus I fain would take my stand,
The shadow of a mighty rock within a weary land;
A home within the wilderness, a rest upon the way,
From the burning of the noontide heat, and the burden of the day.

Upon that cross of Jesus mine eye at times can see
The very dying form of One Who suffered there for me;
And from my stricken heart with tears two wonders I confess;
The wonders of redeeming love and my unworthiness.

I take, O cross, thy shadow for my abiding place;
I ask no other sunshine than the sunshine of His face;
Content to let the world go by to know no gain or loss,
My sinful self my only shame, my glory all the cross.

Prayer: O Lord, forgive me the many times I did not care for my brother and grieved you. Do not let me annoy you again. Amen

JANUARY 24

Overwhelming Betrayal

Bible Text: Genesis 37:25-28

Gen 37:25 And they sat down to eat bread: and they lifted up their eyes and looked, and, behold, a company of Ishmeelites came from Gilead with their camels bearing spicery and balm and myrrh, going to carry it down to Egypt. 26 And Judah said unto his brethren, What profit is it if we slay our brother, and conceal his blood? 27 Come, and let us sell him to the Ishmeelites, and let not our hand be upon him; for he is our brother and our flesh. And his brethren were content. 28 Then there passed by Midianites merchantmen; and they drew and lifted up Joseph out of the pit, and sold Joseph to the Ishmeelites for twenty pieces of silver: and they brought Joseph into Egypt.

Rejoice, when the odds are overwhelming. It suggests God's hand is close to sustain you. Betrayal is ordinarily painful, but there is no betrayal that hurts more than that of your kindred. Few are spared this tough lesson. David is inconsolable when Absalom turns against him. Our Lord Jesus is sold out by Judas Iscariot. It was Mariam, the elder sister of Moses who challenged his leadership. These battles with our own flesh and blood cannot be won and we are slow to bring out the sword of prayers against our own. Beware of covetousness, greed, lusts for power and worldly ambitions - as these are the baits of the devil to recruit his best arrows.

Joseph is handed over to Ishmaelites for twenty pieces of silver. Christ betrayed with a kiss for thirty pieces of silver . . . the souls of men have been items of negotiation for centuries. Normally it is for lucre - money that perishes and is immediately devalued even by the following week. The devil has bought many out of their destiny of life. None us will end like Absalom or Judas . . . hanging dead. But do watch every transaction and check your motives. Ask yourself. Is the Lord and His cause betrayed if I benefit financially from this decision?

There is another transaction that was paid for in full and this time not with perishable currency but with the blood of Jesus. We have been purchased back from the devil by the blood of Jesus that has never lost its power - still as potent as it was thousands of years ago. The precious blood of Jesus was shed to legalize the Lordship of Christ over us. We have been freed to be sons, yet we still elect to be called "the servant of the Lord"

Gal_4:7 Wherefore thou art no more a servant, but a son; and if a son, then an heir of God through Christ. Col_4:12 Epaphras, who is one of you, a servant of Christ, saluteth you . . . 2Ti_2:24 And the servant of the Lord . . . Tit_1:1 Paul, a servant of God, and an apostle of Jesus Christ . . . Heb_3:5 And Moses verily was faithful in all his house, as a servant, for a testimony of those things which were to be spoken after; Jas_1:1 James, a servant of God and of the Lord Jesus Christ, . . . 2Pe_1:1 Simon Peter, a servant and an apostle of Jesus Christ . . . Jud_1:1 Jude, the servant of Jesus Christ

We are devastated by betrayal when we see ourselves as free lords. Indeed we have the choice to be free, but we only come under a different yoke, if we do not take on the yoke of Christ - to be His servant. When overwhelmed with betrayal . . . be led back to Christ and be assured that His yoke of obedience is easy to bear.

Song.

Heir of Salvation, purchase of God, Born of His Spirit - washed in His blood.
This is my story, this is my song, Praising my Savior all the day long

Prayer: O Lord, teach me to serve you as you want to be served. Amen

JANUARY 25

A Scapegoat

Bible Text: Genesis 37:31-34

Gen 37:31 And they took Joseph's coat, and killed a kid of the goats, and dipped the coat in the blood; 32 And they sent the coat of many colors, and they brought it to their father; and said, This have we found: know now whether it be thy son's coat or no. 33 And he knew it, and said, It is my son's coat; an evil beast hath devoured him; Joseph is without doubt rent in pieces. 34 And Jacob rent his clothes, and put sackcloth upon his loins, and mourned for his son many days.

Instead of Joseph to die, another innocent kid of the goats is killed and his blood is shed instead. By this the life of Joseph is preserved and Joseph is released into his true destiny. Jesus Christ was our sin offering like a an innocent kid to replace us who deserved death. When He was crucified our distorted destiny was replaced and we are restored to a new destiny culminating in eternal joy. When Christ was crucified betrayed by Judas Iscariot, it was not known then that this was always the plan of God. In the same way, the brothers of Joseph did not know that Joseph was being sent to be the instrument of their salvation.

Many years later God will instruct Moses . . .

Lev 16:5 And he shall take of the congregation of the children of Israel two kids of the goats for a sin offering, and one ram for a burnt offering. 6 And Aaron shall offer his bullock of the sin offering, which is for himself, and make an atonement for himself, and for his house. 7 And he shall take the two goats, and present them before the LORD at the door of the tabernacle of the congregation. 8 And Aaron shall cast lots upon the two goats; one lot for the LORD, and the other lot for the scapegoat. 9 And Aaron shall bring the goat upon which the LORD'S lot fell, and offer him for a sin offering. 10 But the goat, on which the lot fell to be the scapegoat, shall be presented alive before the LORD, to make an atonement with him, and to let him go for a scapegoat into the wilderness. . . . 21 And Aaron shall lay both his hands upon the head of the live goat, and confess over him all the iniquities of the children of Israel, and all their transgressions in all their sins, putting them upon the head of the goat, and shall send him away by the hand of a fit man into the wilderness: 22 And the goat shall bear upon him all their iniquities unto a land not inhabited: and he shall let go the goat in the wilderness.

Because Christ gave His life to be crucified. Our sins and iniquities have been placed on a scapegoat . . . who has been released far into the wilderness never to be seen. We can rejoice and know they will never be brought up ever again or ever found again. If any brings up your sin . . . tell them because Christ died . . . our iniquities and sorrows have all been carried far away.

Song.

Upon that cross of Jesus, mine eye can sometimes see
The very dying form of One who suffered there for me;
And from my smitten heart with tears two wonders I confess -
The wonders of His glorious love and my own worthlessness.

Prayer: O Lord, I am so unworthy . . . and your love is so glorious. Thank you. May your death for me not be in vain. Amen

JANUARY 26

Change your Seed

Bible Text: Genesis 37:31-34

Gen 37:31 And they took Joseph's coat, and killed a kid of the goats, and dipped the coat in the blood; 32 And they sent the coat of many colors, and they brought it to their father; and said, This have we found: know now whether it be thy son's coat or no. 33 And he knew it, and said, It is my son's coat; an evil beast hath devoured him; Joseph is without doubt rent in pieces. 34 And Jacob rent his clothes, and put sackcloth upon his loins, and mourned for his son many days.

Jacob, the deceiver reaps a cruel deception. Today is a good day to reflect on the seeds you have sown and begin to sow a different seed. Every act of kindness, every act of giving, every act of betrayal - even if men forgive—will have its fruit because of the word of God which says *Gal_6:7 Be not deceived; God is not mocked: for whatsoever a man soweth, that shall he also reap.*

Jacob and Rebekah succeeded to outwit the aging patriarch Isaac, and all seems to have been forgotten. Decades later, a cruel twist of circumstances introduces a more far reaching family deception into the life of Jacob. Begin to sow seeds of forgiveness and mercy. Begin to sow seeds of love especially when this is not returned. The harvest is usually in multiples of the seed, either for good or for evil. Great injustice is harvested by little seeds of unfairness. The coat of many colors given by man to unfairly single out Joseph is also unfairly destroyed by men in far worse circumstances of injustice.

The man who was a master of lies is also drowned in deception. But then Christ paid in full for our redemption and for our eternity in glory. Still our souls must in God's mercy go through a process that brings us to know God and be transformed to be like Him. God's plan is still intact although Jacob reaps a painful betrayal . . . this time he rests in God's benevolence and trusts God fully to still work out His perfect will. David reaped the harvest of the seed of murder and adultery even though he received forgiveness from God.

The Apostle Paul was persecuting and putting Christians in prison and in his future ministry he spent most of his days incarcerated, but it prepared his soul best to be of the greatest use to God. The most important dimension of this lesson is the future and to change our seed for the better.

In Christ, the Bible says the punishment that brought us peace was laid on Christ. i.e. Christ paid for the evil harvest . . . but the Apostle still warns that God is not mocked, He is a God of principles which are beyond our human control and manipulation. But God is also a God of mercy. O how we know in part on how He deals in mercy. Only through mercy will any reach the future glory.

Today, sing of His mercy. Pray for mercy. Give a special offering for mercy even as you change your seed.

Song

The steadfast love of the Lord never ceaseth, His mercy never comes to an end;
They are new every morning . . . Great is thy faithfulness O Lord (2ce)

Prayer: O Lord, Have mercy on me. Amen

JANUARY 27

False Comforters

Bible Text: Genesis 37:35-36

Gen 37:35 And all his sons and all his daughters rose up to comfort him; but he refused to be comforted; and he said, For I will go down into the grave unto my son mourning. Thus his father wept for him. 36 And the Midianites sold him into Egypt unto Potiphar, an officer of Pharaoh's, and captain of the guard.

How could the very sons that masterminded this terrible deed be the same ones that comfort Jacob? This false comfort is so typical. The same that has architected your sorrow is your chief comforter . . . what a deception? Can men truly comfort you? Are not most of their comforts false? How could Jacob be comforted by the same people who almost murdered Joseph and whose prayer was that Joseph will never be seen again. Many brethren and sisters prefer to be comforted by lies instead of going to the word of God for comfort that is true and real.

Are you in grief? Indeed all the people around you may mean well . . . though some are liars . . . but you must go and get the word of God. Find a Bible and read the words of comfort from God. The Bible is so rich in true comfort unlike any other book you will ever find. Many writers in these days want to exclude scripture but there is little comfort outside scripture . . . only lies masked by false compassion. The brothers of Joseph could have won an Oscar for a great dramatic performance. The wicked have become your comforters . . . may God help you. I pray you will learn to go to God and spare yourself the discovery that the best of men are only men. God is waiting for you. He will wipe away your tears and tell you that all is well. You will find that hard to believe just as Jacob did . . . . and perhaps you are justified. But that does not change the situation that all is well. Stop mourning . . . lift up your eyes and be comforted. The dream of God is perfectly intact . . . it only needs to be rescued from your clutches for a while. Soon you will see that God is good . . . and all the time. The Comforter has come. Do not weep anymore.

Song.

O spread the tidings 'round, wherever man is found,
Wherever human hearts and human woes abound;
Let ev'ry Christian tongue proclaim the joyful sound:
The Comforter has come!

The Comforter has come, the Comforter has come!
The Holy Ghost from Heav'n, the Father's promise giv'n;
O spread the tidings 'round, wherever man is found-
The Comforter has come!

The long, long night is past, the morning breaks at last,
And hushed the dreadful wail and fury of the blast,
As o'er the golden hills the day advances fast!
The Comforter has come!

Lo, the great King of kings, with healing in His wings,
To ev'ry captive soul a full deliverance brings;
And through the vacant cells the song of triumph rings;
The Comforter has come!

Prayer: O Lord, often I cannot see your goodness . . . help me to know you are often best when you do not permit me to have my way. Comfort me in all my confusions. Amen

It is not Over

Bible Text: Genesis 37:35-36

Gen 37:35 And all his sons and all his daughters rose up to comfort him; but he refused to be comforted; and he said, For I will go down into the grave unto my son mourning. Thus his father wept for him. 36 And the Midianites sold him into Egypt unto Potiphar, an officer of Pharaoh's, and captain of the guard.

It is not over, my sister. Be strong, my friend. Your pains are baked in the oven of lies, your comforters are liars . . . and all the conclusions of men concerning your situation are vain and untrue. All you have thought and concluded is untrue. It is not over.

Jacob will not be comforted, nor could the perpetrators of evil repent. The tender mercies of the wicked are cruel, saith the Lord . . . all their teachings and sermons to encourage you are wrong. The only truth for you today is that "It is not over." God ignores all your cries and does not reckon with your wrong professions for God knows you are a man . . . and His plans are of Him . . . they were never your plans . . . all your plans and professions are best fitted for shredding and tossed into the trash bin.

Today, be encouraged - even in your pains. I will not ask you to change your conclusions because they are all you can see. Rather, if you are alive to be reading this devotional, then there is great hope. There is hope because of three main reasons.

First, unknown to you, there is a lot that happened, that happens and that will happen that is not for your sorrow but to give you the good end that is expected. Second, amongst your comforters are the traitors that do not have your peace of mind and joy as their priority. Rather, they wait to inherit your substance. But God has reserved your dream in a place that is safe. Third, your tears are for your past wicked ways . . . . the tears you should have cried when you deceived your father and saw his grief, But you will go down into the grave rejoicing and not in mourning.

You may be reading this devotional and wonder how could this be? A huge stone is put to cover the grave of Christ to ensure the story ended in His crucifixion . . . but when God says a new chapter is about to open and it appears to us as though it has all ended in grief . . . be assured that "It is not over." Indeed be not dismayed, a new beginning is about to commence. A new phase is about to start. Your troubles have a life span . . . a short life span.

Song

The race is not to the swift or strong, But to the few who fight the wrong
with revelation from His Word, Reject Baal, and follow on to know the Lord
(Leonard Ravenhill)

Prayer: O Lord, turn all my days of mourning to days of rejoicing and mirth. Amen

JANUARY 29

Fruitfulness least Expected

Bible Text: Genesis 38:25-27

Gen 38:25 When she was brought forth, she sent to her father in law, saying, By the man, whose these are, am I with child: and she said, Discern, I pray thee, whose are these, the signet, and bracelets, and staff. 26 And Judah acknowledged them, and said, She hath been more righteous than I; because that I gave her not to Shelah my son. And he knew her again no more. 27 And it came to pass in the time of her travail, that, behold, twins were in her womb.

The harvest of deception was reaped not only by Jacob, but also by Judah. A chain of deception seems to have been unleashed as Judah encounters this lady called Tamar - who plays the harlot so she can be fruitful. Fruitfulness is important with God. Refusing to be fruitful for God can release unpredictable outcomes and unusual processes. Er, Judah's first born and Onan the second are slain for refusing to bear fruit when God needed a seed. Both are said to be wicked.

Reflect on this. Refusing barrenness is a good mutiny. God must have fruit - souls, increase and expansion. Our lives must not be wasted otherwise you must cry to God and seek all fair means to bear fruit. There are many ways in which the Kingdom of God will be expanded. Through traditional parishes, through books, through online evangelism . . . and even as an Apostle in the market place. You will yet be fruitful for God.

Tamar becomes one of the ancestors of Jesus. What an unusual fruitfulness? The part that is most important in this devotional is recognize that you will be fruitful. Do not assume that God has appointed you for barrenness. He has not. You will not have to play the prostitute for Christ has overcome every infirmity including situations that causes barrenness.

But what should the unfruitful do? Judah means Praise. Learn to praise and when you discover it . . . be given entirely to praising God. Praise God and the God that gives seed to the sower will cause the seeds that must provoke your harvest to be released.

Is it not unusual that Michal was noted as the only barren associated with David? It is instructive that she despised the praise of David who was a King who could not restrain himself from dancing and singing before His God. Today God will bring fruitfulness in the least expected situations . . . just keep on praising God. Your ministry will expand . . . your business will expand . . . you will give birth to twins . . . spiritually and physically you will be fruitful. Amen

Song.

When the Spirit of the Lord moves within my heart, I will dance like David danced
I will dance - I will dance - I will dance like David danced. (2ce)

Prayer: O Lord, Make me fruitful for you. Amen

JANUARY 30

The Scarlet Thread

Bible Text: Genesis 38:27-30

Gen 38:27 And it came to pass in the time of her travail, that, behold, twins were in her womb. 28 And it came to pass, when she travailed, that the one put out his hand: and the midwife took and bound upon his hand a scarlet thread, saying, This came out first. 29 And it came to pass, as he drew back his hand, that, behold, his brother came out: and she said, How hast thou broken forth? this breach be upon thee: therefore his name was called Pharez. 30 And afterward came out his brother, that had the scarlet thread upon his hand: and his name was called Zarah.

The struggle for the birthright is again seen here as it was in the time of Jacob and Esau. These twins are products of an ungodly union . . . examples of grace and memorials to forgiveness and mercy. Judah was to be the ruling tribe and the Lion of Judah . . . Christ emerged as these sons are both named in His genealogy.

The first is marked with a scarlet thread. This points us again to Jesus and His destiny of a cruel crucifixion. His blood to be shed for our sins.

Christ is the first fruits of them that sleep . . . *Rev_1:5 And from Jesus Christ, who is the faithful witness, and the first begotten of the dead, and the prince of the kings of the earth. Unto him that loved us, and washed us from our sins in his own blood,*

After the resurrection of Christ, when he returns at the rapture, the dead in Christ will rise and then others will join Him . . . but the first begotten of the dead . . . the first to taste death and to live never to die again was the one who washed our sins with His own blood. This is the significance of the scarlet thread. By the blood, grace and mercy comes to us in a completely new way that even cause angels to marvel. These twins being in the genealogy are expressions of God's great grace. Marvel at the grace through Christ Jesus and the work that His blood did . . . washing us from our sins. When the saints are breaking out of death and this earthly body to join Christ . . . may you not be missing.

Song.

The blood that Jesus shed for me,
'Way back on Calvary;
The blood that gives me strength from day to day,
It will never lose its power.

It reaches to the highest mountain,
It flows to the lowest valley,
The blood that gives me strength from day to day,
It will never lose its power.

It soothes my doubts and calms my fears,
And it dries all my tears;
The blood that gives me strength from day to day,
It will never lose its power.

It reaches to the highest mountain,
It flows to the lowest valley,
The blood that gives me strength from day to day,
It will never lose its power.

Prayer: O Lord, I plead the blood of Jesus to avail for me . . . Bring me clean to you. Amen

JANUARY 31

Brought Down

Bible Text: Genesis 39:1

Gen 39:1 And Joseph was brought down to Egypt; and Potiphar, an officer of Pharaoh, captain of the guard, an Egyptian, bought him of the hands of the Ishmeelites, which had brought him down thither.

Often we are brought down ... but only to achieve a vital correction or relocation to help us or to position us to be taken up again. Going down into a valley can be a very puzzling experience ... especially when you can find no reason for the descent. Change Management experts have observed that crisis and indeed most change that end positively typically go through a pattern called the Change Curve. This essentially says we initially must go down to come up even stronger or higher. The challenge in managing a bringing down is not to panic but ensure the valley remains a place of hope and thanksgiving ... and the valley is as shallow as possible and the time in it as minimal as needs to be. The desired outcome is to emerge to higher equilibrium as quickly as possible. We often find ourselves resistant to change, until God introduces some sort of crisis. Our initial equilibrium can be the "good" which is the enemy of the "best" that God sees ahead but needs a crisis to manifest. God wanted more for Job but Job was doing well ...

Job 1[1] There was a man in the land of Uz, whose name was Job; and that man was blameless and upright, and one who feared God and shunned evil. [2] And seven sons and three daughters were born to him. [3] Also, his possessions were seven thousand sheep, three thousand camels, five hundred yoke of oxen, five hundred female donkeys, and a very large household, so that this man was the greatest of all the people of the East.

God introduces crisis otherwise Job would have been well contented to be the greatest of all men of the east. But the last chapter in Job's life sees a man at a far higher level ... more than double of where he started. The same was the experience of Joseph and Jacob ... they went through many cycles of being brought down ... always ending much higher than they began.

Psalm 23[4] Yea, though I walk through the valley of the shadow of death, I will fear no evil; for You are with me; Your rod and Your staff, they comfort me.

Song

A pilgrim was I and a-wand'ring,
In the cold night of sin I did roam.
When Jesus, the kind Shepherd, found me,
And now I am on my way home.

Surely goodness and mercy shall follow me
All the days, all the days of my life.
Surely goodness and mercy shall follow me
All the days, all the days of my life.
And I shall dwell in the House of the Lord forever;
And I'll feast at the table spread for me.
Surely goodness and mercy shall follow me
All the days, all the days of my life.

Prayer: O Lord, let me see your goodness and mercy always following me through all my days. Amen.

FEBRUARY 1

Slave

Bible Text: Genesis 39:1

Gen 39:1 And Joseph was brought down to Egypt; and Potiphar, an officer of Pharaoh, captain of the guard, an Egyptian, bought him of the hands of the Ishmeelites, which had brought him down thither.

God often does His work in stages, steps and processes. This is why we must trust Him fully - for we may not know at which stage or section of the process we are in. But we know that we can trust Him. Joseph is now in Egypt and he is initiated into a luxury, culture and beauty that must have completely stunned the Jew who only knew the tents of his fathers. The grandeur of ancient Egypt is unparalleled not only in beauty but in its advancements in medical and scientific feats. But the most seductive aspect of Egypt is its culture or what we call civilization.

The eyes of Joseph are opened to a completely different world with a different set of rules and traditions. He was purchased to be a slave of the Egyptian and so a slave of the Egyptian culture. But He also knew that he could not serve two masters. The God of His family that sold him out and the God of Pharaoh were irreconcilable. Their cultures were completely apart. Like Daniel, he purposed from day one not to defile himself . . . not to partake in the delicacies that the culture offered. Egypt has a lot to offer. Some that looks very harmless and a lot that is quite toxic and obviously undesirable.

There are little victories we must win before we will be permitted to fight the major bouts. If Joseph cannot survive in keeping himself as a slave, how will he cope if he becomes the Prime Minister. I pray that with this devotional God will help you to stay apart for the greater things He wants to do in your future. In the new culture, every day is a test. What we will say, not say. Do or not do. Egypt is a journey down but you do not have to come down . . . you can use it as Joseph did, an opportunity to grow even spiritually and come up even higher. Even in Egypt, you can excel.

Today reflect on men like Daniel who were able to shine in a very different culture. There is a Rock that is higher than I. O then to the Rock I fly.

You can decide today and make a quality decision to cling to the Rock and be unaffected by the culture.

Song.

O sometimes the shadows are deep, and rough seems the path to the goal,
and sorrows, sometimes how they sweep Like tempests down over my soul.
O then to the Rock, let me fly . . . To the Rock that is higher than I.

Prayer: O Lord, hold me in the confusion of the culture. Help me to be fastened to the Rock which cannot move.
Amen.

FEBRUARY 2

The Company of God

Bible Text: Genesis 39:2

Gen 39:2 And the LORD was with Joseph, and he was a prosperous man; and he was in the house of his master the Egyptian.

What does it mean to always have the company of God? There are men who did so many great things and there are men who we are told walked with God. Enoch we are told walked with God . . . Joseph was like Enoch. He enjoyed the company of the most high even as most looked down on him as a Hebrew slave.

Amo 3:3 Can two walk together, except they be agreed?

Having the company of God means to be agreed with God. It means to be on the highway that God walks. It does not mean things will be easy or that we can have whatever we lust for. It means we are protected . . . first and especially from ourselves and our decisions and from external troubles. It means we are comforted and there is an unseen hand that embraces us and wipes away our ears. It means we are covered under a pavilion of safety and hidden in the shadow of the Almighty. But to be agreed with God, we have to accept God's terms. We cannot negotiate lower terms. Many call on the name of God but do not wish to walk with Him because they cannot be agreed with His terms. He has great expectations from those who walk with Him . . . they will not be allowed to stray off . . . and can expect to be swallowed by a whale if in disobedience. Others—he leaves alone.

The best illustration I find of the company of God is to be under a huge refreshing shadow of a mighty unseen being. Imagine an enemy coming to attack suddenly realizing a huge shadow of a mighty unseen presence. The shadow communicates the presence of an awesome defense system that causes trepidation and the enemy flees. The company of God implies the escort of innumerable host of angelic beings awaiting instructions to be executed immediately.

The company of God is an admission into the throne room. Everywhere a king is—no matter how humble - becomes an Imperial Palace. There is a glory that follows the King to defend Him and those in His company. There are chariots of fires and a fiery entourage that establish His majesty - dispensing judgments He permits.

When we have sensed the presence of God, we know that there is no superior experience we can ever have . . . we cannot go higher than the presence of God. We want to preserve the experience and we naturally live a life of worship. David wrote often that he was prepared to lose anything but the presence of God. He did not mind losing the throne of men and going on exile to the hills . . . but groaned in pain and sorrow whenever he sensed God was far from him. God was with Joseph. Are you walking with God or just calling His name?

Song

In the presence of Jehovah - God Almighty Prince of Peace
Troubles vanish—hearts are mended—In the presence of the King.
Troubles vanish—hearts are mended—In the presence of the King.

Prayer: O Lord, may I ever remain in your presence. Amen

FEBRUARY 3

Secret of Prosperity

Bible Text: Genesis 39:2

Gen 39:2 And the LORD was with Joseph, and he was a prosperous man; and he was in the house of his master the Egyptian.

Today, you can discover a secret. Something that is so powerful and true and will bless you. I refer to the secret of prosperity. God does not hate prosperity. Prosperity is not just about having billions. Rather, it is about thriving in the purpose of God - having peace in your body, soul and spirit. Having health and the mental clarity that all is well. Joseph no more lives in a tent and now lives in a house. He is no more a wandering herdsman, but he is now at some peace . . . this is a more luxurious pit. But his rest and peace do not come from Egypt. They come from the presence of God in his life. They come from another person living within him. God is with him to cause all that he does to prosper.

God with you implies, God directing you, God controlling you, God protecting you, God instructing you, God comforting you and also God providing for you. It means being dependent on God for everything. It does not mean calling on God when you perceive you have a need or invoking his presence through music or song. Rather, it suggests a continued presence that makes your worship different and your every moment special. Remember we speak of God and not a prophet, teacher or pastor. But God can be grieved - made sad by your dearest thoughts that exclude Him or your motivations which are primarily to satisfy self and the flesh.

God was not in Joseph's life to lead him back to his family, although God knows the way back. Nor was God available to free him from the shackles of slavery in Potiphar's house. When God is with us, it means we are free from Egypt and only remain because there is a higher purpose in God for it. It implies living and doing everything for a higher purpose, walking on a higher ground and seeing a higher perspective to everything although to everybody else Joseph, like Daniel was just like any other captive in a heathen culture. God with us means that we shine differently because in us, there is a light that shines.

Serving in the house of Potiphar is but another phase - and Joseph must see beyond this phase otherwise he will begin to covet the marble, art and the treasures that could one day be his . . . and begin to notice more the women who now expose their flesh . . . the strange lustful laughter of Egypt and the alluring glances of Potiphar's wife. God must help Joseph. God with us is God helping is to stand in Him daily. The word of God is God. When we study and are filled with it - we have God with us. The word speaks to situations in our lives to always establish God's higher purpose. When we are far from the word of God and we have not reflected on its admonitions and comfort, then we may not have God, rather we may still prosper - but a different type of prosperity. We then rely on our self to sustain what we have begun. In this devotional we see a different way to prosper driven by an inner richness. God with us. Can you say God is with you? God is far from the proud. Humble yourself.

Song.

I need thy presence every passing hour; what but thy grace can foil the tempter's power?
Who like Thyself my guide and stay can be? Through cloud and sunshine, O abide with me.

Prayer: O Lord, do not permit me to stray into pride and lose your presence. Abide always with me. Amen

FEBRUARY 4

Faithful in Little Things

Bible Text: Genesis 39:3-6

Gen 39:3 And his master saw that the LORD was with him, and that the LORD made all that he did to prosper in his hand. 4 And Joseph found grace in his sight, and he served him: and he made him overseer over his house, and all that he had he put into his hand. 5 And it came to pass from the time that he had made him overseer in his house, and over all that he had, that the LORD blessed the Egyptian's house for Joseph's sake; and the blessing of the LORD was upon all that he had in the house, and in the field. 6 And he left all that he had in Joseph's hand; and he knew not ought he had, save the bread which he did eat. And Joseph was a goodly person, and well favored.

How will you lead if you are assigned to lead in slavery or how do you handle small places under serious constraints? Joseph is overseer in captivity. This could have brought out dissatisfaction and sighs but Joseph became God's instrument to bless the house of his captivity. This is a test and one not easy to pass. Often times we know we are going through a phase and that we will move out of a situation . . . but our loyalty in small and restricted scenarios are very critical tests. Joseph was goodly and remained a blessing to all that encountered him. He told no one of his sad unfair past—though he never quite forget his pains.

There is someone reading this devotional. You think life is very unfair and you are overqualified for your present situation . . . it is only a test to see if you will remain a blessing and a giver. Pass this test and watch God move you forward. Where did Joseph learn administration? Where did he learn to lead in the culture of Egypt? Where did the experience that God leveraged in Joseph to manage the economy of Egypt come from? Do not despise the learning and corrections God is exposing you to. Do not say "why have I found myself in this situation?" What you need to learn now is as important for your destiny as all your learning in the best universities. God is preparing you for greatness. Be faithful in little things . . . . soon you will be rewarded and will fully understand why you must first be a blessing in Potiphar's house before being a voice and a blessing to the nations. Examine your situation. Are you being tested? Can you be found faithful when treated unfairly? Joseph was.

Song.

He giveth more grace when the burdens grow greater;
He sendeth more strength when the labors increase.
To added affliction He addeth His mercy;
To multiplied trials, His multiplied peace.

His love has no limit, His grace has no measure,
His pow'r has no boundary known unto men;
For out of His infinite riches in Jesus,
He giveth, and giveth, and giveth again!

When we have exhausted our store of endurance,
When our strength has failed ere the day is half done,
When we reach the end of our hoarded resources,
Our Father's full giving is only begun.

Prayer: O Lord, teach me in all my circumstances to know and shine for you . . . do not despair of training me.
Amen

FEBRUARY 5

The Beginning of Tests

Bible Text: Genesis 39:3-6

Gen 39:3 And his master saw that the LORD was with him, and that the LORD made all that he did to prosper in his hand. 4 And Joseph found grace in his sight, and he served him: and he made him overseer over his house, and all that he had he put into his hand. 5 And it came to pass from the time that he had made him overseer in his house, and over all that he had, that the LORD blessed the Egyptian's house for Joseph's sake; and the blessing of the LORD was upon all that he had in the house, and in the field. 6 And he left all that he had in Joseph's hand; and he knew not ought he had, save the bread which he did eat. And Joseph was a goodly person, and well favored.

God does not promote that which has not been tested. That will be destructive to the individual. God knows what we are made of, but we do not know. Instead we delude ourselves that we are ready when we are far from it. Joseph is showered with advantage and favors, and you could say for a Hebrew slave, he had arrived. Joseph could forget the higher purpose and embrace the immediate offering of a better life. Be careful of doctrines that tell you your best life is now. This is often far from divine truth as God who dwells on high is always taking us higher. In most cases, we are so far from where God wants to take us and even though we are comfortable . . . better than our peers in the dusty tents of Israel - but still we are nowhere near what God has ordained. Joseph is asked to take care of everything for Potiphar . . . this exposed Joseph to all the secrets of Potiphar. It was very easy to divert some of the resources of Potiphar to enrich himself but not Joseph. Joseph could have betrayed Potiphar but he did not.

These were tests. May God help us to see our tests as tests and not fail Him. Joseph scores well only because God is with Him. Everything that Joseph did worked well. Even Potiphar could see the evidence that Joseph was different. Do you appreciate that the best evidence of God in your life is the testimony of the heathen and not your pretensions or confessions?

The heathen watch how you will handle all the opportunities and they observe a difference even when you say nothing. They can see that you fear God in a different way. They can see that there is a protection and guidance for you that cannot be explained. They know the difference because many Hebrew slaves and servants have worked in the house of Potiphar . . . they can see that Joseph is different. The presence of God in your life will cause a marked difference in all that pertains to you. So much so that onlookers cannot but admit the reality of a higher being that is with you.

Ask yourself today. What are the tests that are before me? How am I faring? Is God with me helping me or do I feel myself drifting up and down without an anchor. Go back to God . . . He can point out when the separation occurred and what to do to get God back in your life. Begin with a repentance.

Joseph did well. The presence of God caused much prosperity and favor. Joseph was not spoilt by riches because He had inside him - the one for whom diamonds are like dust. The things that could not impress God could not cause him to gasp in awe. Use your reactions and passions to check what is in you and inspiring you. You will be surprised at your findings. Go back to God. Let Jesus dwell in you.

Song.

I'd rather have Jesus, than silver or gold. I'd rather be His than have riches untold
I'd rather have Jesus, than houses or lands. I'd rather be led by His nail pierced hands.

Prayer: O Lord, teach me and help me to excel in the tests ahead of me. Amen

FEBRUARY 6

Temptations

Bible Text: Genesis 39:7-9

Gen 39:7 And it came to pass after these things, that his master's wife cast her eyes upon Joseph; and she said, Lie with me. 8 But he refused, and said unto his master's wife, Behold, my master wotteth not what is with me in the house, and he hath committed all that he hath to my hand; Gen 39:9 There is none greater in this house than I; neither hath he kept back any thing from me but thee, because thou art his wife: how then can I do this great wickedness, and sin against God?

Temptations are not random tests. They are well studied and arranged to achieve their objective i.e. that we fall. Remember Job and what the devil said concerning him.

Job 1:9 Then Satan answered the LORD, and said, Doth Job fear God for nought? 10 Hast not thou made an hedge about him, and about his house, and about all that he hath on every side? thou hast blessed the work of his hands, and his substance is increased in the land. 11 But put forth thine hand now, and touch all that he hath, and he will curse thee to thy face.

Joseph has already proven that he is a good steward, a diligent man and a honest worker with integrity. He now needed a different test. He had been watched and as he grew with no female company, the best test was prepared to suit his peculiar situation. I observe that many will pass many tests but will fail when subtle lusts are presented. For others the test they will fail relates to pride of life. Satan answers God that Job loves himself and his success more than God and that if he is made a failure—he will abandon God—even as family, friend and supposed religious voices isolate him as a fraud. Will Job hold on to God even if God alone knew what was going on and all men abandoned him? Job passed the test. Joseph passed the test. Tests are packaged after careful study and lifelong observation by the enemy. All our past is available to give indications on where we are most likely to fall. God permits the tests because they are useful to Him. Joseph needed to be in the prisons of Egypt and not the slave of Potiphar. Everything happened as God ordained. Joseph was helped to survive sexual temptation but not protected from false accusation that will send him to prison. May God help us. Lead us not into temptation and deliver us from evil. Amen

Song

The Lord's our Rock, in Him we hide,
A shelter in the time of storm;
Secure whatever ill betide,
A shelter in the time of storm.

Oh, Jesus is a Rock in a weary land,
A weary land, a weary land;
Oh, Jesus is a Rock in a weary land,
A shelter in the time of storm.

A shade by day, defense by night,
A shelter in the time of storm;
No fears alarm, no foes affright,
A shelter in the time of storm.

The raging storms may round us beat,
A shelter in the time of storm;
We'll never leave our safe retreat,
A shelter in the time of storm.

Prayer: O Lord, let me be hidden in the Rock that is Christ. Amen

FEBRUARY 7

Early Victories

Bible Text: Genesis 39:7-9

Gen 39:7 And it came to pass after these things, that his master's wife cast her eyes upon Joseph; and she said, Lie with me. Gen 39:8 But he refused, and said unto his master's wife, Behold, my master wotteth not what is with me in the house, and he hath committed all that he hath to my hand; Gen 39:9 There is none greater in this house than I; neither hath he kept back any thing from me but thee, because thou art his wife: how then can I do this great wickedness, and sin against God?

Joseph has passed the tests for the lower grade and is about to move on to the higher but he must pass the test of compromise. Compromise comes in different shades and is appropriately packaged to be most effective. Joseph is a young man at an age when his mind is beginning to play with strange lusts whetted by the culture. Joseph is not said to be impotent nor is he an eunuch . . . I suspect he had like passions and being a handsome man, it is unlikely that Potiphar's wife is the first to tempt him. Who is the evil destroyer that is asking you to lie with her? Compromise is safe, appears to have no costs - instead it offers significant benefits. There are tests we can easily pass. The test to compromise can be complicated by false assurances. I suspect Joseph would have been well settled in the House of Potiphar. The experienced wife of Potiphar must have had many slaves as her toys - Joseph was to be another. Compromise has already conquered many . . . who been well rewarded, not knowing that their destinies had been truncated. Polluted by compromise, they can no more go far.

Compromise may be in a lustful Delilah and it may be packaged in a safer scenario - the principle is the same. God helps you to conquer it. How do we know that this was God at work for Joseph. We cannot find any guiding mentor, teachings or discipleships schools . . . perhaps Jacob prepared him well. I think differently. God is able to sustain us better than the best human instructions and teachers and uphold us with His own mighty protective arm. Without God . . . we all will fail before the most elementary pressures. The prayer of Satan is for God to leave His own for moment and allow a fair fight . . . to remove all the hedges and not to interfere. The deception many fall into is to see themselves as self-made and strong - having conquered many situations. The difference between Joseph and Samson is the grace and mercy of God that elects to work differently in different situations. May we have grace and mercy in the times we need it the most and never stray to imagine that we can trust in our flesh when compromise deals with its sharpest arrows.

Song.

Did we in our strength confide, our striving would be losing.
Were not the right man on our side, the Man of God's own choosing.
Dost ask who that may be? Christ Jesus, it is He; Lord Sabaoth is His name
From age to age the same. And He must win the battle.
(Martin Luther)

Prayer: O Lord, let me not trust in myself. Rather let your will and truth triumph through me. Amen

FEBRUARY 8

Caught in a Trap

Bible Text: Genesis 39:12

Gen 39:12 And she caught him by his garment, saying, Lie with me: and he left his garment in her hand, and fled, and got him out.

Why is Joseph alone in this situation that easily degenerates quickly? The trap of hell sells a lie that we can resist and run and nothing can go wrong. Many things can and did go wrong. There are many situations that need not arise if we heed the word of God and the Holy Spirit on fashion, decency, music we can listen to, relationships we can have, confidences and friendships we can maintain . . . what we can read etc. It is doubtful that this is a situation that just suddenly emerges. There are many warnings on how to avoid the bait of the enemy in the first place. Was Joseph just an innocent young man attractive to Potiphar's wife . . . perhaps that was so . . . did Joseph know it . . . maybe and perhaps not. Surely a messy situation has developed which may be the harvest of a seed someone somewhere has sown. Many situations can be avoided if we heed to the cautions in the word of God. More importantly single men should not wander into the boudoir of a woman unescorted. I pray you will not be lured into traps of any form and if you are already in one God will make a way of escape. Every trap has a bait . . . the victim must be baited into the trap. Baits are selected based on a study of the victim and determination of the optimum approach. The baits selected by the devil tell a lot about you . . . because the enemy of your soul has been watching you for long. It is silly to just expect you will find yourself victorious if you have not identified the bait early and checked your heart to respond to why this bait was chosen for you.

Joseph was in a trap. Either way he would lose something . . . either his freedom by going to jail or suffering for resisting the advances or worse . . . his integrity and destiny if he chose infidelity. Joseph was wise to choose to be jailed . . . indeed this trap was part of God's process to bring him closer to realizing his destiny. Young men and women—be careful. Heed the warnings. . . . As for Delilahs . . . you can repent or face the ultimate end of a wicked damnation. Be ye holy.

Song.

Take time to be holy,
Speak oft with thy Lord;
Abide in Him always,
And feed on His Word.
Make friends of God's children;
Help those who are weak;
Forgetting in nothing
His blessing to seek.

Take time to be holy,
The world rushes on;
Spend much time in secret
With Jesus alone;
By looking to Jesus,
Like Him thou shalt be;
Thy friends in thy conduct
His likeness shall see.

Prayer: O Lord, teach us and help us to be holy. Amen

FEBRUARY 9

Flee

Bible Text: Genesis 39:12

Gen 39:12 And she caught him by his garment, saying, Lie with me: and he left his garment in her hand, and fled, and got him out.

There are certain situations that require the courage to flee. There are as Spurgeon wrote no other modes of victory but by flight. The ancient naturalists wrote much of basilisks, whose eyes fascinated their victims, so the mere gaze of wickedness can put us in more danger that we think. Many have been hypnotized into situations they did not bargain for ... while others willingly advanced to be slaughtered. The person who would be safe from evil must learn the wisdom of hasting away from certain scenarios. There are things to fight, argue with, preach to, debate and seek reconciliation with and there are things to just simply flee from. A covenant must be made with our eyes not even to look upon potential causes of temptation. If we do not desire to be infected why will we enter a leper's prison. The Pilot does not test the landing gear of the plane and attempt to land on quicksand. Some actions are not in any way related to our faith, but just plainly stupid.

Consider your ways. Joseph did not at any time (even after he became second to Pharaoh) go back to Potiphar's wife for anything. Rather, the jail and dungeons of Egypt were far safer than any suggestion of reconciliation or arguments with a snake. Joseph could have easily lost all the gains and harvest of a painful seed by a short phone call to madame Potiphar. Indeed, Joseph would be far more attractive as a Prime Minister to Potiphar's wife and a more juicy fish to trap in her wicked schemes. Our caution is a lifelong process of continued diligence.

The horrible trinity of the devil, the world and the flesh continue to contrive new contraptions to capture the careless. Madame Potiphar lurks in the corner, perhaps as a counselee in need of help or a supervisor providing extra-zealous hand holding. Be watchful. Do not fight certain experiences for you will certainly lose. Indeed you are right, but it is not every point that needs to be proven. Simply allow God to restore truth in His special way and time - even if it requires years.

Today, if exposed to poisons ... give me the wisdom to take to my heels ... going as far from it as I can possible run ... accepting to be called a coward and a loser - until God justifies His work in my life.

2Ti_2:22 Flee also youthful lusts: but follow righteousness, faith, charity, peace, with them that call on the Lord out of a pure heart.

Song

Father-like He tends and spares us;
Well our feeble frame He knows,
In His hands He gently bears us,
Rescues us from all our foes.
Praise Him! Praise Him!
Widely as His mercy flows.

Prayer: O Lord, rescue us from all our foes. Amen

FEBRUARY 10

Silence

Bible Text: Genesis 39:19-20

Gen 39:19 And it came to pass, when his master heard the words of his wife, which she spake unto him, saying, After this manner did thy servant to me; that his wrath was kindled. 20 And Joseph's master took him, and put him into the prison, a place where the king's prisoners were bound: and he was there in the prison

There is a ministry that is not often spoken about. This is the ministry of silence. This is not the silence of the reserved or the silence of the unlettered. This is not the silence when we do not have anything to say . . . . but when we have a lot but must say absolutely nothing. Joseph is before Potiphar . . . he is not permitted to speak and he does not say anything. Christ was silent before Pilate and all his accusers in a similar way . . . speechless he was as accusations were leveled. Joseph had been trained by his hostile brothers to be silent.

The master's wife must be allowed to have her way in an untruthful accusation. There are times when we will not be permitted to debate the course of our lives and the many inexplicable events. At those times, we should just simply be quiet and watch. Saying nothing is a great virtue of which only a few have the grace. Jesus is not dumbfounded before His accusers. Indeed He had a knowledge and intelligence that none could dispute . . . but He was seen by onlookers as a fool. Everyone knew Barabbas was a wrong choice and that Jesus was innocent . . . but His accusers wanted Him to defend Himself. Similarly, it may have been clear to all that Joseph was not of the character to seduce His master's wife . . . but why would he not say anything and betray his master.

The silence of Joseph saved him. It is not always understood that evil must sometimes be permitted to run its full course. Many are confused at the ministry of silence. But if Joseph had been preserved by simply stating his innocence, he would have missed his divine appointments in the prison. As Joseph is matched to incarceration . . . many onlookers would have mocked him . . . the many who do not agree with his previous elevation in the house of Potiphar will snigger and mock . . . even as he arrives in prison, the welcome of a dangerous pervert would have been given to him . . . but Joseph maintained his silence. May God teach us to be of few words when the Spirit of God demands it . . . especially when we have a lot to say. Soon you will have the opportunity to speak . . . but from the throne. Joseph moves on to greatness . . . nothing is heard of Potiphar and his clever wife after this incident. Lord teach me about silence.

Song

O THOU the God of all my praise,
Do thou not hold thy peace;
For mouths of wicked men to speak
Against me do not cease:
The mouths of vile deceitful men
Against me opened be;
And with a false and lying tongue
They have accused me.

They did beset me round with words
Of hatred and of spite;
And, though to them no cause I gave,
Against me they did fight.
They for my love became my foes:
I set myself to pray.
Evil for good, hatred for love,
To me they did repay.

Prayer: O Lord, strengthen the gift of silence—that your will may prosper. Amen.

FEBRUARY 11

False Accusation

Bible Text: Genesis 39:19-20

Gen 39:19 And it came to pass, when his master heard the words of his wife, which she spake unto him, saying, After this manner did thy servant to me; that his wrath was kindled. 20 And Joseph's master took him, and put him into the prison, a place where the king's prisoners were bound: and he was there in the prison

The imprisonment of Joseph bears some resemblance with the trial and sentencing of Jesus. A lamb is led to the slaughter, but indeed He was the lamb that taketh away the sins of the world. In similar fashion, Joseph must pay the price for the rescue of the Hebrews from a future famine that could wipe out the population. The greater miracle is the lack of resistance and refusal to self-defend when the opportunity was there. If Joseph had not gone to the prison, he could not have met the baker and the butler of Pharaoh. Today is a day to understand more on the tests and trials that come our way and learn what the Bible teaches us to do.

1Pe 1:6 Wherein ye greatly rejoice, though now for a season, if need be, ye are in heaviness through manifold temptations: 7 That the trial of your faith, being much more precious than of gold that perisheth, though it be tried with fire, might be found unto praise and honour and glory at the appearing of Jesus Christ:

Trials, temptations and scourging were the lot of the early Christians. It brought heaviness even as Peter encouraged instead a great rejoicing because these are the things that purify and assure us of the faith we have. Faith in God is a gift of God which is far more precious than gold which perishes. Faith that is not tried is not strong or pure and may not stand in future circumstances that require its value. There are tests and tribulations that come to us - and for which we are able to go through only because we survived previous temptations. God assures us that this will also pass and will make you a stronger Christian. This will be another step on the ladder that will take you higher and higher till Christ returns to take us to the utmost heights. False accusation is the chosen vehicle that sets us to come up and receive the next level of elevation. The assurance that God is with us is strong when in situations that call for Him. The hallmark of godlessness is self-preservation while the evidence of God is the sacrificial life. The knife of false accusation cuts our self-life into pieces - becoming an offering that is placed on the altar for the fire of God to burn. The offering cannot be cut by the offering . . . God must find others to do it for us.

Study the lives of Daniel, the three Hebrew boys with him, Joseph, David and even our Lord Jesus and you will observe false accusation as a precedent to spiritual and eventually physical promotion. Accusation must be false as the Bible warns that we do not suffer for misdoings that cause the name of God to come under reproach. This devotional encourages us to examine our lives and see if we are really being accused falsely or there are legitimate grounds. For most, it is sad that most accusation is not false. The worldly church has absorbed most worldly norms and traditions that it is no more even considered as accusation to raise certain issues. Babyhood is delightful as there is no need to accuse the baby . . . even demons recognize that a Christian who chooses to remain an infant is harmless and should be encouraged to remain in that state. Will you accuse a baby of wetting his nappies or soiling the cot? But observe a man stepping into maturity and the trail of accusations that chase after him. A child cannot inherit riches; he would squander them. As you mature be prepared for accusations. God may want to use accusation to test you. Will you yield or fight to defend yourself?

Song.

Here I give my all to thee - Friends and time and earthly store
Soul and body thine to be - Wholly thine for ever more.

Prayer: O Lord, let me be wholly yours - my rights all cut up - a true living sacrifice.

FEBRUARY 12

New Friends

Bible Text: Genesis 39:21-23

Gen 39:21 But the LORD was with Joseph, and shewed him mercy, and gave him favour in the sight of the keeper of the prison. 22 And the keeper of the prison committed to Joseph's hand all the prisoners that were in the prison; and whatsoever they did there, he was the doer of it. 23 The keeper of the prison looked not to anything that was under his hand; because the LORD was with him, and that which he did, the LORD made it to prosper.

The presence of God in the life of Joseph causes favor and mercy to be showered on him. The keeper commits all the prisoners to Joseph and puts Joseph in charge. Why is this necessary? First the principle of promotion after false accusation is upheld but more importantly Joseph is trained to manage the rejected, the abused and the hopeless. These are God's special people. Murderers and thieves deserve to be in prison and forgotten, but consider that Moses and David were both murderers. Visit the prisons and you will encounter the guilty but also the innocent, the uneducated, the cheated, the unskilled and the deceived. The prostitute introduced into prostitution through rape, starvation and fear. This devotional does not make a case for criminals but did Christ not Himself say . . .

Mat_25:43 I was a stranger, and ye took me not in: naked, and ye clothed me not: sick, and in prison, and ye visited me not. 44 Then shall they also answer him, saying, Lord, when saw we thee an hungred, or athirst, or a stranger, or naked, or sick, or in prison, and did not minister unto thee?

David learnt a lot when in the cave of Adullam with society's rejects. He learnt compassion and his perspectives on social justice were shaped. Joseph will one day be second to Pharaoh, he must learn to have a common touch otherwise the poor will be cheated and the prisoners in the famine will starve to death. The prisoners of Egypt become Joseph's acquaintances and friends - they will be some of his advisers in the future. Many years when Joseph is prime minister, he will not forget them.

God is shaping your life to give you the practical education required for success. Learn an important lesson. God's chosen people do not fail God because there life has been uniquely prepared not to do so - and not because they are better than others. Observe that it was all God's mercy and favor.

Today, thank God for His preparations. Thank Him for His favor and mercy and for leading you into the place of many restrictions and to people special to Him. It is all working together for your good. Ask God to choose your friends.

Song

Lead me through the vale of shadows, bear me o'er life's fitful sea;
Then the gate of life's eternal ; May I enter Lord with thee;
Close to Thee, close to Thee, Close to Thee, Close to Thee
All along my pilgrim journey, Savior, Let me walk with Thee.

Prayer: O Lord, how can I say thanks for all the special training arrangements and favors bestowed on me. Help my ingratitude. Choose my friends for me. Amen

FEBRUARY 13

Character Upholds

Bible Text: Genesis 39:21-23

Gen 39:21 But the LORD was with Joseph, and shewed him mercy, and gave him favour in the sight of the keeper of the prison. 22 And the keeper of the prison committed to Joseph's hand all the prisoners that were in the prison; and whatsoever they did there, he was the doer of it. 23 The keeper of the prison looked not to anything that was under his hand; because the LORD was with him, and that which he did, the LORD made it to prosper.

When Joseph goes into prison, he goes as a convicted rapist and is treated as one. He is observed with suspicion and everyone concludes the need for extra care with him. Things may have been initially rough, but soon his character begins to shine and before long . . . no one cares if Joseph was a rapist or not. Soon they begin to trust him again . . . with a little more here and a little more there. Before long—it becomes clear that the entire prison operation must be handed over to Joseph. The keeper puts everything in the hands of a convicted criminal. Indeed, it may have cross their minds that Joseph was innocent . . . but more importantly, his character begins to glow and soon everyone looks up to him.

Although Joseph is silent. His good deeds and his God are not silent. His character and presence of God in his life defends him and the Spirit of God helps him till he becomes again the most favored in the group. Do you see that false accusation cannot stop your destiny? Instead it will only be a means for your elevation and to correct your location until the appointed time comes. The presence of God impacts our character and becomes a powerful defense that will always answer where we have chosen to be silent.

Song

Go, labor on; spend, and be spent,
Thy joy to do the Father's will;
It is the way the Master went;
Should not the servant tread it still?

Go, labor on; 'tis not for naught;
Thy earthly loss is heav'nly gain;
Men heed thee, love thee, praise thee not,
The Master praises, what are men?

Go, labor on, while yet 'tis day;
The world's dark night is hast'ning on;
Speed, speed thy work, cast sloth away;
It is not thus that souls are won.

Toil on, and in thy toil rejoice;
For toil comes rest, for exile home;
Soon shalt thou hear the Bridegroom's voice,
The midnight peal, "Behold, I come!"

Prayer: O Lord, May your presence shine in my life. Give me a character that is godly. Amen

FEBRUARY 14

After These Things

Bible Text: Genesis 40:1-3

Gen 40:1 And it came to pass after these things, that the butler of the king of Egypt and his baker had offended their lord the king of Egypt. 2 And Pharaoh was wroth against two of his officers, against the chief of the butlers, and against the chief of the bakers. 3 And he put them in ward in the house of the captain of the guard, into the prison, the place where Joseph was bound.

Things do not remain the same. The problems you are currently going through will cease. All the issues you are facing will cease. These things that worry you so much are transient . . . they are events that will pass. Your failures and your successes . . . high and low . . . they will all one day pass. It is pointless to dwell on things that have passed. After all these things . . . something different happens.

Do you see that yesterday has a way of becoming irrelevant? All the accolades and embarrassment may at the moment seem so critical . . . but wait for tomorrow . . . wait a few years and see if anyone remembers your day of honor or day of shame. A few more years and you will need a fading picture to remind yourself that you sat on the high table of honor. The lesson here is to allow things to pass. Allow God to move on into new phases of your victory.

Be careful of bitterness and pains that want to tie you down. Never be tempted to act in revenge or speak out of being tied to an incident. You are simply chaining your destiny down when God wants to move forward. Do you notice that many years later you wonder why certain issues bothered you so much. When you are full of regret and bitterness you waste valuable time and emotions . . . paralyzing yourself where none has paralyzed you. God starts a fresh phase for Joseph by bringing in two inmates into the prison. It has nothing to do with Joseph but in the end it has everything to do with him. Watch out. God is doing something new again. Let go of yesterday.

Song

All the way my Savior leads me; What have I to ask beside?
Can I doubt His tender mercy, Who thro' life has been my Guide?
Heav'nly peace, divinest comfort, Here by faith in Him to dwell!
For I know, whate'er befall me, Jesus doeth all things well;
For I know, whate'er befall me, Jesus doeth all things well.

All the way my Savior leads me, Cheers each winding path I tread,
Gives me grace for ev'ry trial, Feeds me with the living bread.
Though my weary steps may falter, And my soul athirst may be,
Gushing from the Rock before me, Lo! a spring of joy I see;
Gushing from the Rock before me, Lo! a spring of joy I see.

All the way my Savior leads me; Oh, the fullness of His love!
Perfect rest to me is promised In my Father's house above.
When my spirit, clothed immortal, Wings its flight to realms of day,
This my song thro' endless ages: Jesus led me all the way;
This my song thro' endless ages: Jesus led me all the way.

Prayer: O Lord, lead me forward and help me to let go of the past. Amen

FEBRUARY 15

Strange Connections

Bible Text: Genesis 40:1-3

Gen 40:1 And it came to pass after these things, that the butler of the king of Egypt and his baker had offended their lord the king of Egypt. 2 And Pharaoh was wroth against two of his officers, against the chief of the butlers, and against the chief of the bakers. 3 And he put them in ward in the house of the captain of the guard, into the prison, the place where Joseph was bound.

In the palace of Pharaoh, God is preparing strange connections for Joseph. There is a disagreement and a quarrel that leads officers to be sent to prisons. The butler serves and supervises the errands and the wine and the baker the bread. These are influential persons close to the Pharaoh and connected within the politics. The palace politics works against their interest and conflict brews to their disadvantage. The once favored pair are suddenly at a loss.

Do you know that all men, leaders and the led are subject to God. God can raise issues, cause rifts and control even the politics for His higher purpose. Do not imagine that the politics is immune to the power of God's influence. Pharaoh is set up with anger because God has selected a connection for Joseph. Do not attempt to guess how God will raise help for you. Your mind will simply drift to Potiphar's house where you hope in bitterness that someone will speak on your behalf. God's ways are beyond searching. Release the Potiphar experience of injustice to God - who has made it irrelevant. Do not permit the bitterness of the past to confuse your vision.

Your divine connection is the person sent by God and positioned in your prison cell - you cannot miss him. The captain of the guard is instructed to handle their case with extra care - these are VIP prisoners. Many have asked the question. Who is God going to use for my rescue from bondage? A few drift from Church to Church chasing men of God. Some become so worked up with worry. This devotional says "Be still" . . . help is on the way. Help will meet you exactly where you are . . . where you have been sent. Stop pushing issues and seeking to force circumstances. This is the way of the ungodly. The Bible describes the Godly as like a tree planted by the rivers of water, that bringeth forth his fruit in his season; his leaf also shall not wither; and whatsoever he doeth shall prosper. But the ungodly are not so: but are like the chaff which the wind driveth away.

Why do you worry so much about chaff . . . an empty shell that God blows as He wills. Pharaoh is chaff . . . but you are a tree. Pharaoh is angry and tossed up and down but by God only for your connection to be moved effortlessly to where you remain planted. Praise God. Be immoveable in God. Watch the wicked blown away like chaff. Wait on God where he has placed you.

Song

. . . When troubles come and my heart burdened be
and I am still and wait here in the silence until You come to sit awhile with me
You raise me up so I can stand on mountains . . . You raise me up to walk on stormy seas
I am strong when I am on Your shoulders . . . you raise me up to more than I can be.

Prayer: O Lord, teach me to be still and wait on You sometimes even in the silence. Amen

FEBRUARY 16

Service

Bible Text: Genesis 40:4

Gen 40:4 And the captain of the guard charged Joseph with them, and he served them: and they continued a season in ward.

Joseph in earlier days had served Potiphar and then served the Captain of the guards and now he finds himself serving the butler and the baker. The core competence in which he excelled all through his trials was *service*. The Bible teaches that the greatest amongst you will be your servant. Serving is best learnt in harsh environments . . . just as faith grows best not in the summer but the winter seasons. May God teach us to serve. Joseph did not earn any wages. He was serving under a cloud of painful injustice - yet he served so admirably that the most important issues were placed in his care.

Jesus taught the disciples well when he washed their feet . . . knowing one of those feet would betray him with a kiss and the others would deny and desert Him. Service counts more with God when it is as to the unseen invisible God. How would you serve a reigning monarch if appointed his senior adviser? I know you think you will do so excellently, but I dare add you will not serve better that you serve the lowest in the toughest circumstances. Indeed we want to be motivated and encouraged to serve. We want appreciation and we should also give it. But we learn to serve only if we can serve well without these sweeteners. Indeed, our service is as unto God if we can be consistent in all conditions. Do we serve God well only when He smiles at us? Do we serve well when God decides to be silent through our tough seasons?

Joseph did not know he was serving those he would one day rule over as second to Pharaoh. He did not know he would one day allocate resources in a higher role to Potiphar, the captain of the guard and to the butler and baker. He did not serve praying he would one day be their masters as some do. He did not serve despising them for their injustice upon him. He served well and better than the rest.

Have you been given the toughest assignments of service? Have you been unusually consistent especially under pressures and crisis? Do you have the grace to serve even the meanest and harshest of men like you serve God? Ponder on these questions. God needs men for His revival. His men and women who will bring in the harvest of souls will be servants. God is training them. Perhaps you are one of them.

Service like true giving can be hard and unappreciated. True service is neither frivolous or unserious. The Apostle Paul wrote most of the New Testament from the prison cell. A place in which he offered God glorious service that is still blessing mankind.

"The Bible was written in tears and to tears it will yield its best treasure. God has nothing to say to the frivolous man." A.W. Tozer.

Song

Work when the night is coming, Under the sunset skies;
While their bright tints are glowing. Work for daylight flies
Work till the last beam fadeth, fadeth to shine no more;
Work while thenight is darkening, When men's work is o'er.

Prayer: O Lord, I need more grace to serve as you want me to serve. Let me not serve frivolously Amen

FEBRUARY 17

Seasons

Bible Text: Genesis 40:4

Gen 40:4 And the captain of the guard charged Joseph with them, and he served them: and they continued a season in ward.

A season is a period of time marked by certain conditions . . . There are many seasons in life . . . different times. For Joseph it is a season to serve criminals. How will you feel if God permitted such a season in your life?

Ecc 3:1 To every thing there is a season, and a time to every purpose under the Heaven: 2 A time to be born, and a time to die; a time to plant, and a time to pluck up that which is planted; 3 A time to kill, and a time to heal; a time to break down, and a time to build up; 4 A time to weep, and a time to laugh; a time to mourn, and a time to dance; 5 A time to cast away stones, and a time to gather stones together; a time to embrace, and a time to refrain from embracing; 6 A time to get, and a time to lose; a time to keep, and a time to cast away; 7 A time to rend, and a time to sew; a time to keep silence, and a time to speak; 8 A time to love, and a time to hate; a time of war, and a time of peace.

There are times of favor and times of disadvantage. But God appoints the times and seasons. There is no excuse because God provides time for every purpose and for every work. If we say we are faithful, but claim we do not have the opportunity - we lie. Also a man who has no integrity and who is wicked but pretends will also be proven to be so by time. God knows how to bring out our true colors.

Ecc 3:17 I said in mine heart, God shall judge the righteous and the wicked: for there is a time there for every purpose and for every work. Ecc 3:22 Wherefore I perceive that there is nothing better, than that a man should rejoice in his own works; for that is his portion: for who shall bring him to see what shall be after him?

God is in the process of showing what we exactly are - using different seasons to bring out our strengths and sometimes it is our failings that are corrected in the appointed season. Our portion is to rejoice in the present time and accept what God is teaching us. For a season Joseph must serve again . . . a different opportunity to serve for a season unfolds. In this season, the butler and the baker observe Joseph and grow to trust him. Soon they are confiding in him and he becomes their friend. How are you responding in the season before you? Will you be found righteous or wicked? A good thing about seasons is that they change. Soon there shall be a season of showers.

Song

"There shall be showers of blessing:" This is the promise of love;
There shall be seasons refreshing, Sent from the Savior above.

Showers of blessing, Showers of blessing we need:
Mercy drops 'round us are falling, But for the showers we plead.

"There shall be showers of blessing"—Precious reviving again;
Over the hills and the valleys, Sound of abundance of rain.

"There shall be showers of blessing:" Send them upon us, O Lord;
Grant to us now a refreshing; Come, and now honor Thy Word.

"There shall be showers of blessing:" Oh, that today they might fall,
Now as to God we're confessing, Now as on Jesus we call!

Prayer: O Lord, we rejoice and thank you for the seasons. Oh that showers might fall. Amen

FEBRUARY 18

A New Gift

Bible Text: Genesis 40:5-8

Gen 40:5 And they dreamed a dream both of them, each man his dream in one night, each man according to the interpretation of his dream, the butler and the baker of the king of Egypt, which were bound in the prison. 6 And Joseph came in unto them in the morning, and looked upon them, and, behold, they were sad. 7 And he asked Pharaoh's officers that were with him in the ward of his lord's house, saying, Wherefore look ye so sadly to day? 8 And they said unto him, We have dreamed a dream, and there is no interpreter of it. And Joseph said unto them, Do not interpretations belong to God? tell me them, I pray you.

Joseph was not employed to interpret dreams. Indeed he was not employed at all. He was a prisoner serving a sentence, being punished for what He did not do. Why is he now playing the counselor? What kind of spirit is this that cares for the people of the race that has so poorly treated him. Joseph observed the pains and groans of those around him in prison. He was sensitive to the bondage and spiritual defeat. This morning, my question to you is "What are you observing?" ... "What do you notice?" ... "What takes your attention. Joseph expresses a new gift for God. Why is he given this gift?

Many in Joseph's situation will be immersed in bad memories and bitterness. Many will still be asking God "Why me?" Many will be looking at self and be pained at unrealized matters. The temptation to focus on self is more compelling in the prison. But even in the prison, the bridge to a glorious future has been constructed by God. Take your eyes off your issues for a moment and look up ... come higher in your perspective. You will observe the pains and despair of lost souls. You will discern the quiet cries of those who appear to be on top. You will not see their aggression nor their insincerity ... but the root cause of their unspoken sorrows. It is an unselfish man that can be drawn into the pains of others.

We do not know that Joseph had interpreted dreams before. But he knew that interpretations belong to God. Salvation belongs to God. Many flock around you - in need of this salvation but you only see their faults. Shame on you. Joseph noticed the depression of Pharaoh's officers. Lord, help me to be burdened by the sorrow and challenges of others This is what it means to come up higher spiritually. To be able to forget about ourselves and be burdened in intercession for nations, people and situations.

Millions do not know the Lord. They go to Church but have not received the comfort of the Holy Spirit. If you come up higher you will see the heavy luggage weighing them down; that needs to be laid down on the cross. You will not see your own wounds on higher ground. Instead compassion will move you to tears for the barren. Ah ... but you do not know my troubles ... you say. Could you compare them to what Joseph went through and still be moved by compassion for others. I discern a mystery ... how are bitter situations transformed to uncommon compassion? How does sorrow and love meet? Ponder over these and how your trials can be of great value if you go to up to Calvary. You will find as you release them, God can use you in far greater dimensions for others. Receive grace in Christ to focus less on self and be burdened by the pains of others. God has a gift in you waiting to be released.

Song

See from His head, His hands, His feet,
Sorrow and love flow mingled down
Did e'er such love and sorrow meet,
Or thorns compose so rich a crown.

Prayer: O Lord, help me see things you want me to see. Give me compassion for pained souls. Amen

FEBRUARY 19

Two Dreams in a Night

Bible Text: Genesis 40:5-8

Gen 40:5 And they dreamed a dream both of them, each man his dream in one night, each man according to the interpretation of his dream, the butler and the baker of the king of Egypt, which were bound in the prison. 6 And Joseph came in unto them in the morning, and looked upon them, and, behold, they were sad. 7 And he asked Pharaoh's officers that were with him in the ward of his lord's house, saying, Wherefore look ye so sadly to day? 8 And they said unto him, We have dreamed a dream, and there is no interpreter of it. And Joseph said unto them, Do not interpretations belong to God? tell me them, I pray you.

The VIP prisoners are receiving the best treatment in prison. Even in prison, there is a hierarchy and Joseph is assigned to serve and cater for the welfare of the butler and baker of Pharaoh. There are different types of situations in the prison and in life . . . many are happy because they are still being helped by others . . . others also in prison. Joseph should be sad . . . but the Bible does not tell us that he is. Egypt has made special arrangements that though the baker and butler are in prison, they should be well catered for.

God however sends them a troubling dream that makes them sad. Do you wish you are rich and well positioned in society because you think that will make you happy. But peace and joy are with God—and they are not for sale. Because of the destiny of Joseph . . . two VIP prisoners are made sad? They are not sad because they are in prison . . . but because joy is withdrawn from them and troubling dreams sent to them in the same night - but all because of Joseph. God has so many ways of bringing your destiny to pass. The sadness of the world and the gloom of sinners may seem to you justified and at best not your business. You have been warned to stay out of people's issues and not carry burdens that are not yours—but this was not the way of Joseph. Will Joseph pass this test? Will he walk away from this sadness of criminals or will he pass another test set for him. Sometimes your destiny is linked to unusual and exceptional obedience . . . doing what others will ordinarily not do. Look around . . . is someone troubled? Do you care? Are you burdened or too aloof? Bring someone to Calvary. Come yourself and lay down your troubles.

Song

Days are filled with sorrow and care,
Hearts are lonely and drear;
Burdens are lifted at Calvary,
Jesus is very near.

Refrain:
Burdens are lifted at Calvary,
Calvary, Calvary;
Burdens are lifted at Calvary,
Jesus is very near.

Cast your care on Jesus today,
Leave your worry and fear;
Burdens are lifted at Calvary,
Jesus is very near.

Troubled soul, the Savior can see
Ev'ry heartache and tear;
Burdens are lifted at Calvary,
Jesus is very near.

Prayer: O Lord Jesus . . . our burden bearer . . . I bring all the burdens of the many troubled souls around me . . . please lift them all as I lay them at Calvary. Amen

FEBRUARY 20

Linked to the Vine

Bible Text: Genesis 40:9-15

Gen 40:9 And the chief butler told his dream to Joseph, and said to him, In my dream, behold, a vine was before me; 10 And in the vine were three branches: and it was as though it budded, and her blossoms shot forth; and the clusters thereof brought forth ripe grapes: 11 And Pharaoh's cup was in my hand: and I took the grapes, and pressed them into Pharaoh's cup, and I gave the cup into Pharaoh's hand.12 And Joseph said unto him, This is the interpretation of it: The three branches are three days: 13 Yet within three days shall Pharaoh lift up thine head, and restore thee unto thy place: and thou shalt deliver Pharaoh's cup into his hand, after the former manner when thou wast his butler. 14 But think on me when it shall be well with thee, and shew kindness, I pray thee, unto me, and make mention of me unto Pharaoh, and bring me out of this house: 15 For indeed I was stolen away out of the land of the Hebrews: and here also have I done nothing that they should put me into the dungeon.

The Bible often describes Christ as the Vine . . . . and His children are branches that must bear fruit. He laid down His life to be crushed only to be resurrected in three days to report back a finished work that has earned a glorious restoration for all who give their life to Him. Wine is a symbol of joy, restoration and mercy. Christ is good news to be preached to others. In Him is restoration, joy and fresh new beginnings. Christ is joy . . . A Christian cannot be without this joy that is from within. Reflect on this joy and Christ's work of restoration in lives of men. Perhaps someone you know needs to know Him.

Back to Joseph. Joseph interprets a dream and prophesies a restoration in three days - a picture of Christ's resurrection . . . and also an interpretation that releases another series of future events that admits Joseph into a future glory. In similar fashion, when we and all our old passions are crucified with Christ we are resurrected to partake in a present victorious walk and a future glorious destiny. Joseph brings up his situation and pleads for kindness - restating his innocence.

We only need to be born to be captives of the devil. All have fallen and will fall short of the glory because the world has been sold to sin. When one man -Adam fell, mankind's destiny was stolen and all men find themselves in a hopeless spiral without the work of Christ - also one man. Present teachings that suggest there are other good men in Asia etc. by which people will be saved is dangerous poison. Man fell because of one man - the first Adam and because of one man - the second, man can also be restored. We do not need to do anything to be lost without Christ.

In three days, the butler will be restored and later Joseph will also be restored. Similarly, in three days Christ arose from the dead . . . mankind now could be saved and will enter a future glory in Him. It was all the sacrifice of Christ. All the dreams God has given you will one day come to pass. The harvest of souls will be reaped. The future glory with Christ in Eternity will be our portion. The story of the butler was prophesied to end well. All that are in Christ will end well. Let your life be truly given to Him.

Song

Through the love of God our Savior . . . All will be well;
Free and changeless is His favour . . . All, all is well.
Precious is the blood that healed us; Perfect is the grace that sealed us;
Strong the hand stretched forth to shield us; All must be well

Prayer: O Lord, May it be well with all that pertains to us. Amen

FEBRUARY 21

Make mention of me

Bible Text: Genesis 40:14

Gen 40: 14 But think on me when it shall be well with thee, and shew kindness, I pray thee, unto me, and make mention of me unto Pharaoh, and bring me out of this house: 15 For indeed I was stolen away out of the land of the Hebrews: and here also have I done nothing that they should put me into the dungeon.

Joseph voices his inner pains and anguish . . . "make mention of me unto Pharaoh and bring me out" Unfortunately pleas to men are vain. The child of destiny can only be helped by God although he serves Potiphar, the poor prisoner and at last here is the VIP Prisoner . . . but all of them must forget him for a season until Joseph has lost all hope in them. Our hope and trust must be in God. God must move at the time that God has appointed. The lesson is to be good and serve others as though we serve God but to look up to God for His help. God and God alone must help us. Still we are human and our pains will occasionally be voiced . . . the destiny and plans of God would have been marred if Joseph were helped by Potiphar, his wife, the Captain of the guards or the chief butler or baker. We must wait for God. Do you know the inability of people we look up to help us when we want them to can be a good sign that God has something better ahead. I encourage someone in a difficult situation to keep looking up to God as we joyfully serve in the vineyard. It does not matter if you are believed or not. God does not need men the way we perceive He does. His delay is not a denial, but part of His plans.

Song

A Sov'reign Protector I have,
Unseen, yet forever at hand,
Unchangeably faithful to save,
Almighty to rule and command.
He smiles, and my comforts abound;
His grace as the dew shall descend;
And walls of salvation surround
The soul He delights to defend.

Inspirer and Hearer of prayer,
Thou Shepherd and Guardian of Thine,
My all to Thy covenant care
I sleeping and waking resign.
If Thou art my Shield and my Sun,
The night is no darkness to me;
And fast as my moments roll on,
They bring me but nearer to Thee.

Kind Author, and ground of my hope,
Thee, Thee, for my God I avow;
My glad Ebenezer set up,
And own Thou hast helped me till now.
I muse on the years that are past,
Wherein my defense Thou hast proved;
Nor wilt Thou relinquish at last
A sinner so signally loved!

Prayer: Sovereign Protector—Be our constant help . . . may our eyes be lifted up to you. Amen

FEBRUARY 22

Unrealistic Expectations

Bible Text: Genesis 40:16-19

Gen 40:16 When the chief baker saw that the interpretation was good, he said unto Joseph, I also was in my dream, and, behold, I had three white baskets on my head: 17 And in the uppermost basket there was of all manner of bakemeats for Pharaoh; and the birds did eat them out of the basket upon my head. 18 And Joseph answered and said, This is the interpretation thereof: The three baskets are three days: 19 Yet within three days shall Pharaoh lift up thy head from off thee, and shall hang thee on a tree; and the birds shall eat thy flesh from off thee.

Psa_101:1 A Psalm of David. I will sing of mercy and judgment: unto thee, O LORD, will I sing.

The psalmist sings of mercy and judgment. *Psa_89:14 Justice and judgment are the habitation of thy throne: mercy and truth shall go before thy face.* God is merciful and He is just at the same time. He does not wink at evil, yet He forgives like none else. This is a deep mystery. The baker emerges only to be hanged on a tree. God's mercy is based on justice. Christ paid the price for our sins ... the chastisement that brought us peace was laid upon Him, and by His stripes we are healed. Notice chastisement and peace; stripes and healing; his crucifixion and our salvation. As Christ went up to glory, Judas hangs. The unrepentant baker hangs ... his hopes were only presumptions. Do not compare your situation with others or look to men - instead, let the word of God shape your hopes. Mercy and Judgment are twins ... Expect great acts of God's mercy even as judgment also begins in His house—the church ... the same place where His mercy floes like a river. Many preach a God who does not judge ... they are like the chief baker expecting a good interpretation. But sometimes we must face to the reality that God is a righteous judge. He will judge wrong with a commensurate punishment now matches the misdeed. Many persist in evil because all they see is a God who is merciful—they do not repent and keep having an unrealistic expectation that things will end well. We cannot be steeped in idolatry and profanity .... ignoring calls to repent and expect mercy. Judas was offered the forgiveness of Christ on the cross, but He rejected it ... too proud to repent and go back to God for another chance. Saul similarly expected Samuel to cover up for him ... these were unrealistic expectations. Our expectations must tie with the word of God. Ephraim was blessed but eventually was joined to idols ... it will be unrealistic to expect to remain blessed in idolatry but many do. Examine your expectations concerning God. Are they aligned with the word of God and His nature as the God of Mercy and Justice. If your expectations do not match with the word of God ... accept God's corrections quickly. You can begin with humbling yourself and repenting. Do not presume ... instead believe and receive Christ.

Song

"Almost persuaded" now to believe; "Almost persuaded" Christ to receive;
Seems now some soul to say: Go, Spirit, go Thy way;
Some more convenient day On Thee I'll call.

"Almost persuaded," come, come today! "Almost persuaded," turn not away;
Jesus invites you here; Angels are ling'ring near;
Prayers rise from hearts so dear; O wand'rer, come!

"Almost persuaded": harvest is past! "Almost persuaded": doom comes at last;
"Almost" cannot avail;" Almost" is but to fail;
Sad, sad, that bitter wail: "Almost"—but lost

Prayer: O Lord, Open our hearts that many presume for many reasons that in their unbelief they will be saved ... and help us to see our need for repentance. Amen

The Traitor

Bible Text: Genesis 40:16- 19

Gen 40:16 When the chief baker saw that the interpretation was good, he said unto Joseph, I also was in my dream, and, behold, I had three white baskets on my head: 17 And in the uppermost basket there was of all manner of bakemeats for Pharaoh; and the birds did eat them out of the basket upon my head. 18 And Joseph answered and said, This is the interpretation thereof: The three baskets are three days: 19 Yet within three days shall Pharaoh lift up thy head from off thee, and shall hang thee on a tree; and the birds shall eat thy flesh from off thee.

The treachery of Satan is an example that is echoed in all who reject the grace that is freely given in Christ. While in the first dream of the butler, he sees himself serving and pleasing the King - in the dream, Pharaoh; the dream of the baker is different. There were bakemeats meant for the King but which were served to birds.

Centuries later, a man called Judas called and commissioned by Christ to be a disciple but secretly a thief and a traitor, serves the interests of the Pharisees and other agents of hell to betray Christ. Just as Christ is resurrected after three days, Judas ends up hanging, his corpse feeding birds. The lot of a traitor is a bad end. There are many pictures in scripture that point out that it is not all that will end well. For many the end will be fearfully horrible. We are in a time when many question the reality of hell and a horrible end . . . but the types and admonitions in scripture do not support that there is no hell.

Luk_6:25 Woe unto you that are full! for ye shall hunger. Woe unto you that laugh now! for ye shall mourn and weep.

I do pray that your end will be well. Reflect in this devotional on the way you will end. How will my case be? Do not assume or be presumptuous? Ask God who knows the two available paths, the path of life and that of death. David did not take chances. He went to God for answers. You can also discover yourself through the word of God. God judges our ways by His word and there is an illumination for us to correct our deviations. The baker assumed he would also have good news and was bold to reveal his dreams. He was wrong. We can go to God for mercy to help us to be right with Him. Most are too ignorant to do so and would rather just continue in an ignorant presumption that all is well . . . when the word reveals that it is not.

Psa 19:12 Who can understand his errors? cleanse thou me from secret faults. 13 Keep back thy servant also from presumptuous sins; let them not have dominion over me: then shall I be upright, and I shall be innocent from the great transgression. 14 Let the words of my mouth, and the meditation of my heart, be acceptable in thy sight, O LORD, my strength, and my redeemer.

Pray to God for mercy to end well. That which is meant for God - your body is to be His temple—but how come it is served to foul birds? Lord help and change a bad situation.

Song

Yield not to temptation, for yielding is sin; Each victory will help you . . . some other to win
Fight manfully onward, dark passions subdue; Look ever to Jesus, He'll carry you through.
Ask the Savior to help you, Comfort strengthen and keep you;
He is willing to aid you, He will carry you through.

Dr H.R Palmer

Prayer: O Lord, Have mercy on my soul. Let my end be glorious and not shame. Amen

FEBRUARY 24

Unhappy Birthday

Bible Text: Genesis 40:20-22

Gen 40:20 And it came to pass the third day, which was Pharaoh's birthday, that he made a feast unto all his servants: and he lifted up the head of the chief butler and of the chief baker among his servants. 21 And he restored the chief butler unto his butlership again; and he gave the cup into Pharaoh's hand: 22 But he hanged the chief baker: as Joseph had interpreted to them

One is uncomfortable to discover that there are two birthday celebrations mentioned in the Bible. That of Pharaoh and that of Herod. We joyfully celebrate the resurrection of our Lord Jesus on the appointed third day. For some the resurrection of Christ is bad news, a horrible judgment . . . those who will not surrender to Christ. God lifts up one and puts down another. Our birthday is a good day to reflect on our lives, to number them, noting a future accounting is coming at the appointed time.

John was imprisoned and martyred from celebrations from Herod's birthdays. Christ Himself described as greater than all the prophets before him. Although we have no record of the saints in the Bible celebrating their birthday, we see nothing to suggest this is wrong. We are foolish to use it for vain consumption and exhibitions. Unwise to place ourselves on a huge podium as though we are more than grass. One fact to know is that with every passing birthday, we approach an appointed day. The day of the Lord. Even if celebration of birthdays have heathen origin, we can lift up the crucified and risen Lord and take advantage of coming together to share the good news of salvation.

Men give gifts to men which they take away. Pharaoh must have received many beautiful presents . . . many in a museum somewhere forgotten today. Joseph received divine confirmation of the gift of interpretation of dreams as the interpretation of Joseph came to pass. Joseph knew the gifts of the best men will one day be taken - as he reflected on his beautiful coat of many colors . . . now stained in blood and discarded. God can give you a gift that men will not take from you. Ask Him for a special gift, that will be used for His glory.

There was no celebration for Joseph though the Bible confirms a great gift that God will one day use. In the palace Pharaoh received several masterpieces of art and treasures fashioned by men. In the dungeon, Joseph knows he has God. The butler and the baker move forward into different destinies. Laughter and dancing and entertainment continue in the palace. Joseph is not invited but he is hopeful that in the butler he has found a sponsor. Things sometimes do not go as we plan and hope. The sweet wines are enjoyed in the palace of Pharaoh, but for Joseph in a dungeon - only the bitter taste of the prisoner's meal. But if the bud has a bitter taste, sweet will be the flower.

Song

His purpose will ripen fast. Unfolding every hour
The bud may have a bitter taste. But sweet will be the flower.

Prayer: O Lord, Help me to trust you in the winter season. Amen

FEBRUARY 25

God is His own Interpreter

Bible Text: Genesis 40:20-22

Gen 40:20 And it came to pass the third day, which was Pharaoh's birthday, that he made a feast unto all his servants: and he lifted up the head of the chief butler and of the chief baker among his servants. 21 And he restored the chief butler unto his butlership again; and he gave the cup into Pharaoh's hand: 22 But he hanged the chief baker: as Joseph had interpreted to them

We need answers and we read the Bible. But there are now many interpreters and many false comforts. We are in an era where so many different Bibles have been written to make the Bible easy to read . . . this is good, but the Bible still needs to be interpreted. We are sad . . . and in need of comfort to combat the world views from all the religions, people and nations who go to the same Bible but come up with different answers. Joseph's interpretation came true. The Bible tells us who the comforter that will explain our situations and what will happen to us . . . the Comforter tells us the future and sometimes it's good news like it was for the butler . . . but there are times when it isn't. God's interpreter is God—the Holy Spirit.

Psa_51:11 Cast me not away from thy presence; and take not thy holy spirit from me

Joh_14:26 But the Comforter, which is the Holy Ghost, whom the Father will send in my name, he shall teach you all things, and bring all things to your remembrance, whatsoever I have said unto you.

Both the Butler and Baker were sad . . . Joseph provided the correct interpretation just as the Holy Spirit comforts us. We need the comfort of the Holy Spirit because our dreams will only find accurate interpretation if the Holy Spirit helps us to see the way and know what God is asking of us, the corrections He is demanding and the insights he wants us to pick. Many faiths play down the role of the Holy Spirit and play up the intellect of men—the result is more sadness and well-meaning errors. Modern interpretations are based on the perspectives of the prevailing culture and the world view but they are not always based on the comfort of the Holy Spirit. There is nothing—past, present and future that surprises the Holy Spirit. Be filled by the Holy Spirit . . . and guard that relationship. Do not grieve the Holy Spirit.

Song

For Thy Gift of God the Spirit, With us, in us, e'er to be,
Pledge of life and Hope of glory, Savior, we would worship Thee.

He who in Creation's dawning, Brooded o'er the pathless deep,
Still across our nature's darkness - Moves to wake our souls from sleep.

Moves to stir, to draw, to quicken; Thrusts us thro' with sense of sin;
Then, Himself, the Pledge, He seals us—Saving Advocate within.

He, the mighty God, indwells us: His to strengthen, help, empow'r;
His to overcome the Tempter—Ours to call in danger's hour.

He it is, the Living Author, Wakes to life the sacred Word;
Reads with us its holy pages, And reveals our risen Lord.

Prayer: Come Holy Spirit . . . reveal the true interpretations that answer and comfort my daily questions. Amen

FEBRUARY 26

Yet...

Bible Text: Genesis 40:23

Gen 40:23 Yet did not the chief butler remember Joseph, but forgat him.

The most puzzling thing for many to deal with is when they believe God is about to move and He does not. There is perhaps none that has not been humbled by God's strategic intelligence ... His ways are not remotely ours. Even if He explained His ways ... how could we understand an intelligence that created and masters the entire universe. Even Joseph may have been disappointed and so will the best of men. But God has not asked us to be God because we can never.

What do we do when God suspends everything and does nothing for years? How do we deal with God not backing up our understanding of things? These are opportunities for us to be humble and do nothing.

What do you when you have waited, expected and things just seem to be getting worse and there is no help in sight. The answer is ... nothing. Watch, wait ... pray then watch, wait and then pray then watch again ...

There are things we should not do. We should not go around defending self or canvassing those who already will not listen ... we should not stop praising God.

Watching, waiting and praying implies we trust God. In His time, He will come through at the appointed time. God did not help Daniel until He was faced with lions in the den ... many will fairly expect that God should have moved earlier but God had already planned a script which ended with the crushing of his enemies. Daniel simply watched for what God will do ... He prayed and kept praising God and waited for God to do it. It is pointless moving ahead of God even when it is obvious ... we still need the Holy Spirit to tell us to move in a specific direction. Lord teach us to wait as we should ... teach us to pray ... learning to commune and enjoy the communion with God and then show us how to watch ... to be careful not to do something wrong ... teach us to watch ... to watch our tongues, watch our hearts, watch our eyes and watch our actions. Help us to watch and not be provoked by our disappointments and help us not to be baited to act foolishly. Help us to do ... nothing, when that is what is required. To just endure a little longer.

Song

Christian, seek not yet repose, Hear thy gracious Savior say;
Thou art in the midst of foes: Watch and pray.

Principalities and powers, Mustering their unseen array,
Wait for thy unguarded hours: Watch and pray.

Gird thy Heavenly armor on, Wear it ever night and day;
Ambushed lies the evil one: Watch and pray.

Hear the victors who o'ercame, Still they mark each warrior's way;
All with one sweet voice exclaim, Watch and pray.

Hear, above all, hear thy Lord, Him thou lovest to obey;
Hide within thy heart His word: Watch and pray.

Watch, as if on that alone hung the issue of the day;
Pray, that help may be sent down: Watch and pray.

Prayer: O Lord, help us to watch, wait and pray when that is all we can do. Amen

FEBRUARY 27

God needs no Sponsor

Bible Text: Genesis 40:23

Gen 40:23 Yet did not the chief butler remember Joseph, but forgat him.

Many zealots make great exaggerated claims for God. Many promise Heaven and earth. God must wait till all the glory is His before He makes His greatest moves. He therefore needs the defeated Moses in the wilderness, the forgotten Joseph in the dungeon and wandering wanted man - David. Of this we can be sure said an old time preacher. God needs no encouragement; He needs no advice, no comfort and no sponsors. He is never late and never too early. He is always on time. Never expect much from the best meaning of men. They will have to be first proven as only men, for you to be delivered from hero worship. Many men have become vain idols. Lord help me to look up to you.

Joseph expects that his troubles are over but he must still wait for two uneventful years. Joseph imagines that he will be freed to go back home, perhaps helped by the butler to be reunited with his brethren or to start a new life in Egypt. Either way, his vision was far too limited. God had far greater plans than Joseph could ever imagine and God was sponsoring His plan Himself. All the resources and enablement to realize God's plans are with God - to be released in the time He also appoints.

Joseph is forgotten by the butler, forgotten by his Hebrew family, forgotten by the household of Potiphar but God had not forgotten him.

Isa_49:15 Can a woman forget her sucking child, that she should not have compassion on the son of her womb? yea, they may forget, yet will I not forget thee.

We have hardly seen a woman forget her sucking child, but the prophet says this is even possible. Children born and unborn have been forgotten and sacrificed for convenience and financial gratification. Many sell their own into slavery. But God will not forget His own. The attachment of God to His word and His promises to His children cannot be appreciated with human parallel, because there are no illustrations we can use to portray the faithfulness of God. It has never been even remotely stretched.

God causes men to forget us or they will mar his work plan . . . moving too quickly to take us off course. Today, as you reflect on this verse, let it not surprise you when men are not able to keep their word. It may be God behind their folly. Instead, see no man or flesh as the appointed sponsor of God's benevolence - no matter how low or high. Look to God's faithfulness always.

Song

Great is thy faithfulness O God my father.
There is no shadow of turning with thee
Thou changeth not thy compassion they fail not
As thou hast been thou forever will be

Prayer: O Lord, I praise you . . . Great indeed is thy faithfulness. Amen

February 28

More Silence

Bible Text: Genesis 41:1

Gen 41:1 And it came to pass at the end of two full years, that Pharaoh dreamed: and, behold, he stood by the river

Just when you think God is ready to move, then comes two full years of absolute silence. Can God put your life on "pause" for two full years . . . to fit into His purpose. We were created for His pleasure and not vice-versa you know. May we not be noisy when God is silent. I see this as the most complex and mysterious of tests. The Bible does say that they that wait upon the Lord shall be strong, mounting on wings as eagles and soaring higher and higher beyond their dreams. Wait means holding on and enjoying the silent periods with God. Nothing changes for two years. Joseph has been trained in a pit before and knows this two years shall pass and once again he will yet praise his God in freedom. He does not grumble as the time passes and eventually it all comes to an end.

Do you know that it is often we think all is over and lost that God now moves into a completely unexpected high gear. This time it is Pharaoh that is troubled in his sleep with a dream. But before we consider Pharaoh, focus on the expression "full". The years had to be completed . . . every last day and every last minute. Do not permit yourself to be cheated by those who sell you a shortcuts. Shortcuts will cut your destiny, future and glory short. Many characters like Gehazi, Judas, Demas and the destroyed sons of Aaron, Nadab and Abihu and many more wanted short cuts. Every deception of hell must offer a shorter, smoother and wider route that will lead ultimately to damnation. Why can we not learn precept upon precept and line upon line? Why can we not grow like all things in nature grow? Slowly but surely.

In summary, do remember that what you are going through will come to pass. What matters is if you have passed the test of times of silence. I see someone reading this devotional moving up . . . I see someone who thinks surely the end has come suddenly entering a completely new era and phase of glory.

God says it is time for Pharaoh's peace to be arrested until you are repositioned for God's harvest. Why is all this happening? Not for Egypt surely but to preserve the Hebrews. It is all for God, by God and to God. Everything God is doing is towards Revival of His own and taking them to Himself in eternal glory. You can wait on Him or just do your own thing. Those who waited will be glad they did.

Song

I will wait on you, Almighty God in the beauty of your holiness
I will worship you Almighty God in the beauty of your holiness.

Prayer: O Lord, teach me to wait on you in the beauty of your holiness. Amen

MARCH 1

Dreams of Pharaoh

Bible Text: Genesis 41:1

Gen 41:1 And it came to pass at the end of two full years, that Pharaoh dreamed: and, behold, he stood by the river

There are many great dreams that have been dreamt, but there are few who are able to position things to bring the good and avoid the evil associated with our dreams. Pharaoh, the great ruler has dreamed, but he has no understanding on what to do concerning the dreams. God can humble us by giving us great visions and dreams but ensuring someone seeks His face to know the interpretation.

Imagine what would have happened if there was no one to interpret the dreams of Pharaoh. God forbid, the famine would have cost the lives of millions all over the world. Imagine what would have happened if no one remembered Joseph . . . everyone would have perhaps perished with hunger . . . the brother, father . . . Potiphar's household . . . the prisoners and maybe even Joseph himself. A child of destiny has an important role to play . . . and there is a heavy cost to many if that important part is not played.

It takes divine insight to understand God's agenda coded in the dreams he has given, but moreso it also takes the wisdom that only God gives to bring to pass what God ordains. God is also in control of events and knows how to initiate the next phase of events in your life . . . God does not need you to bring His great plans concerning you to fruition . . . but remain obedient and shine as you were created to do. Someone reading this devotional may have forgotten about the destiny of greatness revealed through visions and dreams. You have said how can it be? Joseph will occasionally remember the dreams of his brothers bowing and concluded it cannot come to pass . . . but God is at work in His eternal laboratory arranging all that must be arranged . . . completely beyond our grasp. The time has come for Pharaoh to be given the dreams that is connected to your greatness. It is time for you to rise up from the darkness of the pit. Get ready.

Song

Blessed be the Holy God Jesus Christ, His Son, our Lord
died and rose again for love. By His blood we live assured.

Joy Unspeakable and full of glory that the world can never take away.
Yet believing—joyfully receiving
Even Salvation—the end of our faith.

His power kept us through all the years In temptations His presence near
Tried our faith and made it dear Praise and glory as He appears

Amazing Grace, shall always be my song of praise. For it was grace that bought my liberty.
I do not know just why He came to love me so; He looked beyond my fault and saw my need.

I shall forever lift my eyes to Calvary, To view the cross where Jesus died for me.
How marvellous the grace that caught my falling soul; He looked beyond my fault and saw my need.

Prayer: O Lord, as you work your great works. Let my eyes be lifted to Calvary for grace that brings me out of the pit. Look beyond my faults and see my needs . . . make haste to help me. Amen

MARCH 2

God Moves

Bible Text: Genesis 41:2-8

Gen 41:2 And, behold, there came up out of the river seven well favoured kine and fatfleshed; and they fed in a meadow. 3 And, behold, seven other kine came up after them out of the river, ill favoured and leanfleshed; and stood by the other kine upon the brink of the river. 4 And the ill favoured and leanfleshed kine did eat up the seven well favoured and fat kine. So Pharaoh awoke. 5 And he slept and dreamed the second time: and, behold, seven ears of corn came up upon one stalk, rank and good. 6 And, behold, seven thin ears and blasted with the east wind sprung up after them. 7 And the seven thin ears devoured the seven rank and full ears. And Pharaoh awoke, and, behold, it was a dream. 8 And it came to pass in the morning that his spirit was troubled; and he sent and called for all the magicians of Egypt, and all the wise men thereof: and Pharaoh told them his dream; but there was none that could interpret them unto Pharaoh.

Money, fame and power can do a lot for us, but there are many things that are not for sale. We can have the most luxurious beddings but a minute of sleep is not for sale. We can put everything in order and plan and budget to the last cent . . . but financial peace cannot be bought. Indeed, the best hospitals, doctors and health advise may be available to us . . . still we find health priceless even for the wealthiest of men. I read recently of a great inventor who had become one of the globe's richest men, but an incurable cancer reduces him quickly to nothing. Pharaoh shakes off the first dream and decides to sleep again . . . only to be troubled again. Can you ever escape God? Even if you do not want to see a preacher . . . God can come to you when you cannot stop whatever he wants to paint in your memory. There are many truths, we consider too troubling and we do not want to hear them. But God can force whatever impression he so determines upon us. When God moves, nothing can shut him out.

All the magicians in your life will be disgraced and God proven true. All the wise men are only wise to the extent that God helps them to see. Only God can interpret His own dream and no other intelligence. Someone in contact with God is required to bring that interpretation. Are you troubled? Go to God. Find where God speaks . . . through His word, preacher or prophet. Every trouble has an interpretation. God only moves through our troubled mind to make us seek Him knowing that when we seek Him and do so with all our hearts we will find Him. It is time to seek the face of the Lord. God is moving. Seek Him and find out what to do. Be sensitive to the Holy Spirit speaking to your heart concerning the events troubling your rest.

Song

There's no place I can hide from Your love
I can only survive through Your love
Show me somewhere to go a place You don't know To cover my soul

On the wings of the dawn I might fly
To the ends of the earth beyond the sky
I can go anywhere But You'll always be there Wherever I go

You know where I sit and where I stand
Each moment I live I'm in Your hands
I can't get away from Your sweet Spirit
Lord, you're never sleeping

Prayer: O Lord, lead me to always seek your face. Amen

MARCH 3

Inaccessible Light

Bible Text: Genesis 41:2-8

Gen 41:2 And, behold, there came up out of the river seven well favoured kine and fatfleshed; and they fed in a meadow. 3 And, behold, seven other kine came up after them out of the river, ill favoured and leanfleshed; and stood by the other kine upon the brink of the river. 4 And the ill favoured and leanfleshed kine did eat up the seven well favoured and fat kine. So Pharaoh awoke. 5 And he slept and dreamed the second time: and, behold, seven ears of corn came up upon one stalk, rank and good. 6 And, behold, seven thin ears and blasted with the east wind sprung up after them. 7 And the seven thin ears devoured the seven rank and full ears. And Pharaoh awoke, and, behold, it was a dream. 8 And it came to pass in the morning that his spirit was troubled; and he sent and called for all the magicians of Egypt, and all the wise men thereof: and Pharaoh told them his dream; but there was none that could interpret them unto Pharaoh.

God is the master of all creation. He controls the larger picture that drive the geo-politics, economics and social dynamics in the nations. That is why although He encourages industry, He warns us not to take the work of our hands too seriously and instead trust Him. There are seasons of surprising abundance unrelated to our labors and there are famines that make nonsense of our projections. These are more than economic cycles, but rather ordained events that must occur only as God orders. God is able to make changes that will completely upset the order we are used to. He can turn our cleverest paradigms until we are spinning in confusion. Ask the great thinkers and watch them conclude "we do not know what is going on". I hear too many gurus on the pulpit claiming answers they do not have. The stock markets, weather and other indicators can appear to be predictable . . . but time and time again . . . the surprises have been more compelling. Man does not know how to say "we do not know" . . . but in reality that is the truth.

God is omniscient. He knows all things and is active in all things. He will show His created beings what He is doing . . . but we can only see a shadow of far more complex arrangements. Even if we could see it all, how could we ever be able to understand it. Global Recessions, booms and earthquakes are often described as acts of God. But God likes to disclose His secrets to His generals, His children. Magicians, scientists and wise men will wonder at the depth of understanding of he who possesses the mind of Christ. Similarly the fake, who never knew God and is void of any divine insight, borrows ideas from the world view. We ought to praise God, that is still mindful of us . . . to be even slightly interested in man should cause us to marvel. Still, He shares his secrets with us. We honor the great scientists and their accomplishment but they have not scratched even the fringes of His purposes.

Pharaoh is given a dream so that hidden things of God will be revealed through a prisoner who knows Him - a dream that scientists and wise men will never be able to decipher. Today are there still hidden things that God wants to tell His own? Are there signs that need to be interpreted? Are the press and the intelligentsia giving correct interpretations of the trends and patterns? Do we not see when we look only a little closer that these interpretations are often way off the mark. Praise God for His inaccessible knowledge - His light that only He can give and none can approach.

Song

Immortal Invisible God only wise
In light inaccessible hid from our eyes
Most blessed Most glorious the Ancient of Days
Almighty Victorious - Thy Great name we praise.

Prayer: O Lord, who dwells in light inaccessible - I praise you Amen

MARCH 4

Omniscience

Bible Text: Genesis 41:9-13

Gen 41:9 Then spake the chief butler unto Pharaoh, saying, I do remember my faults this day: 10 Pharaoh was wroth with his servants, and put me in ward in the captain of the guard's house, both me and the chief baker: 11 And we dreamed a dream in one night, I and he; we dreamed each man according to the interpretation of his dream. 12 And there was there with us a young man, an Hebrew, servant to the captain of the guard; and we told him, and he interpreted to us our dreams; to each man according to his dream he did interpret. 13 And it came to pass, as he interpreted to us, so it was; me he restored unto mine office, and him he hanged.

It is one thing to be remembered. It is another to be remembered for good. How we are remembered and the timing and what happens as a result of the memory of our deeds is more important than just being remembered. Mordecai had also done some laudable acts which were forgotten at the time, and not rewarded until the King Ahaseurus is troubled to seek to reward Mordecai . . . but at the exact time when Haman was putting finishing touches to his execution. Do you see that the timing of our remembrance and what it achieves is of extreme importance?

God is not man with imperfect memory. He has scheduled events in a different calendar than what we are familiar with. We say He has forgotten, when our calendar suggests God should be moving and He has a different timetable.

My sister, my brother - be assured that you have not been forgotten. We have heard great prophesies of revival . . . God has not forgotten. His end-time calendar and the glorious future events that will close this dispensation of time . . . . God has not forgotten. Not a single jot of His word will fail. There will be a great revival.

The butler remembers . . . but it is more correct to say God opened his memory for Joseph to be brought forward. God is excellent in all His ways. He is not an absent minded doting old man. How can the God who has numbered our hair with precision and knows the numbers even for all of creation in all of time forget anything? I wonder how many billion gigabytes of memory will contain His thoughts. How much of His thoughts can He possible reveal to man's limited brain? Only a very tiny fraction.

As you reflect on this journal my prayer is that you will not just be remembered for a handshake or thank you but for a greater good. The word says you will receive double for your trouble. Joseph got more than double for his trials. We should thank God if we think a bit deeper - even for the delays He supervises, for our greater good. Praise God for His omniscience.

Song

Remember me O Lord 3ce today.

Prayer: O Lord, remember me for good. Amen

MARCH 5

Controller of Thoughts

Bible Text: Genesis 41:9-13

Gen 41:9 Then spake the chief butler unto Pharaoh, saying, I do remember my faults this day: 10 Pharaoh was wroth with his servants, and put me in ward in the captain of the guard's house, both me and the chief baker: 11 And we dreamed a dream in one night, I and he; we dreamed each man according to the interpretation of his dream. 12 And there was there with us a young man, an Hebrew, servant to the captain of the guard; and we told him, and he interpreted to us our dreams; to each man according to his dream he did interpret. 13 And it came to pass, as he interpreted to us, so it was; me he restored unto mine office, and him he hanged.

God controls every detail. Even our thoughts and our memories. We can forget because God causes us to forget and we can remember because God causes us to remember. Thoughts are extremely powerful levers. Thoughts can destroy and they can change things radically for good. Every awesome revolution starts with a thought . . . similarly every act of destruction and shame also starts with thoughts. We are warned not to just entertain any thoughts and to flee immoral thoughts as these shape futures negatively.

The Bible speaks of thoughts that contradict the will and purpose of God . . . thoughts of discouragement or fears. Thoughts playing with sin in our mind and thoughts that do not enthrone God - are all to be cast down.

2Co 10:5 Casting down imaginations, and every high thing that exalteth itself against the knowledge of God, and bringing into captivity every thought to the obedience of Christ;

Just as God uses thoughts to prosper His plans, the enemy of God also send arrows of thoughts to frustrate them . . . but to no avail. Even if you have been forgotten and it seems all thoughts have conspired against you. Remember that God is sovereign. God had a reason for Joseph to be forgotten and a good reason for him to be remembered. God's thoughts are so far from and advanced compared to ours and so we cannot understand His interventions.

God can raise someone somewhere with the thought to elevate you. God can raise someone somewhere with the thought to promote you. God can raise someone somewhere with the thought to help you. God can raise someone somewhere with the thought to give you exactly what you require. But then we must be discerning with our thoughts . . .

David woke up one day with immoral thoughts and did not cast down these evil imaginations by filling his heart with the desires of God. Before long, he committed adultery with Bathsheba and Urriah was murdered . . . unleashing so many other painful consequences. What is presently dominating your thoughts? God's plans to do good or evil lusts? God's best thoughts are thoughts of thanksgiving and gladness. Are your thoughts dwelling on truth, purity and God's goodness? Spend more time meditating on God's word to correct your thought patterns.

Song

I will enter His gates with thanksgiving in my heart. I will enter His courts with praise
I will say, this is the day that the Lord, has made. I will rejoice for He has made me glad
He has made me glad . . . I am so glad. I will rejoice for He has made me glad. 2ce

Prayer: O Lord, fill me with thoughts of joy, thanksgiving and gladness. Amen

MARCH 6

Change is Inevitable

Bible Text: Genesis 41:14

Gen 41:14 Then Pharaoh sent and called Joseph, and they brought him hastily out of the dungeon: and he shaved himself, and changed his raiment, and came in unto Pharaoh.

Old raiment does not fit in the palace. There are old ways that must not be carried to your next level. There must be change and many elements of our lives that must change dramatically. We must not be afraid of change but rather see change as inevitable. Our ways of thinking and aspects of our character must change. For some location will change, our capabilities and capacities can also change ... careers change ... our aspirations changes. But what about raiment? Raiment represents the first impression we give others ... that which is first concluded about us ... our visible passion. We can begin a give a very different impression such that all who see us only desire to favor us.

Zechariah 3:4 And he answered and spake unto those that stood before him, saying, Take away the filthy garments from him. And unto him he said, Behold, I have caused thine iniquity to pass from thee, and I will clothe thee with change of raiment

Change of raiment also implies forgiveness ... The prison garments of shame and sin are filthy. The devil uses sin to put us in prison and torments us down with poor memories. But ... God causes our iniquity to pass from us .... and clothes us with clean garments. Forgiveness is a very powerful lever for change. Rejoicing is another lever. You are entering a season of change that require you to release several old things you will not need—especially your attitude. How do you change your attitude? By developing and practicing new habits. For example ... begin to pray for those who have hurt you ... begin the habit of regular bible study and praise. Choose to rejoice no matter the outcome ... situations may be unpredictable but your reaction is your choice ... choose new reactions ahead of whatever comes your way ... learn new songs ... begin to declare "no matter what comes my way - my life is safe in God ... I cannot be a victim"

Expect change and expect it to favor you. Your expectations will not be cut off. Preparing for change is an act of faith ... Joseph had a sure faith that this was an important transition. He prepared himself and his garments were changed. Your next level will not be permitted to embrace your old negative habits. Embrace change joyfully.

Song

I know that my Redeemer lives: What joy the blest assurance gives!
He lives, He lives, who once was dead; He lives, my everlasting Head,

He lives, triumphant from the grave; He lives, eternally to save;
He lives, all glorious in the sky; He lives, exalted there on high,

He lives to bless me with His love, And still He pleads for me above;
He lives to raise me from the grave, And me eternally to save,

He lives, my kind, wise, constant Friend, Who still will keep me to the end;
He lives, and while He lives I'll sing, Jesus, my Prophet, Priest, and King,

He lives my mansion to prepare; And He will bring me safely there;
He lives, all glory to His Name! Jesus, unchangeably the same,

We are going higher—Hallelujah Amen - In the name of Jesus—Hallelujah Amen

Prayer: Lord, prepare me for the next level. Amen

MARCH 7

New Garments

Bible Text: Genesis 41:14

Gen 41:14 Then Pharaoh sent and called Joseph, and they brought him hastily out of the dungeon: and he shaved himself, and changed his raiment, and came in unto Pharaoh.

When the day of change comes it will be swift, unhindered and unstoppable. Even appearances change. Garments of shame will be replaced with garments of glory. The attire of a prisoner is a sorry sight that is unsuitable for the palace of Pharaoh. Shame and dirt of the prison are not permitted in the palace. Ponder over this; are we permitted to show up before the King of kings clothed in beggarly garments of sorrow and self-pity. Joseph's garment was given and not earned. What can we do for God that can impress Him? Does the Bible not describe all our best works and achievements as filthy rags . . . . sending out a repulsive odor. But there is a garment given to us for the Palace . . . Christ.

Gal_3:27 For as many of you as have been baptized into Christ have put on Christ.

Like for Joseph, the garment of Christ's righteousness is not of works but given to him that has been called out to salvation by the Holy Spirit of God. It is all grace. Indeed, he that is clothed in Christ by the grace and mercy of God is transformed until the day when we see Christ in glory - by which time we shall be like Him. Be encouraged that you do not need to sew your garment . . . the fine linen is given. When we have put on Christ, then when we are seen, it is Christ that is seen. Lord have mercy. Do people see Christ when they see me?

Deu_22:5 The woman shall not wear that which pertaineth unto a man, neither shall a man put on a woman's garment: for all that do so are abomination unto the LORD thy God

There are many garments and attires described in the Bible. There is the attire of a harlot, babylonish garments, wedding garments, old and new garments. What we wear matters - as it reflects what we have inside. A bad apple is seen on the outside as rotten but it was first bad from the inside. Do not believe that what we wear does not count . . . because it matters to majesty that we are properly dressed - especially God.

Help me to radiate the simplicity, purity and humility of Christ as He reigns within. It is strange that someone can be attired in strange garments with a huge chain and a large gold cross and imagines that he has put on Christ. There is a clear difference between perspectives and even physical garments when we are in the bondage of sin and the dungeon of perversion and when we have received admission by grace into His salvation. It is time to get rid of the wardrobe that does not reflect Christ. You have come out of the dungeon. Stop dressing as though you were still there. Put on the joy of the Lord - the perfect makeup . . . put on Christ . . . the finest white linen.

Song

I am rejoicing my name has been written,
I am rejoicing that I am born again.

Prayer: Lord prepare me to be a sanctuary, pure and holy, tried and true. Amen

MARCH 8

Joseph Speaks

Bible Text: Genesis 41:15

Gen 41:15 And Pharaoh said unto Joseph, I have dreamed a dream, and there is none that can interpret it: and I have heard say of thee, that thou canst understand a dream to interpret it. 16 And Joseph answered Pharaoh, saying, It is not in me: God shall give Pharaoh an answer of peace.

Many years have passed and Joseph is not heard . . . but an end to that period of silence comes. Joseph must now speak. That which was in him is now about to be delivered. We must patiently wait for our time . . . our change—for an end to the time of silence will surely come.

Job 14:14 If a man die, shall he live again? all the days of my appointed time will I wait, till my change come.

The end of silence requires that all the appointed days of waiting be fulfilled. You cannot rush what God in his wisdom has decided to delay. But then, when it is time to take the stage, you must not be absent or be unprepared. Joseph knew what to say and how to say it . . . He knew what to expect and how to deal with it. He had been prepared to emerge as a Prime Minister of Egypt - He was trained in the University of the Pit and Prison. There is someone reading this devotional. Are you tired of your silence and waiting? You must simply endure a little more and then more. The time of waiting is worth it. You will know when Pharaoh himself speaks to you and not through any other . . . that your time to speak has at last come. For now . . . remain still.

Many have delivered prematurely or mismanaged the pregnancy of destiny by unnecessary movements. God uses managed isolation to finish the growth of the embryo until ready for birth. When the time for your baby comes, there is no other than the carrier of the pregnancy that can deliver. It does not matter the good intentions and efforts of other. Only you can deliver your own pregnancy. None could be found to do what Joseph was uniquely destined to do. Likewise it will be for you . . . so relax. Worship your God—who is able to do exceedingly above all our best imaginations. Your delivery time is close.

Song

Lord, Make us instruments of your peace, Where there is hatred, let your love increase
Lord, make us instruments of your peace, Walls of pride and prejudice shall cease
When we are your instruments of peace.

Prayer: O Lord, teach me to be your voice of peace. Let me only speak what I hear you say

MARCH 9

An Answer of Peace

Bible Text: Genesis 41:15

Gen 41:15 And Pharaoh said unto Joseph, I have dreamed a dream, and there is none that can interpret it: and I have heard say of thee, that thou canst understand a dream to interpret it. 16 And Joseph answered Pharaoh, saying, It is not in me: God shall give Pharaoh an answer of peace.

Joseph is before the most powerful of monarchs. He is obviously disarmed by the grandeur of the expensive marble and pillars laid on precious stones - a far cry from the dungeon walls ... but Joseph is careful. He is not carried away. Pharaoh begins with flattery to name Joseph as a great interpreter who knows what all do not. Joseph quickly denies this appellation. He says it is not in me. There is someone else ... God.

Joseph gives glory to God and ascribes all the greatness to Him. He sees Pharaoh in his great riches and royal apparel, yet he can ascribe all greatness to the King of kings. Joseph knows he is as useless or even worse than all the magicians if God is not merciful to reveal the hidden things.

When did you last tell someone you need to pray concerning an issue to hear God before your decision or before you can respond. Are you trusting your intelligence or the God who is omniscient. Joseph is also a man of peace. He emphasizes peace introducing the truth that only those who follow after peace walk with God. Jesus is the Prince of Peace who gives an answer of peace.

God will not give an incomplete answer that causes more anxiety. Even if God speaks in His wrath, it is for a moment. Behind a rough chastening mask, God hides His countenance of love and true peace. There are strange voices that give different answers ... saying there is peace when there is no peace. But God speaks peace to our storms. He speaks peace to our guilt. He speaks peace to our troubles. He speaks peace to our burdens. He knows that the common denominator of all pleas to Him is the need for peace and calm in our spirit. Receive His answer of peace as you reflect on this devotional. Be an instrument of His peace to a world in need of peace. Lord help us to give counsel of peace.

What kind of counsel do you give ? Oftentimes (not always) the peace element that assuages the tossing waves assures us ... when we need to test if the voice we discern is of God. God will give all your issues an answer of peace. Our God is a God of peace.

Song

Where there is hatred, we will show his love - Where there is injury, we will never judge
Where there is striving, we will speak his peace - To the millions crying for release,
We will be his instruments of peace

Prayer: O Lord, teach me to be your voice of peace. Let me only speak what I hear you say

MARCH 10

Seed and Harvest

Bible Text: Genesis 41:22-25

Gen 41:22 And I saw in my dream, and, behold, seven ears came up in one stalk, full and good: 23 And, behold, seven ears, withered, thin, and blasted with the east wind, sprung up after them: 24 And the thin ears devoured the seven good ears: and I told this unto the magicians; but there was none that could declare it to me. 25 And Joseph said unto Pharaoh, The dream of Pharaoh is one: God hath shewed Pharaoh what he is about to do.

Understanding the processes and journey of your life is more important than dwelling on the events. There are so many that start well . . . like the full and good ears. But when we rejoice in our current experience we miss the importance of the process. Are we on a process that ends well? The dream speaks of another seven ears that are not so good but they devour the good ones. There are many seeds we have sown . . . but these also will produce different harvests. In this dream, the bad harvest comes later to devour the good ones. I am not reinterpreting the dream that has already been interpreted, but to bring out another lesson. We must watch the seeds that we sow . . . and be careful of evil seeds that others have sown. There are times when we experience good and think those bad seeds will not germinate. But they are only taking longer to produce their own harvest so that they can destroy the good fruit. This is a good day to say no more evil seeds i.e.wrong actions and decisions. Every seed that is not goodly according to the word of God is not good. Ask for grace. Some evil seeds germinate generations after while some produce fruit immediately. The wrong act of Sarah to introduce Hagar to Abraham to produce Ishmael is still producing its own harvest today.

Mat 15:13 But he answered and said, Every plant, which my Heavenly Father hath not planted, shall be rooted up.

I pray the above shall be answered in your situation. Every evil seed must be uprooted . . . and not permitted to produce its devouring harvest . . . by the power of the Holy Ghost. O Lord, help our future decisions. A good seed is to sow the gospel of Christ. God will not permit evil harvest to destroy present good. Ask Him who sets lawful captives free—for mercy. Remember, watch your seed going forward.

Song

Blessed is the service of our Lord and King,
Precious are the jewels we may help to bring;
Down the passing ages words of counsel ring:
He that winneth souls is wise.

He that winneth souls is wise; In the home beyond the skies,
There's a crown of glory, O the wondrous prize! He that winneth souls is wise.

In the quiet homelife, showing love's bright ray,
More and more like Jesus living ev'ry day,
We may guide a dear one to the heav'nward way:
He that winneth souls is wise.

Sow beside all waters, sow the gospel seed,
Here a word in season, there a loving deed;
Sinners to the Savior be it ours to lead:
He that winneth souls is wise.

Prayer: Lord, in your great power and mercy, destroy every evil plant that you do not plant that they may not produce a harvest of destruction in my life. Amen.

MARCH 11

Higher Ground

Bible Text: Genesis 41:22-25

Gen 41:22 And I saw in my dream, and, behold, seven ears came up in one stalk, full and good: 23 And, behold, seven ears, withered, thin, and blasted with the east wind, sprung up after them: 24 And the thin ears devoured the seven good ears: and I told this unto the magicians; but there was none that could declare it to me. 25 And Joseph said unto Pharaoh, The dream of Pharaoh is one: God hath shewed Pharaoh what he is about to do.

The location of Joseph has changed again. He started in the tents of his father and Hebrew fields, then the pit and then moved to Egypt, the house of Potiphar and then prison, then the two full years in the dungeon and now the palace. Joseph has interpreted dreams before but in bondage, clothed in prison clothes and unshaven. At this stage, we also know Joseph is still self-focused as he seeks the butler to make a case for him. But in the palace, Joseph has gone higher. The way is clear, the chains and guards of the prison are gone, the prison clothes are removed, he is cleaned and well shaved. He does not call himself nor does he make any case for himself. He constantly declares, it is the work of God and God who needs no sponsor or aids has shown Pharaoh what He will do.

Someone reading this devotional has been called by the highest powers to come up. No one can delay or obstruct you, when He that created Pharaoh calls you up. Every garment of sorrow has been replaced with joy and a glowing glory. You are completely God focused on higher ground.

The first interpretation in prison is to the butler and ends with Joseph appealing to be remembered and then two years of nothing. But now, this interpretation is in a place of freedom, joy and glory - there is not the slightest marketing of self in the palace for it is already unnecessary. The same God that has elected to favor you to bring you thus far to use you as His instrument of peace - will that God now desert you?

As Joseph lifted up his God in the palace of Pharaoh, lift up Jesus and see Him draw not just all your lost kin in bondage of sin and shame, but indeed all men unto Him.

Song

Oh! the world is hungry for the living bread, Lift the Savior up for them to see;
Trust Him and do not doubt the words that He said." I'll draw all men all men unto Me."
Lift the precious Jesus up, Still He speaks from eternity:
"And I, if I be lifted up from the earth, Will draw all men unto Me"

Prayer: Lord, may your presence be taken to all the great palaces of the world and even from there draw men from all over the world to you. Amen.

MARCH 12

God the Great Provider

Bible Text: Genesis 41:26-37

Gen 41:26 The seven good kine are seven years; and the seven good ears are seven years: the dream is one. 27 And the seven thin and ill favoured kine that came up after them are seven years; and the seven empty ears blasted with the east wind shall be seven years of famine. 28 This is the thing which I have spoken unto Pharaoh: What God is about to do he sheweth unto Pharaoh. 29 Behold, there come seven years of great plenty throughout all the land of Egypt: 30 And there shall arise after them seven years of famine; and all the plenty shall be forgotten in the land of Egypt; and the famine shall consume the land; 31 And the plenty shall not be known in the land by reason of that famine following; for it shall be very grievous. 32 And for that the dream was doubled unto Pharaoh twice; it is because the thing is established by God, and God will shortly bring it to pass. 33 Now therefore let Pharaoh look out a man discreet and wise, and set him over the land of Egypt. 34 Let Pharaoh do this, and let him appoint officers over the land, and take up the fifth part of the land of Egypt in the seven plenteous years. 35 And let them gather all the food of those good years that come, and lay up corn under the hand of Pharaoh, and let them keep food in the cities. 36 And that food shall be for store to the land against the seven years of famine, which shall be in the land of Egypt; that the land perish not through the famine. 37 And the thing was good in the eyes of Pharaoh, and in the eyes of all his servants.

Joseph hears God and finally gives the solution of God. God does things that no man could possibly do. The prophecies are easy to debunk as all can recognize abundant harvest when it manifests. Also, the years of famine will be equally unmistakable. Egypt will be preserved from a drought that wipes out all memory of good years. As you read this devotional, do remember God in the years of plenty, for God also appoints periods of lack, in which we are sustained by the investments in past giving, worship and honor to Him. In this text, God also establishes the principle of saving for the future and frugal living even in plenty. Today economists all know that there will always be cycles and countries maintain reserves against the day of famine. Families will now set up trusts to cater for children yet unborn. This is wisdom.

What about the bread of life? What do you have in reserve for the unexpected dry periods when you are unable to study and you seem to have been planted in a spiritual desert. Do you know the times of weeks and months of Bible study and meditation which appear needless are in storage for periods when the word needs to answer to sudden unexpected scenarios. Do not miss any opportunity and grace to study the word and store His admonitions and thoughts in your heart.

Mal_3:10 Bring ye all the tithes into the storehouse, that there may be meat in mine house, and prove me now herewith, saith the LORD of hosts, if I will not open you the windows of Heaven, and pour you out a blessing, that there shall not be room enough to receive it.

It is sad these days that many will say the tithe is no more required and God is hard to ask us to make do with only 90%. One day you may have to ask which is better . . . to have 90% of something or be left one day with 100% of nothing. In the economy we will never lack, but God asks us to trust Him by storing a tenth with Him. Some say, this is Old Testament, that God does not call for our tithe. Many now ridicule the principle of bringing to God's storehouses . . . claiming God has no storehouses on earth. But He did in the time of the Israelites and He is the same God. Tithing is scriptural. There are blessings in the Old Testament of the Bible that we still claim today . . . we cannot throw away tithing because it was in the Old Testament.

Song

Great Provider 4ce. He will surely provide for me, He will provide for me.

Prayer: O Lord, teach me to lean on your word for every provision I may need.

MARCH 13

What is in You?

Bible Text: Genesis 41:38

Gen 41:38 And Pharaoh said unto his servants, Can we find such a one as this is, a man in whom the Spirit of God is?

Gen_1:2 And the earth was without form, and void; and darkness was upon the face of the deep. And the Spirit of God moved upon the face of the waters.

In Genesis, the earth was without void ... in confusion. But God desired to have a new beginning. The Bible tells us that the Holy Spirit began to move. The Holy Spirit moves and the stage is set for creation. There are many theories on change and what to do to have change but few remember the vital role of the Holy Spirit. We tend to focus on new ideas, new events or the introduction of new champions. Indeed all these factors may help change, but they are not the prime movers of change.

The Church was born in the new Testament only after Pentecost. Pharaoh identifies the Spirit of God but that does not mean he walks with the Spirit. In summary there are three lessons. One, the Holy Spirit of God is the person that propels all important change in God's agenda. Second, we may be able to identify the work of the Holy Spirit without any personal experience of it ... there is no work of transformation in our own lives ... yet we can appreciate the things of God ... this can lead to self-deception. Third, the Holy Spirit in Genesis is able to work with nothing. Be encouraged, if you have nothing but still see great things. Be encouraged though things are all in confusion—yet you discern God is moving in your life. The contradiction of formlessness and the presence of the God of all creation is explained by the truth that a new reality is about to be birthed. This new birth is not dependent on anything man can make or do ... but it is formed out of nothing. Come Holy Spirit ... I need you. You can ask yourself? Is the Spirit of God dwelling in me? Pray for this indwelling.

Song

Thy Holy Spirit, Lord, alone
Can turn our hearts from sin;
His pow'r alone can sanctify
And keep us pure within.

O Spirit of Faith and Love,
Come in our midst, we pray,
And purify each waiting heart;
Baptize us with pow'r today.

Thy Holy Spirit, Lord, alone
Can deeper love inspire;
His pow'r alone within our souls
Can light the sacred fire.

Thy Holy Spirit, Lord, can bring
The gifts we seek in prayer,
His voice can words of comfort speak
And still each wave of care.

Prayer: Holy Spirit. Come to author the change that my destiny may be fulfilled. Amen

MARCH 14

The Spirit of God

Bible Text: Genesis 41:38

Gen 41:38 And Pharaoh said unto his servants, Can we find such a one as this is, a man in whom the Spirit of God is?

At the time of Joseph, the Spirit of God dwelt in man, on a more selective and strict basis for the purpose of God . . . but the Prophet Joel spoke of a time coming . . .

Joe_2:28 And it shall come to pass afterward, that I will pour out my spirit upon all flesh; and your sons and your daughters shall prophesy, your old men shall dream dreams, your young men shall see visions:

Is it not interesting after the Spirit of God is mentioned in the creation in Genesis with God the Father and the Son, the next mention of the Holy Spirit is in this awesome revelation that completely transforms the nations -preserving millions from death by hunger? This tells me that the Holy Spirit which is promised to all who are in Christ is the doer and enabler of great exploits. But since you claim you have the Spirit - yet it seems nothing noteworthy has been done by His hand. The Holy Spirit comes to fulfill God's agenda. The Spirit controls and rules the vessel that is yielded to it. Still, He is a sweet, gentle Spirit that will not strive, is easy to grieve and is full of patience and kindness that can only have divine origin. The Spirit is the Spirit of Peace that gives answers of peace.

Powerful testimonies of the works of God will come from those who do not have the Spirit but cannot but recognize the difference it makes. Pharaoh was the first mortal man clearly identified as recognizing the Spirit of God in mortal men. Joseph was the one who carried that Spirit in Him. As you ponder over this text, consider what Spirit reigns in you. Indeed there is the evidence of tongues, but what of the evidence of the testimony by those who are close to you. Your wife, your children, your colleagues, your employees and others that observe you will be better able to tell you "Can they find someone as this is".

If your ways are crafty and slippery and your actions devour peace and spread strife, let this be sufficient evidence that you are yet to meet with the Holy Spirit. The Holy Spirit is a transforming Spirit that changes everything . . . making you unrecognizable even by your kin who knew the old you. Old things pass away only because the Holy Spirit achieves this for us.

Do you know Pharaoh (a great King) had to wait for Joseph (a former prisoner)to hear from God. If Joseph was not ready to answer the king, he would simply have to wait until the Spirit speaks . . . . nothing will change until Joseph has given the illumination we all need. The whole of creation is waiting for you - for the revealing of what you carry. Your nation, your chosen area of influence is waiting . . . the revival is waiting for the manifestation of the Holy Spirit through you.

Song

Come Holy Spirit. Come and take control
Come Holy Spirit. Save the sin sick soul.
Come Holy Spirit. Banish fear and shame
By the blood of Jesus. Victory Proclaim

Prayer: Holy Spirit. Come and be in full control of my life. Amen

MARCH 15

Acceptance

Bible Text: Genesis 41:40-44

Gen 41: 40 Thou shalt be over my house, and according unto thy word shall all my people be ruled: only in the throne will I be greater than thou. 41 And Pharaoh said unto Joseph, See, I have set thee over all the land of Egypt. 42 And Pharaoh took off his ring from his hand, and put it upon Joseph's hand, and arrayed him in vestures of fine linen, and put a gold chain about his neck; 43 And he made him to ride in the second chariot which he had; and they cried before him, Bow the knee: and he made him ruler over all the land of Egypt. 44 And Pharaoh said unto Joseph, I am Pharaoh, and without thee shall no man lift up his hand or foot in all the land of Egypt.

After Joseph delivers interpretation, he is silent. Acceptance of Joseph's solution is a different miracle . . . a different work of the Holy Spirit. Joseph does nothing more than to deliver the message of the Holy Spirit. But now Pharaoh acts quickly. He understands and accepts Joseph's interpretation completely . . . he proceeds to honor Joseph and to decorate him with new apparel and jewelry. He gives him authority. Note the process. First Joseph is affirmed, then Joseph is decorated and honored and finally he is given a new level of authority. Joseph does not ask for these things. On the day of your acceptance, you will not clamor . . . nor will you push. There will be no strife or tension or competition. Observe that God has preset this date of acceptance and honor for Joseph. With God all things are possible. When the time of destiny approaches, the strong evidence will be the presence of the Holy Spirit as the helper. You will be easily accepted, decorated, affirmed, honored and ushered into a new level of spiritual authority. When that time comes, all will forget that you were in prison, nor will they be interested in what happened at Potiphar's house . . . the past will be irrelevant. Joseph was not probed on his history. He was simply accepted to enter a role that was destined for him. Even Pharaoh could see that it was God who had preserved a role for Joseph in Egypt. God will today cause His wisdom in your lips to find acceptance amongst men. You will be brought before Kings. Be gone unbelief. It shall be so.

Song

Begone, unbelief; my Savior is near,
And for my relief will surely appear;
By prayer let me wrestle, and He will perform;
With Christ in the vessel, I smile at the storm.

Though dark be my way, since He is my guide,
'Tis mine to obey, 'tis His to provide;
Though cisterns be broken, and creatures all fail,
The word He has spoken shall surely prevail.

Determined to save, He watched o'er my path,
When, Satan's blind slave, I sported with death;
And can He have taught me to trust in His name,
And thus far have brought me to put me to shame?

Why should I complain of want or distress,
Temptation or pain? He told me no less;
The heirs of salvation, I know from His Word,
Through much tribulation must follow their Lord.

Prayer: O Lord, help me . . . let your Spirit be always with me in the day of my acceptance. Amen.

MARCH 16

Raised up to Rule

Bible Text: Genesis 41:40-44

Gen 41: 40 Thou shalt be over my house, and according unto thy word shall all my people be ruled: only in the throne will I be greater than thou. 41 And Pharaoh said unto Joseph, See, I have set thee over all the land of Egypt. 42 And Pharaoh took off his ring from his hand, and put it upon Joseph's hand, and arrayed him in vestures of fine linen, and put a gold chain about his neck; 43 And he made him to ride in the second chariot which he had; and they cried before him, Bow the knee: and he made him ruler over all the land of Egypt. 44 And Pharaoh said unto Joseph, I am Pharaoh, and without thee shall no man lift up his hand or foot in all the land of Egypt.

Joseph was raised up to live henceforth in palatial grandeur, and made ruler over all Egypt. Indeed God is He who raises up from the dung hill to a throne. None is able to stop God when He determines an elevation . . . except you that God determines to elevate. May we not frustrate His grace.

Eph 2:4 But God, who is rich in mercy, for his great love wherewith he loved us, 5 Even when we were dead in sins, hath quickened us together with Christ, (by grace ye are saved;) 6 And hath raised us up together, and made us sit together in Heavenly places in Christ Jesus: 7 That in the ages to come he might shew the exceeding riches of his grace in his kindness toward us through Christ Jesus.

The Bible says when we were dead with no hope, just as Christ was raised up, we were quickened together with Christ by grace. But that is not all. We are raised up together with Christ and made to sit together in Heavenly places. He did this so that the world would see the exceeding riches of his grace towards us through Christ Jesus. Like Jesus we are spiritually in the nest of the eagle, above principalities and powers . . . high up. God did not raise us up because we were great Christians, He raised us up in His mercy when we were dead in sin. Joseph experiences a foretaste of this great wealth by the awesome grace of God. Soon his brothers will also be admitted into this great vault of mercy. The story of Joseph started with mercy on Rachael, continues with mercy and it is also God's rich mercy that brings Him up to rule over all Egypt. We must commit all to the mercy of God, and release our efforts and projects to His mercy. God is rich in mercy, and no one has discovered the depth and limit of this great wealth. Learn to be merciful . . . show mercy not in trickles but let it pour like rushing waves in an inexhaustible ocean. But we also learn that mercy does not deny process. Joseph went through a long process and he grew and learnt progressively. He was not an overnight wonder. God's mercy will not allow us to be thrust into what He has not prepared us for.

Respond to the call of Jesus to come out and be raised. Receive the mercy that destroys bondage and makes us rule over what used to rule and enslave us. Egypt supervised a prison system that kept Joseph incarcerated for years. Now Joseph rules over Egypt and over the prison. Joseph now has the authority to set prisoners free. The Revival is waiting for you to come up higher and walk in the freedom and power to rule in Christ and set neighborhoods free, peoples and nations free. Exercise that opportunity in the place of prayer. The poverty of prayer is the underestimation of mercy and ignorance of our positioning. Begin to rule. Start with yourself. Decree that every dark kingdom oppressing your life should release its hold now. Overturn every word spoken concerning your life that is contrary with God's word. "Our ultimate position as Christians is tested by the power of our prayer life" says Lloyd Jones. It is time to pray for revival and for men to rule over wicked addictions and spiritual slave masters.

Song

Now free from sin, endue within; Give thy compassion - tears
Thou dost, my Lord, Emancipate; Restore my wasted years. (Leonard Ravenhill)

Prayer: O Lord, you have raised me in power in Christ Jesus. Restore O Lord my wasted years.

MARCH 17

The Standards of God.

Bible Text: Genesis 41:45

Gen 41:45 And Pharaoh called Joseph's name Zaphnathpaaneah; and he gave him to wife Asenath the daughter of Potipherah priest of On. And Joseph went out over all the land of Egypt.

A wife from Pharaoh is not a good gift. A daughter of the priest of On would pollute the tribe that was to emerge. There is little in scripture to suggest that God resisted or even queried this action. Idolatry gradually became perhaps the prime weakness of the children of Israel. Moses also had a marriage outside the family of God. It is true that if you do marry the daughter of the devil, he becomes your father-in-law and will seek such rights in your life. The influence of Asenath on Joseph is not quite known . . . but we do know that Joseph does not go the way of polygamy. The marriage seemed necessary to allay concerns in Egypt that this was a stranger. But this is not the way to find a wife . . . for the Bible says *be not unequally yoked*. There are some exceptional situations especially in the New Testament that we should not receive as patterns that please God.

God may not always impose His standard of obedience and may overlook ignorance and weaknesses in mercy—but He appreciates especially those who will keep His standard. See the Rechabites . . . and how God rewards their uncommon obedience on the issue of drinking wine.

Jer 35:5 And I set before the sons of the house of the Rechabites pots full of wine, and cups, and I said unto them, Drink ye wine. 6 But they said, We will drink no wine: for Jonadab the son of Rechab our father commanded us, saying, Ye shall drink no wine, neither ye, nor your sons for ever: . . . Jer 35:18 And Jeremiah said unto the house of the Rechabites, Thus saith the LORD of hosts, the God of Israel; Because ye have obeyed the commandment of Jonadab your father, and kept all his precepts, and done according unto all that he hath commanded you: 19 Therefore thus saith the LORD of hosts, the God of Israel; Jonadab the son of Rechab shall not want a man to stand before me for ever.

God has His standards and waits to reward those who will keep to it and maintain it—no matter the situation. Not because they fear God will hurt or punish them but because they love God. The priesthood of On and Jehovah are not to be put together. Idolatry will, in many future generations, become evident as the weak point of the house of Joseph. May God help us and show us mercy. Do not permit past wrongs to hurt future generations.

Song

Holy are you Lord. All creation calls you Lord
Worthy is your name. We worship your majesty.
Awesome God. How great thou art. You are God
Mighty are your miracles . . . we stand in awe of your Holy Name
Lord, we bow and worship you.

Prayer: Father, Lord teach me your complete ways. Let me be truly set apart for you. Amen

MARCH 18

A New Family

Bible Text: Genesis 41:45

Gen 41:45 And Pharaoh called Joseph's name Zaphnathpaaneah; and he gave him to wife Asenath the daughter of Potipherah priest of On. And Joseph went out over all the land of Egypt.

The name Pharaoh gives to Joseph is said to mean, by some translators "the one who furnishes the nourishment of life," i.e. the chief steward of the realm): Indeed a new birth implies a new name. But scripture only mentions this name once. It is Joseph that is retained in the Bible. Eventually a Pharaoh will come who will forget *Zaphnathpaaneah*, and the name will not be remembered - even in Egypt. Of equal significance is his marriage to the daughter of Potipherah, similar to Moses who was also married to a heathen priest's daughter.

The Bible warns that we are not to be unequally yoked. Eventually, it is Judah that provides the seed and the lineage that produced the Messiah . . . preordained to be the Lion of Judah. Marrying the wrong spouse is of serious implications and selection of a bride is a matter to be handled only after seeking direction from the word of God. We do not know always see the implications of this in our lifetime, but generations unborn may still be affected. The tribe of Ephraim the son of Joseph eventually joins himself to idols. We hear little of what became of the children of Moses. Still God remains faithful to His purposes and merciful to whom He chooses.

There is a marriage we can look forward to. The marriage of the Lamb. Christ joined with the church - a bride without the slightest speck or wrinkle. The ultimate promotion of the saints . . . the final call to come higher will be at the rapture, when we shall be caught up to be with Him . . . never to be apart. I pray you will be among when the church is caught as the bride. Just as the daughter of Potipherah is exalted in marriage to the one second to only Pharaoh, so will we be honored when we are caught up to be joined with Christ, later to return to reign with Him in the millenium and after be with Him forever.

God gives us a new family when we are born again. We have spiritual fathers and elders and we have brothers and sisters in the Lord. But God does not want us to forget our blood relatives who are still yet to be in the Lord. Like Joseph was raised for His family, perhaps God seeks to use you to bring your entire family to know the Lord. The Holy Spirit will make a way for God's purpose to use you for your family. Soon, you will see them drawn to the Lord. Wait on God concerning this issue.

In this devotional, reflect on your marriage or plans for marriage, and pray that it glorifies God. Ask yourself . . . when the rapture happens will I be caught up to be honored for the ultimate marriage. Are there things to be done to make yourself ready? Do them today. Also thank God for the new spiritual family He has ordained for you . . . Thank Him for the salvation of your blood relatives.

Song

Will you be ready when the Lord shall come (4ce)
I will be ready (3ce) when the Lord shall come. (2ce)

Prayer: Father, let my marriage be pleasing unto you and help my preparations for the rapture. Amen

MARCH 19

Leadership Principles

Bible Text: Genesis 41:46-49

Gen 41:46 And Joseph was thirty years old when he stood before Pharaoh king of Egypt. And Joseph went out from the presence of Pharaoh, and went throughout all the land of Egypt. 47 And in the seven plenteous years the earth brought forth by handfuls. 48 And he gathered up all the food of the seven years, which were in the land of Egypt, and laid up the food in the cities: the food of the field, which was round about every city, laid he up in the same. 49 And Joseph gathered corn as the sand of the sea, very much, until he left numbering; for it was without number.

Joseph was only thirty years but prepared by God. He is made ready to be God's instrument for the Hebrews in a period of famine and to bring them into Egypt. He does not know this. He thinks he is Egypt's new prince and rules with the fear of the God that made it all possible. I find some leadership lessons in this text.

Joseph went throughout all the land. He did not remain in the palace . . . he must have visited all the places in which he was hurt . . . releasing the pain and feeling no bitterness. He was a visible leader. He was seen and he was loved. It is good to lead by walking around and be seen even where you may have been mistreated. He went throughout suggests, he sought for a total picture so he could develop a plan that was fair to all. He was not an elite type - far from the common people. He identified with the populace. He had a common touch.

Joseph was involved and hard working. He covered not just the cities, but the fields on the outskirts of the cities. He believed in completeness. He was a thorough leader. He gathered not for himself but established an accounting . . . "he numbered" . . . he was diligent in accounting and did not permit theft, waste or sloth. The harvest was so much that it became pointless to count. Still Joseph knew he was called to lead not just for today but for the future. Leading for the future means having a long-term mindset. Seeing the harvest and the boom of today, high prices and favorable economics within a longer timeframe that recognizes that the future must also be safeguarded. A good leader will lead for the future as well as the present. Are you in a position of leadership? Are you visible? Have you walked around sufficiently around the issues you are responsible for tackling or are you seen only by your friends? Are you comfortable with accounts and numbers? Do you lead only for the short/medium timeframe or can you lead seeing the future good safeguarded? What kind of leader are you?

Christ led by walking around. He did not hide even from the Pharisees . . . He was visible and involved. He was hardworking. He was in the cities and in small villages sometimes going off the expected course so His work will be completed in the sight of God. Christ was a man of the future. He healed many and solved present problems but He did not permit them to make Him a King and went to the cross, so that the future of all mankind would be preserved.

Song

Guide me, O Thou great Jehovah,
Pilgrim through this barren land.
I am weak, but Thou art mighty;
Hold me with Thy powerful hand.
Bread of Heaven, Bread of Heaven,
Feed me till I want no more;
Feed me till I want no more.

Prayer: O Lord, Guide me to lead as you want me to lead—as Christ led. Amen

MARCH 20

Rare Diligence

Bible Text: Genesis 41:46-49

Gen 41:46 And Joseph was thirty years old when he stood before Pharaoh king of Egypt. And Joseph went out from the presence of Pharaoh, and went throughout all the land of Egypt. 47 And in the seven plenteous years the earth brought forth by handfuls. 48 And he gathered up all the food of the seven years, which were in the land of Egypt, and laid up the food in the cities: the food of the field, which was round about every city, laid he up in the same. 49 And Joseph gathered corn as the sand of the sea, very much, until he left numbering; for it was without number.

To store and gather enough reserve for seven years involves several things. The people must be prudent. Huge storage vessels and barns must be constructed and they must do the hard work of moving grains to storage facilities. All this in a period when it does not seem to make sense to do this. Critics of Joseph must have told him that the period of plenty must be enjoyed and that the grains stored will only be wasted as they will not be needed. Storing grain instead of consuming also keeps the price of grain high . . . all these are inconveniences that Joseph imposes. Joseph is also personally involved. No doubt, there must have been some delegation, but he had a hands-on approach. Joseph also ordered that the grain be measured until a time came when it could no more be. Joseph was a great leader not just because he was anointed, but because he was very diligent and hardworking. Not once do we read that he amassed any grain or sought any advantage for himself. He was content with what he had been given. Go ahead. Labor on, for it is the master's will. Joseph exhibited a rare diligence. Be committed to do the same when God helps you to the next level.

Song

Go, labor on; spend, and be spent,
Thy joy to do the Father's will;
It is the way the Master went;
Should not the servant tread it still?

Go, labor on; 'tis not for naught;
Thy earthly loss is heav'nly gain;
Men heed thee, love thee, praise thee not,
The Master praises, what are men?

Go, labor on, while yet 'tis day;
The world's dark night is hast'ning on;
Speed, speed thy work, cast sloth away;
It is not thus that souls are won.

Toil on, and in thy toil rejoice;
For toil comes rest, for exile home;
Soon shalt thou hear the Bridegroom's voice,
The midnight peal, "Behold, I come!"

Prayer: O Lord, Help me to demonstrate a Pilgrim's Work Ethic.

MARCH 21

It was God

Bible Text: Genesis 41:50-52

Gen 41:50 And unto Joseph were born two sons before the years of famine came, which Asenath the daughter of Potipherah priest of On bare unto him. 51 And Joseph called the name of the firstborn Manasseh: For God, said he, hath made me forget all my toil, and all my father's house. 52 And the name of the second called he Ephraim: For God hath caused me to be fruitful in the land of my affliction.

The true mark of a man of God is the glory that goes to God. The worship focus of Joseph is declared in the name of his children. It was God that did it all. Joseph declares the greatness of God and gives God all the glory. Note that Joseph does not ascribe any ill to God. Instead God brings good using whichever method pleases Him. God is faithful. Are you in any way afflicted? Then be assured that God can even cause fruitfulness out of that affliction and make us forget the hardest toils. God can bring us into an oasis of joy even in the most hostile and difficult circumstances. The faithfulness of God is so extensive, it has never been tested to know how far it can reach. God is in control. God is in charge. It was all God. When you have come to this conclusion, you can rest in all your travails and be at peace in the processes you must undergo, knowing in the end it will all be good. God has not abandoned His own and will not forsake you. You will begin to start every sentence with "For God did his ... and for God did that ..." This also means if not for God things could have been much worse.

This is why refusal to praise God as we should is a great injustice and a grievous wickedness. It was all God working a good end concerning your life. Praise Him again and again—even when the methods He uses are not always clear to us and we do not fully understand His appointed processes.

Song

Now in a song of grateful praise To Thee,
O Lord, my voice I'll raise;
With all Thy saints I'll join to tell:
My Jesus hath done all things well.

And above the rest this note shall swell:
My Jesus hath done all things well.

How sov'reign, wonderful and free
Hath been Thy wond'rous love to me!
Thou sav'dst me from the jaws of hell:
My Jesus hath done all things well.

Since e'er my soul has known Thy love,
What mercies Thou hast made me prove:
Thy mercies do all praise excel;
My Jesus hath done all things well.

And when to that bright world I rise,
And join the anthems of the skies,
Above the rest this note shall swell:
My Jesus hath done all things well.

Prayer: O Lord, I praise You. You are indeed faithful ... forever faithful. Help me to also be faithful in all I do.
Amen

MARCH 22

All-round Fruitfulness

Bible Text: Genesis 41:50-52

Gen 41:50 And unto Joseph were born two sons before the years of famine came, which Asenath the daughter of Potipherah priest of On bare unto him. 51 And Joseph called the name of the firstborn Manasseh: For God, said he, hath made me forget all my toil, and all my father's house. 52 And the name of the second called he Ephraim: For God hath caused me to be fruitful in the land of my affliction.

The names given to the children of Joseph reflect the blessings he enjoyed. Joseph was fruitful and in the years before the famine he had two sons. God is a God of all round fruitfulness. He causes you to be fruitful in the body as well as on the field. When He shuts there is none who can open and when He opens, there is none who can shut. As you read, by His grace you will receive new grace and new mercy for all-round fruitfulness.

God can change things but not just that, He can cause fresh events to bring so much comfort that you forget completely the struggles of the past. This means the scars and the visible consequences of past toil will have disappeared. It means God can so solve your problems that you do not remember that they ever existed. Again, this can only be God in action - because memories tend to be strong when past events are extensive in causing pains. But when God says it is over, He causes us to also forget.

Another thing God does is to make us go through several locations in an afflicted state - only to cause us to return to those same places, but this time overwhelmingly fruitful. Egypt was the land of affliction ever since Joseph was brought in as a slave - and in that same place, where Joseph was meant to rot away, he becomes a celebrity and a man of great influence. Again this is a mystery, but the doing of a wonderful God.

As you read this devotional, observe the possibilities if only we trust God. Everywhere in which you broke down in tears - mark the locations, every scenario in which you considered situations tragically hopeless - note the places. In those very same places and situations, God is in action. He makes and He causes events to turnaround for your good. What a great God He is. He is a God of fruitfulness; He is a God of overwhelming mercy and turnaround. Bless His name this morning. Find someone in trouble to encourage with these words of truth. Glory be to God.

Song

He is able more than able to accomplish what concerns me today
He is able more than able to handle everything that comes my way
He is able, more than able to do much more than I could ever dream
He is able more than able to make me what he wants me to be.

Prayer: O Lord, You make and cause things to be only for my good, even where it seems evil plans are thriving -
Do likewise in my situations. Amen

MARCH 23

Knowing God

Bible Text: Genesis 41:53

Gen 41:53 And the seven years of plenteousness, that was in the land of Egypt, were ended.

Times can be very deceptive. Egypt enters a seven year period of boom but Joseph knew it will not last . . . others did not. Many thought Joseph was a joker who would soon be exposed if the period of boom continued. Change is inevitable . . . but how prepared are we for it? Our preparation depends on the accuracy of understanding of the times and this accuracy depends on if we are connected to divine intelligence. When we know God, we know truths that others cannot always discern. Joseph was thinking of the coming famine . . . others were rejoicing and dancing and seeking to consume as much as they could. Find time to seek God and to know Him. Let Him reveal His plans, seasons and timings to you. Learn to see beyond the evidence and to act not just on plain evidence but more on divine insight. God speaks to us individually on issues and He may reveal things others are unfamiliar with. We can have completely different perspectives because we know God resulting in preparations that are equally different. Jesus could look at the Temple in all its glory and see that it would be in ruins in a few years . . . God helps us to see not as ordinary men do. Give us supernatural insights to aid our preparations.

Mat_24:2 And Jesus said unto them, See ye not all these things? verily I say unto you, There shall not be left here one stone upon another, that shall not be thrown down.

In the text, there are seven years of great increase—but these times were about to change. Joseph knew only because he had access to the God who knows all things. Ask God to help you see what He wants you to see to achieve your destiny. In summary, those who know their God are strong and do exploits because they perceive and act on truths hidden to others.

Song

Elijah made a sacrifice
To offer to Jehovah;
It had been wet with water thrice,
Baal's sacrifice was over.
Elijah prayed: the fire came down
And licked the water all around;
So doubting ones believed, and found
Elijah's God was living.
Elijah's God still lives today,
To take the guilt of sin away;
And when I pray my heart's desire,
Upon my soul He sends the fire.

Elijah's God still lives today,
And answers still by fire;
My friend, just let Him have His way;
He'll grant your heart's desire,
Consume the sacrifice you make;
And bid your slumb'ring soul awake:
The chain of inbred sin will break;
Elijah's God is living.

Prayer: O Lord of Elijah - I thirst to know you more . . . fill my thirst. Amen

MARCH 24

The End of plenty

Bible Text: Genesis 41:53

Gen 41:53 And the seven years of plenteousness, that was in the land of Egypt, were ended.

In the end, the saint have the last laugh. God saves the best for the saints for the last days. The glory that is ahead cannot be described. Those in Christ Jesus find a supply that others never discover. After the rapture, when saints are taken away, there will be another seven years. Mid-tribulationists say the rapture will be in the middle of a seven year period. Whatever men have called a boom will not last forever.

You do well to read about this seven year period in the Bible, but suffice it to say that those not in Christ that have not been able to retain their sanctification by His grace will be ushered into a period of trouble. The bliss and joys of modernity, the luxuries - high tech. and delicious living of those who shun God will reach its peak, even as the Bible says the wickedness of the world increases. Then the saints will be taken to be with their Christ - their "Joseph" as a period of tribulation begins. The Bible refers to the Holy Spirit as the restrainer who has been restraining evil. He is now withdrawn.

I asked myself how Joseph would be perceived in the time of plenty. I suspect many will disbelieve him. I expect that some of his advice to gather would be considered unnecessary. I imagine his admonition to be frugal in a time of unbridled excesses would be termed as overly strict. The seven years of plenty would have been like the times of Noah before the flood . . . . few will consider Noah to be in good mental health. Similarly many will wonder what this "crazy" Joseph is gathering and storing things for when there is so much . . . that we cannot number.

In a similar fashion, many wonder in the last days at the sense of being a Christian. Why be lumbered with so many restrictions, why do you need to store so much word in your spirit when scientific advancement has progressed so amazingly forward. Why the tithing, when so many apparently "self-made" billionaires boost that there is no God and teach that the Christian world view is ridiculous and unnecessary. In the last days, the plenty and wealth of nations will mock the teachings and warnings of God.

Joseph was not dancing and enjoying in the time of plenty, rather he was working hard for a future period. Similarly, be diligent in storing the word of God in your heart. It will keep you apart and help you to be prepared for the coming of the Heavenly Bridegroom. Be sure that God has already appointed an end to all the world has called "mighty, pleasing and great" . . . do not set your eyes on them and resist their seductions.

Song

"Called unto holiness" Church of our God,
Purchase of Jesus, redeemed by His blood,
Called from the world and its idols to flee,
Called from the bondage of sin to be free.

Prayer: O Lord, Open my eyes to see the varying and temporal nature of worldly gains. Give me Christ that I may have that which lasts forever. Amen

MARCH 25

Days of Trouble

Bible Text: Genesis 41:54

Gen 41:54 And the seven years of dearth began to come, according as Joseph had said: and the dearth was in all lands; but in all the land of Egypt there was bread.

There are appointed days of trouble. May those days be few. The Bible speaks of the afflictions of the righteous, and that God delivers from them all. The righteous are like those in this world but in Christ. They do not lack any good thing. Just as in all the land there was dearth, those in Egypt - where Joseph was - could get bread not from the fields but from the barns and warehouses. Note that the famine came to all, just as afflictions come to all, but the difference arises from the presence and preparations made by Joseph and those who benefit.

The lesson here is to hold on to Christ and be surrendered to His rule. When the appointed days of trouble come, there will be a deliverance and sustenance from the hunger that kills. Again, we observe another lesson. God may not exempt saints from certain serious trials but the work of the Holy Spirit is a divine comfort that preserves us miraculously. We come through the same situations that completely destroys others

In the seven year period of the tribulation described in the word of God, we know the saints will not be on earth, because the restrainer of evil - the Holy Spirit - will also be removed. In the Heavens, the saints are with their "Joseph". If you have Jesus as your Lord, then you can be assured that in whatever trouble you will have Christ for your comfort and His comfort will be enough.

This verse tells us that the dearth started gradually until it became fully evident. Today, you may have already started observing a dearth in the word of God. Gradually, the true word is gradually becoming scarce as the knowledge and vices of men are increasing in all dimensions. The message is now mixed with philosophies and motivational teachings . . . and I do pray that you will hold on to Jesus to survive the dilution in teachings and the approaching famine of the word.

But there is also a revival of the word, when we discover the reserved barns of Christ to take His own through the difficult seasons. In whatever situation, just look up to Jesus, the author and finisher of our faith. Be encouraged that you will not sink. Christ holds your hands. Feed on His word. Open your Bible and begin to read with a fresh hunger and zeal.

Song

Art thou weary, art thou languid,
Art thou sore distressed?
Come to Me, saith one, and coming,
Be at rest.

Prayer: O Lord Jesus, In appointed days of trouble, call me to you where I will come to be at rest, even amidst the ragings. Amen

MARCH 26

The Salt of the Earth

Bible Text: Genesis 41:54

Gen 41:54 And the seven years of dearth began to come, according as Joseph had said: and the dearth was in all lands; but in all the land of Egypt there was bread.

Christ teaches us that we are to be the salt of the earth. We are to be amongst those who bring a good taste where there would have been none. In this text we note that Egypt is different because of the revelation of Joseph. The Bible says we the children of God have the mind of Christ. That means we have solutions and understandings that meet the needs of people. Just as Christ went around doing good—we are able to do the same with a different renewed mind. A dearth means shortage. When there is dearth, there is sorrow, crime and darkness creeps in. But where there is bread, there is joy, fulfillment and satisfaction. Our Christianity must have a positive influence on our homes and families . . . it must impact our communities positively. The gospel empowers people to live in peace and contentment. The evidence of the Holy Spirit at work can be seen in a visible change for good. Salt must be applied. God applies us to different situations to change that situation. This means we must release our lives to God to use us to His glory. Sometimes it may be in a capacity that we find easy to embrace. But in other situations, it could be in a sacrificial role which demands a heavy cost from us. It is the presence of the Holy Spirit that makes this world bearable and the saints of God make the positive difference. One of the reasons why times of trouble come after the rapture is because the Holy Spirit—the restrainer and born again Christians are no more on the earth. Without the salt and light . . . the earth becomes an unbearable place and chaos takes over. One of the reasons we should thank God includes that we are saved by His grace and we carry a light and comfort that impacts others positively. Imagine what your community will be without you? If there will be no change, then such Christianity must be reexamined. God help us to have the impact that we were destined to have.

Song

Holy Ghost, with light divine
Shine upon this heart of mine;
Chase the shades of night away,
Turn my darkness into day.

Holy Ghost, with pow'r divine
Cleanse this guilty heart of mine;
Long hath sin, without control,
Held dominion o'er my soul.

Holy Ghost, with joy divine
Cheer this sadd'ned heart of mine;
Bid my many woes depart,
Heal my wounded, bleeding heart.

Holy Spirit, all divine,
Dwell within this heart of mine;
Cast down ev'ry idol throne,
Reign supreme, and reign alone.

Prayer: O Holy Spirit. May your impact be felt through us in all the communities you have sent us to go. Amen

MARCH 27

Go to Jesus

Bible Text: Genesis 41:55-57

Gen 41:55 And when all the land of Egypt was famished, the people cried to Pharaoh for bread: and Pharaoh said unto all the Egyptians, Go unto Joseph; what he saith to you, do. 56 And the famine was over all the face of the earth: And Joseph opened all the storehouses, and sold unto the Egyptians; and the famine waxed sore in the land of Egypt. 57 And all countries came into Egypt to Joseph for to buy corn; because that the famine was so sore in all lands

When they wanted wine at a wedding and there was none. Mary stepped up and told them of Christ . . . she said "Go to Him and do whatever He says". Christ is the solution. It was not obvious they needed Joseph until the famine. Today, there is a famine of truth, a famine of love, a famine of integrity, a famine of decency and order . . . there is a decay and a societal malaise that only Christ can arrest. But who is going to point the nations to Jesus. Who is going to ask people to come to Jesus and live? Who is going to suggest that there is hope and that hope is Christ. It does not seem correct to mention Jesus anymore . . . and some ask us not to confuse religion with government as they continually push God out of schools, meetings and more events. How sad. Jesus is still waiting.

If Pharaoh did not point to Joseph what do you think would have happened. Note in the seven years of plenty no one cried to Pharaoh. Many will not cry to the Lord until issues deteriorate significantly. We often wait until it is almost too late. Thankfully—we have a God who reverses the irreversible. Do not waste another minute, in your prayers take the issues of the land, of your church and of your nation to the Lord. Jesus will tell you what to do. Jesus will give answers and guide to a solution of peace. Begin to be the salt of the earth that carries the solution that arrests the decay.

Song

Jesus is the answer; Jesus is the way
He knows what to do when we have gone astray
Give all your worship. Listen for His word
Jesus is the answer; Jesus is the Lord

Jesus is the answer; Jesus is the way
It's never too late to come to Him do not delay
He turns water to wine and sets the captives free
Jesus is the answer; and He reigns supreme

Jesus is the answer; Jesus is the way
Shout a loud Hallelujah—Praise His holy name
He is coming back to reign with all the raptured saints
Jesus is the answer that the world needs today

Prayer: O Lord, Take control of all issues in my life. Lord Jesus tell me what to do. I come for help and salvation. Let me be guided by you. Amen.

MARCH 28

All countries come

Bible Text: Genesis 41:55-57

Gen 41:55 And when all the land of Egypt was famished, the people cried to Pharaoh for bread: and Pharaoh said unto all the Egyptians, Go unto Joseph; what he saith to you, do. 56 And the famine was over all the face of the earth: And Joseph opened all the storehouses, and sold unto the Egyptians; and the famine waxed sore in the land of Egypt. 57 And all countries came into Egypt to Joseph for to buy corn; because that the famine was so sore in all lands

Isa_60:3 And the Gentiles shall come to thy light, and kings to the brightness of thy rising.

We tend not to truly come to Christ until we see that all other alternatives have failed. We tend not to seek the bread of Heaven until our own bread is finished. Joseph opened the storehouses, indeed he had the keys. When the famine waxed sore in the land, Joseph opened the storehouses. Jesus is offering His own bread even now, the bread of Heaven is given to us. It cost the blood of Jesus Christ. It was not free, only someone else paid the price. All have been invited to be saved from all over the world. Only if they will come to Jesus and be surrendered to Him. Whatever He says do and see water turn to wine, experience the dead come back to life and transformations.

Many go to Christ because of the coming famine - physical and spiritual. God is reviving His own. In every nation of the earth, there are people who come to Jesus. God is going to cause nations to come to Him. Will you be part of his great work? Would you be a co-laborer as the Holy Spirit ministers, bringing many rare and rich blessings with it. Blessings such as the convictions of evil and vileness of sin, the Redeemer's glory, many crowns of victory and triumph to Christ, great additions to his friends and laborers ... will all soon be seen. see. Jesus is coming for a Bride and not a beggar .... not a hungry and sick Church. Ponder over this truth, what must be your part in partnering with Him to feed the world with restoring truth.

God has created the saints to be part of the answer in Christ and not to complain like others or to analyze the famine. Christianity brings solutions to issues. That is why we are described as the salt of the earth and the light of the world. Lord help us to shine with Christ.

Somehow the news spread that there was bread in Egypt. Will you be amongst those Christ needs to spread the word all over the world that the answer is Jesus. Spread the news far and near. In Egypt people heard, in distant lands people also heard and they all came.

Pray for the coming Revival.

Song

Great is the need of our nations,
Great is the need of this hour
Lord, we abhor our stagnation.
Answer with Holy Ghost power.

Prayer: O Lord, Empower me to spread the good news. The bread of life is Jesus Christ that satisfies. Grant me grace to carry that word even to distant lands using all possible means.

MARCH 29

God has a Way

Bible Text: Genesis 42:1

Gen 42:1 Now when Jacob saw that there was corn in Egypt, Jacob said unto his sons, Why do ye look one upon another?

Even in the worst of situations, God has a way. Egypt was the last place Jacob and his family would have thought of, because they had been told never to go down to Egypt. The earlier patriarchs who went down to Egypt erred to do so.

When Abram went down to Egypt because of famine, he came up with a deception that Sarai was his sister . . . God had to help him to survive that mistake. Abram had a son by the Egyptian Hagar—another wrong and costly move. God told Isaac specifically not to go to Egypt.

Gen 26:1 And there was a famine in the land, beside the first famine that was in the days of Abraham. And Isaac went unto Abimelech king of the Philistines unto Gerar. 2 And the LORD appeared unto him, and said, Go not down into Egypt; dwell in the land which I shall tell thee of:

But God did not tell Jacob not to consider Egypt. Be careful of traditions and patterns that tie us down. God does not need to do things as He has done before. We need grace to understand His ways and hear Him specifically for our individual situations. I have often wondered . . . why is it that every time there was famine . . . it was always Egypt that came up as a solution. Egypt is a place of unusual testing to bring out what is in our heart and to birth a new move to the next level when we have passed divine examination. For Jacob, it was clear . . . it was Egypt or death. What matters is that we do what God wants us to do. Go to God on the specific matter you are dealing with and get a clear picture of where you need to be. Get your answers from God and be at peace knowing He will still work out His promises at the appointed time. May God also anoint our instincts to respond to Him . . . especially in critical situations.

Song

I am trusting Thee, Lord Jesus, Trusting only Thee,
Trusting Thee for full salvation, Great and free.

I am trusting Thee for pardon, At Thy feet I bow;
For Thy grace and tender mercy, Trusting now.

I am trusting Thee for cleansing - In the crimson flood;
Trusting Thee to make me holy By Thy blood.

I am trusting Thee to guide me: Thou alone shalt lead,
Ev'ry day and hour supplying All my need.

I am trusting Thee for power; Thine shall never fail;
Words which Thou Thyself shalt give me Must prevail.

I am trusting Thee, Lord Jesus; Never let me fall;
I am trusting Thee forever, And for all.

Prayer: O Lord, I need more grace to trust you to guide me in situations calling for unusual actions. Amen

MARCH 30

The Beginning of Restoration

Bible Text: Genesis 42:1

Gen 42:1 Now when Jacob saw that there was corn in Egypt, Jacob said unto his sons, Why do ye look one upon another?

In this text, we see the initial stages for revival and restoration - no matter how bad or deteriorated the situation. First we thank God that Jacob is still alive for it is only the living that can come to God. If you are still breathing then God can still rescue you from whatever damage or destructions lie at your door. Death was waiting to snatch the victims of the famine—a famine which had spread even to the tents of Jacob.

The first stage is realizing that Jesus has His salvation and only waits for us to come to Him. There is no other first step. The prodigal son received grace for that first stage. That is why the gospel must be preached with every means possible to tell all that the bread of Heaven is available. Nothing must be allowed to stop the preaching of the gospel, there is no barrier that must be permitted to get in the way of hearing the gospel. Entertainment and variety shows masquerading as the gospel provide confusing alternatives. Today, many now tell people in faraway lands like China and Japan that there may be other ways apart from Christ for their salvation. How wicked this is. For in these far way lands, they groan under a bondage for which only Christ has the answer. Look to Jesus and Live.

The second stage is to question our wanderings. The most common error is to look up to people, often ourselves. Our leaders - good as they may be, or even your pastor is not the answer and all must be pointed to Christ. Why do you look elsewhere for restoration? Why not lift up your eyes to the hills from whence cometh your help. What is the reason for not going to Jesus.

There are many reasons. Some have not really heard that the gospel is good news for all sinners that come to Jesus. Many have misrepresented the gospel as negative and faultfinding. It is not. All - even witches and wizards . . . all can come to Him and receive transforming grace in the bread that satisfies. Some have been impressed by the achievements of people and the intelligence and brilliance of human inventions and ideas. Excellent as all these may be, you will need grace to take your eyes off them. Churches have built men focused ministries and many miss the Lord of the Church. In this text, be sure you understand that Christ is waiting for you to come to Him for what you need, and you must take your eyes off whatever stops you from coming.

I know, you say . . . you are not clean to come. Your hunger is your qualification and not your virtue. Receive grace to come to Christ. Go on your knees. Now. Go and find the resting place waiting for you. Have you heard the news. Jesus saves. Have you spread the message to far lands. Tweet: Jesus Saves today. Stop looking around—look to Jesus.

Song

"I've a message from the Lord, Hallelujah! The message;unto you I'll give
'Tis recorded in His word, Halleluyah.! It is only that you "look and live"
"Look and live "my brother live, look to Jesus now and live
Tis recorded in His word Halleluyah; it is only that you "look and live"

Prayer: O Lord, Begin a work of restoration as I commune afresh with Christ . . . looking up to Him for grace for myself and for my Church and nation. Amen

MARCH 31

The Ultimate Assignment

Bible Text: Genesis 42:2

Gen 42:2 And he said, Behold, I have heard that there is corn in Egypt: get you down thither, and buy for us from thence; that we may live, and not die.

God has assignments for us in different forms, but there is one destiny changing assignment. Often it does not seem to be important but our obedience is so critical now. God may have to surround these assignments with unusual circumstances that will compel us to behave as He wants us to . . . this is to help us. In this situation, the threat of death looms over the household of Jacob and a desperate move to go to a strange land did not appear to be of any value apart from arresting starvation.

Training our children to be obedient is important. There is a generation that believes parents do not have a role but to just guide and present options to their children. Children are to be instructed in the way of the Lord and especially taught to obey their parents. Parents must seek God and provide Godly example. The house of Jacob is still united, but incomplete in that Joseph was missing. Destiny was about to be fulfilled and the key was obedience to an assignment that looked trivial . . . but it was the ultimate assignment. I suspect that a generation that is not sensitive to obedience to parents is a generation that will not fulfill its destiny. Obedience is much better than sacrifice. Be accustomed to obeying first rather than packaging gifts to leaders or honoring men of God . . . our first question to be answered is "Have we listened carefully to all the instructions given to us? Have we obeyed them all?" May God help us to hearken and obey Him always.

Song

Have Thine own way, Lord, Have Thine own way;
Thou art the Potter; I am the clay.
Mould me and make me After Thy will,
While I am waiting, Yielded and still.

Have Thine own way, Lord, Have Thine own way;
Search me and try me, Master, today.
Whiter than snow, Lord, Wash me just now,
As in Thy presence Humbly I bow.

Have Thine own way, Lord, Have Thine own way;
Wounded and weary, Help me, I pray.
Power, all power, Surely is Thine;
Touch me and heal me, Savior divine.

Have Thine own way, Lord, Have Thine own way;
Hold o'er my being Absolute sway.
Fill with Thy Spirit Till all shall see
Christ only, always, Living in me.

Prayer: O Lord, release more grace for obedience to saints all over the world. Amen

APRIL 1

Help our Doubts

Bible Text: Genesis 42:2

Gen 42:2 And he said, Behold, I have heard that there is corn in Egypt: get you down thither, and buy for us from thence; that we may live, and not die.

We reap what we sow. Jacob the former deceiver was now under the lie that Joseph was dead. His conclusions were wrong. His utterances were misplaced, but God remains merciful. God sees our struggles and failings and has not decided to abandon us. He works above our very limited appreciation of His wonderful works. He is indeed a great God. The wrong conclusions of Jacob are based on his incomplete picture.

Jacob says he has heard that there is corn in Egypt but he does not know the greater refreshing truth that Joseph is alive and ruling in Egypt. He has doubts as to whether the Hebrews will be well received by the Egyptians, he has doubts whether the corn will be available and affordable for them - we know this because they had been ravaged also by the famine.

Jacob asks his sons to go and buy. He has doubts of how much they will be able to procure and how long it will last. He does not know that the price has already been paid by Joseph his son that was "dead". Jacob was already seeing death and had doubts on how long they would be sustained - even if they found food in Egypt . . . would it be enough, would it be too late . . . how would they obtain a continued supply for their sustenance. More doubts. Jacob does not know that God has made an elaborate provision to ensure that they do not die, rather they would live the rest of their lives in the best of Egypt.

My God help our doubts for they appear so legitimate. Meanwhile God has made extraordinary provisions ahead for His own. Well in excess of our understanding. A full price has been paid for our salvation, the word is forever settled and we only need to trust it . . . and we shall not die, rather we live to declare the word of God and His praises even until eternity. But today, many want to buy salvation with works or other things. Today, we have doubts if God truly desires to save us - because we are so bad. Today we have doubts if we will live through the issues and problems.

Cast away your doubts. You do not have the full picture things. Instead believe His word which gives you His revealed agenda. Pray for more understanding and revelation - but meanwhile, simply trust that He whom you have trusted - our Lord Jesus Christ - He will come through. Very soon all the provisions that have been made ahead will soon manifest their purpose. Soon you will be ashamed that you ever doubted Him.

Song

Faint not, nor fear, his arms are near,
He changeth not, and thou art dear;
Only believe, and thou shalt see
That Christ is all in all to thee.

Prayer: O Lord, Help my doubts. Strengthen my faith. I want to believe. Help me. Amen

APRIL 2

A Free Salvation

Bible Text: Genesis 42:3

Gen 42:3 And Joseph's ten brethren went down to buy corn in Egypt

The blessings of God are not cheap. The most precious is completely unaffordable - our salvation, and that is why Jesus Christ had to pay the price. There are many ways we misrepresent the price of salvation. Many for years have been coming to Christ with an action or a sacrifice or a contribution. But salvation is full and free to us because of Jesus. All the corn in Egypt was free and available to the sons of Jacob only and only because Joseph paid the price and went to the pit, and to the dungeons of Egypt, suffering as a lamb that goes to the slaughter. It was Jesus and His work on the cross that bought our salvation.

When we seek a salvation without Christ Jesus, we present a salvation that we must work for. When we think we are just the right person for salvation, we present our human goodness as a price. When we believe we are too bad for salvation, we declare that the blood of Jesus could not possibly be adequate for our salvation. How is it that we bear so many needless burdens? We want a salvation that some man somewhere can take some credit for, but this cannot be the salvation of God.

Note from the text though that the sons of Jacob did what was reasonable within the context of the understanding that they had of the situation. May God give us an understanding that is true and complete. Our salvation is free but must be worked with fear and trembling. There are labors in the vineyard and battles with the one who contends for our soul. But our salvation remains a free gift of God. The brothers obeyed their father and went down to Egypt. It was a long tedious and risky journey, but God had preordained it to prosper their way.

There are no devices, there are no creeds, there are no offerings or spiritual arguments for salvation beyond the death of Christ on the Cross of Calvary for the sinner. Reflect on this.

Song

Enough for me that Jesus saves; This ends my fear and doubt;
A sinful soul I come to Him, He'll never cast me out.
I need no other argument, I need no other plea
It is enough that Jesus died and that He died for me.

Prayer: O Lord, in the past I was ungrateful and misguided, presenting works of self-improvement - instead of my whole life. Jesus I now come to you - with nothing else but as a sinful soul. Save me Lord Jesus and do not cast me out. Amen

APRIL 3

Hidden Agenda

Bible Text: Genesis 42:3

Gen 42:3 And Joseph's ten brethren went down to buy corn in Egypt

Many times we are convinced we know what we are being asked to do and we obey . . . but what we do not know is the hidden objective of God. God is known to hide His objectives from the eyes of men until the appointed time to do so.

1Sa_9:3 And the asses of Kish Saul's father were lost. And Kish said to Saul his son, Take now one of the servants with thee, and arise, go seek the asses.

Saul has been sent to seek the asses that were lost. This was the assignment given by Kish and Saul obeys . . . but God has planned a completely different objective to lift Saul up to the throne of Israel. Samuel meets Saul to prepare him for the throne only because Saul obeys His father, Kish. The assignment is a trivial assignment . . . not in the least kingly you may add . . . but it will lead to the throne. When faced with assignments, do not ever forget that God may have a completely different and hidden agenda for that assignment . . . do not judge assignments by your perception of what they could accomplish. Rather, be sure that God is with you. Going to Egypt is described as going down . . . because it is a spiritually inferior location . . . a place of idols and witchcraft. But God has an important hidden agenda. Reflect on what God has asked you to do . . . lean not to your understanding. Things are not as they seem.

Song

Glorious things of thee are spoken, Zion, city of our God!
He, whose Word cannot be broken, Formed thee for His own abode.
On the Rock of Ages founded, What can shake thy sure repose?
With salvation's walls surrounded, Thou may'st smile at all thy foes.

See! the streams of living waters, springing from eternal love,
Well supply thy sons and daughters, and all fear of want remove:
Who can faint while such a river ever flows their thirst to assuage—
Grace which, like the Lord, the Giver, Never fails from age to age?

Round each habitation hov'ring, See! the cloud and fire appear
For a glory and a cov'ring, Showing that the Lord is near:
Blest inhabitants of Zion, Washed in the Redeemer's blood—
Jesus, whom their souls rely on, Makes them kings and priests to God.

Savior, if of Zion's city - I thro' grace a member am,
Let the world deride or pity, I will glory in Thy Name:
Fading is the worldling's pleasure, all his boasted pomp and show;
Solid joys and lasting treasure none but Zion's children know.

Prayer: O Lord, your agenda is a great, awesome and hidden one . . . but always working for our joys and good. Help me to acknowledge you in all my ways and know that you are always working something for my good. Amen

APRIL 4

Experience is not our Teacher

Bible Text: Genesis 42:4

Gen 42:4 But Benjamin, Joseph's brother, Jacob sent not with his brethren; for he said, Lest peradventure mischief befall him.

Jacob cannot trust his sons to look after Benjamin. It is not unlikely that he has seen the animosity between the houses of Leah and Rachel and the envy of Rachel's children. He also senses that Benjamin, being the only surviving son (in his mind) of the children of Rachel, must be preserved—but he is wrong. His experience tells him to keep Benjamin also to preserve the tribe perhaps if all the other brothers are killed. The strange land of Egypt did not bring any good to the ancestors of Jacob . . . Benjamin one way or the other would be safer at home. But experience is not our teacher. God is our teacher. God does not interfere in the wrong conclusions of Jacob because they will still work for His good. Beware of conclusions based only on experience . . . we should form the habit of checking our actions with God. The house of Jacob was torn with envy, sorrow and fears . . . this is not a good platform for good decisions. We must ask God—especially when our experiences make us suspicious of others—and we need God to divorce our thinking from pains and distortions of the past. Meditate on the decisions you have made based on suspicions and past hurts and anxieties. Did they end up right? Ask God to help you make the right decision. Experience can of course be useful. But do not permit it to be your teacher. Instead let your Savior lead you. Let the word of God be your tutor. Help us to forgive past hurts and forget all that must be forgotten.

Song

All the way my Savior leads me;
What have I to ask beside?
Can I doubt His tender mercy,
Who thro' life has been my Guide?
Heav'nly peace, divinest comfort,
Here by faith in Him to dwell!
For I know, whate'er befall me, Jesus doeth all things well;
For I know, whate'er befall me, Jesus doeth all things well.

All the way my Savior leads me,
Cheers each winding path I tread,
Gives me grace for ev'ry trial,
Feeds me with the living bread.
Though my weary steps may falter,
And my soul athirst may be,
Gushing from the Rock before me, Lo! a spring of joy I see;
Gushing from the Rock before me, Lo! a spring of joy I see.

All the way my Savior leads me;
Oh, the fullness of His love!
Perfect rest to me is promised
In my Father's house above.
When my spirit, clothed immortal,
Wings its flight to realms of day,
This my song thro' endless ages: Jesus led me all the way;
This my song thro' endless ages: Jesus led me all the way.

Prayer: O Lord, Lead us all the way. Amen

APRIL 5

Hold nothing back

Bible Text: Genesis 42:4

Gen 42:4 But Benjamin, Joseph's brother, Jacob sent not with his brethren; for he said, Lest peradventure mischief befall him.

What are you holding back and shielding from the Lord's use? Which area of your life do you think you must protect by yourself? We must come completely and fully. Many times we hold back two categories of things. We hold back our priciest treasures, our career, our dreams, our long held agendas. We fear God will tear them up, just as Jacob's coat of many colors were torn apart by mischief. We do not want to take the full risk, and so we hold back our cultural traditions and areas we think God has no interest. But God wants all of us as an offering laid on the altar - chopped up and put on the wood - awaiting the fire of God.

Another thing that many hold back are sins and ways that we have become so accustomed to having with us, that so easily beset us and in some cases private sins that we fear God may choose to bring to the open. The brothers of Joseph could not admit that they had lied and Joseph may not be dead. Come before God and be plain in your confessions. He knows anyway . . . everything. Nothing is hidden from Him.

As you meditate on this devotional, what aspect of your life have you not handed to God - what are you still trying to protect from God's salvation. All must be brought and be crucified with Christ to experience the same power of resurrection in Him. Our "Benjamins" which we feel we can manage without the salvation of God tend to be our weakest targets—most vulnerable to the enemies arrows.

Jacob was wrong again in his conclusions that if Benjamin travelled to Egypt, he would be hurt. If only he could see that Benjamin was about to be rejoined with the senior offspring of his late mother Rachel. Benjamin would have missed his brother Joseph and it seems Jacob passed his preferential love for Joseph now to Benjamin. Jacob did not know he was delaying Benjamin from the happiest union he could ever have. What joys we hold back, when we keep our best away from Christ - hidden in the closet of our hearts. Lord, today I pray - take my all.

Song

Faith in Christ will save me!
Let me trust Thy weeping Son
Trust the work that he has done,
To His arms, Lord help me run
Faith in Christ will save me!

Prayer: O Lord, give me grace to surrender all to Christ. My ups, downs, dreams, wealth, hopes, victories and disappointments - let me hold nothing back. Amen

APRIL 6

Famine in Canaan.

Bible Text: Genesis 42:5

Gen 42:5 And the sons of Israel came to buy corn among those that came: for the famine was in the land of Canaan.

I observe a mystery here. Why does God use Egypt to protect His own in a global famine? Why does God permit famine in the land of Canaan. The only answer I dare suggest is that "It pleased God to do so" . . . it was the plan of God. There are many bruising things that happen but for God it brings pleasure.

Isa_53:10 Yet it pleased the LORD to bruise him; he hath put him to grief: when thou shalt make his soul an offering for sin, he shall see his seed, he shall prolong his days, and the pleasure of the LORD shall prosper in his hand.

The pain, hunger and thirst of famine may have destroyed many, but it caused the family of Joseph to come to him and the greatest joys. Many families of thieves were thrown into grief when their sons were crucified, but the crucifixion of Christ ushered the beginning of a return to glory for the family of God and this pleased God.

God has need of famines not just to bring his own to Him, but for opportunities to demonstrate His mighty provisions to them that trust Him. God has need of famines to separate those on the narrow path of trusting Him from those who really serve their belly. Remember Job. A famine came into his life as a test. But what did Job say?

Job_13:15 Though he slay me, yet will I trust in him: but I will maintain mine own ways before him.

Consider this devotional. Have you gone through famine situations in your life? Did you pass the examination of God? Were your ways maintained or did they change? Did you curse God or were you steadfast knowing this will also pass.

Song

Set thou thy trust upon the Lord, and be thou doing good;
And so thou in the land shalt dwell, and verily have food.
Delight thyself in God; he'll give thine heart's desire to thee.
Thy way to God commit, him trust, it bring to pass shall he.

And, like unto the light, he shall thy righteousness display;
And he thy judgment shall bring forth, like noon-tide of the day.
Rest in the Lord, and patiently wait for him: do not fret
For him who, prospering in his way, success in sin doth get.

Let anger cease within thy heart, and wrath forsake thou too:
Fret not thyself in any wise, that evil thou should'st do.
For those that evil-doers are shall be cut off and fall:
But those that wait upon the Lord, the earth inherit shall.

Prayer: O Lord, send your comforter The Holy Spirit . . . to comfort many Christians in pain and anguish. Amen

APRIL 7

Not all that come

Bible Text: Genesis 42:5

Gen 42:5 And the sons of Israel came to buy corn among those that came: for the famine was in the land of Canaan.

The Bible says that God foreknew all that would be saved and that these He sanctified and subsequently glorified. Only those drawn by the Spirit of God can come to His salvation. There were so many that say that they came to God but they came not by the door, but they jumped over the fence. In times of difficulty many will say they serve God, but those that truly love God will be known by God, set apart by God and eventually glorified by God.

The Bible says concerning the congregation, many will say they did great exploits in the name of Christ, but Christ knows all that are His. Just as Joseph knows His brothers. There were many others that came and bought so much corn. These are like the many that come to the word of God and use its principles to improve their life and even did many exploits - but God did not know them. They did not obey Him, and were not assigned tasks by God. These are like wandering stars . . . they are uncontrolled even in the sanctuary.

The main difference between Joseph's brothers and the rest that came is that Joseph knew his bothers. God had pre-chosen them as his brothers - they did not qualify themselves by any performance or lack of it. It was all grace that elected them into the family of Joseph. They are the ones who will find a bread that is already paid for and ushered to live for the rest of their lives in Goshen.

As you reflect on this short text, reflect that it is not all that cry Lord, Lord that will be joint heirs with Him. Dearth can bring many mercenaries to come for what they need to survive. Hunger attracts wolves as well as sheep. Goats will look for pasture just as lambs need to feed. It is not ours to judge, for we do not know. God gives the toughest assignments to His cherished ones, because He foreknew them that they will remain faithful even if faced with death. His own are His special army - co-workers in His Revival. A pastor once put up a sign board "This Church will have either a revival or a funeral." . . . It had a Revival. God knows those who care for Him than their very lives. Are you one of those to whom He will say "I never knew you"?

Many have come to the Church and find only food . . . true salvation reunites us with the family of Christ—we find a brother.

Song

The saints of old were beaten, tried, condemned and even crucified.
These martyr men beat no retreat when flames were licking at their feet
They saw the tyrant's brandished steel, But still they offered no appeal.

They struck no bargain for their lives, For heir children or their wives.
All slowly roasted in the flames. While angels wrote each of their names.
Within a book God calls His own - To be proclaimed before His throne.

Prayer: O Lord, teach us to pray the desperate prayers that will bring your Revival. Amen

APRIL 8

Joseph - Governor (Part 1)

Bible Text: Genesis 42:6

Gen 42:6 And Joseph was the governor over the land, and he it was that sold to all the people of the land: and Joseph's brethren came, and bowed down themselves before him with their faces to the earth

There are many categories of power. The Bible declares that all power belongs to God - whichever the category. There is the lowest category which is economic power. This is wealth and financial means that enable us not just to be sustained but to accomplish exploits such as feeding others. The Bible tells us that poverty does not glorify God nor will His own lack for bread or beg. Our Father is a great provider. There is also political power which is higher than economic power. Political power will often equate to economic power. This is power to rule over territories and demand obedience of populations. Joseph had political power as governor over the land. But there is a third category of power. This is Spiritual power i.e. power with God to decree and shape history from the spiritual realms. This is the highest power. People will bow before all categories of power. The higher the category level the more people will be subjects.

The brothers of Joseph, lacked every category of power. The famine had wiped out economic power that they may have had, they had no political power in the foreign land of Egypt, they were subjects and so they bowed before Joseph their junior brother. God does not want us to be powerless, robbed of all our powers. A powerless Christian is weak, vulnerable and will fall into many traps and temptations. It is not that he wants to be unreliable, but he lacks the power to sustain his resolve in whatever he sets his mind to. He ends up double minded - weak in all His ways.

How long will you bow to forces you should reign over? How long will you be subject to even the lower powers. Is it not God who gives power to make wealth? In this earlier part of this devotional reflect on the first two categories of power. Perhaps you are failing because you find yourself always oppressed and made to give in - even when you see otherwise, you cannot backup your decision with action. You have no means to look after your home and feed your children. You need to pay the rent. You want to build a church for God and give even more to others but you have no power to do so. Instead you borrow and bow to crippling debts.

Today by the mercy and grace of God you are coming up higher. God will empower you financially to supply all your needs according to His riches in glory. Go to the God who empowers, tell him what you want to do for Him with the power that He will grant.

Song

All hail the power of Jesus name
Let Angels prostrate fall 2ce
Bring forth the royal diadem
and crown Him Lord of all.

Prayer: O Lord, I am tired of the valley of powerlessness . . . raise me up in your power. Amen

APRIL 9

Joseph - Governor (Part 11)

Bible Text: Genesis 42:6

Gen 42:6 And Joseph was the governor over the land, and he it was that sold to all the people of the land: and Joseph's brethren came, and bowed down themselves before him with their faces to the earth

There is another category of power, the highest category. This is spiritual power. We can have power with God operating from Heavenly places where we have been seated with Christ. This is the highest seat of power from which we challenge principalities and wicked powers, rulers over nations and villages and tribes and religious devilry. This category is the highest category of all. Indeed political and economic powers are subject to spiritual powers. If you find yourself still standing in spite of all that has come against you, it may be you have a reservoir of spiritual strength given by God that has not been allowed to fail. Do not laugh at those who have fallen, lest you lose the grace that kept you standing. All power including spiritual power belongs to God.

Jesus walked as the example of how we should walk in spiritual power. He did not judge by sight and mere human senses. He waited always on God, his Father. In the same way, we should wait always on the Holy Spirit. If we are seated with Christ, it means we have been already given the permission to operate at the highest but still we refuse to come up higher. God is inviting us to come up.

The brothers of Joseph and indeed all who came . . . bowed to Joseph - but we see this as only a political power. Indeed it released great wealth but we are told little of what was happening spiritually. Everything on the earth will bow to political power. But how about the things in the Heavens and under the earth. It should not surprise us that several years after Joseph died a Pharaoh arose which did not know him and erased his legacy. Power can also change hands. Politically and spiritually.

Php_2:10 That at the name of Jesus every knee should bow, of things in Heaven, and things in earth, and things under the earth;

Jesus is the model given to the Christian. We are to walk in spiritual power with Christ. Every knee includes sickness, poverty, enchantments, curses . . . they all must bow to the name of Jesus. The things in the Heavens and the worst of hell must all bow before Jesus. There is an appointed day in eternity where every knee will literally bow to Jesus at the gates of eternal judgment. I urge you to flee from teachings that suggest another name has been given to some for salvation -- but the name of Jesus. When we operate in spiritual power, even the economic and the political must bow to the glory of Christ Jesus.

Song

All power! All power belongs to God. (Chorus)

Prayer: O Lord, I am weak but thou art mighty - connect me again to your spiritual reservoir of great power and switch on the flow of current. Amen

APRIL 10

Joseph - Governor (Part 111)

Bible Text: Genesis 42:6

Gen 42:6 And Joseph was the governor over the land, and he it was that sold to all the people of the land: and Joseph's brethren came, and bowed down themselves before him with their faces to the earth

In the previous study, we considered the different categories of power. The highest is spiritual power, the others political and least is economic power. The lower powers are subject to the highest powers and spiritual power is the highest. We can also move up and go higher. We need to operate at spiritual levels that permit us to challenge wickedness tormenting nations and devils behind evils in the land. But how do we go higher?

Luk 14:10 But when thou art bidden, go and sit down in the lowest room; that when he that bade thee cometh, he may say unto thee, Friend, go up higher: then shalt thou have worship in the presence of them that sit at meat with thee. 11 For whosoever exalteth himself shall be abased; and he that humbleth himself shall be exalted.

The secret of positioning for elevation by God is in humility. When we read Matthew 5, we see that all the attributes in the beatitudes—the poor in spirit, mourn, meek, hunger and thirst for righteousness, merciful, pure in heart, peacemakers, the persecuted all point to humility.

Humility is not poverty nor weakness. Humility is turning away from self and our wicked ways and praying. It is time to humble yourself, be quiet before God, be obedient to His leading. He will call you up to go higher and even higher. With spiritual power you can be on your knees and decree changes cause earthly kings to tremble and demonic plans to collapse. What a difference you will make in your family, marriage, church and the nations.

Jesus went down several steps till he ended in the grave . . . but He was raised to the highest levels. He did not just grab power - even though it was offered to Him by the people, He preferred to die, to come down even more. Christ did this because He knew God's ways and principles or elevation. Jesus operated in the highest of spiritual realms. He spoke truths boldly and accepted His crucifixion like a meek lamb for the slaughter. Yet He was the mighty Lord of Hosts with innumerable angels waiting for His orders.

As they all bowed to Joseph. God will help us to reign over wickedness rather than have them reign over us.

Song

At the Name of Jesus
Every knee shall bow,
Every tongue confess Him
King of glory now;
'Tis the Father's pleasure
We should call Him Lord,
Who from the beginning
Was the mighty Word.

Prayer: O Lord, teach me how to come up higher and higher every day. Amen

APRIL 11

God knows His Own.

Bible Text: Genesis 42:7

Gen 42:7 And Joseph saw his brethren, and he knew them, but made himself strange unto them, and spake roughly unto them; and he said unto them, Whence come ye? And they said, From the land of Canaan to buy food.

Jesus knows them that are His. The Bible says they were already given to Him before the foundations of the earth. Joseph can recognize His family although many years have passed. He knew what they had done to him and their wicked thoughts. Joseph could recognize their features and their way of dressing, their way of speaking . . . in Egypt they were strange . . . but not to Joseph.

If the brothers of Joseph had perhaps changed their clothing to fit better with Egypt . . . learnt their language and accent and hide their own . . . if they had borrowed some attributes from Egypt . . . perhaps supposing this will help their mission . . . if they had done these things, Joseph who was not expecting to see them in his palace may not have recognized them and they may have just come and gone . . . with food, but never knowing that Joseph was alive and well. How peculiar are you in Egypt? How easy is it to identify you as a Christian? Many say what we wear does not matter and how we look does not matter . . . and that it is what is in us that counts. I pray this is so but suspect otherwise. Joseph did not know his brothers by some inspiration . . . he could recognize them because they dressed as their father had taught them to dress . . . with the same manners as they had been trained to exhibit. Joseph knew these mannerisms and ways and knew they were not Egyptian . . . He also knew these were the ways of the tribe of Canaan. This caused him to look again at their faces and complexion . . . they did not have strange tattoos, nor did they swear like desert men. Also consider that Joseph was not recognizable because he had completely changed his clothes and appeared to them as an Egyptian. Our appearance affects our recognition. There is a major lesson here. We are a peculiar people, a chosen nation, a holy priesthood . . . do we communicate this identity or are we easily confused with others.

A day comes when Jesus says He knows us not because we say so but because internally and externally we are truly like Him . . . we love His teachings and obey his words. There are many who profess Him, but to whom He says . . . I knew you not.

Song

Lord, I want to be a Christian in my heart, in my heart,
Lord, I want to be a Christian in my heart, in my heart. In my heart, in my heart,
Lord, I want to be a Christian in my heart, in my heart.

Lord, I want to be more loving in my heart, in my heart,
Lord, I want to be more loving in my heart, in my heart. In my heart, in my heart,
Lord, I want to be more loving in my heart, in my heart.

Lord, I want to be more holy in my heart, in my heart,
Lord, I want to be more holy in my heart, in my heart. In my heart, in my heart,
Lord, I want to be more holy in my heart, in my heart.

Lord, I want to be like Jesus in my heart, in my heart,
Lord, I want to be like Jesus in my heart, in my heart.In my heart, in my heart,
Lord, I want to be like Jesus in my heart, in my heart.

Prayer: O Lord, Help me to be different—peculiar . . . like Jesus. Amen

APRIL 12

A Frowning Providence

Bible Text: Genesis 42:7

Gen 42:7 And Joseph saw his brethren, and he knew them, but made himself strange unto them, and spake roughly unto them; and he said unto them, Whence come ye? And they said, From the land of Canaan to buy food.

Why does God frown when He is overwhelmed with joy? The mission of our Lord Jesus is only truly accomplished when sinners come home. Have you ever felt a sense of a job well done? Has it ever become clear to you why certain things had to be the way they were? This feeling comes with a sense of joy. Yet, Joseph spoke roughly and strangely to His brothers.

There are times when the voice of God is harsh and cold, when it does not seem like we have anything to do with Jesus. There are times when we feel Jesus cannot want us and prefers to be distant for us. We sometimes imagine there is some sin that Jesus must know about and he cannot want us anymore. These are not just all untrue but very far from what is really occurring.

There is nothing we can do that Christ has not paid in full for. Joseph missed his brothers and in a strange land yearned for the company of His blood relatives. He missed his father, he missed Benjamin and could barely resist the temptation to fully reveal himself. There must be tests in our Christian walk. There is a process of growing, chastening and getting us perfect. Some of this comes at early stages of growth, some come in our latter years. Could mankind do more to God than kill His own only begotten son sent to seek and save them? If mankind could be forgiven for crucifying Jesus, could they not be forgiven anything by God. In similar fashion the brothers "killed" the favorite son of their father. Could they still do more or worse. God forgives sin if we confess them to Him. There is nothing that God cannot give us, if He gave us His only son. When we see that the value of the painful death of Christ is only realized when the prodigal son returns home, then we can understand that behind God's hard chastening is a great joy that the sinner is returning home.

It is often true when we come to Christ in our initial experiences that we do not really know Him, and Christ has to send His Holy Spirit to do the work of transformation and help our perfection . . . as we are changed from glory to glory. Rejoice. The chastening you are going through is a good sign. Joseph did not speak roughly to any other person but his brothers. Also note that Joseph wanted all his family with him and needed an approach that would not incur the wrath of the Egyptians or even bring hurt to them. He was still uncertain of the reactions of his brothers or even of the Egyptians to them. Would his brothers go back and tell another lie to their father, never to return, Joseph works a plan that will - in the end - bring the entire family to safety. Do not be sad when God seems rough, He is working out His great plans that you come to the beautiful end that is expected.

Song

Judge not the Lord by feeble sense,
But trust Him for His grace
Behind a frowning providence
He hides a smiling face

Prayer: O Lord, you are chastening me so that I can be perfected and partake in a greater glory. Help me to see and know this. Amen

APRIL 13

Do you know Him?

Bible Text: Genesis 42:8

Gen 42:8 And Joseph knew his brethren, but they knew not him

How can we know someone as awesome, as mighty, as limitless, as infinite as God except that He reveals Himself to us. God is great. We are grass. How much of God will grass ever discover. Yet God reveals Himself to us by His creation, by His living word and by His innumerable hosts of messengers and ministering angels, watching over us. Indeed, much of our wanderings and problems arise from poor knowledge of God. The enemy of our soul, he himself having been one of his most trusted angels before, does know well that those that know their God will be undefeatable in their exploits.

The result of not knowing God is that we fret, we fear, we are too easily discouraged and place too much emphasis on our deeds - good or bad, as if they could do anything to God's infinite purposes. If we knew God, then we will know that God sees our thoughts clearly from afar - even before the thoughts came to us. God is so complex and so simple. He is so big and so small. He does not need a microscope to manage the unseen cells and organisms yet to be discovered. He does not need a telescope or a space ship to reach out to galaxies that fit into his hands. How could we describe Him. All our words are too limited, because we can only use our experience and created senses to observe that which created us and is well beyond our experience. All our words fail.

If God does not reveal Himself to us, then seeking to know Him would be fruitless. But in Christ we see God walk the earth. In His word, we see God in print. In His Holy Spirit we see God as our comforter. The Son, the Father and the Holy Spirit ... all the same God. The Bible says that mankind is different in that we were made in His own image. Even angels were not said to be made in the image of God. Do you know that angels marvel at humanity and learn about God from observing us.

Satan fights the knowledge of God in our lives more than any other attribute. He fills our minds with knowledge ... so much vain knowledge, so we are limited. Can you imagine the difference to the brothers of Joseph when they knew God and knew they were forgiven and all is well. When we know God, we will realize we need not walk in guilt. He has forgiven us. When we walk in guilt, we walk in fear and continually carry burdens we are not even meant to lift.

Song

Knowing you, Jesus, knowing you, There is no greater thing
You're my all, you're the best - You're my joy, my righteousness ... And I love you, Lord

All I once held dear, built my life upon - All this world reveres, and wars to own
All I once thought gain I have counted loss - Spent and worthless now, compared to this

Knowing you, Jesus, knowing you, There is no greater thing
You're my all, you're the best You're my joy, my righteousness ... And I love you, Lord

Prayer: O Lord, reveal Yourself even more in my life. Amen

APRIL 14

The Lamb upon the Throne

Bible Text: Genesis 42:8

Gen 42:8 And Joseph knew his brethren, but they knew not him

How can we see that the Lamb that was slain, is now risen—Jesus and is upon the throne. We have mocked Christ, ignored Him, crucified Him and often betrayed Him. We eventually fail to recognize that He that we maltreated and disdained is upon the throne. Why do we fail to see Christ upon the throne? Is it because He is so gentle and loving. He forgives us so easily and gives us another chance to come to Him. Is it because He comes to us as a brother and a friend that we cannot also see Him as a King. But the King of kings is our brother, our own friend that is closer than any brother we have and can ever know. Don't you see the joy this should cause knowing the authority in Egypt is not in the hands of a stranger? But then we forgo so many benefits and carry so many needless pains simply because we do not see the one on the throne as our friend, brother, King and our Lord.

Why is it that Joseph is not recognized? Perhaps because it was the very last place they thought Joseph will ever be. Similarly, many do not expect Christ to be on the throne and so imagine themselves to be victims when in reality they are being helped by the Lord. We do not praise God as we should because we do not see Him as we should. The reason the angels worship in a different more respectful manner is because they know whom they bow to—The Almighty.

Jesus is on the throne. Look again and you will see He rules and reigns undisputed even amongst the heathen. What if they had recognized Joseph immediately ? Joseph would have welcomed them warmly like the father welcoming the fearful prodigal son. Have no fear . . . Jesus knows all about you—everything you have done and can do . . . and still says He hates sin but loves you—the sinner. Sinner come home to Jesus. Do not waste another minute. He rules over all . . . including his enemies.

Song

Before the throne of God above I have a strong, a perfect plea,
A great High Priest, whose name is love, Whoever lives and pleads for me.

My name is graven in His hands, My name is written on His heart;
I know that, while in heav'n He stands, No tongue can bid me thence depart.

When Satan tempts me to despair, and tells me of the guilt within, I look
Up ward above and see Him there who made an end of all my sin.

Because the sinless Savior died, my sinful soul is counted free;
For God the Just is satisfied to look on Him, and pardon me.

Behold Him there! the risen Lamb! My perfect, spotless righteousness,
The great unchangeable I Am, The King of glory and of grace!

One with Himself, I cannot die, My soul is purchased by His blood;
My life is hid with Christ on high, With Christ, my Savior and my God

Prayer: O Lord, reign and rule forever. Grant me mercy from your throne of grace. Amen

APRIL 15

Pass your Test

Bible Text: Genesis 42:9

Gen 42:9 And Joseph remembered the dreams which he dreamed of them, and said unto them, Ye are spies; to see the nakedness of the land ye are come.

What would you do if you were connected to all power and the greatest might? Would you use this connection to do more good and obey God or would you have your own agenda? Would you forgive your enemies and pray for those who curse you or will you embark on a journey of revenge? Would you be as harmless as a dove or would you oppress the harmless? These questions do not have obvious answers.

Indeed, as many things will not be revealed till the end, we are warned to test every spirit . . . whether they be of God. Many have come to the kingdom for salvation because they need help. There is nothing wrong with this. But who is of God and who is not - is known to God and is not be known to even us and others. The Bible warns of great betrayals of faith in the last days. Spies will be revealed.

Who are spies? Spies have another hidden master who has given them instructions on how to infiltrate the camp. Satan understands the Church and has observed people for centuries. His spies know what to do . . . how to sing the songs and talk the talk. But they cannot stand the heat. Spies have covered the body of Christ, offering all sorts of placebos to soothe Christians and balms that make people feel good but without salvation. Spies have risen to high levels of authority, and have been lifted high in the Church by mortals. Many will be shown to be spies at the appointed time.

Spies want to know the weakness of the Kingdom, so that temptations can be fashioned in the pits of hell to bring you down. We must be cautious and guard our tongues. Out testimonies sometimes are not ripe to be shared because of spies. The enemy is not omniscient and he must infiltrate and come close to obtain information to destroy us. The Bible therefore has the answer - test every spirit. All - without exception . . . whether in leaders or in young Christians. We are not told to test the spirit in new converts only. All spirits. God will help you to stand and remain standing. When tested, do not be offended. Simply pass your test.

Song

I need thee ev'ry hour,
Stay thou near by;
Temptations lose their pow'r
When thou art nigh.

I need thee, Oh I need thee
Every hour I need thee!
O bless me now my Savior,
I come to thee.

Prayer: O Lord, teach me to pass all the tests before me. Prove me and let it be known that I am truly yours. Amen

APRIL 16

Spies or Pilgrims

Bible Text: Genesis 42:9

Gen 42:9 And Joseph remembered the dreams which he dreamed of them, and said unto them, Ye are spies; to see the nakedness of the land ye are come.

A pilgrim is a person who journeys, especially from a long distance, to some place as an act of obedience. The pilgrim has his homeland and does not disguise his identity. He has an assignment and will return after the assignment . . . in many ways he is like an ambassador. A spy is different. First, he hides his true identity and not just identity but most importantly his mission. He partakes in everything that other citizens partake in as though he were like them and blends. None identifies him as different. But a pilgrim looks different. He has no agenda but to bless the place he visits, often bringing gifts and offerings from his homeland. But a spy is a secret destroyer. Which are you? Some say neither. The one that is lukewarm . . . is useless for both purposes in that he neither represents the homeland of the pilgrim as he should nor is he effective as a spy, perhaps because in some ways he is too easy to spot. In many cases, he weakens the resolve and zeal of other pilgrims who begin to relax their peculiarity and begin to copy the lukewarm. Spies are eventually caught and executed or retire in the home of the destroyer—Satan which the Bible says is hell fire. Pilgrims also have their own place of retirement—in a blissful eternity. Are you a pilgrim? I pray you are not a spy. When He sent spies to look at the promised land of Canaan, the majority brought back an evil report. The pilgrims live by faith.

Song

The Church from her dear Master
Received the gift divine,
And still that light she lifteth
O'er all the earth to shine.
It is the golden casket
Where gems of truth are stored;
It is the heav'n-drawn picture
Of Christ, the living Word.

It floateth like a banner
Before God's host unfurled;
It shineth like a beacon
Above the darkling world.
It is the chart and compass
That o'er life's surging sea,
'Mid mists and rocks and quicksands,
Still guides, O Christ, to Thee.

O make Thy Church, dear Savior,
A lamp of purest gold,
To bear before the nations
Thy true light, as of old.
O teach thy wand'ring pilgrims
By this their path to trace,
Till, clouds and darkness ended,
They see Thee face to face.

Prayer: O Lord, am I a spy or a pilgrim . . . speak to my heart ? Amen

APRIL 17

The Throne Room

Bible Text: Genesis 42:10-12

Gen 42:10 And they said unto him, Nay, my lord, but to buy food are thy servants come. 11 We are all one man's sons; we are true men, thy servants are no spies. 12 And he said unto them, Nay, but to see the nakedness of the land ye are come.

The brothers of Joseph say they are not spies and refer to Joseph as lord and his servants. But Joseph persists in his testing. They say they are true men . . . but Joseph knows that they are not true men. They have lied before, and will lie again.

When the Prophet Isaiah came before the throne of God in a vision, he said "Woes is me for I am undone". He does not say he is a true man. Before men, we are virtuous in our eyes in spite of the wickedness of our heart. But we cannot come before God with that attitude. When God reveals Himself afresh to you - humble yourself before Him. Be undone before Him for He looks for who to send into His Revival. When we come with our virtues and works, it only shows we have a long distance yet.

No man in himself is true before God. The blood of Christ and His righteousness is our only way of access to remain in His presence. All those who claim they have not sinned, and have a truth of their own are spies, for they have not known redeeming salvation. It is enough that Joseph is before them, they did not need to plead their poor credentials. Similarly, it is more than sufficient that Jesus died and His blood was shed for all our sins. Spies deny the grace in God. Spies deny the complete work of Christ and the liberty therein. They will present their own goodness and see themselves as superior to others . . . when indeed, all the brothers and family of Joseph would be equivalently saved and totally forgiven. Spies will probe for the past and fish for issues that the blood has dealt with.

As you ponder over this text, it is enough to accept the wickedness of your heart from which everything emanates and the redemption and saving grace of Christ which has forgiven you, now and even in the future when you confess your sins and truly belong to Him. Do not pretend to be better than how the Bible has described you, instead enjoy the grace that is transforming you from glory to glory until we are indeed without blemish, ready for the Heavenly bridegroom. May you walk not in your own truth, but the righteousness that was purchased for you at Calvary.

Grace will make you more like Christ every day and not leave you still as the child of the devil.

Song

He has paid it all,
He has paid it all,
The Lamb of Calvary,
He has paid it all.

Prayer: O Lord, woe is me for I am undone before You. I need more grace. Amen

APRIL 18

The Family of God

Bible Text: Genesis 42:10-12

Gen 42:10 And they said unto him, Nay, my lord, but to buy food are thy servants come. 11 We are all one man's sons; we are true men, thy servants are no spies. 12 And he said unto them, Nay, but to see the nakedness of the land ye are come.

God has a family . . . there is one father—God who has only one begotten son—Jesus. We are His children, joint heirs with Christ. Christ is also God. Through Christ we have been reconciled back to this family. This is what the Bible teaches us. We are brothers and sisters—not in competition. When a family member suffers, then all suffer. When a family member is in need . . . all will come together to meet that need. When the Holy Spirit comes upon the Church, there is a sense of oneness and unity not previously known . . . all possessions are held in common for the entire family . . . all give generously to others as God has given to them.

Are we all the sons of one man—the God of all the earth? Brothers and sisters will dwell in family love and not seek to hurt each other. We are not spies . . . we are of one family—God is our father. As you read this devotional ask yourself some questions. Can you stand to see another brother in pain or anguish? Can you help your brother sacrificially? Are you happy to see your brother get ahead of you? The most compelling evidence of Christianity is the love between brothers and brethren. When others see this love, they will come gladly and want to be part of the family. Those who have been chosen will come back home when they sense there is a family somewhere. Have you strayed from your family like the lost son . . . come home.

Song

Belovèd, let us love: love is of God;
In God alone hath love its true abode.

Belovèd, let us love: for they who love,
They only, are His sons, born from above.

Belovèd, let us love: for love is rest,
And he who loveth not abides unblest.

Belovèd, let us love: for love is light,
And he who loveth not dwelleth in night.

Belovèd, let us love: for only thus
Shall we behold that God Who loveth us.

Prayer: O Lord, strengthen the bond of love in the family of God. Amen

APRIL 19

Puzzling Conversations

Bible Text: Genesis 42:13

Gen 42:13 And they said, Thy servants are twelve brethren, the sons of one man in the land of Canaan; and, behold, the youngest is this day with our father, and one is not. 14 And Joseph said unto them, That is it that I spake unto you, saying, Ye are spies:

There are times when we are having our conversations with God and God is testing us . . . seeking to bring out that which is in our hearts. At those times, it appears God does not care or deliberately wants to belittle or hurt us. We are confused and wonder what is going on. The brothers do not understand why Joseph insists that they are spies. They have not dressed as spies nor have they comported themselves as such . . . they have come openly as pilgrims, brethren of one family but Joseph insists they are spies.

What do we do when it seems we are being accused by none other than God himself? How do we react? Are there times in ministry when we are a puzzled at what God seems to be saying. How do we make progress when we are being accused by those who must help us? We must remember that it may be that we are being tested and our hearts can deceive us. We need stillness and patience before God. We cannot come to God expecting God to just respond as we want and quickly too. This would mean we are God and He is not. We need to be reverent in the throne room . . . waiting upon Him who must have mercy on whom He chooses. The brothers are not innocent and the one before them knows this to be so. Neither are you dear reader. You have sinned and deserve only death, but God is so full of great mercy and He waits to pour mercy upon you? What do you do in these times of waiting . . . keep serving Him, keep loving Him . . . keep honoring Him . . . keep praising Him. Job went through a time of not just failing but of accusations and puzzling examinations. But he held on to the end. Also consider your ways. Repent and seek forgiveness for past misdeeds. The brothers have come before Joseph as if they are completely innocent of all wrongs . . . there is no remorse for the ill treatment of their brother. Many times we come to God as if God owes us and we have every reason to be answered with favor when the truth is that we first need mercy for all the evils we have done. May God help us. Remain humble . . . behind the frowning face is a smile. Wait for the smile.

Song

Approach, my soul, the mercy seat,
Where Jesus answers prayer;
There humbly fall before His feet,
For none can perish there.

Thy promise is my only plea;
With this I venture nigh;
Thou callest burdened souls to Thee,
And such, O Lord, am I!

Bowed down beneath a load of sin,
By Satan sorely pressed,
By war without and fears within,
I come to Thee for rest.

Be Thou my shield and hiding-place,
That, sheltered near Thy side,
I may my fierce accuser face,
And tell him Thou hast died.

Prayer: O merciful Lord, when I come before your throne of mercy—do not refuse my plea. Amen

APRIL 20

A little Lie

Bible Text: Genesis 42:13-14

Gen 42:13 And they said, Thy servants are twelve brethren, the sons of one man in the land of Canaan; and, behold, the youngest is this day with our father, and one is not. 14 And Joseph said unto them, That is it that I spake unto you, saying, Ye are spies:

A little lie or omission appears innocent enough. The brothers of Joseph have not told the whole story - they say one is not. They seem to want it understood that Joseph is dead. Probably the lie they told their father. A minor lie you may think but still a lie. The spies of the enemy of our soul are liars for it is their very nature to lie. Their father being the father of liars. There are many things considered not to be lies. Subtle exaggerations, little omissions, minor deviations and so on. Some of this have been carried on for many years. This does not make them true. A lie that has been sustained over decades still remains a lie. Christ taught that let your yes be yes and nay nay. It means we are to be consistent and truthful. Indeed there is nothing to fear if we remain on the side of truth. Joseph calls his brothers spies. he wants to know more. The brothers had become a blood cult bound by the lie that their brother was killed in the wilderness, when they had sold their brothers into slavery and he may still be alive. Lies only ensure we remain captive to the father of liars - the devil.

Christ is merciful. Even the lawful captives shall be set free. Do you have a secret that has kept you bound in lies?. Go and tell all to Jesus. Joseph knew the full truth just as Joseph knows the complete story of his brothers. Confess all to Jesus and experience the joy and relief and pardon from Christ who is only saddened by the cords of deception. He will help us to come out with the truth. Is it not easier on their conscience to confess the truth to their old father?

Christ has paid it all. Tell Him all. Especially that little lie.

Song

You came from Heaven to Earth to show the way
From the earth to the Cross, my debt you paid
From the cross to the grave, from the grave to the sky
Lord, I lift your name on High.

Prayer: O Lord, woe is me for I am undone before You. I need more grace to stand before you. Amen

APRIL 21

Ye shall be Proved

Bible Text: Genesis 42:15

Gen 42:15 Hereby ye shall be proved: By the life of Pharaoh ye shall not go forth hence, except your youngest brother come hither.

All will be tested. There will be no exemptions. Old Christians, new Christians . . . the mature and the toddler. The one who has passed many tests and the one who has failed . . . All will be tested. Many think that the passing of a test means an end to further testing. Rather, it means we are ready for a higher test. Why does God test us? God is omniscient and knows us already . . . he knows exactly at what stage we are and what we are capable of doing even in the far future. So why does He need to test us?

He tests us to teach us and to allow us to see ourselves. Our tests are like mirrors placed before us that help us to adjust as required. But this mirror probes into the heart and can reflect for us to see what is really deep inside. Our hearts will often deceive us to suggest we are ready for another higher level . . . until we understand we need to wait to overcome our greed and selfishness. Tests also help us discipline ourselves in study and preparation. A student will probably not read as hard or study the syllabus if he could be offered a medical degree without an examination. But imagine what kind of surgeon such a person will be. Tests encourage us to go deeper into the word of God. Many deep truths will not have been uncovered or known by you if you had not gone through tough periods of trials. Tests enable us to experience the rare joy of experiencing success. Have you seen a student going to the notice board to check his score soon to be excited that he has passed . . . and with flying colors? But tests are also God's brakes . . . to stop us - when we are going too fast and close to confronting issues we are not ready for. We are full of zeal and will not be stopped. God must arrange a small test . . . our failure only means we are going too fast . . . sometimes we just need to slow down and consider some other matters needing attention . . . like our family or the less privileged we refuse to see. Enjoy the next test and pass with flying colors knowing that . . . ye shall be proved and the same God who proves us also helps us to pass.

Song

Take the world, but give me Jesus! All its joys are but a name;
But His love abideth ever, Thro' eternal years the same.

O the height and depth of mercy! O the length and breadth of love!
O the fullness of redemption, Pledge of endless life above!

Take the world, but give me Jesus, Sweetest comfort of my soul;
With my Savior watching o'er me I can sing, tho' billows roll.

Take the world, but give me Jesus! Let me view His constant smile;
Then thro'out my pilgrim journey Light will cheer me all the while.

Take the world, but give me Jesus! In His cross my trust shall be,
Till, with clearer, brighter vision, Face to face my Lord I see.

Prayer: O Lord, move me up only as you have tested and found me ready. But help me to be ready. Amen

APRIL 22

Where is your brother ?

Bible Text: Genesis 42:15

Gen 42:15 Hereby ye shall be proved: By the life of Pharaoh ye shall not go forth hence, except your youngest brother come hither.

The proof of the Christian is in the doing. The question that beats at the door of our hearts today is . . . where are our brothers? There are many Christians who are too busy with their Christian walk to think about evangelism and helping others. Helping others delays our speed and curtails our progress. Many are confident they will beat their chest at the gates of eternity only to be asked . . . where is your brother? Yes, your brother the village drunkard, your sister the city prostitute . . . your brother the brothel manager . . . your sister the high fashion model. Indeed, you reckoned they would not be interested in the gospel or you were daunted at how you would follow them up. But the records of Heaven indicate they were to have received the gospel through you and that is why you had all the opportunities.

But then you who read this devotional cannot be said to be a spy of the enemy. Go then and look for your brother. Bring him also to be refreshed by the living waters and taste the bread of Heaven. I sometimes guess that the best evidence of salvation is being an incurable evangelist . . . telling as many as you can that Jesus saves.

I also suspect the trait to easily spot a spy is the quietness that has no converts, no disciple . . . nothing to show the master if He asks . . . where is your brother. Prove your faith by sharing it.

Song

Is your life a channel of blessing? Is the love of God flowing through you?
Are you telling the lost of the Savior? Are you ready His service to do?

Make me a channel of blessing today, Make me a channel of blessing, I pray;
My life possessing, my service blessing, Make me a channel of blessing today.

Is your life a channel of blessing? Are you burdened for those that are lost?
Have you urged upon those who are straying, The Savior who died on the cross?

We cannot be channels of blessing If our lives are not free from all sin;
We will barriers be and a hindrance To those we are trying to win.

Prayer: O Lord, make me a channel of blessing - give me a burden for the lost. Amen

APRIL 23

Do not Despair

Bible Text: Genesis 42:16

Gen 42:16 Send one of you, and let him fetch your brother, and ye shall be kept in prison, that your words may be proved, whether there be any truth in you: or else by the life of Pharaoh surely ye are spies. 17 And he put them all together into ward three days.

It is wise to be a man of few words. We must learn silence and how to speak few words. Words have weight and the fewer the better. Our words will also be tested. Joseph tells his brothers that their words will be tested . . . probed further. Our professions of faith will be tested. Our sermons will be tested. Our declaration of truth will be tested. God does this that we may be proven to be people of integrity. Every higher level of truth will have a higher practical examination. All are to speak truth in love knowing we may sometime in future fail the tests associated with these same truths. The test seems harsh—to be imprisoned for three days, but when one considers the future bliss in Goshen ahead of them and the joys of being saved from a famine that was destroying others, then the three days seems not as tough. What are you going through now? God already had determined to move you into a position of such joy and wellness to make the present hardships appear only as a bearable inconvenience. Keep singing your song—even in the prison—when all the issues have been proven you will be exalted with Christ. Do not despair—O tested saint, you will yet celebrate and be celebrated. You will yet dance and jump for joy. Three days in the prison of Egypt will soon be wiped out of your memory as God takes you up again. Things are about to change. Only seek grace to respond well to the matters facing you today. Do not despair. God is with you.

Song

Why pour'st thou forth thine anxious plaint,
Despairing of relief,
As if the Lord o'erlooked thy cause,
And did not heed thy grief?
Hast thou not known, hast thou not heard,
That firm remains on high
The everlasting throne of Him
Who formed the earth and sky?

Art thou afraid his pow'r shall fail
When comes thy evil day?
And can an all-creating arm
Grow weary or decay?
Supreme in wisdom as in pow'r
The Rock of ages stands;
Though him thou canst not see,
nor trace The working of his hands.

He gives the conquest to the weak,
Supports the fainting heart;
And courage in the evil hour
His heav'nly aids impart.
Mere human pow'r shall fast decay,
And youthful vigor cease;
But they who wait upon the Lord,
In strength shall still increase.

Prayer: O Lord, make haste to help the weak and fainting reader. Amen

APRIL 24

Time to Reap

Bible Text: Genesis 42:16

Gen 42:16 Send one of you, and let him fetch your brother, and ye shall be kept in prison, that your words may be proved, whether there be any truth in you: or else by the life of Pharaoh surely ye are spies. 17 And he put them all together into ward three days.

The brothers that put Joseph in prison are now arrested and jailed. Destiny is not immune to certain divine principles. One of such is sowing and reaping. The Bible encourages us not to be weary in good deeds. We are to scatter our seeds as we do not know when it will spring forth . . . sometimes at the least expected time to favor us. There are many acts of kindness that you have done that you will soon see the harvest coming back to you as God multiplies the seed. You who could not see your brother in lack will also not lack. You who did not permit the stranger to be without a home will also never be homeless. You who gave a home as a facility for the work of the Kingdom will find homes equally given to you. You who cared for the helpless will always find help.

But there are wicked seeds. Alas we pray God will forget them. Indeed He forgives, but we need the learning that reaping provides to us. The brothers who facilitated the imprisonment of the innocent now will go to prison. Paul who arrests many Christian in a previous era now finds himself writing the Epistles in a prison in Rome. God is not mocked and we do not need to clamor for justice as He is always just. He is ever merciful to sustain us through our learning.

The most important thing is to change our seed if we need to. You can sow a kind word, instead of criticism. You can sow mercy instead of justice. You can give generously and scatter even more of that which others have a desperate need. You can give a room to a friend . . . you can sow a visit to that elderly man with no relatives to care for him.

If you are reaping the wrong seed of yesterday . . . you can go to God for mercy . . . but learn. Do not be hasty to do unto someone else that which you will not want done to you . . . and in multiples too. The harvest is always much more . . . many multiples of the seed. Mercifully, the brothers are put in prison for only three days. Joseph has truly paid the price and cannot bear to see his own incarcerated.

Isa_53:5 But he was wounded for our transgressions, he was bruised for our iniquities: the chastisement of our peace was upon him; and with his stripes we are healed

Song

You are going to reap - just what you sow 2ce
Up in the mountain . . . or down in the valley
You are going to reap - just what you sow

Prayer: O Lord, help me to change my seed today. Amen

APRIL 25

Jesus, my Surety Stands

Bible Text: Genesis 42:18-19

Gen 42:18 And Joseph said unto them the third day, This do, and live; for I fear God: 19 If ye be true men, let one of your brethren be bound in the house of your prison: go ye, carry corn for the famine of your houses:

Joseph gives his brothers instructions on what to do if they must live. Someone must be held as a surety while others go with corn. This is a picture of salvation in Christ. There is a better testament but it requires a surety. Jesus was made a surety of this better testament. Only He is able to save to the uttermost. Come to Him and live.

Heb 7:22 By so much was Jesus made a surety of a better testament. 23 And they truly were many priests, because they were not suffered to continue by reason of death: 24 But this man, because he continueth ever, hath an unchangeable priesthood. 25 Wherefore he is able also to save them to the uttermost that come unto God by him, seeing he ever liveth to make intercession for them.

Christ stood in our place, suffered in our place, was punished in our place and died in our place. He paid the price while we could go free. He came bound in the body of mortality—a prison he accepted and into the womb of a woman. He lived a blameless life only to be arrested, mocked, spat at and reviled by sinful man . . . eventually to be crucified. He went to the grave and the dark chambers of death to face principalities and made a shew of them . . . He took the keys of death and the grave so that we - His own will no more fear these evils. He had victory and rose the third day and ascended into the greatest glory.

He did all this so we can live. So we can carry corn in times of famine. Yet many prefer still not to accept His offer of salvation. Joseph gives the brethren instructions on what to do if they must go . . . they need a surety. You need a surety in the courts of Heaven to live forever. Let Jesus be your surety.

Song

Arise, my soul, arise;
Shake off thy guilty fears;
The bleeding Sacrifice
In my behalf appears:
Before the throne my Surety stands,
Before the throne my Surety stands;
My name is written on His hands.

Five bleeding wounds He bears,
Received on Calvary,
They pour effectual prayers,
They strongly plead for me:
"Forgive him, O forgive," they cry,
"Forgive him, O forgive," they cry,
"Nor let that ransomed sinner die!"

Prayer: O Lord, help me . . . Stand as my Surety before the throne. Amen

APRIL 26

Suffering for the Gospel

Bible Text: Genesis 42:18-19

Gen 42:18 And Joseph said unto them the third day, This do, and live; for I fear God: 19 If ye be true men, let one of your brethren be bound in the house of your prison: go ye, carry corn for the famine of your houses:

There are instances when we are called upon to suffer for the gospel. We are puzzled at the value of this suffering, nor do we understand why this particular challenge has become so immovable . . . that we feel demobilized for a while. To wait for what we do not know. Waiting on God - not being able to make the progress we see ahead or holding on until we have a desired clarity - is sometimes our lot.

There are tests that appear to be prisons when we are not free to pursue our dreams and must only see others advance forward while we remain. At these times, it is good to know that what we do for God is not in vain. No sacrifice will be unrewarded by the righteous judge. If indeed we are part of the brethren we must see persecution as part of what we can expect. Jesus Christ wrote . . .

Mat 5:11 Blessed are ye, when men shall revile you, and persecute you, and shall say all manner of evil against you falsely, for my sake. 12 Rejoice, and be exceeding glad: for great is your reward in Heaven: for so persecuted they the prophets which were before you.

Why then will you shun being reviled, maligned or persecuted . . . . if this is a means to being blessed. Instead rejoice that Jesus is alive. Your future rewarder sees all and does not miss any details. But do not suffer for being a busy body or a meddler in the affairs of others. The toughest assignments for the kingdom are reserved for the choicest saints. The closest friends to Jesus must consider Patmos as a necessary stop on the pilgrim's journey. If ye be true men, then be prepared to bear some of the burdens and suffer. The stories of the martyrdom of many continually remind us that for many who went ahead . . . they allowed their personal dreams to die or put on hold . . . indeed many died - so that the gospel could reach us. These were true men. How does your testimony compare?

Song

Toss'd with rough winds, and faint with fear, Above the tempest, soft and clear,
What still small accents greet mine ear? 'Tis I; be not afraid.

'Tis I, who washed thy spirit white;'Tis I, who gave thy blind eyes sight;
'Tis I, thy Lord, thy life, thy light:'Tis I; be not afraid

These raging winds, this surging sea, Have spent their deadly force on Me:
They bear no breath of wrath to thee:'Tis I; be not afraid.

This bitter cup, I drank it first; To thee it is no draught accurst;
The hand that gives it thee is pierced:'Tis I; be not afraid.

Mine eyes are watching by thy bed,Mine arms are underneath thy head,
My blessing is around thee shed:'Tis I, be not afraid.

When on the other side thy feet shall rest mid thousand welcomes sweet,
One well-known Voice thy heart shall greet,'Tis I; be not afraid.

Prayer: O Lord, help me to stand in the tough times. Amen

APRIL 27

Free Free Free

Bible Text: Genesis 42:20-21

Gen 42:20 But bring your youngest brother unto me; so shall your words be verified, and ye shall not die. And they did so. 21 And they said one to another, We are verily guilty concerning our brother, in that we saw the anguish of his soul, when he besought us, and we would not hear; therefore is this distress come upon us.

Guilt is a powerful emotion that enslaves all that have not been mercifully delivered. We are often guilty of what we did and did not do . . . things we said or did not say . . . places we went to or did not go to. We are guilty of prayers we said and did not say . . . sermons we preached and did not preach . . . mistakes we make, initiatives we failed to take . . . we are guilty of being too quiet or too noisy. We are guilty of not forgiving and being too lax in discipline. There is none who will not say *we are verily guilty* and the devil likes it so. Satan does not want us to see that without Christ - we are only his pawns to be manipulated through our flesh and worldly seductions. Satan does not want us to know that he is the author of all evil thoughts and the mastermind behind every addiction and for centuries we have been in his laboratory of destruction. Satan does not want us to see that he is behind every damage of destiny and when we think we are making our own decision, we are only yielding to his demonic enchantments.

No man can be your enemy. It is vain to strive or be upset with men when the architect of troubles and disappointments is the enemy of our soul. He tells us to sleep and not go to church and lie to the pastor and then the same Satan heaps the guilt of failure on us. He makes us weak and fall and then he reminds us every day that we have fallen. He twists our thinking with discouraging thoughts until we are vulnerable and offers some alcohol for our relief . . . and then mocks us that we drunkards and not fit to be saints.

Joseph has not pronounced any guilt on his brothers. Indeed he knows that that they helped him to his destiny. Repent of past failures and ask receive strength to depart from evil. And when the devil seeks to remind you of the past, remind him that he is the architect of your failures and has no right to now accuse you when Jesus has acquitted you of wrong by His blood. Practice this thought and learn to enjoy the peace of a life without guilt in Christ. Celebrate your freedom.

Song

Hark! sinner, hark! we have tidings so true, Tidings of pardon and blessings for you!
God in His word says that Christ on the tree, Died for guilty sinners, and "Salvation is free."

Hear the news, sinner, free! free! free! Why not believe it? 'Tis good news for thee.
Jesus the Just One has died on the tree, Died for guilty sinners, and "Salvation is free."

Guilty you are, yet you know very well Jesus has suffered to save you from hell;
Tho' now condemned, justified you may be, Jesus paid the ransom, and "Salvation is free."

Trust not in "doing," it cannot avail. Good resolutions and works can but fail;
"Grace, grace alone," is the saved sinner's plea, "Not of works," the Scriptures say, "Salvation is free."

Trust not in feelings, your heart is depraved. Trust only Jesus, who now lives to save;
Tears of repentance, tho' real they may be, Ne'er can purchase Heaven, for "Salvation is free."

Prayer: O Lord, Let your salvation replace every sense of guilt that I may sing "free . . . free . . . free". Amen

Trusting God

Bible Text: Genesis 42:20-21

Gen 42:20 But bring your youngest brother unto me; so shall your words be verified, and ye shall not die. And they did so. 21 And they said one to another, We are verily guilty concerning our brother, in that we saw the anguish of his soul, when he besought us, and we would not hear; therefore is this distress come upon us.

It is easier to trust when we get what we want or we understand God's dealings with us. But this tends to be the more rare instances. When we are in trouble or face storms and droughts, we are quick to come to wrong conclusions. Our thoughts are flooded with self-doubts and many sins of the past are flashed before us. But God's mercy does not fish in the lake of yesterday to torment you. When we fail Him He does not rake up old scores to imprison us in old fears. Oh that we may learn to trust Him when it seems that all has failed, for he never fails.

Still, our consciences will not be silenced until we discover our salvation. Do not imagine that the unsaved soul enjoys his rest. Even without the famine, he lies tormented day and night with memories that cause him to wake up in cold sweat. He is troubled with secrets that only he can unlock. Because he knows himself well, he doubts and questions himself and others . . . unable to trust anyone. The unsaved have no anchor that holds. They must drift and be tossed with imagined and real waves . . . hoping to berth safely someday somewhere. They want peace . . . but the Bible says there is no peace for the wicked.

As you read this devotional. Learn to trust God and just put things in His hands. To obey God by doing many things can be easier for some than to obey God by just doing nothing. There are too many vain worries that cost us lost sleep and many cares and burdens that we are not designed to carry. Indeed His beloved is given a restful sleep knowing all is safe in the arms of Jesus Christ.

Song

What a Friend we have in Jesus, all our sins and griefs to bear!
What a privilege to carry everything to God in prayer!
O what peace we often forfeit, O what needless pain we bear,
All because we do not carry everything to God in prayer.

Have we trials and temptations? Is there trouble anywhere?
We should never be discouraged; take it to the Lord in prayer.
Can we find a friend so faithful who will all our sorrows share?
Jesus knows our every weakness; take it to the Lord in prayer.

Are we weak and heavy laden, cumbered with a load of care?
Precious Savior, still our refuge, take it to the Lord in prayer.
Do your friends despise, forsake you? Take it to the Lord in prayer!
In His arms He'll take and shield you; you will find a solace there.

Prayer: O Lord, when overwhelmed with perplexities - teach me to lay them all down at Calvary as I take all to you in prayer. Amen

APRIL 29

Trusting God - Part II

Bible Text: Genesis 42:22

Gen 42:22 And Reuben answered them, saying, Spake I not unto you, saying, Do not sin against the child; and ye would not hear? therefore, behold, also his blood is required.

When raking the past does not seem to address our trials, we are tempted to bring up our good deeds. But God works outside the realms of our deed and intentions. Reuben reminds them that he warned against hurting Joseph. But he was wrong to imagine the selling of Joseph was anything but a preordained event - concluded before the world began. We should trust God when we cannot have our way and when our ideas are not accepted. Saying "I told you so" is a heathen's response or an insult to a God who has unlimited permutations to work through and still achieve the end He had predetermined. Trusting God when the way seems far from our expected track can be difficult. But remember God has told us that His ways differ from ours . . . as far as the earth is from the Heavens . . . an irreconcilable gap needs to be closed. The Holy Spirit helps us.

The sermon of Reuben is good but is irrelevant . . . it only prolongs pain but offers no comfort. Many times, Jesus is present to soothe and comfort us - but "Reubens" must drag in old failings. The Reubens must learn to trust God as well as the other brothers who failed to heed the good advice. May be you are like Reuben. Indeed you do well to point out the warnings of consequences for sin, but we fail when we do not reveal the comforting truths of Christ's death and resurrection . . . His blood shed as a double cure to break the addictive strength of sin and its power to destroy. Whether the people hear or not - God continues His work unimpeded. We see that sin disturbs and hurts us . . . but not God or His eternal purposes. The wages of sin is indeed death . . . but death is still only an angel waiting for God's directions.

Reuben is partially right, but has incomplete information to conclude that Joseph's blood was shed and that Joseph is dead. He is unaware perhaps that their brother was sold for money. God has all the information and you may unknowingly be speaking from a position already corrupted with misrepresentation. We may be sincere but still wrong or have very incomplete knowledge. The solution is to learn in all things to just trust Him who knows all and perfectly too.

Song

But we never can prove the delights of His love
Until all on the altar we lay;
For the favor He shows, for the joy He bestows,
Are for them who will trust and obey.

Trust and obey, for there is no other way,
To be happy in Jesus - But to trust and obey.

Prayer: O Lord, when overwhelmed with perplexities - teach me to lay them all down at Calvary as I take all to you in prayer. Amen

APRIL 30

The Omniscient God

Bible Text: Genesis 42:23

Gen 42:23 And they knew not that Joseph understood them; for he spake unto them by an interpreter.

Joseph understands perfectly all that is happening but the brothers do not know. That is because they did not know that it was Joseph before them. Many times we think God does not understand . . . but it is us that does not understand. The brothers are in the dark concerning what was going on but Joseph is not. The plot is now in the hands of Joseph . . . no more in the hands of his brethren who plotted his end.

God knows it all and controls all the events and plots. There are many things we do not know around our destiny and it is good also that we do not know these things. But there are things we can know. We can know the word of God. We can know God by His Spirit. But we will not know everything about Him. But we must never think that God is short of knowledge—He is not. Because He will not take certain decisions as you believe He must does not mean He does not understand. Joseph understand his brothers so much better that they think. God knows you better than you think you know yourself. God knows you situation better than you think you do. God knows what you do not know about all you are going through. God knows not just what you do not know about your past, but He also knows our future and what you do not know about your future. He knows what you are facing and the great warfare concerning your family. He knows every plot to destroy your destiny and every agenda to scatter your future . . . He also knows what needs to be done so your end is good as expected. We know so little and imagine vainly that we are not understood. In truth, it does not matter much that men misunderstand us . . . even if they understood, their knowledge would still be very limited. Our God is omniscient—He knows ALL about our struggles.

Song

Not now, but in the coming years, It may be in the better land,
We'll read the meaning of our tears, And there, sometime, we'll understand.

Then trust in God through all thy days; Fear not, for He doth hold thy hand;
Though dark thy way, still sing and praise; Sometime, sometime, we'll understand.

We'll catch the broken threads again, And finish what we here began;
Heav'n will the mysteries explain, And then, ah, then we'll understand.

We'll know why clouds instead of sun Were over many a cherished plan;
Why song has ceased when scarce begun: 'Tis there, sometime, we'll understand.

Why what we long for most of all eludes so oft our eager hand;
Why hopes are crushed and castles fall Up there, sometime, we'll understand.

God knows the way, He holds the key, He guides us with unerring hand;
Sometime, with tearless eyes we'll see: Yes, there, up there, we'll understand.

Prayer: O Lord, thank you for helping me see that you understand—but it is I that need your illumination. Amen

MAY 1
Spirit of Truth

Bible Text: Genesis 42:23

Gen 42:23 And they knew not that Joseph understood them; for he spake unto them by an interpreter.

In a previous dispensation, God spoke primarily through His selected prophets and the Holy Spirit filled individually for divine purpose—but not in a general outpouring. But the Prophet Joel spoke of another era.

Joe_2:28 And it shall come to pass afterward, that I will pour out my spirit upon all flesh; and your sons and your daughters shall prophesy, your old men shall dream dreams, your young men shall see visions:

From the day of Pentecost, God has sent His Spirit, the Spirit of Christ to indwell us. We have the best interpreter of God's word in us. God Himself with us. But this is granted only to His children. Many read the Bible and have provided their own interpretation of texts . . . even significantly editing the text to make it more acceptable or friendly for readers. This is all good. Many commentaries have provided alternative revisions and interpretations to the word of God. This should not confuse you . . . God is not confused and knows all our thoughts and motivations talk less of our words.

But God has only one interpreter - God. Not our favorite teacher, preacher or commentary author. In the times when Nigeria was a colony of the British and the officials spoke through interpreters, these were often prone to coloring the words from their own selfish perspective. But the Holy Spirit will always magnify God in His word. The Bible warns us to test the spirits. This is done when we study the word of God, meditating on it . . . day and night. We are helped by the word to spot false spirits . . . for they contradict the word of God.

The word of God is not just a history book though it contains historical facts. It is coded, many parts await the revelation and interpretation of God Himself at the appointed time. As you read the word of God, pray for the help of the Holy Spirit, the Spirit of Truth so we do not just judge by our senses. It is thus fruitless to debate the Bible with scholars . . . when we discern that these interpretations have not come from the Holy Spirit.

When God finds an obedient servant - like He did with Moses, He speaks plainly. Christ spoke in parables - but interpreted them to His disciples. Indeed, it is one thing to hear God, and another to understand and have the wisdom for obedience as God directs and supervises Himself. Obeying God is not obeying men . . . we need God to hear Him, love him, understand Him and obey Him.

Song

Blind unbelief is sure to err, and scan His work in vain
God is His own interpreter, And he will make it plain.

Prayer: O Lord, make your words plain to me - I am ready to fully obey. Amen

MAY 2

When God Turns Away

Bible Text: Genesis 42:24

Gen 42:24 And he turned himself about from them, and wept; and returned to them again, and communed with them, and took from them Simeon, and bound him before their eyes.

There are times when it seems God has turned away but He returns again. Christ exclaimed "My God, my God why has thou forsaken me?" but it was for a purpose. The Bible says God neither slumbers or sleeps. It takes only a second for the destroyer to pounce on the unprotected. The Bible says mothers can forsake their children but God cannot. Joseph turns away for a brief moment only to weep for a love that he could not openly express.

God loves us so much that He must sometimes leave us alone so we can grow. The story was once told of a mother eagle training her eaglets. She would take the young eaglet who is yet to learn to fly to a high altitude and drop her only to watch her flap her wings clumsily and just before she hits the ground the mother eagle will catch her eaglet and carry her up again only to be dropped again. Where God has turned away—He is still closely watching over us. He observes the attacks and how we struggle on our own to stand. He weeps at our bruises and hurts and wishes He could shorten the period of our pain . . . but He knows we need the experience of loneliness to truly appreciate His presence. Do you feel God has turned away from you? He has not abandoned you? He is training you? He is helping you? Like Job, perhaps you have been identified for a double increase in the end but a process of exposure to Satan's arrows is appointed. When God turns away—Satan strikes because He knows your defenses are inadequate. But God still limits his progress . . . when God has accomplished the purpose and the appointed time is spent . . . He returns again with double for all our troubles. We cannot be killed at those times because we must still be preserved to obtain our double portion and give our testimony of the God who never abandons His own.

Song

A Rock that stands forever
Is Christ, my Righteousness!
In Him I stand un-fearing, In everlasting bliss!
Christ is my boast and glory—All wrath for me is o'er;
The judgment of the sinner
Affrighteth me no more.

There is no condemnation,
There is no hell for me!
The torment and the fire—My eyes shall never see!
For me there is no sentence, For me there is no sting,
For Christ, my Lord, who saved me,
Will shield me with His wing!

No hunger, Lord, nor thirsting,
No danger, fear, nor fight,
No foe, no tribulation, No throne, nor pow'r, nor might,
No height, no depth, no creature That has been or can be.
Can pluck me from Thy bosom—
Can sever me from Thee!

Prayer: O Lord, Let me always know you as my Rock that stands forever. Amen

MAY 3

Joseph weeps

Bible Text: Genesis 42:24

Gen 42:24 And he turned himself about from them, and wept; and returned to them again, and communed with them, and took from them Simeon, and bound him before their eyes.

The Bible speaks of a time when all the tears of the saints will be wiped away. There are many categories of tears and different sources of pain. There are also tears of overwhelming joy. May we cry for joy someday. Joseph cannot bear that He must cause such pain and such discomfort to his brother Simeon and looks away for a season. God also looked away as Christ was subjected to the most cruel death man could devise for His only begotten son. How true it is that blood relations have strong feelings for each other.

What are your feelings concerning other brethren? Are you pained at their wanderings which God permits. Do we sorrow for souls still enjoying sin, knowing many are chosen by God for salvation. Or do we weep only for ourselves and our perceived losses. The love of God that is in us separates us with a compassion for the lost and for other brethren . . . a compassion that has caused many to abandon great treasures and take great risks . . . crossing vast oceans to strange lands.

The Christian is not always happy . . . but the root of his tears are unique and peculiar. Most importantly, his tears are all destined to be wiped away. Not so for the lost soul. He may never have cause to cry in his wickedness, but he will weep bitterly at the non-negotiable prospect of admission into eternal damnation. His cynical and wicked grins will all be wiped off his face forever.

All weep. The question is what for and when? How will it be in your case? When will you weep?

Song

Though with a scornful wonder, men see her sore oppressed
By schisms rent asunder, by heresies distressed,
Yet saints their watch a keeping, their cry goes up "how long?",
And soon the night of weeping shall be the morn of song.

'Mid toil and tribulation, And tumult of her war,
She wait the consummation of peace for evermore
Till with the vision glorious . . . her longing eyes are blest,
And the Great Church victorious . . . shall be the Church at rest.

Prayer: O Lord, Comfort me. Amen

MAY 4

Commander in Chief

Bible Text: Genesis 42:25-26

Gen 42:25 Then Joseph commanded to fill their sacks with corn, and to restore every man's money into his sack, and to give them provision for the way: and thus did he unto them. 26 And they laded their asses with the corn, and departed thence.

Joseph issues a command and it is so. He does not need suggestions or advisors. He does not require to canvass for support or lobby for obedience. He is God. He decrees something and it is so. He knows that you must move forward and He commands your elevation. He knows you need preservation and so He commands your barns to be filled. Even in famine . . . Egyptians will begin to fill your sacks—because He has commanded it to be so. He is not an adviser . . . he commands.

But the same way He commands blessings, He commands with laws that must not be disputed. God issues commands and laws . . . and we are not being advised or urged . . . we are being commanded. Our God is commander in Chief. This is why our problems can be stopped in an instant command . . . our restoration only needs a word from Him. Our prosperity awaits His commandments . . . our lifting up awaits His commandments. When He has said Yes . . . who can say No. When He decrees your deliverance . . . who can say it is not to be so. None dare.

Joseph commands that sacks to be filled with corn and it was done. For some reading, God is announcing an end to your hunger and giving commands for your deliverance and sustenance.

The Commander in Chief commands "Hold the fort—for I am coming" He says

Song

Ho, my comrades! see the signal
Waving in the sky!
Reinforcements now appearing,
Victory is nigh!

Hold the fort, for I am coming,
Jesus signals still;
Wave the answer back to Heaven,
By Thy grace we will.

See the mighty host advancing,
Satan leading on;
Mighty men around us falling,
Courage almost gone!

See the glorious banner waving!
Hear the trumpet blow!
In our Leader's name we'll triumph
Over ev'ry foe!

Fierce and long the battle rages,
But our help is near:
Onward comes our great Commander,
Cheer, my comrades, cheer!

Prayer: O Great Commander and Lord, give your army grace to bow to all your commands. Amen

MAY 5

The Great Restorer

Bible Text: Genesis 42:25-26

Gen 42:25 Then Joseph commanded to fill their sacks with corn, and to restore every man's money into his sack, and to give them provision for the way: and thus did he unto them. 26 And they laded their asses with the corn, and departed thence.

God is the Great Restorer. His very nature is to restore. Observe even in nature. Every damage seems to self-repair. Barren hills are soon covered with lilies, damaged body cells seem to instinctively work to repair themselves. It seems God has put in all His creation, the nature to restore damage. Look at the oceans and the rivers, can they ever run dry or be reduced in their capacities? Perhaps in unusual circumstances they can . . . but the resources of God can never be reduced. That is why God is not competitive - He has no need to be. He has no needs and His assets can never be reduced or increased. His nature is to pour out from an inexhaustible storage.

One moment, Simeon was being bound and in another Joseph was commanding restoration of funds and as much corn as they could possibly carry. I want to encourage the reader of this devotional. God will surprise you with His restoration. You are weighed down by losses and lack . . . soon you will taste restoration and plenty. There are many scriptures that tell us of the abundance that is in God. He can never be in debt to anyone. We can never out give Him who sustains our hands.

The brothers leave Egypt uncertain of what to make of their experience. They think they have no more funds and fear the shock of the unpleasant news that Simeon has been held hostage. They are confused at the request to bring their youngest brother knowing this will not be granted by their still grieving father. They feel as if they are under a curse. How utterly unreliable are our feelings and perceptions. Feelings may be justified and the evidence may be contrary but the word of God is the only thing that is forever settled. Cling to the word of God as your constant truth in a world of diverse and changing traditions. Did He not promise in His word to supply all your needs according to His riches in glory . . . and not based on the economy; why are your eyes saddened at the market indices and the limited funds eroded daily by inflation, when you have resources that can never be touched by inflation. Instead rejoice, look up to Him, the Great Restorer. He is already at work, though you do not perceive it to be so.

Song

He's the Great Provider . . . the Great Provider . . . the Great Provider.
He will surely provide for me - The Great Provider.

He's the Mighty Provider . . . the Mighty Provider . . . the Mighty Provider.
He will surely provide for me - The Mighty Provider.

He's the Sure Provider . . . the Sure Provider . . . the Sure Provider.
He will surely provide for me - The Sure Provider.

Prayer: O Lord, Restore O Lord Restore. Amen

MAY 6

A Pleasant Surprise

Bible Text: Genesis 42:27

Gen 42:27 And as one of them opened his sack to give his ass provender in the inn, he espied his money; for, behold, it was in his sack's mouth

Our days are filled with long journeys and we all can do with some refreshing. On the way back, they find an inn. Can you catch a sense of the situation. I see someone exhausted reading this short page. You are in a process filled with burdens and fears, uncertain about so many things. You are beginning to be short of funds as you are spending your very last in a tough season. You are uncertain that you will be replenished and cannot think of where your help will come from. God has not deserted you. You see a nice inn far away. You can catch a rest, but you wonder how you will pay for a meal and a good rest . . . Indeed it is a lovely restaurant, and there is a lovely menu. Also the garage will tune up your car and fix some leaks . . . overheating. But how will you pay for the oil change you need. You stop at the resort and walk to the reception . . . and bring out your purse only to find all the money you started with intact. You had spent the money to purchase the supplies you needed. How come the money is back in your purse? Strange parable.

It is enough to simply enjoy and not cross examine the providence of God. A couple once gave a testimony of a meal in very difficult times, but as they ate God told them not to look into the bowl, only to discover that they ate to their fill from what they thought was barely enough. Have we not read of how Elijah was provided for by the widow with barely nothing. God can work with zero. He can replenish from His secret storage. The brothers are pleasantly surprised - at least one problem is solved . . . and they enjoy a good meal and the ass is well taken care of. The same God that surprised you yesterday has not finished with you. Trust Him. Expect a pleasant surprise today.

Song

I have made you too small in my eyes ; Oh Lord, forgive me,
And I have believed in a lie, that you were unable to help me,
But thou Oh Lord I see my wrong, Heal my heart and show yourself strong.
And in my heart and in my song - Oh Lord be magnified 2ce,

Be magnified Oh Lord; You are highly exalted
And there is nothing you can do.
Oh Lord my eyes are on you
Be magnified Oh Lord Be magnified.

Prayer: O Lord, Be magnified in all my situations today. Amen

MAY 7

Fear Not

Bible Text: Genesis 42:28

Gen 42:28 And he said unto his brethren, My money is restored; and, lo, it is even in my sack: and their heart failed them, and they were afraid, saying one to another, What is this that God hath done unto us?

The deeds of an awesome God in our lives can be fearsome. Realizing we are all within easy reach of a powerful God who does not leave things to run neutral to His control. On the contrary, God is the driver in full control of events. Even when He works to our favor, we still have fears - for our conscience knows we are not so true before Him. We wonder . . . how is it that we are still alive? Why has God permitted certain evils to continue if He can stop what He wills. Why are many innocent afflicted with ills, hunger, abuse and disease . . . if God is not distant to us? These are good questions and I have no answers as I am not God . . . neither are you. Is it not sufficient to know that He is a God whose mercy endures forever. Why must I question His grace if He has given me one more opportunity to get right. One day in eternity, none will be able to question His administration of justice . . .

Many scriptures tell us "fear not" when our hearts fail us. The source of fear is our wrong doing. Why then do we not depart from evil. The evil doer that persists in wickedness should be afraid as he has chosen a path that leads certainly into a dark spiral down into hell. But God deals with the brothers of Joseph in mercy. His word says He will have mercy on whosoever He wills.

There is someone reading this devotional. You know what you truly deserve and how evil your ways have been. But God is calling you to return to Him still. Like the prodigal son, you expect to be harshly treated and punished for your ways. True you deserve punishment but the sufferings of Christ are enough to more than cover for you. That is if you surrender to Him and ask Him to take over your life. He will banish all your fears.

But if you do not. Even the days of mercy for you will continue to be days of fear - for even you suspect that that there is the most High God - and He is a righteous judge and He will give you what you deserve in the end. Exchange your life of tensions for a time of rest, forgiveness and peace in Christ. Fear not.

Song

My sin - *Oh, the bliss of this glorious thought*
My sin not in part, but the whole.
Is nailed to the cross; and I bear it no more;
Praise the Lord, praise the Lord, O my soul

It is well . . . with my soul.
It is well, it is well with my soul.

Prayer: O Lord, may your presence calm all the fears in my soul. Amen

MAY 8

Facts are not Truth

Bible Text: Genesis 42:29-35

Gen 42:29 And they came unto Jacob their father unto the land of Canaan, and told him all that befell unto them; saying, 30 The man, who is the lord of the land, spake roughly to us, and took us for spies of the country. 31 And we said unto him, We are true men; we are no spies: 32 We be twelve brethren, sons of our father; one is not, and the youngest is this day with our father in the land of Canaan. 33 And the man, the lord of the country, said unto us, Hereby shall I know that ye are true men; leave one of your brethren here with me, and take food for the famine of your households, and be gone: 34 And bring your youngest brother unto me: then shall I know that ye are no spies, but that ye are true men: so will I deliver you your brother, and ye shall traffick in the land. 35 And it came to pass as they emptied their sacks, that, behold, every man's bundle of money was in his sack: and when both they and their father saw the bundles of money, they were afraid.

A preacher once explained to me the difference between truth and facts. Facts are an accurate narration of what happened from the record of the perspective of the recorder. Truth is the complete picture of reality. Christ says He is the Truth. We deal often only with facts. All that was relayed to Jacob are the facts of the trip to Egypt, but only from the perspective of the brothers of Joseph. The truth is far from the facts in this situation and indeed in many cases. The brothers do not lie this time, neither do they exaggerate . . . but facts are easy to twist and history has suffered much in the hands of the humanity of its authors. Jesus Christ says . . . He is the same, yesterday, today and forever. The Rock of Ages. Unchangeable, immutable, faithful and ever true.

I do not deny the facts of the situation before you nor do I controvert the evidence you are faced with. I agree you have been given a report - but factual as it may be . . . it is very untrue. Whose report will you believe? The word of God - the truth that remains forever or a situation report that will be updated tomorrow. The facts are not useless, nor are we to shun ourselves from the news . . . but we need to hear the truth - the word of God constantly to interpret the facts and not base all we know and feel on a temporal scenario.

Be strong - even though the facts are flooded with the fears of the brethren. The truth remains firmly unchanged even though we do not seem to discern it. The report of Jacob's sons were far from the truth. Find the truth today in the word of God. His report speaks of healing, restoration and another chance.

Song

It is not meet for Saints to fear, Nor for them to despair
For when they least expect His help; The Savior will appear.

When Abraham took up his knife, God's voice said to him "stop"
The yonder ram caught by the horn shall substitute thy son.

With such great might and love as this - abounding in His word;
I pray to bring my anxious cares and leave them all to Him.

Lift up your eyes and wait His help - it may be long but wait;
Though the promse may tarry long, It shall soon come to pass.

Prayer: O Lord, Lord help my unbelief. Amen

MAY 9

No more Bereaved

Bible Text: Genesis 42:36

Gen 42:36 And Jacob their father said unto them, Me have ye bereaved of my children: Joseph is not, and Simeon is not, and ye will take Benjamin away: all these things are against me.

We often conclude that all our dreams have one by one been dashed. We are bereaved and despondent and will conclude there is a plot against us. What else could we possibly believe? Jacob is under a shadow but it is a shadow of lies.

Be no more bereaved. The helper of the helpless is in control. All your God given dreams are perfectly intact none can die or be buried . . . rather they are hidden in the hands of the one who gives dreams and makes them come true. The guilt of the misdeeds also floods the mind of Jacob. Dear saint, God has not stored up your sins in a bottle to later afflict you. Be no more bereaved . . . Joseph, Simeon and Benjamin are safe but only in the hands of God. Your dreams are not safe in your care . . . they must be released to God.

Be not bereaved that which has been released to God cannot be lost. Never!!!

Song

Safe in the arms of Jesus,
Safe on His gentle breast,
There, by His love o'ershaded,
Sweetly my soul shall rest.
Hark! 'tis the voice of angels
Borne in a song to me
Over the fields of glory,
Over the jasper sea.

Safe in the arms of Jesus,
Safe on His gentle breast,
There, by His love o'ershaded,
Sweetly my soul shall rest.

Safe in the arms of Jesus,
Safe from corroding care,
Safe from the world's temptations—
Sin cannot harm me there.
Free from the blight of sorrow,
Free from my doubts and fears;
Only a few more trials,
Only a few more tears!

Prayer: O Lord, keep everything that pertains to us, our homes and our families—Keep them all safe. Amen

MAY 10

The Shadows of Lies

Bible Text: Genesis 42:36

Gen 42:36 And Jacob their father said unto them, Me have ye bereaved of my children: Joseph is not, and Simeon is not, and ye will take Benjamin away: all these things are against me.

The facts are too compelling. There seems to be no hope. It is over. But watch your tongue. The power of life and death lies therein. Jacob concludes before his children in an expression of great despair. His sorrow is so deep . . . all hope is lost. The tongue of Jacob releases a wrong conclusion.

Jacob has not forgotten Joseph. How could he? He sums up the entire story of his life as a catalogue of losses. He wonders at God for rewarding Him with such pain. He recalls the manipulations he engineered in his own past. He focuses on Himself and again wrongly concludes this is all a reaping for his own wicked acts. Indeed, we reap what we sow, but we do not serve a wicked God. His ways are mysterious and past finding out in many ways. Jacob now projects the loss of Benjamin.

Enough of Jacob. How about you? What have you been told? What have you concluded? Have you decided that all is against you and useless . . . your life is a waste. Your ministry is not worth a dime? It is best to die . . . the devil offers you a rope. But wait, which company are you in? You are in the company of men and women like David, Naomi, Daniel, John the Baptist, the Apostle Paul . . . God's special generals. Did the Lord Jesus Christ Himself not see the facts and say 'My God . . . my God why hast thou forsaken me?" . . . Facts are powerful but can be very deceiving. This is why the devil works well with the facts and will do everything to hide the Bible and its truths from all who permit him to do so.

It is pointless to examine the facts sometimes. They will only point to a terrifying future. My friend, be encouraged to know that in all these situations before us - the facts were soon proven to be true. This would have been a good time perhaps for Jacob to find some relief in his sons' admissions that Joseph was sold to slavery and may still be alive somewhere. But as the flesh cannot and is unable to agree with the Spirit so will facts remain in opposition to truth until God chooses Himself to work out His truth in the situation. There is no comfort for Jacob but His God. He learns at times like this to just wait. For the impatient, hasty Jacob, used to having his way - this is a great learning point. Joseph lives . . . if only Jacob knew . . . . Jesus lives, if only you know the full implication of this. Jacob is in the shadows of lies. You need not be there.

Song

Because He lives I can face tomorrow
Because He lives . . . all fear is gone
Because I know He holds the future; And life is worth the living, just
Because He lives.

Prayer: O Lord, The empty grave proves you are alive. I chose to trust the work that you have done in your resurrection power. Call and help me come up above the shadow of wicked facts. Amen

MAY 11

Rash Promises

Bible Text: Genesis 42:37

Gen 42:37 And Reuben spake unto his father, saying, Slay my two sons, if I bring him not to thee: deliver him into my hand, and I will bring him to thee again.

Reuben makes rash promises ignorant of what God has already done. It does not occur to them to simply trust their God. The family had descended into a sort of godlessness that arises when things are bitter and hard. Jacob does not say God will bring Benjamin back, nor does any consult God for direction. But God is merciful and remembers His promises even when men forget theirs. Indeed how many times do men abandon a God that remains still there with them - helping them in spite of their rash words.

To offer the life of two sons as a surety is again unnecessary. God is our surety - for indeed only He can be so. The Bible does not ask us for strange offerings, nor is there any other sacrifice required for our sins. They have been paid in full, if only we will confess them to Him and accept His forgiveness. Failure to confess to God pulls us into various activities and promises which no one has required from us.

What sin are you hiding? One of the fruits of deception to others is a harvest of self-deception. The family of Jacob was reaping a downpour of exactly what they had sown. Perhaps as a family, a vigil of joint repentance crying out to God and to each other to seek forgiveness which is already waiting to be offered . . . would do far more good than promising to climb the Mt Everest for God.

Reuben has no power to do that which he advocates. The absence of God is to live without power. The absence of God is to dwell in foolishness. The absence of God is to speak empty things. When will you remember to return to Him, O prodigal son. Still, the mercy of God appears again as an inexhaustibly vast supply from which the family of Jacob continues to draw from. The mercy of God is truly amazing. Soon the days of fears and tensions will be over.

Mat 5:36 Neither shalt thou swear by thy head, because thou canst not make one hair white or black.

Jas_5:12 But above all things, my brethren, swear not, neither by Heaven, neither by the earth, neither by any other oath: but let your yea be yea; and your nay, nay; lest ye fall into condemnation.

Song

I have no power of my own
I have no power of my own
Holy Spirit; I look up to you - Help me
I have no power of my own.

Prayer: O Lord, you are my refuge when I do not know what to do. I will be still and know that you are God. Help me. Amen

MAY 12

No Wasteful Emotions

Bible Text: Genesis 42:37

Gen 42:37 And Reuben spake unto his father, saying, Slay my two sons, if I bring him not to thee: deliver him into my hand, and I will bring him to thee again.

Rachel had two sons. One is Joseph and the other is Benjamin. If both are lost . . . Rachel's line will be completely cut off. Reuben offers his own two sons to be slain if for any reason Benjamin does not return. But this is so far from the will and purpose of God who was working out an awesome preservation of all 12 brothers and an expansion into a great people that will fill the earth.

What kind of pledges are we making to God? Are we offering God a plan that opposes His will? Have we offered to help prosper evil by slaying innocent brethren? How can life not mean anything to us that we can offer to destroy one to appease for the loss of another? At the root of this horrible promise are the suspicions and bitterness that has poisoned the family. Reuben is responding to an unspoken belief that Benjamin will not be protected by his brothers. Jacob has come to the conclusion that somehow the brothers who hated Joseph have some hand in some way in his death and Benjamin may fall in a similar situation.

In Jacob's heart, he accuses his ten sons . . . day and night for the death of Joseph. But again Jacob is unaware of God's master plans that are walking according to schedule. If he did, he would not waste his emotions in regret, unspoken accusations and pitiful statements. If only we know God at work . . . we will not engage in wasteful emotions such as unforgiveness. Jacob has not forgiven his sons even though he is uncertain of their crime. Jacob has suffered much and Reuben knows it. Hence he makes a desperate offer that was vain and unrequired. Are you engaging in emotions that waste our lives such as unforgiveness, suspicion, fear, accusation and envy? Or enjoying the knowledge that you have a shelter in the worst storms.

Song

The Lord's our Rock, in Him we hide,
A shelter in the time of storm;
Secure whatever ill betide,
A shelter in the time of storm.

Refrain:
Oh, Jesus is a Rock in a weary land,
A weary land, a weary land;
Oh, Jesus is a Rock in a weary land,
A shelter in the time of storm.

A shade by day, defense by night,
A shelter in the time of storm;
No fears alarm, no foes affright,
A shelter in the time of storm.

The raging storms may round us beat,
A shelter in the time of storm;
We'll never leave our safe retreat,
A shelter in the time of storm.

Prayer: O Lord, Be my shelter when my emotions are attacked and I find it hard not to fear or to release wrong thoughts. Amen

MAY 13

Arrest Wrong Conclusions

Bible Text: Genesis 42:38

Gen 42:38 And he said, My son shall not go down with you; for his brother is dead, and he is left alone: if mischief befall him by the way in the which ye go, then shall ye bring down my gray hairs with sorrow to the grave.

Sincerity can still be very alien to truth. Jacob voices the feelings that are not backed up with reality. He is ignorant and so confused. Our dreams are not dead neither are we left alone. None reading this devotional will go to the grave with sorrow.

Mat 5:41 And whosoever shall compel thee to go a mile, go with him twain. 42 Give to him that asketh thee, and from him that would borrow of thee turn not thou away.

Giving away your son is a fearful proposition. Who can pass such a test? But whatever we give away that is ours will come back to us . . . as all are safe in the hands of the keeper of Israel. We must not cling to blessings as though we were the sources of them. The one that gives may want to borrow them for a while from us. Jacob had no cause to grieve . . . both his two sons were safe.

It is vain for saints to grieve for losses - even before they have manifested. Our projections are negative. My question is that where is your faith. The Bible says the just shall live by faith. Our faith must be tried and found to be true so we can build on it and not on our perceptions. If circumstances have imposed certain challenges that seem to have scattered your home . . . I encourage you to trust God, you will be reunited with your sons and daughters again. The plan of God is a good plan . . . the end He is working out is a good end. Jacob is at his lowest but does the Bible does not say - even from the dunghill He raises up. God has not forgotten you. Release what you must and look up to God. Soon the beautiful plans of the most High will be revealed and you will only marvel at His benevolence and most kind hand coated in bitter pills.

Song

Be not dismayed whate'er betide, God will take care of you!
Beneath His wings of love abide, God will take care of you!

God will take care of you, Through every day o'er all the way;
He will take care of you; God will take care of you!

Through days of toil when heart doth fail, God will take care of you!
When dangers fierce your path assail, God will take care of you!

All you may need He will provide, God will take care of you!
Trust Him, and you will be satisfied, God will take care of you!

Lonely and sad, from friends apart, God will take care of you!
He will give peace to your aching heart, God will take care of you!

Prayer: O Lord, I place my life in your hands. Take care of me. Amen

MAY 14

Far from the Grave

Bible Text: Genesis 42:38

Gen 42:38 And he said, My son shall not go down with you; for his brother is dead, and he is left alone: if mischief befall him by the way in the which ye go, then shall ye bring down my gray hairs with sorrow to the grave.

Have you recently been having thoughts of death? Do you contemplate suicide? Do you think you are soon to descend to the grave. Let me let you know. You are far from the grave. There are still many good years ahead of you that you are unaware of. You have work to do. Joseph must be blessed ... Ephraim is going to be blessed ... Manasseh will be blessed. You must pronounce blessings on all your children ... they are all going to father great tribes. All this does not seem to possible ... he has no interest to bless any of his children knowing Joseph is dead. But all this must still change. Jacob cannot die yet. You cannot die yet because your story is only midway. You cannot go the grave because destiny still needs your contribution at a future appointed date. There is a role God has preserved for you. You are far from the grave ... do not permit strange thoughts of death to confuse you. You will still live to declare great testimonies of the truths in the word of the Lord. You cannot die. Not now.

Your appointment with the grave will not be escorted by sorrow but the joy of completing a glorious destiny in Christ. Perish the thought of death dear reader ... instead God is about to start something new and fresh in your life. Wait patiently for it.

Song

Ho, reapers in the whitened harvest!
Oft feeble, faint, and few;
Come, wait upon the blessed Master,
Our strength He will renew.

Refrain:
For "They that wait upon the Lord
Shall renew their strength;
They shall mount up with wings,
They shall mount up with wings as eagles:
They shall run and not be weary;
They shall walk and not faint;
They shall run and not be weary;
They shall walk and not faint;
They shall run and not be weary,
shall walk and not faint."

Too oft a-weary and discouraged,
We pour a sad complaint;
Believing in a living Savior,
Why should we ever faint?

Rejoice! for He is with us always,
Lo, even to the end!
Look up! take courage and go forward.
All needed grace He'll send!

Prayer: O Lord, renew my strength for the new thing you are beginning. Amen

MAY 15

God works all for our Good.

Bible Text: Genesis 43:1

Gen 43:1 And the famine was sore in the land.

Things went from bad to worse until they become really terrible. How are things with you? Have they gone from bad to worse, and have you decided to just give up completely. Have you considered there is a decision that God wants you to make? Is there something you should do still undone? Is God trying to provoke an action from you. Why are you facing a deteriorating situation? What is the root cause?

In this case, it appears the famine is sore to force Jacob to revisit his earlier decision not to release Benjamin. God has planned that the family will be restored and united in Egypt, but Jacob does not know this. God needs a scenario to force Jacob to rethink his earlier decision. What is it that you consider to be evil and hard, but God permits only so that the expected end will be realized for your greater good. Indeed, the ways of God are past finding, they will remain mysteries in God's workshop to which no human mind is admitted.

But we have the word of God that declares that all things will work together for the good of the righteous who truly love God. Our righteousness is given and not earned. Jacob and his sons are seen as righteous because of Joseph - who paid the price for their righteousness. Jacob comes to the wrong conclusions that God is punishing him and has abandoned him. But he fails to see that God has not. Rather God was putting final touches to their restoration.

Every day of hunger in the tent of Jacob was of needless pain. Are you suffering unnecessarily for that which you need not suffer for. Is your delay in aligning with the will of God causing more pain and risk to others and especially yourself.

Do not despair. Have faith in God. The famine is to connect you to the new phase you so desperately need to put the sadness of the past, completely behind. The famine is sore . . . but for your good.

Song

Though we pass through tribulation, All will be well
Ours is such a full salvation, All, all is well.
Happy still in God confiding;
Fruitful if in Christ abiding;
Holy through the Spirit's guiding;
All must be well.

On our Father's love relying,
Jesus every need supplying,
Or in living or in dying,
All must be well.

Prayer: O Lord, Let me sing a new song that says . . . I never knew all was indeed well by His grace. Amen

MAY 16

The Narrow Way

Bible Text: Genesis 43:2

Gen 43:2 And it came to pass, when they had eaten up the corn which they had brought out of Egypt, their father said unto them, Go again, buy us a little food. 3 And Judah spake unto him, saying, The man did solemnly protest unto us, saying, Ye shall not see my face, except your brother be with you. 4 If thou wilt send our brother with us, we will go down and buy thee food

After many days of careful rationing and austere meals, everything eventually finishes. I remember the story of the prodigal son. After even the food of pigs became scarce - he eventually came to his senses, Indeed, returning to the will and purpose of God could be challenging and there could be loss of face, we may not be welcome and in some cases restitution will be costly. Judah speaks of the situation awaiting them in Egypt and the conditions that have been laid down.

Why does God place difficult conditions for our ultimate glorification? Why is it that the way to Heaven is narrow and few find and walk it? Why is it that Christianity in its truest form is also about painful sacrifices? A casual approach to God that costs us nothing is a fake experience. Christianity is not a tea party and that which costs nothing is worthless to us. But we say Christ has paid a price and he paid it all . . . very true . . . salvation cost God all. But how about us . . . will we value that which we are accustomed to taking so lightly . . . that which demanded nothing from us. Will we worship a God and appreciate the value a God we gave up nothing for.

God asks that we present what we cherish most . . . our bodies as a living sacrifice and be holy. He knows it is in our power to do so. But like Jacob, we have no intention to release the beloved Benjamin until the famine gets sore. I have encountered Christians with salvation experiences which seemed to be just God giving everything to them . . . they saw the need for no sacrifice, they protected their lives and sought to use God to obtain things. I doubt if this is real. When God puts us on the narrow way, we are living sacrifices and must lay all down and learn self-denial . . . crucifying the flesh, daily.

The pain of living a life set apart, consecrated and given totally to God . . . releasing all that we cherish to Him eventually becomes the bridge to a beautiful new beginning. You must thank God for the famines that force the right response. You love to sing I surrender all—but what about your Benjamin?

Song

All to Jesus I surrender, All to Him I freely give
I will ever love and trust Him, in His presence daily live.

All to Jesus I surrender, Humbly at His feet I bow,
Worldly pleasures all forsaken, Take me Jesus, take me now.

I surrender all 2ce
All to thee, my blessed Savior,
I surrender all.

Prayer: O Lord, Let my life be all surrendered to you. Nothing held back. Amen

MAY 17
Dealings of Israel

Bible Text: Genesis 43:6-7

Gen 43:6 And Israel said, Wherefore dealt ye so ill with me, as to tell the man whether ye had yet a brother? 7 And they said, The man asked us straitly of our state, and of our kindred, saying, Is your father yet alive? have ye another brother? and we told him according to the tenor of these words: could we certainly know that he would say, Bring your brother down?

Israel is confused. How is it that this stranger knows exactly how to question the brothers to focus on Benjamin. As far as Israel can perceive this is a plot and perhaps another engineered by his wicked sons. Israel has lived with the pain of watching his sons grow and observing the harvest of his life manifest in his children. The man of guile can only see more guile. Jacob may now be Israel but he knows the way of the trickster. The struggles for rights in a large polygamous home are not lost to him and Benjamin seems to be the next target.

Ask God to help you renew your mind to free your thoughts from demonic suspicions entrenched by years of unforgiveness and bitterness. But there is a worsening famine and the threat of death looms in the house of Israel. Israel descends further into wrong imaginations. At the heart of Israel's confusion is the lie that God hates him and wants to destroy him. This is the greatest lie that the devil plants in the hearts of His children especially when they have fallen into sin. Unfortunately it is a lie that is not helped my many well-meaning counselors. Our enemy is sin and the devil and not people. God waits for us to return to Him and to put off wicked imaginations. Unfortunately Jacob afflicts himself and causes even more hurt on his family by delaying the release of Benjamin. I pray that God will help us to cast off every wrong imagination. Soon Israel will be relieved. Soon you will be dancing and singing new songs. God still loves you.

Song

What the Lord has done for me I cannot tell it all
What the Lord has done for me—I cannot tell it all
What the Lord has done for me—I cannot tell it all
He saved me and washed me in His blood
So I can shout Hallelujah 3ce
I can shout—Praise the Lord 2ce

Jesus loves me, this I know,
Though my hair is white as snow.
Though my sight is growing dim,
Still He bids me trust in him.

Yes, Jesus loves me! 3ce
The Bible tells me so.

Though my steps are oh, so slow,
With my hand in his I'll go.
On through life, let come what may,
He'll be there to lead the way.

Prayer: O Lord, Be always there to lead and guide all my ways. Amen

MAY 18

Release your Burdens

Bible Text: Genesis 43:6-7

Gen 43:6 And Israel said, Wherefore dealt ye so ill with me, as to tell the man whether ye had yet a brother? 7 And they said, The man asked us straitly of our state, and of our kindred, saying, Is your father yet alive? have ye another brother? and we told him according to the tenor of these words: could we certainly know that he would say, Bring your brother down?

What is it that we would rather men did not know about? Knowing about these things will put us at a disadvantage. Perhaps an indiscretion, or a lie or something we have and do not want to release. Are you like the couple - Ananias and Sapphira who thought to lie to the Church. Many are like Jesus, we suspect that if certain information is released it would lead to future loss of reputation or we may be asked to give more than we intend to give.

What an unfortunate conclusion ... another self-deception. The most High knows all already. Did Joseph not know that they had another brother who was not with them? Does Jesus not know what you are keeping back from Him. He does and He asks you not because He does not know but because He does.

Did our maker not give all to us? Why is it so tough to surrender all to Him. Can He not give us again and again? He who gave us our very breath and created all ... is it too much for Him to ask us to surrender all to Him. He said He made all for his pleasure not for ours. It pleased God to scar the soul of Jacob in demanding the release of Benjamin ... but it was too small to ask for given what He had planned ahead ... a pleasant surprise in Egypt.

Release all you burdens to Jesus. He is so real and so full of mercy. Jesus knows it all and has a solution in store in the future if only you will stop blaming circumstances and raking up your past. At the heart of inability to see the beautiful provisions for God is our past guilt. The devil loves to assail our joys with snippets of the past so we will not be able to enter into his merciful provisions and remain tied in bitter memories. Jacob has no expectation of any good from God because of his guilt. His sons likewise. Let go of the guilt. Release the past and enjoy a new provisions ahead. It may not be clear to you how God will move. The famine may be more real than the comforts of Goshen, but still be assured that His word and promises will come to pass.

Also, God loves a joyful giver ... may we have more grace to give our life and place everything totally in your hands. God will help you come out gloriously. Stand on His word. Stop blaming people ... your sons, brothers or pastor ... stop blaming yourself. Release the guilt. Soon it will be time for rejoicing. Release what He has asked of you ... whatever is released to Christ is safe and ultimately returns blessed, increased and strengthened.

Song

Were the whole realm of nature mine
It were an offering far too small.
Love so amazing so divine
Demands my soul, my life, my all.

Prayer: O Lord, That which I cherish the most, I give it to you. Help me to give joyfully and not grudgingly. Amen

MAY 19

That We May live

Bible Text: Genesis 43:8-9

Gen 43:8 And Judah said unto Israel his father, Send the lad with me, and we will arise and go; that we may live, and not die, both we, and thou, and also our little ones. 9 I will be surety for him; of my hand shalt thou require him: if I bring him not unto thee, and set him before thee, then let me bear the blame for ever:

We shall not die but live. But there are things to be done to be spiritually alive. What has Jesus said we should do? Joseph asked them to bring Benjamin but they feared to do so . . . only to slowly die of hunger. Jesus has taught and asked for obedience on so many things. Jesus asked his disciples "do you love me . . . then feed my sheep" He said you are my friends if you do whatsoever I command you. He asks us to pray even for our enemies and bless those who curse us. How many things have we been told to do that we have failed to do? But in not doing so we have suffered much until we went back to the original instruction. God will not change his instruction to us. Rather we will have to go and dig up what we have been told to do and simply do it - no matter how painful or dangerous it seems . . . that we may live. God uses the famine to ensure they do not forget Joseph's instruction. I suspect they would have abandoned Simeon in Egypt for nothing will compel Jacob to release Benjamin.

There is an obedience to God in which you have failed that is holding up your breakthrough in life . . . why don't you simply rediscover what it is . . . God is simply using your frustration to draw attention to that action that you need to do. Many have already started to picture your death—but they will only be proven wrong. God will give you more grace. As Israel eventually agrees to send Benjamin, you will be strengthened in the area of weakness and will live, you and your entire family will live. But for the sons of Israel, not without going to Joseph - a shadow of Christ. God bless you.

Song

Under the burdens of guilt and care
Many a spirit is grieving,
Who in the joy of the Lord might share,
Life everlasting receiving.

Life, life, eternal life!
Jesus alone is the giver;
Life, life, abundant life!
Glory to Jesus forever!

Bearing our burden of guilt,
there came One who is strong to deliver;
Bringing to men, through His wondrous name,
Life "more abundant" than ever.

Burdened one, why will you longer bear
Sorrows from which He releases?
Open your heart and, rejoicing,
share Life "more abundant" in Jesus!

Prayer: O Lord Jesus, as we come to you, bless us with abundant life. Amen

MAY 20

Our Surety the Lion

Bible Text: Genesis 43:8-9

Gen 43:8 And Judah said unto Israel his father, Send the lad with me, and we will arise and go; that we may live, and not die, both we, and thou, and also our little ones. 9 I will be surety for him; of my hand shalt thou require him: if I bring him not unto thee, and set him before thee, then let me bear the blame for ever:

Joseph was already given for them. He went through pits, prison and slavery and came out for them. There is no need for Benjamin to do the same. God will not need another sacrifice for sin after Christ. Christ has already paid it all. This is a different sacrifice. When we come as a living sacrifice offering sacrifices of praise, obedience and joy, we do so because we love God. We are filled with the love of God and will do anything for Him. We will keep ourselves for Him who first loved us. When we obey His commandments we do so out of love, for how can we say we love Him we do not want to please.

There is no other sacrifice for sin. Benjamin will not go the same path as Joseph. Judah promises to watch over Benjamin. I do not know what Judah can do . . . but the coming Lion of the Tribe of Judah is however a sure protection. He will watch over all our giving and gifts and our seed. By His Spirit, we will not end up giving and then sorrowing for losses. Instead, we will see His harvest.

Luk_6:38 Give, and it shall be given unto you; good measure, pressed down, and shaken together, and running over, shall men give into your bosom. For with the same measure that ye mete withal it shall be measured to you again.

The surety is the word of the Lion of the tribe of Judah. Do not despair. Indeed, everywhere you have given, you will reap a bountiful harvest. It does not matter what the evidence presents to you. You will not lose when you surrender anything to Jesus.

Did you read about the boy who brought his little lunch and placed it in the hands of the Lion of Judah? Did you read about the widow who surrendered her last meal to the Prophet. Jacob is forced to release a son and got back three sons (Benjamin, Simeon and Joseph) . . . and two more grandsons (Ephraim and Manasseh) through Joseph. The once considered barren - Hannah released Samuel and out of her womb came forth five others. God multiplies what we give. So give.

1Sa_2:21 And the LORD visited Hannah, so that she conceived, and bare three sons and two daughters. And the child Samuel grew before the LORD.

Your release will link you to a harvest you least expect. You can rely on the Lion of Judah. He is truly able to multiply the life given as a living sacrifice to be far more fulfilling than it could ever possibly have been. Do not grieve. Release that which you hold with joy.

Song

What shall I render to my God,
For all His mercy's store?
I'll take the gifts He hath bestowed,
And humbly ask for more.

Prayer: O Lord, May all my giving be truly multiplied in your hands. Amen

MAY 21

Delays are costly

Bible Text: Genesis 43:10

Gen 43:10 For except we had lingered, surely now we had returned this second time.

Delays are often costly. Our giving and release is best when it is immediate and not compelled by circumstances. The Bible does not tell us how long they lingered, but we know the famine became worse. So many other things lingered. Fears and anxieties in the famine lingered. The imprisonment of Simeon lingered. The mourning for Joseph lingered. There are many reasons we give for delays in obedience to God. The most common helper of our delays is our flesh. When we perceive disadvantage we prefer to stay our action. But time passes and God keeps our breakthroughs awaiting in mercy our obedience.

Another manifestation of delay we see when Rebekah lingers in following the servant of Abraham to meet her bridegroom. We know that this delay is external for Laban and the household contrive all means to keep Rebekah from going.

Gen 24:56 And he said unto them, Hinder me not, seeing the LORD hath prospered my way; send me away that I may go to my master

There are hindrances from the devil. Indeed God must conceal His plans so well that the devil is unaware and helps even to accelerate it. If the devil knew better, He would have hindered the arrest and crucifixion of Christ . . . but he facilitated it, instead. Paul was hindered several times in ministry.

1Th_2:18 Wherefore we would have come unto you, even I Paul, once and again; but Satan hindered us.

What the flesh, Satan, and his agents . . . some in your family plan to hinder the most is our coming to Jesus in repentance. He knows Christ is coming soon and when the trumpet sounds, it will be too late for any repentance. Do not permit anything to delay your return to Christ for you do not know when Christ will return and it will be over.

Do not delay the freedom of your brothers languishing in the prison of sin. Go and tell the good news. Do not linger at giving God praises for the Lord arises in the praises of His children and His enemies scatter. When we linger to praise God, so much unnecessary havoc persists. Now is the time to go to Jesus . . . Now is the time to obey Him . . . do not wait another moment. Praise Him Now.

Song

My God, how wonderful Thou art, Thy majesty, how bright;
How beautiful Thy mercy seat In depths of burning light!

How dread are Thy eternal years,O everlasting Lord,
By prostrate spirits day and night Incessantly adored!

How wonderful, how beautiful,The sight of Thee must be;
Thy endless wisdom, boundless power, And glorious purity!

Father of Jesus, love's Reward! What rapture it will be
Prostrate before Thy throne to lie, And gaze, and gaze on Thee!

Prayer: O Lord, Let nothing be able to hinder me from worshipping and serving you. Amen

MAY 22

Pleasing God

Bible Text: Genesis 43:11

Gen 43:11 And their father Israel said unto them, If it must be so now, do this; take of the best fruits in the land in your vessels, and carry down the man a present, a little balm, and a little honey, spices, and myrrh, nuts, and almonds:

What would compare to the joy of Joseph seeing his brethren and his father. He already has the best balms, spices and choicest fruits of Egypt. Joseph misses His own and not their assets or what they have. In similar fashion, Christ wants our soul. He misses our company and desires our love and presence. He has no need of our service, offerings or even our sacrifices. His greatest joy is when we are given to Him. Many do not have time to make available for Jesus, in devotion. They hurriedly bring things to the altar and wonder why the meetings are so long. They want to go back to their other pursuits. Jesus wants them and not what they can bring. His greatest joy is in our surrendered life and time and not in what we do for Him. Does he derive pleasure in our offerings and sacrifices when he discerns we do not know that He is our brother who wants to be reunited with us.

We seek to please God and that is good . . . but what gives Him greatest delight . . . is the love that He observes in our heart for Him that provokes our obedience.

1Sa_15:22 And Samuel said, Hath the LORD as great delight in burnt offerings and sacrifices, as in obeying the voice of the LORD? Behold, to obey is better than sacrifice, and to hearken than the fat of rams.

Rom_8:8 So then they that are in the flesh cannot please God.

The brothers gave as though they were giving to a strange king, there was nothing in their heart . . . only a fear that they would be treated unkindly. Many come to God like this . . . with many gifts. But God wants us to know Him first before we give to Him. We then see that we need not give to bribe Him for He has already freely given us His best . . . His own life He gave when we hated Him . . . what will He not freely now give us.

Friend, keep your gift for now and get to know that your God is your friend, your brother . . . Christ, and you will one day be joint-heirs with Him. Perhaps your obedience will be different if you knew Him more . . . perhaps your giving will be more joyful and sacrificial and painless . . . if you truly knew Him to whom you give. Give Him whom you know and love as the Savior, who died for the salvation of your soul . . . your brother crucified for your sins. Now . . . consider . . . is anything too much to be offered to Him.

Song

What shall we offer our good Lord, Poor nothings! for His boundless grace!
Fain would we His great Name record, And worthily set forth His praise.
Great object of our growing love, To Whom our more than all we owe,
Open the fountain from above, And let it our full souls o'erflow.

So shall our lives Thy power proclaim, Thy grace for every sinner free;
Till all mankind shall learn Thy Name, Shall all stretch out their hands to Thee.

Prayer: O Lord, preserve me from vain offerings . . . teach me instead to know you. Amen

MAY 23
Double Money

Bible Text: Genesis 43:12

Gen 43:12 And take double money in your hand; and the money that was brought again in the mouth of your sacks, carry it again in your hand; peradventure it was an oversight:

Often we are tempted to believe we can buy our way to salvation. We offer a kind of bail to free us from the guilt of the past . . . only to realize that we need to come again. The things of God are not for sale. There are examples of many who sought to buy the anointing or some other spiritual virtue. They were all disappointed.

God desires praise from our heart. God does not need to be bribed or compensated by the mortals He created. Do we forget that He said the silver and the gold is already His. The gestures by the brothers of Joseph are well meaning and are full of the right intentions. But the Bible asks us to make peace with our brother before we come with any sacrifice.

Far too many sacrifices and offerings cannot be accepted by God although useful to the recipient. Indeed, our motives are like Jacob's . . . perhaps He will be moved by the offering to provide in the famine and release our loved ones from bondage. Someone did ask . . . why did God accept a generous offering from Solomon? It was not because of its size, rather the later request by Solomon for divine wisdom to lead God's people showed that Solomon had an uncommon heart after God - to do God's will.

Have you given God your heart? Have you sought Him first? Do you have grievances yet to be resolved? Are you not at peace with any? Then hold back your offering and your lavish giving. Do not put the cart before the horse. Go and make peace with your brother or sister.

Jas 3:18 And the fruit of righteousness is sown in peace of them that make peace.

Song

Deeper, deeper in the love of Jesus
Daily let me go;
Higher Higher in the school of wisdom
More of you to know.
O deeeper yet I pray
And higher every day,
And wiser Lord
In the precious Holy Word.

Prayer: O Lord, Let me know you even more . . . let this be my top priority. Amen

MAY 24

Empty Handed

Bible Text: Genesis 43:13

Gen 43:13 Take also your brother, and arise, go again unto the man:

There is a song that goes thus

Must I go empty handed?
Thus my dear Redeemer meet?
Not one day of service give Him
Lay no trophy at His feet?

Must I go and empty handed?
Must I meet my Savior so?
Not one soul with which to greet Him?
Must I empty handed go?

O ye saints, arouse, be earnest
Up and work while yet t'is day
Ere the night of death o'er take thee
Strive for souls while still you may.

Indeed just as Joseph wanted his brother brought to him, Christ yearns for souls. His delight is that His own repent and return to Him. Note that it has to be Benjamin and no one else. We cannot bring wolves to Jesus when he knows His sheep. Evangelism in all forms must be His top priority assignment. What will you have to present to Him at His throne room?

May we receive fresh grace to daily win souls for Jesus

Song

Come soul and find thy rest
No longer be distressed
Come to thy Savior's breast
Oh don't stay away.

Prayer: O Lord, may I not come empty handed before you. Amen

MAY 25

Choose Obedience

Bible Text: Genesis 43:14

Gen 43:14 And God Almighty give you mercy before the man, that he may send away your other brother, and Benjamin. If I be bereaved of my children, I am bereaved.

There are times that you do not know what to do. You have to make a choice to do something that is personally costly and an easier choice but that which is leading to death. But the decision to disobey God is to choose death anyway even obedience is personally costly. Sometimes the evidence confuses us. If Jacob does not release Benjamin they will die of hunger, but if Benjamin is released Jacob sees a high chance that he will be bereaved. But the act that God desires is that which will lead to life. If Jacob had sought God for direction, he would have been told to release Benjamin. Of course we can suspect that Jacob did not pray concerning this decision because he did not want to release Benjamin.

May you always choose obedience or risk death. Seek the face of God on what to do and then do it . . . no matter the personal cost to you or what you perceive to be the risk. When we chose obedience to God, we are protected by the God we obey and our obedience ultimately leads to life. It is good to wait until we have heard God clearly before we act . . . but when we have, we should obey. We can discover God's will in the word of God. The path of obedience to God is the path out of trouble. Find that path.

Song.

I can hear my Savior calling,
I can hear my Savior calling,
I can hear my Savior calling,
"Take thy cross and follow, follow Me."

Where He leads me I will follow,
Where He leads me I will follow,
Where He leads me I will follow,
I'll go with Him, with Him all the way.

I'll go with Him thro' the garden,
I'll go with Him thro' the garden,
I'll go with Him thro' the garden,
I'll go with Him, with Him all the way.

I'll go with Him thro' the judgment,
I'll go with Him thro' the judgment,
I'll go with Him thro' the judgment,
I'll go with Him, with Him all the way.

He will give me grace and glory,
He will give me grace and glory,
He will give me grace and glory,
And go with me, with me all the way.

Prayer: O Lord, Give me grace to go with you all the way. Amen

MAY 26

If I perish I perish

Bible Text: Genesis 43:14

Gen 43:14 And God Almighty give you mercy before the man, that he may send away your other brother, and Benjamin. If I be bereaved of my children, I am bereaved.

Is it not strange that many that said "If I perish I perish" do not perish . . . rather they go from glory to glory. Falling into the plans of God is not a descent into an abyss, but a rediscovery of His mercy. Jacob mentions the name of the Almighty God . . . He remembers His covenant and speaks according to that covenant. Our God is a God of mercy . . . Indeed, His mercy endures forever.

David once had to choose between falling into the hands of men or God and he chose God. You will not be bereaved as you imagine. Jacob already expected the worst would happen . . . but God's mercy had already gone ahead of all the issues. God's mercy has gone even before your prayers to do what you have not, indeed cannot ask for. God was preparing a union that was so glorious and had not entered the heart of Jacob even once. Do you know a day like that is coming for all saints.

God is indeed all mighty. He has all might and power and is more than able to do exceedingly more than we can ever ask or imagine. God has might to reverse the irreversible, to turnaround situations and completely bring new dimensions that never were remotely considered. God has limitless avenues to bring about His divine purposes and intentions.

Jacob called the name of the Almighty God. As you praise Him as the Almighty expect his sure mercies. David was renowned for praise and also became the beneficiary of very lavish mercies from the throne room of the Almighty. As you praise Him, God will go well beyond all your limited expectations and surprise you for great good.

Why don't you praise Him . . . Now.

Song

Almighty God, Almighty King
You are the Lord of everything
The highest praise to you I bring
Almighty God, Almighty King

Prayer: O Lord, May you grant me mercy . . . uncommon mercies . . . enduring mercies. Like you gave David and Jacob. Amen

MAY 27

The Ultimate Present

Bible Text: Genesis 43:15

Gen 43:15 And the men took that present, and they took double money in their hand, and Benjamin; and rose up, and went down to Egypt, and stood before Joseph. 16 And when Joseph saw Benjamin with them, he said to the ruler of his house, Bring these men home, and slay, and make ready; for these men shall dine with me at noon.

What God is looking for is quite different from what men value. Presents, money . . . even double would have demonstrated appreciation to Joseph, but it was Benjamin that his heart longed for. Christ longed for souls because He died for them. Christ is expecting us to work and bring to Him those He died for. There are rewards in eternity that are not equivalent for all. Those who excel in winning souls or evangelism will have a unique welcome.

Jesus is not expecting us to bring to Him those we are unable to bring. He has already created the famines in the world system to help us receive a more positive response when we share the good news of the gospel. Also, we see the that we must be persistent in soul winning . . . Benjamin was not released immediately . . . keep going. Indeed you have a younger brother who does not know the Lord. In eternity Christ will say well done for all the service you rendered, but for him and indeed other souls . . . He will arrange a special reception. I often wonder what happens at the death of soul winners . . . I suspect it will be different. I also wonder at those who travel to far lands to save souls but ignore the cries of their neighbors and relations.

1Pe 5:2 Feed the flock of God which is among you, taking the oversight thereof, not by constraint, but willingly; not for filthy lucre, but of a ready mind; 3 Neither as being lords over God's heritage, but being ensamples to the flock. 4 And when the chief Shepherd shall appear, ye shall receive a crown of glory that fadeth not away.

There is a satisfaction found in soul winning that is found nowhere else! *Jas 5:20 Let him know, that he which converteth the sinner from the error of his way shall save a soul from death, and shall hide a multitude of sins.*

Also, there is the affection and gratitude of those whom we influenced and won to the Lord. But in eternity there will be the Lord's commendation and the joy and honor that will accompany it as well as the thrill of meeting those who have been blessed and won to the Lord through us.

Reconsider what you are focusing your life on.

Song

Lord, I'm available to you
My will I give to you
I'll do what you say do -use me Lord
To show someone the way and enable me to say
My storage is empty and I am available to you.

Prayer: O Lord, Use me to show someone the way back to you. Amen

MAY 28

Fear

Bible Text: Genesis 43:17-18

Gen 43:17 And the man did as Joseph bade; and the man brought the men into Joseph's house. 18 And the men were afraid, because they were brought into Joseph's house; and they said, Because of the money that was returned in our sacks at the first time are we brought in; that he may seek occasion against us, and fall upon us, and take us for bondmen, and our asses

Even as Joseph has ordered a feast . . . only fear fills the brethren . . . they expect the worst. God has not given you fear. The enemy shows you things that have not happened . . . how old foes still await to kill you . . . how old grievances will be raked up again and you will be put on trial . . . how you are being hunted by those you have offended in the past . . . how you will only fail if you try to get up again. Fear is so potent even in an atmosphere of feasting. As the men go to prepare a great dinner . . . the brothers are suicidal with fears.

They wonder what it will be like to be slaves in Egypt and prepare to be made bondmen. Fear causes you to prepare for the worst . . . but this is not the mind that God has given . . . where does fear come from. The vendor of fear is the devil. He tells you your marriage will fail . . . he tells you of your failure . . . he tells you your church will fail . . . he brings bad news even before they have been announced.

Christ taught us to tell Satan "get thee behind me" . . . and not permit him any ground. Immediately you sense fear, know this is not of God. Indeed, the brothers have done much wrong . . . but Joseph knew all this and had forgiven them and had prepared a feast for them. Do not permit fear to ruin your life and paralyze your progress. Move forward. Be of good courage . . . a feast that awaits you.

Song

God is calling the prodigal: come without delay!
Hear, O hear Him calling, calling now for thee;
Tho' you've wandered so far from His presence, come today,
Hear His loving voice calling still.

Refrain:
Calling now for thee: O weary prodigal come!
Calling now for thee: O weary prodigal come!

Patient, loving, and tenderly still the Father pleads;
Hear, O hear Him calling, calling now for thee;
O return while the Spirit in mercy intercedes,
Hear His loving voice calling still.

Come, there's bread in the house of thy Father, and to spare;
Hear, O hear Him calling, calling now for thee;
Lo! the table is spread and the feast is waiting there,
Hear His loving voice calling still.

Prayer: O Lord, bring all the prodigals, still living in fear. Amen

MAY 29

Grace

Bible Text: Genesis 43:17-18

Gen 43:17 And the man did as Joseph bade; and the man brought the men into Joseph's house. 18 And the men were afraid, because they were brought into Joseph's house; and they said, Because of the money that was returned in our sacks at the first time are we brought in; that he may seek occasion against us, and fall upon us, and take us for bondmen, and our asses

Do you see how men continue to doubt God. Even when His mercies are already evident, we still return these gestures with doubts. There is something about us that makes us expect the worst and to doubt the sincerity and forgiveness of God. The reason is our guilty conscience. Why will God forgive us? We do not deserve the forgiveness . . . but we forget we do not deserve the reward either. It was God that helped us to win souls. All is grace and mercy and nothing more. The mystery of grace. We need to meditate that we are all subject to the mercy of the one who saves who He will. Many cannot receive salvation not because it was not offered but they cannot accept why it was offered. They see traps where these are non-existent.

God forgives and forgives totally and completely. He forgave the brothers of Joseph, but they could not forgive themselves. Even when we do right we are arrogant to look down at another who did not do as well - forgetting it was the same God that helped us that withdrew that same grace from others. Not accepting God's forgiveness is also a sign of pride - that prefers to suffer for wrong rather than be positioned eternally to be grateful to the God who can forgive us.

Have you gone to God for forgiveness? Have you received His forgiveness? Are you doubting His forgiveness? This devotional is for someone who is at the brink of being targeted for a great act of mercy and restoration. Do not ask why? or why not? Let the truth that it is all grace be more than sufficient for you. Do forgive others as you have also been forgiven. Trust His word that says His blood was shed for all your sins. Past, present and future. Amazing, inexplicable, unbelievable, but still true.

Song

Amazing grace! How sweet the sound that saved a wretch like me!
I once was lost, but now am found; Was blind, but now I see.

'Twas grace that taught my heart to fear, And grace my fears relieved;
How precious did that grace appear the hour I first believed!

Through many dangers, toils and snares, I have already come;
'Tis grace hath brought me safe thus far, and grace will lead me home.

The earth shall soon dissolve like snow, The sun forbear to shine;
But God, who called me here below,Will be forever mine.

When we've been there ten thousand years,Bright shining as the sun,
We've no less days to sing God's praise Than when we'd first begun.

Prayer: O Lord, Help me to understand and receive your grace. Amen

The Ministry of the Holy Spirit

Bible Text: Genesis 43:17

Gen 43:17 And the man did as Joseph bade; and the man brought the men into Joseph's house

Christ told the disciples to wait for the Holy Spirit. He is described as the comforter who will lead us to our first Husband - Jesus Christ Himself.

1Co 12:7 But the manifestation of the Spirit is given to every man to profit withal. 8 For to one is given by the Spirit the word of wisdom; to another the word of knowledge by the same Spirit; 9 To another faith by the same Spirit; to another the gifts of healing by the same Spirit; 10 To another the working of miracles; to another prophecy; to another discerning of spirits; to another divers kinds of tongues; to another the interpretation of tongues: 11 But all these worketh that one and the selfsame Spirit, dividing to every man severally as he will.

The Bible says none can come to Christ except they are drawn by the Holy Spirit. The Bible also teaches about several gifts that He gives and that it is only those who are led by the Spirit of God that are the children of God. Who is leading you in that venture? There may be struggles, but everyone knows who has the upper hand in our lives challenges. Is it the spirit of the antichrist, the flesh or the world or the Spirit of God? Which home will you end up in? The home prepared by Christ where there are many mansions . . . and a place prepared for you or hell fire. Learn to embrace the friendship of the Holy Spirit. As you meditate on His word, you will understand better why He must disagree with many of your natural preferences. The Spirit of God is a Spirit of grace. It does not work based on the merit of our performances but is instructed to help us and comfort us through our trials and ultimately bring us home.

Reflect today on the Holy Spirit. Make sure He is more real to you than any other personality. He can be grieved, and can ultimately leave. It is a sad thing if we ever grieve the Holy Spirit so much that He must leave us. Being a Holy Spirit, what grieves Him is sin - particularly secret sins that are hidden from external view but serve to repel the one that must help us. The tragedy of sin is more compelling when we understand how it separates us from the Holy one we need to succeed and be comforted in the inevitable famines of life.

When you stop sensing the direction of the Holy Spirit and the subtle checks and nods and sometimes the strong rod of His discipline - beware.

Song

Come Holy Spirit I need you
Come Holy Spirit I pray
Come in your strength and your power
Come in your own special way.

Prayer: O Lord, Do not permit me to do anything that will grieve your Spirit in my life. Amen

MAY 31

Revealer of Truths

Bible Text: Genesis 43:19-23

Gen 43:19 And they came near to the steward of Joseph's house, and they communed with him at the door of the house, 20 And said, O sir, we came indeed down at the first time to buy food: 21 And it came to pass, when we came to the inn, that we opened our sacks, and, behold, every man's money was in the mouth of his sack, our money in full weight: and we have brought it again in our hand. 22 And other money have we brought down in our hands to buy food: we cannot tell who put our money in our sacks. 23 And he said, Peace be to you, fear not: your God, and the God of your father, hath given you treasure in your sacks: I had your money. And he brought Simeon out unto them.

All scripture is inspired by the Holy Spirit. This is why your meditations on the word of God are in fact a communion with an unseen person, the third person of the Trinity, God Himself. As you read the word of God, bring your situations in into a different perspective as you allow God to reveal the many things you will never know. The brothers of Joseph are puzzled concerning so many things that are happening to them?

But the word of God gives an answer of peace to God's children. Are you filled with fears? Go and meditate on the word of God? Do you wake up feeling tensions and worried? Start your day with the word of God. You will find a peace that the world can never be able to give and a blessed assurance you will never find elsewhere. When we fail to read the word of God, we drift into needless painful imaginations or are misguided into thrills that do not last. The Holy Spirit inspired the word of God and is the only interpreter of the same word. We are in times when many want to claim that the Bible is another storybook. This is dangerous for your peace as it attacks the only source that can calm all your fears. Eventually men resort to pills, addictions, lusts and other regimes that will never satisfy to find the answers they need in the word of God.

The unnamed man tells them "fear not . . . you have been given treasure . . . and Simeon is returned . . .". The Holy Spirit is telling someone . . . that which you feared would be lost is not lost but safe in the hands of Jesus. Expect surprises of restoration. Expect treasures to be further revealed through the word of God. God has reserved many beautiful treasures for His saints . . . do not imagine that God starves us from that which will gladden our hearts on the earth. The Holy Spirit will not give us what will destroy us. His treasure is good treasure and is the best we can ever hope to have.

Receive your Simeon. Receive your brother lost in drugs, lost to sin, trapped in the prison of bondage. Receive your loved ones back . . . and rejoice - for things are going to get even better.

Song

Holy Spirit, breathe on me.Until my heart is clean
Let Sunshine fill its inmost part . . . with not a cloud between

Prayer: Holy Spirit, banish all the clouds with your divine illumination in my life. Amen

JUNE 1

Peace be to You.

Bible Text: Genesis 43:19-23

Gen 43:19 And they came near to the steward of Joseph's house, and they communed with him at the door of the house, 20 And said, O sir, we came indeed down at the first time to buy food: 21 And it came to pass, when we came to the inn, that we opened our sacks, and, behold, every man's money was in the mouth of his sack, our money in full weight: and we have brought it again in our hand. 22 And other money have we brought down in our hands to buy food: we cannot tell who put our money in our sacks. 23 And he said, Peace be to you, fear not: your God, and the God of your father, hath given you treasure in your sacks: I had your money. And he brought Simeon out unto them.

Be comforted and may the peace of God be with you. Joseph only speaks peace to you ... why are you so worried? What do you have to fear? But they cannot receive this peace because they do not know who the giver is—of what value is a word of peace from an Egyptian officer. The one who does not know you and what you have been through, your guilt and your fears cannot promise you peace.

But it is Jesus who promises you—dear reader ... peace. You will not be destroyed nor will you end badly ... Receive the peace of Christ even though it passes understanding. It is a peace that the world cannot give nor can it be taken away. Receive the peace of Christ for you have found favor in the eyes of your God. Remember this is not the peace of men nor is it the peace of the world. This is the peace of God ... the Prince of Peace offers you a sure peace ... receive that sure peace ... even as Simeon appears. Let His peace banish all your fears ... you will sing for joy and will rediscover laughter and dancing ... just wait on Him. Meanwhile hold on to His peace ... soon it will be clear that your maker is your Husband ... the Lord of Hosts is His name. He has forgiven and will restore you fully.

Song.

He is my peace He has broken down every wall
He is my peace He is my peace.
He is my peace He has broken down every wall
He is my peace He is my peace
Cast all your cares on Him
For He cares for you
He is my peace He is my peace 2ce.

Prayer: Holy Spirit, Move and make my life at peace again .... Amen

JUNE 2

The Journey Home

Bible Text: Genesis 43:24

Gen 43:24 And the man brought the men into Joseph's house, and gave them water, and they washed their feet; and he gave their asses provender.

In this text, we see several characters and elements with much significance. We see the man that brings, which I had earlier said was representative of the Holy Spirit that must guide His own to eternity. It will never be by our understanding, no matter how sanctified that understanding may be. We are told never to lean on it. Then we see the water that cleanses representing the blood of Jesus, the cleansing fluid ever so potent to wash away our sins and bring us clean before God.

But there are other dimensions, the man led them on a journey home. Which journey are we on? Do we have a direction to our lives and is this direction to Heaven. The feet represent the hunger and the zeal to please God, the readiness and equipment to move in the direction that we are led. Many are too lazy or appear paralyzed and refuse to move ... lack of zeal can be the undoing of many. This devotional reminds us that God is a Holy God and all who come to him must be Holy. One of the assignments of the Holy Spirit is to take us through a journey of sanctification - getting rid of sinful weights.

You can examine your life and see if you are on a path as has been described. What is your focus? Is it Heaven or something else? Do we trust and love Jesus as our Savior? Do you have a sense of the dirt that is on your feet - sin ... that must be cleansed and stopped ... or do you not care for your sanctification? Do you sense the zeal of the Lord of Hosts telling you there is little time and you must do all you can quickly as you have been led to do ... or are you still always procrastinating.

Many will cry in Heaven when they see the opportunities lost and frittered in vanity. We will wish we had been more zealous for the things of God, wish we had been more careful with sin and shunned more the world ... we will wish we had not permitted our lives to be distracted by the many toys competing with God's assignment in our lives.

Ponder over these and make sure you are not on your own. When God says "leave him alone" in frustration, then one has entered already into the trap of Satan. If you are not on the journey to the home prepared by Christ and escorted by the Holy Spirit, then you are on the road to a horrible damnation. You can get back on track as you receive grace to repent.

Song

Lord, we are hungry for blessing,
This is in tune with Thy Word;
Now as our need we're confessing,
Give us new hearts, cleansed and stirred.

Prayer: Holy Spirit, give us new hearts, cleansed and stirred to follow you till we reach our Heavenly home. Amen

JUNE 3

Is your Focus Right?

Bible Text: Genesis 43:25

Gen 43:25 And they made ready the present against Joseph came at noon: for they heard that they should eat bread there.

As the brothers got ready to meet with Joseph, we read that they made ready their presents. It is a good tradition to go before men of honor with gifts. Visitors do not normally approach Kings empty handed. Our offerings to the King of kings should reflect the great honor we accord to our God. But in this story, there is a different dimension in that they did not know Joseph was their brother. This was a very material fact that made them focus on how to win the acceptance and favor of Joseph, who was already set to favor them. Ignorance affects our attitude.

There are still many today trying to please God with things, performances and service. Many have focused on what money can buy and have pledged to do impressive things for the Lord. This is all commendable, but is not the best we can be for God. God is not so impressed with our gifts as He is excited about us. We should focus on our lives, and the lives of others to make them sanctuaries that please the most high to dwell in. If they knew this was their brother and that he had forgiven them, they would have prepared their hearts to meet him, to be pleasing to him who they had ill-treated.

We tend to focus on the material but God is focused on us. What impresses men tends to be of silver and gold . . . what pleases God is faith that He is our father who sent His son, our Lord Jesus Christ as our senior brother . . . the second Adam to die and be raised that we may be ever saved. Without this faith, it is impossible to please God. Our faith therefore looks up to Christ, the Lamb of Calvary.

Faith is the most attacked and underestimated of virtues. Because all power belongs to God and Satan has no power to defeat us, he tricks and discourages us with wiles to erode faith. When we have no faith, we will soon search for other ways to please God only to embark on futile journeys. We then become discouraged and become vulnerable to Satan's deceptions. Lord increase our faith. Faith comes by hearing—therefore ensure you are constantly exposed to expository teachings of God's word. The measure of your faith is linked to the word you regularly receive.

Song

My faith looks up to thee,
thou Lamb of Calvary,
Savior divine!
Now hear me while I pray,
take all my guilt away,
O let me from this day
be wholly thine!

May thy rich grace impart
strength to my fainting heart,
my zeal inspire!
As thou hast died for me,
O may my love to thee
pure, warm, and changeless be,
a living fire!

Prayer: Holy Spirit, Help me to prepare my heart to be pure and faithful always pleasing to my Savior. Amen

JUNE 4

Joseph's Home

Bible Text: Genesis 43:26

Gen 43:26 And when Joseph came home, they brought him the present which was in their hand into the house, and bowed themselves to him to the earth.

Earthly monarchs are known to be given the highest levels of worship. Those who must come before them do not go empty-handed . . . they come with gifts and presents. They come in uncertainty that they will be received and bow to the earth . . . all this for a king with a time limit to reign and even if he reigns all his life, that life is limited . . . even powers and ability to favor are also limited. Joseph's home can be seen as a shadow of our Heavenly home

How do we come before the limitless God. David comes humbly before Him, remembering that He is our Maker. *Ps. 95:6. [6] O come, let us worship and bow down: let us kneel before the LORD our maker.*

Only with a humble attitude will we offer true worship unto God realizing His greatness and holiness, and our own insignificance and sinfulness. As we appear before the gates of the temple of God, we must be prepared to bow down and kneel in the worship of the Lord. The reason for this is that the Lord alone is God, a mighty God, and a great King, and the whole universe lies under His control. What prevails in some sanctuaries today insults God as regards His worship. People participate with enthusiasm in worship service while hearts are very far away from God in daily living. Worship is flippant.

Can you imagine situations whereby someone has the rare privilege to be in the presence of God in worship and runs out to answer a phone call from someone of a mortal body - even if from a close relative or related to an urgent issue? How do you expect God to honor that kind of worship? Yet this continues in Church services today. This could explain why there is limited or no impact as can be expected from the manifest presence of the most high. Indeed, most are only present physically but their hearts remain very far from God. Informality and careless familiarity has combined to create an atmosphere that ridicules the reality that God is supreme and above all. How much you know about God will determine the kind of glory that you will give Him and the honor you will ascribe to His Holy Name. Do not come before the presence of God empty handed. The very first offering God expected from you is by presenting yourself as a living sacrifice, Holy, acceptable unto God . . .

Rom. 12:1 I beseech you therefore, brethren, by the mercies of God, that ye present your bodies a living sacrifice, holy, acceptable unto God, which is your reasonable service.

Indeed, we often call people to sing praises and songs unto God and this invitation has made many people from all works of life to be engaged in singing new songs unto God in response to that call and invitation. However, people turn the praises and worship of God to a circus whereas Jesus has given vital clues in His word to recognizing true worship, the heart desire of God.

Song

All creatures of our God and King -Lift up your voice and with us sing Al-le-lu-jah, Al-lelu-jah!
Thou burning sun with soft-er gleam; O praise Him, O praise Him; Al-lelujah; Al-le-lujah; Al-le-lu-jah;
Thou rush-ing wind that art so strong - Ye clouds that sail in heav'n a-long O praise Him! Alleluia!
Thou ri-sing morn, in praise re-joice Ye-lights of eve-nings, find a voice, O praise Him! O praise Him

Prayer: Lord, Help me to prepare my heart to come before your presence and worship always in Spirit and in Truth. Amen

JUNE 5

Heavenly Worship

Bible Text: Genesis 43:26

Gen 43:26 And when Joseph came home, they brought him the present which was in their hand into the house, and bowed themselves to him to the earth.

Our worship tells us whether we are citizens of Heaven or not. Worship is not performance, but the work of the Spirit of God having its way in our lives as we yield to Him. We worship according to the truth and revelation of God. Heavenly worship involves the presence of the Most High God. Psalm 22:3 says "But thou art holy, O thou that inhabitest the praises of Israel." In 2 Chronicles 5:11-14, when the Israelites worshipped God in one accord, singing of the mercy of God that endureth forever, the presence of God was manifested to the extent that the glory of God filled the temple of the house of God. This will be your experience.

Heavenly worship opens the Heavens even for others to benefit, releasing freedom from bondage and giving victory over incredible opposition. In Acts 16:25-26, Paul and Silas were in prison and as they rendered praises, God paid them a visit and they and other prisoners were free. King Jehoshaphat through worship was also victorious over major opposition. 2 Chro. 20:20-25.

Heavenly worship releases the grace of genuine repentance and conviction which paves the way for true salvation. In Acts 16:27-34, the keeper of the prison was saved and his household. A grace released after Paul and Silas worshipped. In Revelation 1:10 John said he was in the Spirit on the Lord's day . . . Heavenly worship experiences begin with the Heavens opening and divine visitation i.e. the Holy Ghost the presence of God descending and filling us afresh. We are freshly anointed and empowered and so direct our expressions and talents to the glory of God who sits on the throne and unto the Lamb of God forever and ever. The Heavens are very selective and open only to genuine citizens of Heaven. Again, I urge all to begin by ensuring their passport is genuine.

Song

No more night No more pain No more tears never crying again
Praises to the great I am. We will live in the light of the risen Lamb.

Prayer: Lord, may I never lose my citizenship in your Heaven. Amen

JUNE 6

The Tears of Joseph

Bible Text: Genesis 43:27

Gen 43:27 And he asked them of their welfare, and said, Is your father well, the old man of whom ye spake? Is he yet alive? 28 And they answered, Thy servant our father is in good health, he is yet alive. And they bowed down their heads, and made obeisance. 29 And he lifted up his eyes, and saw his brother Benjamin, his mother's son, and said, Is this your younger brother, of whom ye spake unto me? And he said, God be gracious unto thee, my son. 30 And Joseph made haste; for his bowels did yearn upon his brother: and he sought where to weep; and he entered into his chamber, and wept there.

Why does Joseph weep? Was he ever tempted to deny his own brothers? Did he feel any need for revenge? We do not know but we do know these are normal human reactions. Joseph had nothing to gain it seemed from the tribe of Israel and could easily have pretended that he did not know them. But Joseph felt their pains. One can discern from the answers of his brothers that they were desperate, afraid and panicked. It was not clear what would happen to them. They did not even feel covered by the God they had betrayed in getting rid of their brother and lying to their father. God is able to make every dream He gives come true . . . no matter how unlikely or improbable. The brothers were crying inside and Joseph could feel their sorrow, their pains and fears. The fact that he had the power to restore their situation did not stop him feeling their anguish. Others in the palace did not cry because there was no connection to this untidy rabble in the Royal Palace.

Do also remember that Jesus was similarly overcome with sorrow and wept when called to the tomb of Lazarus . . . even though He knew He had power over death. Brothers feel for each other. When a brother in the body weeps, the other must also feel the hurt. We are indeed a family and the pains of Christians in North Korea or other denominations should touch us. The tears of Joseph were not selfish tears. We are not told even once that Joseph cried in the pit or during his trials. "Jesus wept" comes up only once at the tomb of Lazarus and nowhere else . . . no doubt the inner cries can be even deeper than the shedding of tears. Our God sees all our pains and feels all our struggles. As our brother, He is touched by all our weaknesses and is more anxious to see us restored than we can ever imagine.

It is not unlikely that at least one of the brothers of Joseph . . . maybe Benjamin was so frightened and that fear did not permit the tears of sorrow to rush down his cheeks. What can we learn? First Christ feels all the pains you go through and sees all the needless burdens we refuse to bring to Him and this causes Him more sorrow. The restoration of a brother is of importance as Christ feels for the brother in the pit of shame and confusion. Brethren - living in bondage does not make Christ happy . . . and he who works to lift the veil of sorrow and bitterness by extending help and the gospel is a rare gem. The gospel of Christ is good news . . . go and spread it. Do the work of wiping sorrow from the face of others. Christ will reward you well.

Song

Take my hands, and let them move
At the impulse of Thy love
Take my feet, and let them be
Swift and beautiful for Thee.

Prayer: Lord, be forever magnified in our worship. Let every living soul praise you for ever and ever. Amen.

JUNE 7

An Unusual Banquet

Bible Text: Genesis 43:31-33

Gen 43:31 And he washed his face, and went out, and refrained himself, and said, Set on bread. 32 And they set on for him by himself, and for them by themselves, and for the Egyptians, which did eat with him, by themselves: because the Egyptians might not eat bread with the Hebrews; for that is an abomination unto the Egyptians. 33 And they sat before him, the firstborn according to his birthright, and the youngest according to his youth: and the men marvelled one at another.

Joseph hosts an unusual banquet with arrangements made for three different sections. One setting for Joseph, another for his brothers and a third for the Egyptians. Meditate on this unusual arrangement and you will find some lessons on how we live in the present dispensation.

The children of Israel could not be accepted, yet their brother was lord over the Egyptians. In a similar fashion, Christians are considered abomination to many but Jesus is still Lord of all - whether they are His or not. Also in this text we see the pattern of no meeting point between darkness and light, and why our Lord urges us to be separate, distinct, sanctified . . . apart.

But there is again the separation between us and our Lord Jesus. Though we are His, our knowledge of Him can only be still in part until the appointed time. This should create a longing and a desire for us to want to know Him. Paul had this desire when he said in Philippians . . . *Php_3:10 That I may know him, and the power of his resurrection, and the fellowship of his sufferings, being made conformable unto his death;*

The brothers did not know it was Joseph their brother they had betrayed. They did not know what it means to suffer in prisons and pits for years. They did not know the power that can bring out of the pit. If they knew, their lives would have been transformed. When they eventually know their appreciation of God would completely change.

A good question to meditate on is to ask yourself. What knowledge are you seeking? Knowledge on earthy matters is very useful but is very different from seeking to knowing God. Understanding our traditions is very different from the fellowship of suffering which is to express love and communion with God and saints by voluntarily bearing painful inconveniences. To know the power of men and the great things men can do is also very different from understanding the power of God to raise back that which is dead, decomposed and has become dried up bones in a desolate valley. Ask God for revelation at a higher level. There is more to God than simply answering our prayers concerning our needs. God does the impossible, reverses the irreversible and is in a separate class to Himself in His wonders. Joseph sits in a separate class as well.

Song

I just want to be where you are - Dwelling daily in your presence
I don't want to worship from afar -Draw me near to where you are.

I just want to be where you are - In your dwelling place forever
Take me to the place where you are - Cause I just want to be with you.

Chorus: I want to be where you are - Dwelling in your presence,
Feasting at your table, Surrounded by your glory
In your presence, That's where I always want to be, I just want to be, I just want to be with you

Prayer: Lord, I do not want to remain apart from you. Take me higher to where you are. Amen

June 8

God of Order

Bible Text: Genesis 43:31-33

Gen 43:31 And he washed his face, and went out, and refrained himself, and said, Set on bread. 32 And they set on for him by himself, and for them by themselves, and for the Egyptians, which did eat with him, by themselves: because the Egyptians might not eat bread with the Hebrews; for that is an abomination unto the Egyptians. 33 And they sat before him, the firstborn according to his birthright, and the youngest according to his youth: and the men marvelled one at another.

God loves order. The Hebrew brethren are seated according to their seniority . . . the eldest according to His birthright and the youngest according to His youth. *1Co_14:40 Let all things be done decently and in order.*

There is a new love for informality that does not respect elders or order in worship. The brothers marveled at the order because this is a Hebrew tradition and must have wondered how Joseph knew of it. Decency and order which respects elders are good and important traditions. Decency can be lost in our comportment . . . order requires planning and diligence. All things are to be done decently . . . there are no exceptions. Consider every aspect of all that you do. Ask God to teach you His decency . . . this does not mean we are not to rejoice or dance ecstatically for our deliverance . . . but by His spirit we can still learn of decency and order and how to reflect this not just in Church but in all we do.

Song

All things bright and beautiful,
All creatures great and small,
All things wise and wonderful,
The Lord God made them all.
Each little flow'r that opens,
Each little bird that sings,
He made their glowing colors,
He made their tiny wings.

All things bright and beautiful, All creatures great and small,
All things wise and wonderful, The Lord God made them all.
All things bright and beautiful,
All creatures great and small,
All things wise and wonderful,
The Lord God made them all.
The purple-headed mountain,
The river running by,
The sunset, and the morning
That brightens up the sky.

All things bright and beautiful,
All creatures great and small,
All things wise and wonderful,
The Lord God made them all.
The cold wind in the winter,
The pleasant summer sun,
The ripe fruits in the garden,
He made them ev'ry one:

Prayer: Lord, teach me your order . . . let me learn of your decency. Amen

JUNE 9

God has Favorites

Bible Text: Genesis 43:33-34

Gen 43:33 And they sat before him, the firstborn according to his birthright, and the youngest according to his youth: and the men marvelled one at another. 34 And he took and sent messes unto them from before him: but Benjamin's mess was five times so much as any of theirs. And they drank, and were merry with him.

As we study the word of God, we discover more and more that God has favorites. Somehow we always find some characters in the Bible that seem to enjoy a different largesse and provision. The many that are called will often wonder at the few that are chosen. Benjamin is the least ... low in the hierarchy and seated farthest from the head of the table. The Jewish society did everything based on a hierarchy ... but God will often go to the low and sometimes the very least and raise as the head. The neglected can become the celebrated.

In this devotional, do not despair at how low you have had to descend and the position that has humbled you. It is only a set up by God to be able to raise you up in His blessings. He that is low is lifted. Jesus was brought down to be a man and even further to the depths of the grave only to be raised up over all of creation - in Heaven and on earth. The favorites of God have received help to be humble and lowly ... like the lowly Jesus Himself.

They drank and were merry with Benjamin. They were not jealous nor did they wonder that Benjamin had five times as much as they had. The old character of the brothers would have been envious ... God had transformed even the wicked brother's hearts. Do not despair or write brethren off - you may not know His own ... for He will remove the heart of stone from His own and replace with a heart of flesh and call them to go up higher ... and this after you have written them off.

Song

Jesus is calling - give Him your heart - Leave the past ways behind
He breaks the chains - soothes the pain - and says "Go up Higher"

Chorus
Friend ... Go up higher - Honor awaits you now
He that is low - is lifted up - So friend - Go up Higher and Higher
friend - Go up higher.

Worship the Lord - wait on His word - Please Him in all your ways
Give Him your all to hear Him call - you Friend "Go up Higher"

There is not a friend like the lowly Jesus   Not a friend like Him
Wonder of wonders - how can it be - That He died for me

He died but He rose - He conquered death
Now He lives enthroned - My Savior my King is coming again - to say "Friend Go up higher"

Prayer: Lord, I need more grace to humble myself and receive that brokenness - to be one of your favorites. Amen.

JUNE 10
The Steward of His House (Part 1)

Bible Text: Genesis 44:1

Gen 44:1 And he commanded the steward of his house, saying, Fill the men's sacks with food, as much as they can carry, and put every man's money in his sack's mouth.

There is a principle of Stewardship concerning the assets of God. Stewards execute the agenda of God for God the owner. This suggests that God is interested in things others overlook as insignificant or as the accountant would say "immaterial". He wants us to be faithful in a few things.

Luke 16[10] He who is faithful in what is least is faithful also in much; and he who is unjust in what is least is unjust also in much.

Someone who will divert $10 will if given the right opportunity steal $10 million. How we handle little amounts is very important to God and tells us what we will do in larger scenarios. We learn by starting with managing small units. God gives according to abilities. This implies He expects us to do only what He has uniquely enabled and gifted us to do and not everything. This suggests that the ways of focus and divine specialization lend to more Godliness and faithfulness rather than broad finger-in-every-pie approaches. Every steward has some competitive advantage to trade and which he must find and leverage for increase. Increase can be partly invested to enhance competitive strength—this is self-development. Competitive strength refers to what we can do better than someone else and this can be increased as we leverage technology, resources, skills and more research. Competitive strength can decay to nothing if not well applied or developed. Operating out of divinely given advantage is wastage as someone can and should be making better use of the resources in your hands in that area. This is well understood if not obvious in agrarian mindsets for the farmer will never plant seeds suited for temperate conditions in the tropics. Nor will the farmer embark on a large scale field until he has mastered the crop in a more manageable scale.

Before the oil boom in many developing countries, agriculture boomed and distinct competences developed. These competencies and skill advantages faded as oil wealth brought the prospect of accelerated prosperity in the cities where trading and supplies in a rich and corrupt environment were seen to be more lucrative. Skills and technology for oil production were imported and the nations remained poor. Nations like Brazil succeeded in the oil sector in impacting local wealth and value as opposed to other developing countries because they nurtured small local enterprise as suppliers to the industry who later grew to be sizable companies. They encouraged bio-fuels thus rewarding small local farmers specialized in farming the local terrain. In addition, they did not favor international oil giants and imported technology. Soon they had mastered local technologies suited to their own oil fields and began to export expertise. Success in mobilizing small local enterprise and nurturing them to grow only as they become better (not better connected) is God's path. This does not mean God is against growth and size - only that competitive and sustainable growth must be progressively earned and not suddenly blossom through clever dealing and opportunist positioning.

Song

Jehovah Jireh my provider . . . His grace is sufficient for me
The Lord will supply all my need . . . according to His riches in glory
He will give His angels charge over me . . . His grace is sufficient for me.

Prayer: Lord, Bless me . . . O Bless me indeed even as you help me to be your faithful steward. Amen

JUNE 11

The Steward of His House (Part 2)

Bible Text: Genesis 44:1

Gen 44:1 And he commanded the steward of his house, saying, Fill the men's sacks with food, as much as they can carry, and put every man's money in his sack's mouth.

We are given talents . . . opportunities and open doors in the same measure that we have the ability to do what is required with it. God does not give the same to all and we must not expect that God will bless someone else in the same measure as He blessed us. God may give us even more and may consider it prudent to give less. Actions and habits that repel God's power also diminish what we can get from His hidden riches. We can therefore increase wealth by expanding our abilities-connection to divine power or by trading existing talents for more. One value focuses on nearness to God and deep faith in the unseen while the other focuses on innovation, obedience, diligence and persistent hardworking of our gifts. Both must work together - otherwise faith without works will produce zealous error and poverty arising from lack of action. Works without spiritual depth or strength could result in a large bag with many holes and much sorrow.

Meanwhile the owner has said in; *Proverbs 10[22] The blessing of the LORD makes one rich, and He adds no sorrow with it.*

Note, the disciples did not store up wealth for the future but lived in communal love, making available to every man as they had need.

Acts 2[41] Then those who gladly received his word were baptized; and that day about three thousand souls were added to them. [42] And they continued steadfastly in the apostles' doctrine and fellowship, in the breaking of bread, and in prayers. [43] Then fear came upon every soul, and many wonders and signs were done through the apostles. [44] Now all who believed were together, and had all things in common, [45] and sold their possessions and goods, and divided them among all, as anyone had need.

The word "needs" is very different in its meaning from "desires and wants" . . . again this is another concept important for reconstruction of our mindset. As long as our desires and wants remain well programmed by consumption advertising and modern appetites and lusts, God will not send down strength for true communal love and giving as we saw in the first century. If He does it will only cause chaos as many are misled in their needs and there can be no agreement on the meaning of this word. Paul wrote the masterpieces of faith - most of the New Testament from either prison or severely limited circumstance—yet all his needs were met for his peculiar journey.

Reflect on the truth that God seeks Stewards who will do His will. Will He find us faithful?

Song.

Oh, what can little hands do
To please the King of heav'n Heaven?
The little hands some work may try,
To help the poor in misery:
Such grace to mine be giv'n.

Oh, what can little lips do
To please the King of heav'n Heaven?
The little lips can praise and pray,
And gentle words of kindness say:
Such grace to mine be giv'n.

Prayer: Lord, bless me . . . help me to be your steward. Amen.

JUNE 12

Lord, Expand our Coasts

Bible Text: Genesis 44:1

Gen 44:1 And he commanded the steward of his house, saying, Fill the men's sacks with food, as much as they can carry, and put every man's money in his sack's mouth.

God is unlimited but we are not. We are severely limited in terms of how much blessing, anointing, wealth and strength we can retain or manage. We can compare our capacity to a man going to the ocean with a large bucket - what can he possibly do to diminish the waters in the ocean. God understands our limitations and seeks the man who desires for an expansion in capacity to work for God. This man will be fulfilled no matter the scale of the depression inflicted on him. Consider Jabez.

I Chronicles 4[9] And Jabez was more honourable than his brethren: and his mother called his name Jabez, saying, Because I bare him with sorrow. [10] And Jabez called on the God of Israel, saying, Oh that thou wouldest bless me indeed, and enlarge my coast, and that thine hand might be with me, and that thou wouldest keep me from evil, that it may not grieve me! And God granted him that which he requested.

Jabez excelled though born in very depressive circumstances (details are not given of causes of a deep sorrow that typified his early days—it does not seem to matter) for it is said he was in spite of this—more honorable than his siblings. He did not need to seek expansion because he was already ahead in many ways, but Jabez was one to take risks to move forward. He did not thirst for blessings because he was in a rut . . . he simply wanted what God wanted for his life . . . knowing that God's desire is far more than we often imagine. Therein lies an important principle to shine out of depressive circumstances and that is to cultivate the habit of *going to God for more. Going to God for more* is neither pride nor disobedience. Rather it tells God who always has far more to give that we can ever be ready for, that we are set to be equipped for another *mission impossible.*

Jabez was not just asking for resources, but by seeking an enlargement of his coast, he was seeking God for expanded accountability. Seeking a greater and farther reach for impact and influence is not cheap . . . it will require more—emotionally, physically, financially . . . in all categories—and especially in our mind-set. Jabez wanted God's hand with him i.e. to be God's battle axe, acknowledging that evil was present all around him and especially in the places God's hand will move him, but God will keep him from evil. Many do not see evil as evil and rather justify it or downplay it. Finally, Jabez acknowledges that blessings can cause even more depression without God's help. God must grant our pleas.

Joseph asks that his brothers should have their sacks filled with as much as they could possibly carry and to return their money. Joseph a mortal King is so immensely able to bless his brothers well beyond what they prepared for. If they had brought larger sacks, they would have carried more. They brought only what their money could buy. Indeed, their money was a limiting factor. God has no use for what limits us, as He is unlimited by anything but by our capacity and faith. Begin to expand your thoughts and possibilities of doing much more for God than previously envisaged.

Song

The Lord's my Shepherd I'll not want - He makes me down to lie
In pastures green He leadeth me - the quiet waters by.

Prayer: Lord, Show me how to expand my coast for greater provisions that I may serve you at a higher level. Amen.

JUNE 13

Getting Ready to be Tested

Bible Text: Genesis 44:2-5

Gen 44:2 And put my cup, the silver cup, in the sack's mouth of the youngest, and his corn money. And he did according to the word that Joseph had spoken. 3 As soon as the morning was light, the men were sent away, they and their asses. 4 And when they were gone out of the city, and not yet far off, Joseph said unto his steward, Up, follow after the men; and when thou dost overtake them, say unto them, Wherefore have ye rewarded evil for good? 5 Is not this it in which my lord drinketh, and whereby indeed he divineth? ye have done evil in so doing.

It is one thing to know that you will be tested and it is another to get ready for that testing. The brothers were taken unawares by the test, but we need not be unprepared as they were. Every examination is based on a curriculum . . . and God's curriculum is the word of God—the Bible. We need to read it and know exactly what it says. Every examination also has a timetable for written and practical tests. God has appointed dates for our testing and he will prove our teachings first in our own lives . . . the songs we have sung will be tested . . . the revelation we claim to know will be tested. Many examinations tend to have surprise questions . . . even though we prepared well by studying model answers there will be questions we tend to be unfamiliar with and we wish were not asked. Model answers are discovered when we study the actors in the word of God, the teachings of Christ, the dealings of Prophets . . . and we understand what they went through and how they responded . . . and how Christ would have responded. When we see surprise questions that are unfamiliar and we do not know what to do, we are tested not on model answers but on what we have learnt so far . . . God is able to help us discover how far we have developed in an area and where we are still wanting. God will test our integrity . . . what we will do when no one sees us. God will test our patience and attitude to suffering . . . God will test our love for the unlovable . . . He will test faithfulness in a little . . . He will test our humility and how we correct our wrongs. Perhaps the most advanced of tests focuses on handling aggressive accusation—whether they be true or not. He will test if we want glory for self or if we can release issues to God. Our preparation in prayer and the reading and studying of the word is most helpful or we would be clueless to respond. Our readiness for the surprise unexpected test shows we have grown and God can trust even more difficult environments in our care. Jesus will test us to see if we will be ashamed of Him when things do not go as we expect . . . in times of disgrace and pain . . . will we still sing of His glory?

Song.

Jesus, and shall it ever be, A mortal man ashamed of Thee?
Ashamed of Thee, whom angels praise, Whose glories shine thro' endless days?

Ashamed of Jesus! sooner far - Let evening blush to own a star;
He sheds the beams of light divine O'er this benighted soul of mine.

Ashamed of Jesus! that dear Friend - On whom my hopes of heav'n depend!
No; when I blush, be this my shame, That I no more revere His name.

Ashamed of Jesus! yes, I may, When I've no guilt to wash away;
No tear to wipe, no good to crave, No fears to quell, no soul to save.

Prayer. Lord, Teach me to prepare and to await patiently to excel in all the tests you have set for me. Amen.

JUNE 14

Final Examinations

Bible Text: Genesis 44:2-5

Gen 44:2 And put my cup, the silver cup, in the sack's mouth of the youngest, and his corn money. And he did according to the word that Joseph had spoken. 3 As soon as the morning was light, the men were sent away, they and their asses. 4 And when they were gone out of the city, and not yet far off, Joseph said unto his steward, Up, follow after the men; and when thou dost overtake them, say unto them, Wherefore have ye rewarded evil for good? 5 Is not this it in which my lord drinketh, and whereby indeed he divineth? ye have done evil in so doing.

There are many tests that God administers and God has an array of angels, men and even controls demons and the devil himself - all to bring His purpose to pass. Scriptures teach us that God does not bring out what has not been tested to be His own. We see this pattern even in the life of His only begotten son . . . where the Bible tells us that Christ was led by God to be tested. One of the greatest test we face is to establish if we will be ruled by our faith in God and His word or by our feelings based on how we perceive evidence before us. What does the bible teach us to do when faced with accusations and inexplicable turmoil? Can we still praise him knowing His word says all things must work out for our good . . . All things . . . even if the evidence does not prove so.

David said I will wait on thy name . . . *Psa 52:9 I will praise thee for ever, because thou hast done it: and I will wait on thy name; for it is good before thy saints.*

The brothers are about to undergo a tough test. There are times that what we go through is not our fault but we need go through them for our own good. God knows the processes and tests that all will need for the next level of elevation. We cannot be in a postgraduate class when we have not passed O-levels . . . surely our answers to the lecturer would only cause him to wonder . . . how did we get there . . . could we have possibly passed the basic undergraduate courses. If we cheat to come up, we will only find ourselves bewildered in a situation we have not been tested and proven ready to handle.

Do not be bewildered . . . just trust and obey God. God will still come through, in spite of the many conspiracies. God knows best when He insists that we reap what we have sown . . . the brothers having majored in intrigue are now the victims. Be still and know that He is God.

Song.

Be still and know that I am God 3ce
In you O Lord I put my trust 3ce
You are the Lord that healeth me 3ce

Prayer: Lord, Help me to trust and obey you always and to be still to know your processes and pass your tests. Amen.

JUNE 15

Benjamin's Cross

Bible Text: Genesis 44:2

Gen 44:2 And put my cup, the silver cup, in the sack's mouth of the youngest, and his corn money. And he did according to the word that Joseph had spoken.

Benjamin is chosen as a favorite of Joseph. Suddenly that choice which led to extra supplies, five times more than the other brothers is becoming what looks like a nightmare. Have you ever faced a situation of accusation in which you must simply be speechless and expect a punishment you do not understand. Christ asked us to take up our cross and follow Him. This is not an option, but a command.

Salvation is free . . . but what is the cross. Indeed, there are basic truths of free salvation . . . but also higher truths of testing and burdens that we must bear. One of these burdens is that of restitution to prove repentance and appease what would have been the harvest of wrong past actions. Christ bore His cross of cruel accusation and indictment without a whimper but He saw a glory ahead. Benjamin and the other brothers did not see the glory ahead, and must have been afraid at this sudden turn of ill-luck.

The choice of Benjamin is not accidental. The choice of the cross is equally deliberate. But even in all the cross you carry, there is the master architect - God still in charge, and who loves us dearly giving us a grace that will be more than sufficient. "Take up your cross and follow Me" means being willing to die in order to follow Jesus. This is called "dying to self." It's a call to absolute surrender. Although the call is tough, the reward is matchless.

Wherever Jesus went, He drew crowds. Although these multitudes often followed Him as Messiah, their view of who the Messiah really was—and what He would do—was distorted. They thought the Christ would usher in the restored kingdom. They believed He would free them from the oppressive rule of their Roman occupiers. Even Christ's own inner circle of disciples thought the kingdom was coming soon (Luke 19:11). When Jesus began teaching that He was going to die at the hands of the Jewish leaders and their Gentile overlords (Luke 9:22), His popularity sank. Many of the shocked followers rejected Him. Truly, they were not able to put to death their own ideas, plans, and desires, and exchange them for His.

Following Jesus is easy when life runs smoothly; our true commitment to Him is revealed during trials. Jesus assured us that trials will come to His followers. Discipleship demands sacrifice, and Jesus never hid that cost. In Luke 9:57-62, three people seemed willing to follow Jesus. When Jesus questioned them further, their commitment was half-hearted at best. They failed to count the cost of following Him. None was willing to take up his cross and crucify upon it his own interests.

If you wonder if you are ready to take up your cross, consider these questions: Are you willing to follow Jesus if it means losing some of your closest friends? Are you willing to follow Jesus if it means alienation from your family? Are you willing to follow Jesus if it means the loss of your reputation? Are you willing to follow Jesus if it means losing your job? Are you willing to follow Jesus if it means losing your life?

Song.

Fear not when shadows on your pathway fall, look to the lamb of God
In joy or sorrow Christ is all in all, look to the Lamb of God

Prayer: Lord, Help me to be courageous and to look to the Lamb of God always. Amen.

JUNE 16

Godliness Eclipses Self Part I

Bible Text: Genesis 44:16-33

Gen 44:16 And Judah said, What shall we say unto my lord? what shall we speak? or how shall we clear ourselves? God hath found out the iniquity of thy servants: behold, we are my lord's servants, both we, and he also with whom the cup is found. 17 And he said, God forbid that I should do so: but the man in whose hand the cup is found, he shall be my servant; and as for you, get you up in peace unto your father. 18 Then Judah came near unto him, and said, Oh my lord, let thy servant, I pray thee, speak a word in my lord's ears, and let not thine anger burn against thy servant: for thou art even as Pharaoh. 19 My lord asked his servants, saying, Have ye a father, or a brother? 20 And we said unto my lord, We have a father, an old man, and a child of his old age, a little one; and his brother is dead, and he alone is left of his mother, and his father loveth him. 21 And thou saidst unto thy servants, Bring him down unto me, that I may set mine eyes upon him. 22 And we said unto my lord, The lad cannot leave his father: for if he should leave his father, his father would die. 23 And thou saidst unto thy servants, Except your youngest brother come down with you, ye shall see my face no more. 24 And it came to pass when we came up unto thy servant my father, we told him the words of my lord. 25 And our father said, Go again, and buy us a little food. 26 And we said, We cannot go down: if our youngest brother be with us, then will we go down: for we may not see the man's face, except our youngest brother be with us. 27 And thy servant my father said unto us, Ye know that my wife bare me two sons: 28 And the one went out from me, and I said, Surely he is torn in pieces; and I saw him not since: 29 And if ye take this also from me, and mischief befall him, ye shall bring down my gray hairs with sorrow to the grave. 30 Now therefore when I come to thy servant my father, and the lad be not with us; seeing that his life is bound up in the lad's life; 31 It shall come to pass, when he seeth that the lad is not with us, that he will die: and thy servants shall bring down the gray hairs of thy servant our father with sorrow to the grave. :32 For thy servant became surety for the lad unto my father, saying, If I bring him not unto thee, then I shall bear the blame to my father forever. 33 Now therefore, I pray thee, let thy servant abide instead of the lad a bondman to my lord; and let the lad go up with his brethren

Spend some time to reflect on this lengthy narration. The old Judah initiated the plan to sell off Joseph for his own selfish need to retain the love of a father and preserve his inheritance, or just an unresolved. This is the old man, the first man . . . Adam who disobeys God and ends up running from God, fallen. The old Judah is not just ungodly but has come under a satanic influence to murder his own blood and bring deep sorrow to an aging father.

Do not assume that time changes people for the better or that crisis births saints. More likely, it breeds even greater plots and opens doors to worse habits. The old Judah is wicked and disobedient. Benjamin could be so easily disposable as Joseph was. This was yet another opportunity for revenge on the children of Rachel so obviously preferred by their father. The old man is selfish, it seeks its own and puts God out of his thoughts. Every sin, be it lust, murder, lies or others is rooted on the desire to simply please self and disregard God. All sins. Selfishness is at the core of the hardened heart of stone. Not everyone changes for the better. Indeed, most are like King Saul, they only get worse until they are found in a cave with witches. But Judah had found grace with God . . . and the opportunity to prove the new heart he has received. Has God given you another chance to prove a new heart? Are you getting worse like King Saul or better?

Song.

Room for pleasure, Room for business - But for Christ the Crucified
Not a place that he can enter - In your heart for which He died

Prayer: Lord, Occupy all the rooms in me . . . Give me a heart of flesh - A new heart for you. Amen

JUNE 17

Godliness Eclipses Self Part II

Bible Text: Genesis 44:16-33

Gen 44:16 And Judah said, What shall we say unto my lord? what shall we speak? or how shall we clear ourselves? God hath found out the iniquity of thy servants: behold, we are my lord's servants, both we, and he also with whom the cup is found. 17 And he said, God forbid that I should do so: but the man in whose hand the cup is found, he shall be my servant; and as for you, get you up in peace unto your father. 18 Then Judah came near unto him, and said, Oh my lord, let thy servant, I pray thee, speak a word in my lord's ears, and let not thine anger burn against thy servant: for thou art even as Pharaoh. 19 My lord asked his servants, saying, Have ye a father, or a brother? 20 And we said unto my lord, We have a father, an old man, and a child of his old age, a little one; and his brother is dead, and he alone is left of his mother, and his father loveth him. 21 And thou saidst unto thy servants, Bring him down unto me, that I may set mine eyes upon him. 22 And we said unto my lord, The lad cannot leave his father: for if he should leave his father, his father would die. 23 And thou saidst unto thy servants, Except your youngest brother come down with you, ye shall see my face no more. 24 And it came to pass when we came up unto thy servant my father, we told him the words of my lord. 25 And our father said, Go again, and buy us a little food. 26 And we said, We cannot go down: if our youngest brother be with us, then will we go down: for we may not see the man's face, except our youngest brother be with us. 27 And thy servant my father said unto us, Ye know that my wife bare me two sons: 28 And the one went out from me, and I said, Surely he is torn in pieces; and I saw him not since: 29 And if ye take this also from me, and mischief befall him, ye shall bring down my gray hairs with sorrow to the grave. 30 Now therefore when I come to thy servant my father, and the lad be not with us; seeing that his life is bound up in the lad's life; 31 It shall come to pass, when he seeth that the lad is not with us, that he will die: and thy servants shall bring down the gray hairs of thy servant our father with sorrow to the grave. :32 For thy servant became surety for the lad unto my father, saying, If I bring him not unto thee, then I shall bear the blame to my father forever. 33 Now therefore, I pray thee, let thy servant abide instead of the lad a bondman to my lord; and let the lad go up with his brethren

Judah speaks of God. He has rediscovered God. He expresses the divine truth that this is the hand of God on them. If self is at the heart of all sin, then rediscovering and returning to God is at the heart of true repentance. The old Judah can kill to protect self . . . the new Judah, the second man, like the Lion of Judah, the King Christ offers His own life that his brother may be released. Judah no more thinks of himself as anything but a sacrifice that his father may not mourn the loss of Benjamin again.

Christ, the Lion of Judah came to establish the pattern of being the sacrifice for our sin. We are asked to be living sacrifices, crucified with Christ . . . our self, nailed to the cross. The Christian is a new person, the old has passed away. He has received the miracle of transformation, He is a changed man, bearing no resemblance to his old wild nature, having received grace, cleansing and the renewal of his mind to put God first, God always and God alone.

Have you received that salvation, that transformation. This is a supernatural change of character and not something that events can produce. The saints have been helped by God to be changed persons, having received a new heart and a renewed spirit. There are occasions when this new man will be tested and demonstrated to amazed angels watching to see that mankind has indeed received a transformation by the mercy and grace of God - to a restoration back to the image of God. Angels will be amazed at your transformation.

Song

Thine forever! Thou our guide, All our wants by thee supplied,
All our sins by Thee forgiven, Lead us, lord, from earth to Heaven.

Prayer: Lord, You created me to be in your image. Lord, let your restoration be complete. Amen

JUNE 18

The Mission of Christ

Bible Text: Genesis 44:34

Gen 44:34 For how shall I go up to my father, and the lad be not with me? lest peradventure I see the evil that shall come on my father.

The Lion of Judah was sent on an assignment to restore the chosen of God back to God. God wanted the family of many like Christ with Him in eternity. The Lion of Judah would go and pay the necessary prize, His very life. Consider the mission of Christ. It is a mission that can never fail. I am not encouraging your complacency but I want to assure you that there is enough power to restore you to what you were meant to be. The legal ground has also been fully perfected. The redemption can be fulfilled because the previous contract of bondage has been cancelled.

Can evil now befall God? God forbid. Is it possible that Christ will not be able to present you - pure and holy, blameless before His Father. The blood of Jesus cannot be in vain. It is a most excellent and precious blood indeed, that of the only begotten of the Father. There is no need for any other sacrifice . . . all that is needed is for the good news to be spread far and near. Salvation has come to mankind.

How can Christ go up to say "It is not yet finished" . . . or "there were some too tough and sinful to be restored" . . . Even concerning His disciples, except the one He called another's son - the child of perdition. After His death, in the first century of Christianity, a terrible persecution arose against the first leaders causing almost all of them to face very violent and horrible deaths and still found to be standing for Christ. If they made it, you will also do the same. Drop the weights and the sins that so easily beset you. Arise to be what God had designed you to be . . . one day to be presented to God - without speck or wrinkle.

If the grace of our Lord Jesus proved insufficient for you. it may only mean you never knew that grace in the first place. May none reading this devotional be identified as children of perdition.

Song.

Jesus, my heart's dear refuge, Jesus has died for me;
Firm on the Rock of Ages, Ever my trust shall be.
Here let me wait with patience, wait till the night is o'er;
Wait till I see the morning - Break on the golden shore.

Safe in the arms of Jesus - Safe on His gentle breast
There by His love o'er shaded - sweetly my soul shall rest.

Prayer: Lord, May the mission of the Lion of Judah never fail concerning my soul. Amen

JUNE 19

Giving Account of Service

Bible Text: Genesis 44:34

Gen 44:34 For how shall I go up to my father, and the lad be not with me? lest peradventure I see the evil that shall come on my father.

There is a sense of giving account of service that is getting lost to many. There is an accounting for all we say, all we do not say, what we have been asked to do or not do and how we discharge duties given to us. There is an account on if we succeeded based on the indicator of the one who sent us—God. Judah knows his work is a failure if he brings back sacks of food and great treasures from Egypt and Benjamin is absent. Unfortunately, many in ministry now accord emphasis to human indicators of success—size of our church, funds in the bank, how quickly we climbed the church career totem pole and our acceptance and popularity. These are good but not always God's measures and can actually lead to corruption. God may have set a target for you to watch over one soul in your 1000 man church and if that soul is lost to the enemy you have failed. God may have set a target to impact a small community by selfless giving and showing Christian love . . . and even if you did not receive any applause God can check if His targets were met.

We need a personal walk with God to know what God has asked us to do and how we are to do it. God gives instructions, gives us His goals and explains the methods we are to use. We fail if we deviate from any of these . . . and the end does NOT justify the means. Judah has a sense of accountability and fears to fail . . . his measure of failure is linked to Benjamin his brother. In similar fashion, I suspect God cares for people—especially those we do not care for . . . .much more than we think. He may be more interested in how you look after that widow than the size of your church. May God help us to truly know Him.

Song.

Rescue the perishing, care for the dying,
Snatch them in pity from sin and the grave;
Weep o'er the erring one, lift up the fallen,
Tell them of Jesus, the mighty to save.

Rescue the perishing, care for the dying;
Jesus is merciful, Jesus will save.

Tho' they are slighting Him, still He is waiting,
Waiting the penitent child to receive;
Plead with them earnestly, plead with them gently:
He will forgive if they only believe.

Down in the human heart, crushed by the tempter,
Feelings lie buried that grace can restore;
Touched by a loving heart, wakened by kindness,
Chords that were broken will vibrate once more.

Rescue the perishing, duty demands it;
Strength for thy labor the Lord will provide;
Back to the narrow way patiently win them;
Tell the poor wand'rer a Savior has died.

Prayer: Lord, May I not fail in my responsibility for the perishing. Amen

JUNE 20
The Final Cry

Bible Text: Genesis 45:1

Gen 45:1 Then Joseph could not refrain himself before all them that stood by him; and he cried, Cause every man to go out from me. And there stood no man with him, while Joseph made himself known unto his brethren. 2 And he wept aloud: and the Egyptians and the house of Pharaoh heard.

The Egyptians did not suspect that Joseph had any relationship with these tent dwellers and had no reaction for what was going on until they hear the loud cry of Joseph - who could no more restrain himself. This was no ordinary cry nor was it an expression of sorrow or loss. This cry was loud the Bible tells us and gets the attention of the house of Pharaoh.

This was a cry of victory. The victory of God over every plan of hell to destroy the destiny of men. Joseph could see that the father he missed was alive and well, the brother he missed was right in front of him, his other brothers had been transformed . . . and that God had used him to preserve the clan from death in the seven year famine. It was a cry of joy, to suddenly realize that the years of sacrifice and waiting on God was not in vain. It was a cry to announce that destiny has at last been fulfilled and dreams have come true. It was a cry that had never been heard before - that the salvation of God is real, complete and beyond the comprehension and manipulation of men. It was a loud cry to declare that Jehovah indeed reigns in all the affairs of men, and above every other god . . . including the gods of Egypt. It was a cry that wiped out every previous cry ushering a new era -an end to pain, toil and conflict.

But this sound also has a significance to Egypt . . . the Bible says in *Rev_8:13 And I beheld, and heard an angel flying through the midst of Heaven, saying with a loud voice, Woe, woe, woe, to the inhabiters of the earth by reason of the other voices of the trumpet of the three angels, which are yet to sound!*

For the unsaved, there will be an appointed day of loud sounds, trumpets and cries. But it will be a day of woe. A day of sudden realization that the Most High reigns forever and ever, and He rules over every other god including the gods of Egypt and their evil princes of lust, mammon and religious deception. A day that marks the beginning of an eternal damnation and wails of regret - the shrieks in hell fire. The unsaved will one day hear . . . the announcement of a woe that has come upon them. A final cry is coming with different implications for different people. May God have mercy on us when the trumpet sounds.

Song

Jesus cries out that "I am come . . . I am come with great love"
My heart in answer says come Lord - And bring salvation nigh

Will you be ready when the Lord shall come
Will you be ready when the Lord shall come
I will be ready I will be ready I will be ready when the Lord shall come 2ce

Prayer: Lord, May I be in the assembly that will rejoice forever at the final cry. Amen

JUNE 21

I am

Bible Text: Genesis 45:3

Gen 45:3 And Joseph said unto his brethren, I am Joseph; doth my father yet live? And his brethren could not answer him; for they were troubled at his presence.

Joseph tells his brethren . . . I am Joseph. God revealed himself to Moses who feared to begin his assignment as was commissioned . . .

Exo_3:14 And God said unto Moses, I AM THAT I AM: and he said, Thus shalt thou say unto the children of Israel, I AM hath sent me unto you.

Everything changed when Joseph revealed himself. Their understanding of God changed. Their understanding of themselves and their situations also changed. Their understanding of their mission in life . . . and in Egypt also changed. Their vision of life and their hopes for tomorrow also changed. The correct revelation of identity affects how we see ourselves and others. For the brothers . . . the revelation of Joseph as alive and a leader in Egypt proved to be a troubling shock.

God tells Moses to introduce Him as I AM—the everlasting, self-sufficient, self-existent, eternal, inexhaustible. He is the unchangeable, faithful and true God. Joseph declares that God has protected him, helped him, sustained him and eventually promoted him. Joseph declares that there is a supreme all-knowing ever powerful intelligence that watches over His purposes and causes His will to prosper. Joseph reveals in this troubling revelation that they cannot stop what God has purposed and men do not present any threat to the Most High God in the very least. At this stage in history, knowledge of God was somewhat limited . . . and the brothers of Joseph do not know how to answer . . . they oscillate between sheer disbelief and wonder . . . can it be true was the question on their mind. I pray God will reveal himself to you in a way that silences all opposition to simply bow and honor Him. Praise the great I AM.

Song

God of earth, God of sky: Lord, on Thee all things rely.
God of time, God of space: Father Thou of Adam's race;
Torn from Thee by Adam's fall, Lord, to Thee we raise the call:
"God of time, God of space, Meet with us in this place."

Spotless Lamb come for me, Reconcile my debt to Thee.
Sinful men, helpless, lost, With Thy life's blood paid the cost;
Take away our bent to sin: Wash our hearts and cleanse with in.
Lamb of God slain for me, Lamb of Life, hear my plea.

Bread of Life, Daily Bread, By Thy grace our souls are fed.
Broken once all to feed, Give us strength for ev'ry need.
Blest communion thro' the Son, All our hearts are knit as one:
Bread of Life, Dai ly Bread, To Thy feast we are led.

King of kings, Lord of lords—Heaven's anthems shout the chords.
Holy God, Angel Bright; Conqu'ror of the Hosts of Night.
Alleluia! Praise the Lamb! God of Ages, Great "I AM!"
Master, Lord, claim Thine own: Take my heart as Thy throne

Prayer: Lord, Be forever praised . . . The Great I AM. Amen

JUNE 22

The Troubles of The Redeemed

Bible Text: Genesis 45:3

Gen 45:3 And Joseph said unto his brethren, I am Joseph; doth my father yet live? And his brethren could not answer him; for they were troubled at his presence.

As soon as we know Christ as our Lord and Savior, we enter into His salvation, but we are also soon afflicted with troubles. We fight many doubts. Are we really delivered? Has Christ completely forgiven us? Will we make it to the end? What if we suddenly fall by the wayside? What if we are not His chosen? We sometimes have memories that haunt us? Even as we mature in our walk with the Lord, we can face situations that cause us to wonder if the Lord will turn against us. Are we his enemies knowing how we have hurt and disobeyed Him.

On hearing this strange revelation of Joseph, many questions immediately arose . . . many troubling questions? Will Joseph forgive us? How will their father take the whole story? Will there be revenge? Is this the beginning of sorrow? Indeed, there will be many questions requiring answers. Doubts to many doubts. Now Joseph controls the machinery of Egypt - will he use his power to punish them? Although it appears Joseph will spare them, the brothers remember all the tests - and wish they had performed better. The brothers will wish they had treated Joseph better. Those who wanted to say a word to defend Joseph but kept quiet will now regret.

Someone said once in eternity, all will wish they had loved Jesus more. All will wish they had served Him better. All will wish they had given more to Him, defended Him more. We will regret our lack of zeal and wish we had spent more of our wealth and time on evangelism and souls. We will all wish we had put in much more than we did into the service of the Kingdom of Heaven. We will be apprehensive when our works are burnt, how much will really remain. What will be left behind?

But in all these troubles, the presence of the Prince of Peace brings us an assurance that all is well. The Bible says when we see Him we shall be like Him. We have been changed, redeemed, sanctified, transformed to His likeness. We are no more slaves to sin . . . we are the bride dressed in a gown without spot or any wrinkle. The bible says the righteous are delivered from all their afflictions and troubles. This revelation was the most awesome event in the history of the family - yet it initially only caused troubling thoughts to attack the mind of his brothers. In conclusion, do not dwell on your feelings, do not dwell on your hunches, do not believe the evidence that contradicts the word of God. Simply continue to live by faith. Our feelings can run riot at times polluted with guilt and corrupted memories. Dwell instead on the word and promises of God - be firmly planted on the Rock of Ages. Soon you will hear the Master say "Peace be still" to all your troubles.

Song

Master, with anguish in spirit, I bow in my grief today;
The depths of my sad heart are troubled, O waken and save, I pray;
Torrents of sin and of anguish, Sweep o'er my sinking soul!
And I perish! I perish! dear Master; O hasten, and take control!

Master, the terror is over, The elements sweetly rest;
Earth's sun in the calm lake is mirrored, And Heaven's within my breast.
Linger, O blessed Redeemer, Leave me alone no more;
And with joy I shall make the blest harbor, And rest on the blissful shore.

Prayer: Lord, Speak your peace to all my troubles. Amen

JUNE 23

What to do when troubled.

Bible Text: Genesis 45:4

Gen 45:4 And Joseph said unto his brethren, Come near to me, I pray you. And they came near. And he said, I am Joseph your brother, whom ye sold into Egypt.

What do you do when you sense troubles in your spirit. When you feel overwhelmed and suddenly out of words … when you do not know what to do? The answer is to come nearer to Jesus. Coming nearer to Jesus could imply many things … separation from other and previous centers of focus. It could be taking time off to be alone with God or just being silent before Him or worshipping and resting in His presence. This does not seem to appease the trouble but it will allow comfort from the wells of God's presence bringing a relief we cannot explain.

When we come near to Jesus, we discover a love, grace and forgiveness that disarms us. Soon we wonder why we need be troubled in the presence of such power and might that offers a hand of friendship. We discover that the king of all Kings is also our brother and our friend. As we get closer and sense the dwellings under His mighty shadow, our troubles begin to vanish, and our fears begin to fade. But God must draw us close to Him … He invites us and awaits our response … to end our troubles and find the rest that we need. He also corrects us, chastens us and His sayings will be hard … but we can sense that this is the truth that sets free.

Song

Draw me close to You
Never let me go
I lay it all down again
To hear You say that I'm Your friend

You are my desire
No one else will do
'Cause nothing else could take Your place
To feel the warmth of Your embrace
Help me find the way
Bring me back to You

You're all I want
You're all I've ever needed
You're all I want
Help me know You are near

Prayer: Lord, draw me closer to you and calm my troubled heart. Amen

JUNE 24

Come Near to Jesus

Bible Text: Genesis 45:4

Gen 45:4 And Joseph said unto his brethren, Come near to me, I pray you. And they came near. And he said, I am Joseph your brother, whom ye sold into Egypt.

Jesus once told the disciples when He rose from the dead that it is He that they crucified. Doubting Thomas needed to touch His hands and feel the nail prints, the wounds that were still visible on His body. Jesus wants us to come nearer to Him to discover that indeed He has died for our sins and is calling us to be cleansed by the blood that He shed at Calvary. We must come up higher to He that dwells on high. As we come higher to Him, we drop the weights of fear, doubt, sin and foolishness. As we come nearer we see Christ has been glorified. He is not bitter or vengeful about His crucifixion, but more concerned that His work be not in vain. He does not want us in pain, fear or sin again. He is sad when we enter into bondages He has already paid for.

Joseph has similar feelings towards his brothers and wants them to see that God only used the situation to cause Him to protect and raise them up to join him albeit in a time of famine. Joseph wants them to come close to examine him well . . . indeed there are marks that only brethren can identify. Joseph reminds them that it was their wicked actions God used to bring Him to this exalted place.

When we come near to Jesus, we feel His compassion, His love, His forgiveness . . . we hear Him, we begin to know Him and love Him. When we come near to Jesus, darkness flees from our heart as darkness cannot come close to Jesus. We come near to Jesus by meditating more on the word of God as He is the word made flesh. We understand and have a deeper revelation of the fellowship of His suffering and the power of His resurrection. We are crucified with Him - therefore we no longer live, Christ lives in us. Christ becomes everything . . . our all in all. Lord draw me nearer to you today.

Song

I am Thine, O Lord, I have heard Thy voice, And it told Thy love to me;
But I long to rise in the arms of faith And be closer drawn to Thee.

Draw me nearer, nearer blessèd Lord, To the cross where Thou hast died.
Draw me nearer, nearer, nearer blessèd Lord, To Thy precious, bleeding side.

Consecrate me now to Thy service, Lord, By the power of grace divine;
Let my soul look up with a steadfast hope, And my will be lost in Thine.

O the pure delight of a single hour That before Thy throne I spend,
When I kneel in prayer, and with Thee, my God I commune as friend with friend!

There are depths of love that I cannot know Till I cross the narrow sea;
There are heights of joy that I may not reach - Till I rest in peace with Thee.

Prayer: Lord, Draw me nearer to you never to be apart from you, again. Amen

JUNE 25

Be not Grieved nor Angry.

Bible Text: Genesis 45:5

Gen 45:5 Now therefore be not grieved, nor angry with yourselves, that ye sold me hither: for God did send me before you to preserve life.

What great words of comfort. Do not be sad, angry or troubled. many are angry with God and with themselves at how their lives had turned out. Was it really their fault that they had to fight forces that overcame them even from early years ... where was Jesus when temptations seem to rage and lead them into wickedness ... Why did we have to suffer so much losses? There are so many things that cause us much sorrowing, grief, anger and confusion. We have been overcome by bondage, sin and the terror of darkness. Jesus does not condemn anyone. His words to His own are comforting. I died and suffered for those things you did wrong - your sins - so that you will one day come higher to me. God already sent Jesus ahead to preserve our lives in a wicked world already sold to sin and destruction.

Joseph does not condemn his brothers. He reminds them instead that God has already gone ahead to preserve their lives. Judah's family must be preserved for the coming Savior - the Lion of Judah - Jesus was to be born through the lineage of Judah. Joseph must be raised up for God's divine purpose to prosper.

The Bible says all things work together for the good of the righteous, the chosen that love God. All things and not some. Even the things that should make you angry are working for your good. The things that should make you grieve in sorrow are working for your good. Your mistakes are also working for your good - bad as they are. Do not try and apportion blame to any and be angry with your pastor or leader or wife or whoever it seems is at fault . . . . are we not all faulty in one way. Instead simply thank God that He is working His great work through your life even though you do not yet see all the pieces falling as you expect.

Joseph says all the brothers did to him was simply be an instrument of God. This is rather deep. Joseph says God sent him ... when did God call Joseph? I do not recall any commissioning. But in all the cruel dealings and submission to the ill treatment and accusations and imprisonment and being forgotten, Joseph was being sent ahead to preserve life. There is a purpose to the victory ahead ... to serve the purpose of God. God has apprehended your life for a reason. Soon it will be clear to you. Be not grieved nor angry.

Song

Art thou weary, art thou languid, Art thou sore distressed? "Come to Me," saith One, "and coming, Be at rest."
Hath He marks to lead me to Him, If He be my Guide? In His feet and hands are wound prints - And His side.
Hath He diadem, as monarch, That His brow adorns? Yes, a crown in very surety, But of thorns.
If I find Him, if I follow, What His guerdon here? Many a sorrow, many a labor, Many a tear.
If I still hold closely to Him, What hath He at last? Sorrow vanquished, labor ended, Jordan passed.
If I ask Him to receive me, Will He say me nay? Not till earth and not till Heaven Pass away.
Finding, following, keeping, struggling, Is He sure to bless? Saints, apostles, prophets, martyrs, Answer, Yes!

Prayer: Lord, Be glorified in my thoughts ... put an end to grief and anger. Amen

JUNE 26

God Preserves Life.

Bible Text: Genesis 45:5

Gen 45:5 Now therefore be not grieved, nor angry with yourselves, that ye sold me hither: for God did send me before you to preserve life.

There are many things God has done just to preserve your life. We do not appreciate them many of these things or we see them as against us, but God knows how to ensure we live to declare His glory and purpose. He has ways to preserve our destiny that He must hide from even our perceptions. He knows that often we can be our own worst enemy. In the story of Joseph, God uses accusation, hatred, delays, pain, forced separation, imprisonment, temptation, abandonment and the foolishness of speaking of our dreams too early to ensure that the tribe of Israel is preserved. He may use different ways but He is faithful. God is sovereign and we should not fight tough circumstances because we do not know if he is using these very circumstances to progress our destiny in a way we can never imagine. God may be using a delay or He may be using an accusation or He may be using a cruel rejection. I observe that God must use even our inclinations to promote His agenda. The brothers were sure they were in control and all their hatred and plots only served God well. This is a mystery and points us to remember God's sovereignty in all issues … knowing He preserves His own using ways and methods we cannot predict, stop or even discern at times. In the end the great and mighty God must have His way—and His expected end is a noble one. Glory be to God.

Song

Glory be to God the Father,
Glory be to God the Son,
Glory be to God the Spirit—
Great Jehovah, Three in One!
Hallelujah! Hallelujah!
While eternal ages run!

Glory be to Him who loved us,
Washed us from each spot and stain!
Glory be to Him who bought us,
Made us kings with Him to reign!
Hallelujah! Hallelujah!
To the Lamb that once was slain!

Glory to the King of angels,
Glory to the Church's King,
Glory to the King of nations!
Heaven and earth, your praises bring;
Hallelujah! Hallelujah!
To the King of Glory bring!

"Glory, blessing, praise eternal!"
Thus the choir of angels sings;
"Honor, riches, power, dominion!"
Thus its praise creation brings.
Hallelujah! Hallelujah!
Glory to the King of kings.

Prayer: Lord, All the glory, all the honor and power belongs to you forever. Be magnified in our lives. Amen

JUNE 27

A Great Deliverance

Bible Text: Genesis 45:6-7

Gen 45:6 For these two years hath the famine been in the land: and yet there are five years, in the which there shall neither be earing nor harvest. 7 And God sent me before you to preserve you a posterity in the earth, and to save your lives by a great deliverance.

Joseph explains that his brothers only facilitated a great deliverance. The brothers did not know that the famine was to last five more years, and without Joseph they would all have died of hunger. What lessons emerge from his text in today's devotional? Let us meditate on only three.

1. Life and death is in the hands of God. Indeed many would have perished during this seven year famine. The years of plenty and harvest were all decreed and controlled by God.

2. God will preserve His own - one way or another. None that ever puts His trust in Him will ever regret or suffer a lack of divine provision.

3. A great deliverance counters a great famine - both ordained of God. There is no problem too vast for which a matching deliverance has not already been put in place ahead. The Almighty does not work in time. He can start the work of deliverance decades ahead of any sign of trouble.

Why is this called a great deliverance? It is great in its concealment . . . no one could ever discover this deliverance. It is great in its magnitude. God translates a tribe of hungry wandering tent dwellers who were an abomination to Egypt into people who bask in the best of royal provisions and stores/barns of a wealthy civilization that abhorred their very existence. It is great in its authorship. It was all the work of a great and mighty God. We need to appreciate the great deliverances of the Almighty to see how puny our thinking can be. How can we ever do anything but worship a God that can begin a work of protection over ten years before we even perceive the need for deliverance. God is truly awesome - even Joseph does not know the plan until he sees his brothers in need of provisions at a time of great death. Jehovah is not an ordinary deliverer. He is a great deliverer - an awesome deliverer.

Now compare your challenges of today to what God did in this text and observe that your issues are elementary, way too easy for God to deal with and bring the required restoration. He can store the food, supplies in hidden places waiting for you. Israel and his clan did not labor a single day for the provisions they enjoyed . . . provisions Egypt gathered and stored for seven years. Perhaps you only need to wait a few more years for what you will enjoy to be fully stored up by those that cannot even stand your presence. God is awesome.

Song

My God is awesome, He can move the mountains,
Keep me in the valley, hide me from the rain,
My God is awesome, heals me when I'm broken,
Strength where I've been weakened
Forever He will reign

My God is awesome, Savior of the whole world,
Giver of salvation, by His stripes I am healed
My God is awesome, today I'm forgiven
His grace is why I'm living
Praise His Holy Name.

Prayer: Great Deliverer - Be my strength, my shield and my helper. Amen

JUNE 28

Let God make You.

Bible Text: Genesis 45:8

Gen 45:8 So now it was not you that sent me hither, but God: and he hath made me a father to Pharaoh, and lord of all his house, and a ruler throughout all the land of Egypt.

Joseph was not self-made but made my God. We can make ourselves into many things but still far from what God can make us. God made Joseph a father to Pharaoh . . . meaning he was head over Pharaoh's family, lord of the house of Pharaoh . . . meaning He controlled all the wealth and resources, nothing could be spent without his permission and Joseph was also ruler - prime minister of Egypt. He was in charge. Do you see that Joseph could not in his wildest dreams have made himself more than a senior servant in the house of Potiphar - with the help of Potiphar's wife . . . and even with the help of everyone he ever met . . . perhaps they could have made him captain over the prisons. But compare this to what God made Him.

The Bible says we have been wonderfully made to be Kings and priests . . . a royal priesthood, a holy nation . . . a peculiar nation, called out of darkness to a marvelous light. Our Lord the King of kings, our High Priest. But what have we made ourselves? Professors, engineers, farmers, business men etc. God is not against professions but are we functioning in what God has made us or making ourselves into something else.

The enemy of our true destiny loves to see us grovel below what we are meant to be. He loves it when we do not understand what God has promised to make us and all the compromises that eventually leaves us short of the glory we should have had. If only we knew what disobedience and careless wandering is really costing us, we would never stray a moment from our prime calling. We are not arrows shooting blindly but well targeted to achieve a glorious purpose. In reality, the one who is most powerful to tamper with our destiny is us. When we play with Potiphar's wife or slide into bitter murmurings in the prison cell . . . we unknowingly truncate our destiny. Sin is a destiny stealer. Yet God is merciful to raise Joseph against all odds to rule over the vast empire of Egypt. What has God planned to make you? What are you planning to make yourself? Be amazed at the wide gulf as you compare both. Lean on God.

Song

He is able more than able to accomplish what concerns me today
He is able more than able to handle everything that comes my way
He is able more than able to do much more than I could ever dream
He is able more than able to make me what He wants me to be . . .

Prayer: All Powerful God - Make me as you had ordained before the foundations of the earth. Amen

JUNE 29

Secrets of Wealth

Bible Text: Genesis 45:9-11

Gen 45:9 Haste ye, and go up to my father, and say unto him, Thus saith thy son Joseph, God hath made me lord of all Egypt: come down unto me, tarry not: 10 And thou shalt dwell in the land of Goshen, and thou shalt be near unto me, thou, and thy children, and thy children's children, and thy flocks, and thy herds, and all that thou hast: 11 And there will I nourish thee; for yet there are five years of famine; lest thou, and thy household, and all that thou hast, come to poverty.

Is God concerned about things like our wealth and supplying our needs? Indeed He must be. This Bible text shows He cares that we do not fall into poverty. There are some principles worth considering from this passage.

1. Those who will prosper are diligent. Men who can make haste to obey God and do things quickly. The slothful and procrastinator will find wealth elusive. Make haste to do as God has revealed to you.

   1Sa_21:8 And David said unto Ahimelech, And is there not here under thine hand spear or sword? for I have neither brought my sword nor my weapons with me, because the king's business required haste.

2. Those who will remain close to God. Living a life of close fellowship with the Holy God can open doors. God is far from the proud and cannot behold sin . . . Be watchful especially of pride.

3. Depending fully on God for nourishment as He knows where the green pastures are. To depend on God is not an elementary issue. We have been programmed from birth to be self-made and at best use God to fill in the gaps. Many who claim to depend and have given testimonies of provision actually have not given the full picture. When you are able to give out your last meal uncertain of where the next will come from, it is more indicative that your eyes are on God. When you say no to what men can do for you - then see God say yes.

   3Jn_1:2 Beloved, I wish above all things that thou mayest prosper and be in health, even as thy soul prospereth

God emphasizes the prosperity of the soul first. Salvation, sanctification and assurance of a future glorification counts far more as foundational matters for which material wealth can be laid. But for the one who is fully set apart to obey God, the God who says the silver and the gold belongs to Him and watches all the resources mismanaged by Pharaohs and Barons. What do you think will be His greatest wish? God will not want His name embarrassed as will happen if He gives wealth to those who eventually bring His name to disrepute . . . for Him these are worse than outright devils. But when God finds a David or a Nehemiah or someone dedicated to the finer points of hearing God, God must then rush resources as this wealth will be properly utilized and not consumed on lusts. Indeed, these are a rare breed even in the Church. I perceive that is why God is more anxious to make the obedient wealthy as He wants to be magnified and there is purpose to wealth - to establish His covenant. It is an anomaly that God's wealth is in the hands of the wicked. Discover and apply His principles.

Song

Take my silver and my gold;
Not a mite would I withhold;
Take my intellect, and use
Every power as Thou shalt choose,

Prayer: Lord, I need my soul to prosper first. Help me to be fully set apart for you. Amen.

JUNE 30

Goshen

Bible Text: Genesis 45:9-11

Gen 45:9 Haste ye, and go up to my father, and say unto him, Thus saith thy son Joseph, God hath made me lord of all Egypt: come down unto me, tarry not: 10 And thou shalt dwell in the land of Goshen, and thou shalt be near unto me, thou, and thy children, and thy children's children, and thy flocks, and thy herds, and all that thou hast: 11 And there will I nourish thee; for yet there are five years of famine; lest thou, and thy household, and all that thou hast, come to poverty.

Location is important to God. Are you properly located. How and if you survive difficult will greatly depend on your location. Are you in the Goshen that God has made for you. Remember Naomi who left Bethlehem in the famine and went to the land of Moab. This was the wrong move and the wrong location. It only brought death. But relocating can be positive if it is a Goshen we find but Moab can resemble Goshen. Still we need to know that location matters. There is a place of divine nourishment and there is a place of death. Check with God. Goshen is a place where you are near to God as well as your household to be nourished spiritually and physically by Him.

A few more words on Moab. It is a location of self-will. A place of alluring pleasures and excess. May God open our eyes to relocate before we are devoured—if in Moab . . . and to seek fresh insight from Him to discover our Goshen. Goshen is the place of grace . . . the price and cost has been fully settled at Calvary.

Song

Far dearer than all that the world can impart
Was the message came to my heart.
How that Jesus alone for my sin did atone,
And Calvary covers it all.

Calvary covers it all, My past with its sin and stain;
My guilt and despair Jesus took on Him there,
And Calvary covers it all.

The stripes that He bore and the thorns that He wore
Told His mercy and lover evermore
And my heart bowed in shame as I called on His name,
And Calvary covers it all.

How matchless the grace, when I looked in the face
Of this Jesus, my crucified Lord;
My redemption complete I then found at His feet,
And Calvary covers it all.

How blessed the thought, that my soul by Him bought,
Shall be His in the glory on high;
Where with gladness and song, I'll be one of the throng
And Calvary covers it all.

And Calvary covers it all

Prayer: Lord, lead me to the locations covered by Calvary . . . my Goshen. The place of nourishments that you paid for. Amen.

JULY 1

The Mouth of Joseph

Bible Text: Genesis 45:12-13

Gen 45:12 And, behold, your eyes see, and the eyes of my brother Benjamin, that it is my mouth that speaketh unto you. 13 And ye shall tell my father of all my glory in Egypt, and of all that ye have seen; and ye shall haste and bring down my father hither.

O tongue . . . this potent instrument for good or evil. A destroyer and yet a builder - the driver of many woes and the builder of many lives. There are times when our mouth should just be shut so that there will be future opportunities for glorious words. May our mouths be transformed and our manner of speaking be delivered.

Many say they have been saved but their mouth is filled with guile. Others cannot control the gates of their lips and speak too soon when they should be silent. It is not every sermon that should be preached, nor is it every observation that must be voiced. Why does Joseph ask that they see that it is Joseph that speaks. His words are now seasoned with grace and wisdom. All Joseph says is what God has asked him to say and not what he feels or discerns or observes. The mouth of Joseph was not always harmless . . . it was a mouth that brought evil reports of his brothers. Indeed, the greatest seed are our words . . . and Joseph reaped what he sowed. His mouth spoke too soon of his dreams . . . we are not told God told him to speak of his dreams to his brethren or indeed to any. . . . but as he went through the pit, prison and eventually palace - his mouth had been completely transformed for the better. It was God that did it as prison and tragic experiences can even cause the bitterness of sorrow to cause worse utterances.

The Joseph that speaks does not speak to promote guilt or avenge ills. The mouth that speaks is simple, plain, honest, kind and does not repeat the evil things afflicted on Him. This mouth seeks not to satisfy his thirst for vengeance but to promote the welfare of brothers that despised him, his father and Benjamin. His words are full of assurance that all is now well. This mouth has forgotten all the past false accusations and the hell of being hated with a passion. A transformed mouth is a transformed life. Joseph speaks with grace and tells his brothers to go and report their father that the Joseph that was termed foolish has changed . . . He is now filled with a divine and kind wisdom, and his words are different. He now dwells in a high glory but remains so humble . . . all he clamors for is to see the father he loves dearly.

We must be patient with God to change what must change in our lives. His greatest works are not material provisions but healings of our character flaws . . . The brothers have also changed, by the grace of God. They can receive the brother they once hated and embrace him. You will change as well.

Song

Take my voice, and let me sing
Always, only, for my King;
Take my lips, and let them be
Filled with messages from Thee,

Prayer: Lord, May my lips be always and only filled with messages from you. Amen.

JULY 2

Moreover . . . a Higher Love.

Bible Text: Genesis 45:14-15

Gen 45:14 And he fell upon his brother Benjamin's neck, and wept; and Benjamin wept upon his neck. 15 Moreover he kissed all his brethren, and wept upon them: and after that his brethren talked with him.

Someone said once that true love for others will often manifest itself in tears. There is a fake love that merely seeks its own but wears a mask of compassion for others. But we cannot fake tears when we are in the midst of brethren we truly love. There is love that wants to be proven as superior or better than others . . . and there is the higher love. What is a higher love?

It is good to fall upon Benjamin and smother him with kisses and to cry . . . weeping upon his neck. But it is more difficult to even look at the eyes of his brothers who filled all his early life with pains. The Bible says "Moreover . . ." as if to draw our attention to something unusual. Joseph embraced his brothers, kissed them and wept upon them. Amazing by any standards the world has seen.

True Christians will amaze the world not by their songs and words or by their great deeds, but by the love they have - especially for those they cannot ordinarily stand or be with. Especially for those who had hurt them and targeted evil at them. But, today - is the altar of God not an the oven for great hatreds and long standing grudges? We cannot be open to brethren or expose our vulnerabilities to others - for we fear betrayal. Yet Christ said love your enemies. Do good to them that hurt you. When a man demands your shirt, give your coat as well. Perhaps that is easy. But to fall on your brethren that has hurt you in a deep love that expresses itself in tears is so deep and so high. No other testimony on earth so deeply matches this.

It was after this expression of a higher and shocking demonstration of love that the brothers of Joseph open up completely to Joseph seeing that they are safe. What a lesson. Meditate on this expression of love and consider the great evidence it confers on the recipient. It is the power of the gospel, helped by a practical demonstration of a high love that brings souls to restoration. How can we say we love God when we are cold to our brethren? Meditate on this. Christ did not just weep but He endured a horrible and painful death for love. It is this love that causes us to go to the mission field to serve God in extremely hostile territories . . . sowing in tears. Great revivalists - Evan Roberts, Jonathan Edwards and George Whitfield - were all great reapers in public because they were all great weepers in private. Joseph was a great weeper.

Do note as well - Joseph did not weep or fall on Egyptians. Be watchful in love . . . Joseph remained aloof to the Egyptian elite - separated.

Song

There is love within Thy store house,
But Thy people are so dry.
There's compassion in Thy storehouse
Then, my Savior, why, oh, why
Are Thy people stony-hearted
And our eyes so desert dry?

Prayer: Lord, May my eyes not be dry for souls and my brethren destined to be one with Christ. Amen

JULY 3

The Fame of the Gospel.

Bible Text: Genesis 45:16

Gen 45:16 And the fame thereof was heard in Pharaoh's house, saying, Joseph's brethren are come: and it pleased Pharaoh well, and his servants.

The Gospel is a beautiful story, but it is more than story. It is the power of God to save and transform lives. The story of Joseph was spread all over Egypt. This gladdened the hearts of the Egyptians. The gospel has the power even to gladden the soul of the heathen who continue to serve their own God. Society will change and rejoice if the gospel is preached. Governments will hear and rejoice when the gospel is preached. Far and near all who hear the word of God will be touched that this is truth. But who will come to God?

Not all who hear come . . . many are glad, and even pleased with the truths of God. Did you read that Herod was a disciple of John and loved to hear him. The governor Felix heard as Paul preached for years but said . . . at a convenient time, I will call for thee. Many have itching ears like the Greeks and fascinated with the romance and suspense or perhaps the morality and wisdom. The fame of the gospel is very different from revival when people come to God.

Do not mistake pleasure of men to hear the truth - with a decision to abandon sin and a commitment to serve the Almighty who will not share His throne with another. I have met so many who love truth, are pleased with the gospel and will even preach it - they gather always to hear God's word . . . but they retain the wickedness in their heart. Lord, may the Holy Spirit draw us . . . for the Bible says none can come except they are drawn by the Holy Spirit but we also cannot we put the Holy Spirit in our box. He calls unlettered fishermen like Peter as well as scholars like Paul. He calls dubious men like Zaccheaus and tax collectors like Matthew but called Judas to perdition and Herod was never convicted. Indeed, there is no heart that can withstand the call that brought Paul to his knees on the road to Damascus without any preacher.

Do not confuse the fame of the Gospel for the revival. They are related but not always the same. In Revival the evidence of the Holy Spirit is manifest in the fruits that are tough to fake.

Song

When I survey the wondrous cross
On which the Prince of Glory died
My richest gain I count but loss
And pour contempt on all my pride

Forbid it Lord, that I should boast
Save in the death of Christ
All the vain things that charm me most
I sacrifice them to His blood

If the whole realm of nature were mine
It were an offering far too small
Love so amazing so divine
Demands my soul my life my all

Prayer: Lord, Let the Revival begin with me . . . your words have pleased me . . . let it revive me. Amen

JULY 4

The Invitation of Egypt.

Bible Text: Genesis 45:17-20

Gen 45:17 And Pharaoh said unto Joseph, Say unto thy brethren, This do ye; lade your beasts, and go, get you unto the land of Canaan; 18 And take your father and your households, and come unto me: and I will give you the good of the land of Egypt, and ye shall eat the fat of the land. 19 Now thou art commanded, this do ye; take you wagons out of the land of Egypt for your little ones, and for your wives, and bring your father, and come. 20 Also regard not your stuff; for the good of all the land of Egypt is yours.

It is Pharaoh that invites the family of Joseph to be preserved by all the good of the land. It is the will of God for the children to be preserved, but this is meant to be for a period after which they would move on. We often miss out the details when we are victorious and gloss over the important elements. God preserved Israel for Himself and not for Israel. Israel was a chosen special race with eternal significance. Egypt was preselected as a ransom for Israel's redemption.

Pharaoh no doubt had his reasons for inviting the family of Joseph. Who were these strange people with such a powerful God? Could this God be harnessed for the greatness of Egypt? Imagine what it would be like if such an intelligent civilization were slaves in Egypt? They will be fed with cucumbers and delicacies and ecstasies that will be impossible for them to abandon and leave . . . then they will be enslaved. We can only guess at the real reasons behind the generosity for Pharaoh but we also know it was the plan of God that this should be so, but the higher plans of God remained intact.

Gifts, fatness and prosperity can be more dangerous than the snakes in the wilderness. Invitations to prosper are good but consider the end of most situations like this. As soon as the prospered taste Egypt, they are hooked to the sweet baits . . . and soon caught in nets of bondage. We love good endings so much that we forget altars and truths that must be preserved so generations after us will be preserved.

The devils of the Nile are left with no option as they need to be preserved by the wisdom that has proved superior to all the magicians of Egypt. But they remain alert still driven by an age old hatred for Israel's God. They are patient and need a plan that must span generations. This devotional alerts you to be cautious with wealth and open invitations to prosperity that do not require a consecration to God as it may indeed be well with the present generation. But a generation will still come that does not know and has forgotten his contributions. Have you received an invitation that glorifies God from Egypt? Accept it but take heed for the future. Remember your God . . . ensure the fire on the altar of God in your heart is kept burning.

Song

I'd rather have Jesus than silver or gold; I'd rather be His than have riches untold;
I'd rather have Jesus than houses or lands; I'd rather be led by His nail-pierced hand

Refrain:
Than to be the king of a vast domain - And be held in sin's dread sway;
I'd rather have Jesus than anything - This world affords today.

I'd rather have Jesus than men's applause; I'd rather be faithful to His dear cause;
I'd rather have Jesus than worldwide fame; I'd rather be true to His holy name

Prayer: Lord, Let the invitation of Egypt not ruin me. Help me to be ever faithful to your dear cause. Amen

JULY 5

The Good of The Land

Bible Text: Genesis 45:17-20

Gen 45:17 And Pharaoh said unto Joseph, Say unto thy brethren, This do ye; lade your beasts, and go, get you unto the land of Canaan; 18 And take your father and your households, and come unto me: and I will give you the good of the land of Egypt, and ye shall eat the fat of the land. 19 Now thou art commanded, this do ye; take you wagons out of the land of Egypt for your little ones, and for your wives, and bring your father, and come. 20 Also regard not your stuff; for the good of all the land of Egypt is yours.

The Bible tells us that the earth is the Lord's. There is no section of the earth that does not belong to God. All the fullness of the fields, mines, oil, gold, precious minerals all belongs to God. If the wealth of the earth is ours ... why do so many saints lack. The Bible also says that for lack of knowledge the people perish. We do not know that which belongs to our father ... and have no interest to enjoy that which is our inheritance. It is sad that many Christians do not know how to enjoy the goodness of God's provision. God will often admit us into times to enjoy wealth and provisions that are part of our heritage. Many are embarrassed to possess wealth because they imagine it to be evil. How can that which God put in the land for us be evil?

All the goodness of all the land was offered for the enjoyment of the Hebrews. They are told to stop fretting about their limited paltry baggage and instead to consider there is a vast river of resources available for their comfort. This is still God's promise to His children. It does not mean that God will grant us access to that which we are not prepared for ... but it certainly means that wealth and possessions controlled by children of darkness is an anomaly. We pray and ask for souls ... but are too shy to ask for resources to be transferred into the hands of kingdom stewards for His work. Remember I used the word stewards ... because God can instruct and command His stewards concerning the use of His goods.

If God loved us so much that He can give us His most precious son, there is nothing else He can deny us. God is good and all the goodness of the earth belongs to Him.

Song

I have a Father—The Almighty Father
He is King of King and Lord of Lords
I have a Father.
He is so good and so kind ... Almighty God 2ce

Prayer: Lord, Let your saints enjoy and be satisfied with your abundant goodness all over the earth. Amen

JULY 6

The First Exodus.

Bible Text: Genesis 45:21-25

Gen 45:21 And the children of Israel did so: and Joseph gave them wagons, according to the commandment of Pharaoh, and gave them provision for the way. 22 To all of them he gave each man changes of raiment; but to Benjamin he gave three hundred pieces of silver, and five changes of raiment. 23 And to his father he sent after this manner; ten asses laden with the good things of Egypt, and ten she asses laden with corn and bread and meat for his father by the way. 24 So he sent his brethren away, and they departed: and he said unto them, See that ye fall not out by the way. 25 And they went up out of Egypt, and came into the land of Canaan unto Jacob their father.

There will be many great trips out of Egypt. Notably three are worth mentioning because they occurred with much fanfare. The first was this trip to escort the brothers to bring Jacob and the family of Israel to Egypt. The second was the burial of Jacob ... which was also with a great procession and the third worth mentioning was several centuries later when Moses led the Children of Israel out of Egypt. God used this trips to bless the children of Israel as all entailed much transfer of the wealth of Egypt to the Hebrews. The final Exodus was a great spoiling of Egypt.

It is the way of God to often transfer resources to the hands of His covenant children to establish His covenant. These are often voluntary transfers and gifts that fiancé His purposes. The wealth of the wicked is often laid up for the just. But this is not a covetousness or a robbery of Egypt ... but in all trips out of Egypt, we read that voluntary deposits of great substance ... asses laden with all the good things of Egypt. God was building a consciousness of prosperity in the minds of His own ... a prosperity that will be stewarded someday to ensure that the gospel goes around the entire world.

Reflect on this devotional. Consider wealth that God has graciously permitted to be legitimately transferred to you. How are you stewarding that wealth? Is that wealth playing its part in the financing of the final harvest.

Song

Come, ye thankful people, come,
Raise the song of harvest home;
All is safely gathered in,
Ere the winter storms begin.
God our Maker doth provide
For our wants to be supplied;
Come to God's own temple, come,
Raise the song of harvest home.

Even so, Lord, quickly come,
Bring Thy final harvest home;
Gather Thou Thy people in,
Free from sorrow, free from sin,
There, forever purified,
In Thy garner to abide;
Come, with all Thine angels come,
Raise the glorious harvest home.

Prayer: Lord, make me one of your treasurers who will finance the final harvests. Amen

JULY 7

Up to Canaan.

Bible Text: Genesis 45:21-25

Gen 45:21 *And the children of Israel did so: and Joseph gave them wagons, according to the commandment of Pharaoh, and gave them provision for the way. 22 To all of them he gave each man changes of raiment; but to Benjamin he gave three hundred pieces of silver, and five changes of raiment. 23 And to his father he sent after this manner; ten asses laden with the good things of Egypt, and ten she asses laden with corn and bread and meat for his father by the way. 24 So he sent his brethren away, and they departed: and he said unto them, See that ye fall not out by the way. 25 And they went up out of Egypt, and came into the land of Canaan unto Jacob their father.*

Everywhere the Bible speaks of Egypt it says "come down" . . . but when it speaks of Israel it says "go up". This is strange as Israel is geographically south of Egypt. Also the leaving of Egypt is with spoil . . . this happened again in Exodus. I sense that all wealth belongs to God, but the true heirs to this wealth have been robbed by deceptions that lure them into disobedience. The main purpose of this wealth is to comfort Jacob their father . . . perhaps the unhappiest soul in this saga. Wealth always has purpose . . . do not ever be deluded to think wealth is for selfish consumption. Jacob was old, tired and despondent . . . in a chronic depression and inconsolable state. How will he be convinced that God had not forsaken His covenant?

Joseph understands that prosperity is to be used to serve God. The giving and spending of wealth in our hands tells a lot of our true identity as children of God. Note the brothers are convinced but will Jacob believe this is a trick and follow them . . . not until he sees the camels.

The blessings of God have purpose. Do not seek for idle blessings. These are the sorts of riches that cause pain and sorrow. Indeed it is enough that Jacob is convinced that Joseph is alive. No money or riches will ever be able to provoke the great joy that is ahead of him.

Journeys out of Egypt are times of glorious transitions. There is a final journey to the Heavenly Canaan to be one with our Heavenly Father. Will you be among those making the journey? Will you have souls and a service that can be presented to the Father or will you be empty handed? Indeed all sorrow in the house of Jacob is soon to be over.

Song

I shall wear a golden crown, When I get home; I shall lay my burdens down, When I get home;
Clad in robes of glory, I shall sing the story Of the Lord who bought me, When I get home.

When I get home, when I get home, All sorrow will be over when I get home;
When I get home, when I get home, All sorrow will be over when I get home.

All the darkness will be past, When I get home; I shall see the light at last, When I get home;
Light from Heaven streaming, O'er my pathway beaming, Ever guides me onward, Till I get home

Prayer: Lord, In the final journey up to the Heavenly Canaan. Do not let me be left behind. Amen

JULY 8

Good News

Bible Text: Genesis 45:26

Gen 45:26 And told him, saying, Joseph is yet alive, and he is governor over all the land of Egypt. And Jacob's heart fainted, for he believed them not.

The word of God . . . the gospel of Christ is good news. If it does not sound like good news to you, then it is not the gospel of our Lord Jesus Christ. If it leaves a sour taste, then this may be your pastor's personal thoughts but not the gospel of Christ. The message of salvation is unbelievably good. The mercy and grace in the salvation of Christ is not just good but should sound too good to be true. But the Holy Spirit draws the elect to believe that indeed this is true.

Many have heard a gospel that speaks of a hell that scares the believer . . . but indeed Jacob is preserved from hunger and death in a famine but the more exciting news is that Joseph is alive. Like Jesus who resurrected from the grave and is alive to make intercession for us in the presence of god. All who believe in Him will not perish but have everlasting life. It sounds too simple to just expect that everything is suddenly going to be fine for Jacob after years of a tormenting grief and deepest sorrow. Nights in which Jacob cried unceasingly . . . months of sighing and quiet sorrowing and regretting . . . if only I had not sent Joseph out on that day . . . if only this and if only that. And then this news that all is well. I agree with a pastor who once taught that if you are hearing a gospel that sounds weak and you do not get the feeling of a gift that is too good and merciful to be true . . . then it is perhaps not the gospel and it is time to find another church where the good news is preached. But the good news is Christ and faith in His word and not psychology and motivational speeches of men. Jacob heard the news that Joseph was not just alive (that would have been good enough) but that he was also Governor of perhaps the greatest nation of that time . . . Jacob was already weak from grief, fear and old age . . . saddened and praying to God to take him home for everyday was an extension of grieving. This news sounded like a cruel joke . . . such that he fainted. Have you heard the gospel of Christ. It is good news . . . too good to be true . . . . you could say but I tell you, the gospel is true. Jesus loves you and invites you to come to Him for salvation.

Song

Sinners Jesus will receive; Sound this word of grace to all
Who the heav'nly pathway leave, All who linger, all who fall!

Sing it o'er and o'er again: Christ receiveth sinful men;
Make the message clear and plain: Christ receiveth sinful men.

Come, and He will give you rest; Trust Him, for His Word is plain;
He will take the sinfullest; Christ receiveth sinful men.

Now my heart condemns me not; Pure before the law I stand;
He who cleansed me from all spot satisfied its last demand.

Christ receiveth sinful men, Even me with all my sin;
Purged from ev'ry spot and stain, Heav'n with Him I enter in.

Prayer: Holy Spirit, draw your own to Christ as ways are made for the gospel to be heard in the nations. Amen

JULY 9

Unbelievable but True.

Bible Text: Genesis 45:26

Gen 45:26 And told him, saying, Joseph is yet alive, and he is governor over all the land of Egypt. And Jacob's heart fainted, for he believed them not.

The news is brought to Jacob. Already weary with fears and further weakened with hunger. When he hears the story of his sons, indeed the great former trickster can only see that this is another deception - knowing what his sons are capable of. Instead his heart faints and he sinks further into grief wondering why would his sons chose to remind him of Joseph at this vulnerable moment.

Someone reading this devotional has completely written off a situation as absolutely hopeless and only remembers in great grief. But God has completely transformed the situation to beyond what you can ever believe possible. The works of God continue to be astonishing to men . . . unbelievable and amazing. Everyone knew that the tent dwelling Israelites were an abomination to the Egyptians . . . how then, this story that Joseph is not just alive but governor over Egypt. His sons were sent to buy food . . . Jacob was more interested to see the provisions that will sustain them for a few months or so . . . not even knowing that there were still five more years of famine. Jacob had even forgotten the dreams of Joseph and was having no expectation to ever see Joseph alive.

Like Thomas, Jacob will need to see the evidence. Meanwhile his heart sank, his mind confused . . . his hopes at its lowest ebb. But none of this stops God. Jacob is self-deceived by his feelings - but God has already gone beyond his illusions to bring a glorious testimony into reality for him.

Do not give up on God. God is not man. Let your heart not faint. The revival you long to see, you will still see. Jesus is alive and well at work. His Spirit of Revival has not been chained by any. The lies that His church is dead is still debunked by awesome moves of God. Perhaps you have been convinced by your past that you will not see Christ. It seems He is a dead relic, a painting, a story that modern thinkers have mocked and you seem to have lost your once living hope. Do not abandon the hope to see your Savior's face . . . to see His revivals in your Church. O hope of glory do not depart from my life.

Song

Hope, as an anchor so steadfast, rends the dark veil for the soul
Whither the Master has entered, Robbing the grave of its goal;
Come then, O come glad fruition, Come to my sad weary heart;
Come, O Thou blest hope of glory,
Never, o never depart.

Whispering hope,
O how welcome thy voice,
Making my heart in it sorrow rejoice.

Prayer: Lord, Blessed Hope of glory. May you never depart from my life. Amen

JULY 10

Signs and Wonders.

Bible Text: Genesis 45:27

Gen 45:27 And they told him all the words of Joseph, which he had said unto them: and when he saw the wagons which Joseph had sent to carry him, the spirit of Jacob their father revived.

Preaching the gospel without God's signs and wonders following can make the great news of God sound to hearers like another myth. It is true that when the power of God is demonstrated in signs and wonders, this makes a difference to faith and hearts are revived. When we see the ten plagues of Egypt and the parting of the Red Sea and ask why did God do these things? It was not so that Pharaoh would release the children of Israel . . . indeed God actually hardened Pharaoh's heart not to allow the freedom of the children of Israel until the appointed time. It was to revive the Israelites. The great display of signs such as the ten plagues of Egypt was to demonstrate to the Israelites - the greatness of their God. For many years they had seen the greatness of Egyptian witchcraft, God needed to show them the unsurpassed might of the great I AM. When signs and wonders demonstrate the power of God . . . it is easier for the chosen of God to surrender to Him. Jacob was revived as he saw the miracle of God's providence hidden over the years but working so powerfully to bring the expected end to pass. I pray for a time of God's power in the nations, for a time of great signs and wonders that millions will come to know to the Lord. I pray many that have backslidden will come home when they see again the power of God.

Song

Great God of wonders! all Thy ways
Are matchless, Godlike, and divine;
But the bright glories of Thy grace
Above thine other wonders shine,
Above thine other wonders shine.

Who is a pard'ning God like Thee?
Or who has grace so rich and free?
Or who has grace so rich and free?

Such deep transgressions to forgive!
Such guilty sinners thus to spare!
This is Thy grand prerogative,
And in this honor none shall share;
And in this honor none shall share.

In wonder lost, with trembling joy,
We take the pardon of our God:
Pardon for crimes of deepest dye,
A pardon bought with Jesus' blood,
A pardon bought with Jesus' blood.

O may this glorious, matchless love,
This God-like miracle of grace,
Teach mortal tongues, like those above,
To raise this song of lofty praise,
To raise this song of lofty praise

Prayer: Lord, May that happy day that wipes away all previous days come. Amen

JULY 11

God shows Evidence.

Bible Text: Genesis 45:27

Gen 45:27 And they told him all the words of Joseph, which he had said unto them: and when he saw the wagons which Joseph had sent to carry him, the spirit of Jacob their father revived.

For there to be revival there must be evidence of the unstoppable moves of God and not just words and pleadings. Sermons are great, but evidence of the mighty presence of God is better. The skills and talents of men may be persuasive but that is not evidence that can revive a man whose heart is already fainting. Words can be shared but there are things we must see.

I am praying that as you read this devotional you will be given a sign that will encourage you to believe that God has truly gone ahead to help you. If you are in ministry I pray that signs will follow your work and you will witness the move of God in ways that are truly remarkable.

In the Acts of Apostles, we read for the first time that handkerchiefs were brought from Paul and many were healed by God working through these handkerchiefs. God did a new thing and the people saw it and were revived. God will revive your ministry, your congregation, your neighborhood, your family and your nation. This time it will not just be words as good and important as preaching is, but it will be by visual evidence of the omnipotence of the great God that we serve.

I prophesy to the life of a reader, you will be so amazed for good . . . your amazement will heal all your depressions and you will be revived - launched into a new great beginning. This day was a day never to be forgotten by Jacob. God has appointed certain days when things are completely changed for our good. May your day of joy come and soon. You will not just hear but will see.

Song

O happy day, that fixed my choice on Thee, my Savior and my God!
Well may this glowing heart rejoice, and tell its raptures all abroad.

Happy day, happy day, when Jesus washed my sins away!
He taught me how to watch and pray, and live rejoicing every day
Happy day, happy day, when Jesus washed my sins away.

O happy bond, that seals my vows to Him Who merits all my love!
Let cheerful anthems fill His house, while to that sacred shrine I move.

'Tis done: the great transaction's done! I am the Lord's and He is mine;
He drew me, and I followed on; Charmed to confess the voice divine.

Now rest, my long divided heart, fixed on this blissful center, rest.
Here have I found a nobler part; here Heavenly pleasures fill my breast.

High Heaven, that heard the solemn vow, That vow renewed shall daily hear,
Till in life's latest hour I bow and bless in death a bond so dear.

Prayer: Lord, Make it clear beyond all doubts that I belong to you and you alone. Amen

JULY 12

It is Enough

Bible Text: Genesis 45:28

Gen 45:28 And Israel said, It is enough; Joseph my son is yet alive: I will go and see him before I die

There are times you feel as though more needs to be done either for good or for bad. You want to reward and encourage someone or you feel additional reprimand or a stern reaction is called for. And then you realize . . . it is enough. Jacob discovered two main things - first that Joseph is alive and then the wickedness of his children must have shocked him. This could also have been so disappointing to Jacob. I would have expected some reaction or comment concerning the hatred that caused him so much pain.

Perhaps he remembered how he treated Joseph so specially and how that may have provoked much jealousy. I also remember a story I heard, of a man in a town known for being very hard and tough. This man arrives one day to discover that his home had been robbed, his wife killed and his only daughter severely wounded by the robbers weapons. The entire village expected trouble but the man simply said "It is enough that my daughter is alive" . . . the neighbors who knew this man well were shocked as the man confessed, that many years ago in his teens - he was in a gang that violently attacked many homes.

Jacob said "it is enough" as he heard again the loud cries of Esau his cheated brother and the sorrow of Isaac his father who he deceived into releasing the blessing. Jacob saw that he had only reaped the seed he had sown in a previous era. The Apostle Paul before he became a Christian, was putting Christians in prison eventually to find himself frequenting prisons all through his ministry. There are times we come face to face with the harvest of past seeds that God in His wisdom, insists that we harvest. Even in these His grace will be enough. At those times we should remember to be quiet and to say . . . "it is enough that Jesus died and that he died for me . . . and that He lives and reign forever that I may reign with Him".

For Jacob, it was enough that Joseph had been miraculously preserved for their posterity. It was easy for Jacob to release the past and move forward. Putting the past behind is important. Look forward.

Song

My faith has found a resting place, not in device or creed;
I trust the ever living One, His wounds for me shall plead.

I need no other argument, I need no other plea,
It is enough that Jesus died, And that He died for me.

Enough for me that Jesus saves, This ends my fear and doubt;
A sinful soul I come to Him, He'll never cast me out.

My heart is leaning on the Word, The living Word of God,
Salvation by my Savior's Name, Salvation through His blood.

Prayer: Lord, May your grace and the truth that you reign forever, be sufficient for me . . . especially when I should be greatly disappointed. Amen

JULY 13

Begin again with God

Bible Text: Genesis 46:1

Gen 46:1 And Israel took his journey with all that he had, and came to Beersheba, and offered sacrifices unto the God of his father Isaac.

As you begin a journey, there are many things we include on our checklist. The excited Israel would not want to ensure he did not forget anything as chances were that they would not be returning . . . not very soon.

But Israel does not forget God. It is easy to forget God when things are upbeat and seem to be working right, but God watches us closely for our first moves . . . the hordes of hell are also interested in new beginnings and ready to target the most wicked temptations to scuttle any real progress. I also notice the name Israel is used and no more Jacob. This is the new covenant name. Our progress into new things also must leave behind old identities. We must learn to start afresh with God to commit all in His hands. Israel offered sacrifices, bringing offerings and burning them on the altar. We are living sacrifices and there are times when we should go to God afresh . . . putting our lives afresh on the altar of God. We should tell God that indeed He is God and we are just His creation . . . to use us as He wills. Sacrifice represents an expensive gift . . . our lives being the most important offering of all. Why is it important to start in times of new beginnings with communion with God? Because new beginnings involve new apprehensions, new devils, new encounters, new troubles and new challenges . . . and we need the assurance of God. The place chosen for the sacrifice was Beersheba. God appoints the sacrifice and the place. As you read this devotional . . . are you at the verge of a new beginning ? If so, then find the location and time to quickly go to God in communion. Surrender your life completely to Him and His agenda. Let God know by your sacrifice that He is in control and the future of all that pertains to you is safe in his hands. Praise Him, worship Him . . . declare His majesty and greatness. Worshipping God is another way to present a pleasing sacrifice. Sing hymns of praise to Him.

Song

Praise, my soul, the King of Heaven;
To His feet thy tribute bring.
Ransomed, healed, restored, forgiven,
Evermore His praises sing:
Alleluia! Alleluia!
Praise the everlasting King.

Praise Him for His grace and favor
To our fathers in distress.
Praise Him still the same as ever,
Slow to chide, and swift to bless.
Alleluia! Alleluia!
Glorious in His faithfulness.

Fatherlike He tends and spares us;
Well our feeble frame He knows.
In His hands He gently bears us,
Rescues us from all our foes.
Alleluia! Alleluia!
Widely yet His mercy flows.

Prayer: Lord, May your grace and truth that you reign forever, be sufficient at all times for me. Especially when I should be greatly disappointed. Amen

JULY 14

I am God

Bible Text: Genesis 46:2

Gen 46:2 And God spake unto Israel in the visions of the night, and said, Jacob, Jacob. And he said, Here am I. 46:3 And he said, I am God, the God of thy father: fear not to go down into Egypt; for I will there make of thee a great nation:

I pray that God reintroduces Himself to you. It is an awesome thing, to hear I am God . . . to realize that God is incomparable to any and not limited by time, space or location. God called the doubting nature, the scheming nature trying to return . . . Jacob, Jacob. He reminds Jacob. I am God and not you. I am God who told you not to go down at any time to Egypt . . . but I now tell you that in Egypt I will make you - there - a great nation.

Ponder on these words and you will see the dangers on dwelling on past encounters and promises. The worst situations we fall into is to stop hearing God. God has too many different ways of progressing His agenda. Do not ever fall into the trap of thinking you know it all, or have heard it all. We are only as good as the assurance and leading we received yesterday . . . we need to continually hear God . . . especially at new beginnings. Israel is wise to fear entering Egypt without hearing from God. God comes to assure him that He is the same God that was faithful to his ancestors.

It is foolish not to fear the power of evil and to tread carelessly where you have been asked not to go simply because a door opens. It is even more reckless to dare go without clearly hearing the "fear not" of God.

God is telling someone "I am God" and not a man . . . I can make a way where there is no way . . . even in the wilderness, I am supreme . . . I am God, and do not fear. It is in the place where you least expect that I will bless you. Praise God from whom all blessings flow and who is unstoppable to do all He purposes in any time, location or situation notwithstanding the witchcraft and opposition. Check again with God . . . He has a fresh word for you.

Song

All people that on earth do dwell, Sing to the Lord with cheerful voice.
Him serve with fear, His praise forth tell; Come ye before Him and rejoice.

The Lord, ye know, is God indeed; Without our aid He did us make;
We are His folk, He doth us feed, And for His sheep He doth us take.

O enter then His gates with praise; Approach with joy His courts unto;
Praise, laud, and bless His Name always, For it is seemly so to do.

For why? the Lord our God is good; His mercy is forever sure;
His truth at all times firmly stood, And shall from age to age endure.

To Father, Son and Holy Ghost, The God Whom Heaven and earth adore,
From men and from the angel host Be praise and glory evermore.

Praise God from whom all blessings flow. Praise Him all creatures there below
Praise Him above ye Heavenly hosts. Praise Father, Son and Holy Ghost

Prayer: Lord, May your great name be forever praised. Amen

JULY 15

Blessed Assurance

Bible Text: Genesis 46:4-5

Gen 46:4 I will go down with thee into Egypt; and I will also surely bring thee up again: and Joseph shall put his hand upon thine eyes. 5 And Jacob rose up from Beersheba: and the sons of Israel carried Jacob their father, and their little ones, and their wives, in the wagons which Pharaoh had sent to carry him.

The sons of Jacob have assured him, all is well. The wagons and goods and treasures brought as gifts for Jacob, hint that all will indeed be well and that it is safe to leave for Egypt. But there is a voice Jacob is still waiting for and that is the voice of God. At Beersheba, Jacob waits on God. Time and life has taught Jacob that all that glitters may not be gold. God must give His own blessed assurance . . . and the merciful God speaks.

Jacob is reassured that God will be with him and the family will be preserved in Egypt. Jacob knows that God is the one at work and not Pharaoh. We need to wait on God and recognize His voice as He gives His blessed assurance. There are times when God speaks to warn us against the direction we feel convinced to take. The fact that the evidence shows all is well is not indicator that the direction is right. God who sees the future must confirm our journeys so we do not drift into errors or worse go alone without His defending presence.

Reflect on the words of the text and the importance of hearing God for yourself on the things that concern you and may God help you to know Him. God will speak and make it clear to you when He knows you are truly waiting on Him and not just seeking to validate your already decided proposal of action. What will you do if God gives you an instruction contrary to your plans? Will you set your plans aside and obey God?

Song

Blessèd assurance, Jesus is mine! O what a foretaste of glory divine!
Heir of salvation, purchase of God, Born of His Spirit, washed in His blood.

This is my story, this is my song, Praising my Savior, all the day long;
This is my story, this is my song, Praising my Savior, all the day long.

Perfect submission, perfect delight, Visions of rapture now burst on my sight;
Angels descending bring from above - Echoes of mercy, whispers of love.

Perfect submission, all is at rest - I in my Savior am happy and blest,
Watching and waiting, looking above, Filled with His goodness, lost in His love.

Prayer: Lord, Speak . . . thy servant listens. Guide me as I rise up again. Amen

JULY 16

Rising up into Glory

Bible Text: Genesis 46:4-5

Gen 46:4 I will go down with thee into Egypt; and I will also surely bring thee up again: and Joseph shall put his hand upon thine eyes. 5 And Jacob rose up from Beersheba: and the sons of Israel carried Jacob their father, and their little ones, and their wives, in the wagons which Pharaoh had sent to carry him.

Israel is keen only to the extent that God backs him up. God tells Israel that He will not be alone and that he will spend the rest of His life in Egypt, Joseph His beloved son who thought to be dead will be there for him even in his old age and dying moments. God also wants Israel to know that the sojourn in Egypt will only be for a period and that God again will bring them up . . . again. Is it not wise to hear God clearly before making your moves?

Wagons, riches and doors can be seductive, but they can be only great traps if we do not know what God is doing. How do we hear God in a noisy world? To hear God we need altars, we need a place of silence . . . a place of devotion. God still speaks. He speaks through His word powerfully if only we will spend time reading the Bible. He speaks through the pulpit if we do not have a puppet of men preaching. He speaks through His creation if we can be silent to discern his leadings.

God predicts the Exodus, many generations earlier. Indeed Abraham was also given this prophecy of the future. God sees the future and He does not hide this vision from His own. As you read this devotional, it is pertinent to hear what God is speaking to you. If you are not hearing anything and must go blind, then consider that Egypt is a dangerous territory . . . Pharaoh is presented so far as a mild gentle monarch. but let the Bible tell you who Pharaoh really is . . .

Eze_29:3 Speak, and say, Thus saith the Lord GOD; Behold, I am against thee, Pharaoh king of Egypt, the great dragon that lieth in the midst of his rivers, which hath said, My river is mine own, and I have made it for myself.

Without God on your side and without His help . . . put plainly you do not stand a chance. The great dragon has sent wagons and a lavish entourage to receive you . . . you are foolish to be impressed and lured into a scenario that has not been checked with God. It is time to rise up to glory - but not before hearing God and receiving His assurances.

Song

Call Jehovah thy salvation, Rest beneath th'Almighty's shade,
In His secret habitation - Dwell and never be dismayed:
There no tumult shall alarm thee, thou shalt dread no hidden snare;
Guile nor violence can harm thee, in eternal safeguard there.

From the sword at noonday wasting, from the noisome pestilence,
In the depth of midnight blasting, God shall be thy sure defense:
He shall charge His angel legions watch and ward o'er thee to keep;
Tho' thou walk thro' lonesome regions, tho' in desert wilds thou sleep.

Since with pure and firm affection, thou on God hast set thy love,
With the wings of His protection He will shield thee from above:
Thou shalt call on Him in trouble, He will hearken, He will save;
Here for grief reward thee double, crown with life beyond the grave.

Prayer: Lord, Speak . . . thy servant listens. Guide me as I rise up again. Amen

JULY 17

Beneficiaries

Bible Text: Genesis 46:6-7

Gen 46:6 *And they took their cattle, and their goods, which they had gotten in the land of Canaan, and came into Egypt, Jacob, and all his seed with him: 7 His sons, and his sons' sons with him, his daughters, and his sons' daughters, and all his seed brought he with him into Egypt.*

This text describes the many that were preserved by the pains of only one man. The sons and daughters and grandchildren all benefited. Indeed, there are beneficiaries . . . our children and even their seed who benefit from the covenants we make with God. Also, when we stray . . . the consequences are not limited to us. It also means we are benefitting from many things we know nothing about but could also imply we groan under negative covenants.

If Joseph had disobeyed God . . . in the famine of the next five years, the entire clan may have been completely wiped out. Do you see that though your obedience may not be appreciated by relations and at the time they did not understand what God was demanding from your life. But they benefit from your obedience and may even suffer from curses if you disregard the commandments of God. When people are blessed they are typically not blessed alone . . . the overflowing nature of God's blessings pours into the lives of thousands but the anger of God which thankfully is only for a moment can be catastrophic for many generations unborn.

Do not take God lightly . . . think of your children and grandchildren before indulging in those few minutes of sin. The entire seed were brought out of a horrible famine . . . not just the brothers of Joseph. Reflect on this when next Potiphar's wife approaches you . . . consider the real cost. There are indeed thousands you have never seen that will benefit from your obedience to pray for revival and do the work entrusted in your hands faithfully. The faithfulness of God is great.

Song

Great is thy faithfulness, O Lord my Father - there is no shadow of turning with thee
Thou changest not, thy compassion they fail not. As thou hast been thou forever will be

Great is thy faithfulness 2ce Morning by morning new mercies I see
All I have needed thy hands have provided. Great is thy faithfulness, Lord unto me.

Pardon for sin and peace that endureth
Thine own dear presence to cheer and to guide
Strength for today and bright hopes for tomorrow
Blessings all mine and ten thousands beside.

Prayer: Lord, Help me to be faithful . . . for the sake of generations after me . . . Keep me faithful. Amen.

JULY 18

Let none call you Barren

Bible Text: Genesis 46:20-22

Gen 46:20 And unto Joseph in the land of Egypt were born Manasseh and Ephraim, which Asenath the daughter of Potipherah priest of On bare unto him. Gen 46:21 And the sons of Benjamin were Belah, and Becher, and Ashbel, Gera, and Naaman, Ehi, and Rosh, Muppim, and Huppim, and Ard. Gen 46:22 These are the sons of Rachel, which were born to Jacob: all the souls were fourteen

Rachel at a time was written off as barren . . . later she receives mercy and gives birth to Joseph. She eventually dies giving birth to Benjamin. A sad story . . . she was late in being fruitful but her life was pivotal to the history of Israel. Her first son has only two sons, but Joseph becomes the strategic lever that delivers Israel from a seven tear famine. Benjamin has ten sons. The souls that came through Rachel are counted as 14. Have things appeared to be late for you? Did you start too late? Like Rachel's life was suddenly terminated at birth of her son . . . have your dreams been suddenly cut off. Do not despair. Reflect that much fruitfulness came after her death. Still I pray that God will cause you to enjoy fruitfulness in your lifetime and not after your death.

Imagine the joy for Joseph who did not know her mother . . . if Rachel had been there to share the days of glory. You will not sow and another reap. You will be blessed and see the glory of God at work in your lifetime. You will be fruitful beyond your dreams in your lifetime. Out of your seed, God will raise an army for Himself. Those who wrote you off once will be amazed at the unprecedented turnaround in your situation. You will not die a premature death nor will any reading die at child birth. All your deliveries will be attended by divine midwives . . . angels assigned by God to help. Your sons will not become street urchins or drop outs . . . they will be successful.

One day, your blessings will be counted and you will say - see what the Lord has done.

Song

Count your blessings, name them one by one
Count your blessings see what God has done
Count your blessings; name them one by one
And it will surprise you what the Lord has done.

Prayer: Lord, Let it be said that God has been good to me in His blessings. Give me all round fruitfulness. Amen

JULY 19

A Place of Nourishment

Bible Text: Genesis 46:28

Gen 46:28 And he sent Judah before him unto Joseph, to direct his face unto Goshen; and they came into the land of Goshen

The Bible tells us that 70 souls came to Egypt of the House of Israel. From the onset they were to be separated from the rest of Egypt in a beautiful place called Goshen. Israel was particularly interested in the plan of separation and sent Judah in advance to know the territory. The understanding of the command - Be ye separate, has always been a doctrinal issue that has been at the core of many controversies in the Church. How do we become separate and be effective in evangelism?

Our evangelism must also involve letting the world see that we are different in every regard. We dwell in a land with different rules and abide with different regulations. The Bible is our constitution and the weapons of our warfare are not carnal. We are pilgrims - and our home is a distinctively different place. This should give us encouragement . . . knowing we came from a better place and will one day return there.

But there are more lessons. Judah is to be directed to Goshen. God wants us focused and directed on our Heavenly home. Not enough is written or preached about Heaven, but I tell you, I wish you could imagine how beautiful Heaven must really be. I wish your focus and attention could be more directed on Heaven. It is a myth that the Church is too Heaven minded. Indeed, there are far too many distractions even in the church for that to be true. The idea of a separate place called Heaven is now perceived even in many congregations as allegorical and not a literal place. Many Christians believe the earth is all that there is. Do not fall into this trap. Learn to live separately in your lifestyle and manner even from now . . . knowing you will be eternally separated from unbelievers eventually. But from now, even if you sense you are in Egypt, there is still a place God has reserved for you. You can be different, worship God as He has demanded to be worshipped - in Spirit and in Truth . . . and live as His chosen race and not as men and women of Egypt. Sing about your home in Heaven . . . even when you are here on earth. Enjoy the separated sanctified life of the chosen of God.

Song

I shall wear a golden crown, When I get home; I shall lay my burdens down, When I get home;
Clad in robes of glory, I shall sing the story - Of the Lord who bought me, When I get home.

Refrain:
When I get home, when I get home,
All sorrow will be over when I get home;
When I get home, when I get home,
All sorrow will be over when I get home.

All the darkness will be past, When I get home; I shall see the light at last, When I get home;
Light from Heaven streaming, O'er my pathway beaming, Ever guides me onward, Till I get home.

I shall see my Savior's face, When I get home; Sing again of saving grace, When I get home;
I shall stand before Him; Gladly I'll adore Him, Ever to be with Him, When I get home.

Prayer: Lord, as you use me on this earth for your glory, let my life be directed on my Heavenly home.

JULY 20

Face to Face

Bible Text: Genesis 46:29

Gen 46:29 And Joseph made ready his chariot, and went up to meet Israel his father, to Goshen, and presented himself unto him; and he fell on his neck, and wept on his neck a good while.

What would it be like when we meet someone we love so dearly and have longed to see someday - uncertain if you will ever meet . . . but still it remains the greatest hope of joy - that someday you will behold him. The joy when we behold the Lord is so indescribable, the tears of happiness . . . the realization that we made it . . . and forever. This joy is that which exceeds the unspeakable joy and full of glory mentioned in 1 Peter 1:8. If though we see Him not, but having the assurance that one day we will - already fills us with unspeakable joy . . . imagine how it will be when we actually see our master face to face.

1Pe_1:8 Whom having not seen, ye love; in whom, though now ye see him not, yet believing, ye rejoice with joy unspeakable and full of glory

There are no words to describe this meeting. We know it was in Goshen - the separated place . . . where there were no Egyptians. There will be tears . . . tears of Christ all over our neck . . . and our tears as well . . . but for joy. These are the tears mentioned in Revelation 7:17 that will be wiped away. There will be a personal welcome embrace . . . Christ drawing us into His arms . . . welcoming us like a lost son anxiously awaited - who has just returned home. The early Christians as they faced martyrdom believed so much in this coming joyful union that they asked those who were being burnt on the stake to give a sign that the end was as glorious as they expected it will be . . . and many as they perished did . . . just like Stephen to encourage others . . . no wonder many rejected deliverance.

Act 7:54 When they heard these things, they were cut to the heart, and they gnashed on him with their teeth. 55 But he, being full of the Holy Ghost, looked up stedfastly into Heaven, and saw the glory of God, and Jesus standing on the right hand of God, 56 And said, Behold, I see the Heavens opened, and the Son of man standing on the right hand of God. 57 Then they cried out with a loud voice, and stopped their ears, and ran upon him with one accord,

Even before they started stoning Stephen, Jesus was already waiting for Him at "Goshen" . . . knowing he was about to be martyred. If we ever saw what Stephen saw as he looked steadfastly into Heaven . . . we will all wish we had been martyred . . . a crown was waiting for him. Lord give a revelation of the joy that is ahead . . . that has never been told by any.

Song

I have found His grace is all complete, He supplieth every need;
While I sit and learn at Jesus' feet, I am free, yes, free indeed

Refrain:
It is joy unspeakable and full of glory, Full of glory, full of glory;
It is joy unspeakable and full of glory, Oh, the half has never yet been told.

I have found that hope so bright and clear, Living in the realm of grace;
Oh, the Savior's presence is so near, I can see His smiling face.

I have found the joy no tongue can tell, How its waves of glory roll;
It is like a great o'erflowing well, Springing up within my soul.

Prayer: Lord, keep me singing for joy, even now and into an even more joyful union with you. Amen

JULY 21

Now let me die

Bible Text: Genesis 46:30

Gen 46:30 And Israel said unto Joseph, Now let me die, since I have seen thy face, because thou art yet alive.

When we catch a glimpse of eternity, we are immediately freed of all the shackles and attractions of the earth. Our clamoring to be something or to live very long or to do this or that is really a sign that we are yet to see the spiritual Goshen. The early Christians and I believe Christians in tough periods or hostile locations are helped by the gift of this rare vision. It is easy to release everything including our earthly suit of mud if we caught a glimpse of our eternal body waiting for us to last all through eternity without aging. Sin loses all attraction and is seen as the enemy it is. Like Esther, we can say if I perish I perish.

This proclamation really means, Lord tear apart if you wish - all my ambitions . . . and the Jacob who out-schemed Esau and Laban understood ambitions . . . like most of us. Jacob declares that God is more than able to bring all His plans to pass without our slightest maneuvers except that we simply trust Him. All our maneuvers must die, all our ambitions must bow to His will, all our projections must be buried . . . and all placed in the casket of divine providence to be resurrected as God desires.

Note that the previously fainting Israel lived well over a decade after this declaration. Esther lived to become a heroine after she buried her ambitions. God is waiting for us to catch a glimpse of what He has already prepared for us. We will equally say . . . "Now, let me die" . . . but God has now found a rare instrument for His glory - an uncommon ally . . . If only we declared this earlier, when we are younger. Teach your children and youths more about Heaven . . . and see the difference in how God is able to use lives that are "dead" to the world's magnetic pull. Because Jesus is alive . . . we can face tomorrow whatsoever it brings - even death has lost all its sting . . . it will only one day be a glorious transition. Halleluyah to the Lamb . . .

Song

Let us, then be true and faithful - Trusting serving every day
Just one glimpse of Him in glory - will the toils of life repay.

When we all get to Heaven, What a day of rejoicing that will be!
When we all see Jesus, We'll sing and shout the victory.

Onward to the prize before us! Soon His beauty we'll behold;
Soon the pearly gates will open, we shall tread the streets of gold.

When we all get to Heaven, What a day of rejoicing that will be!
When we all see Jesus, We'll sing and shout the victory.

Prayer: Lord, Help me to release all my selfish ambitions and fears . . . knowing that Jesus is alive to see me through whatever comes - even death. Amen

JULY 22

Shepherds

Bible Text: Genesis 46:31

Gen 46:31 And Joseph said unto his brethren, and unto his father's house, I will go up, and shew Pharaoh, and say unto him, My brethren, and my father's house, which were in the land of Canaan, are come unto me;32 And the men are shepherds, for their trade hath been to feed cattle; and they have brought their flocks, and their herds, and all that they have. 33 And it shall come to pass, when Pharaoh shall call you, and shall say, What is your occupation? 34 That ye shall say, Thy servants' trade hath been about cattle from our youth even until now, both we, and also our fathers: that ye may dwell in the land of Goshen; for every shepherd is an abomination unto the Egyptians.

Shepherds are nomadic tribesmen, going from place to place, setting up tents to dwell and not builders of cities and civilizations. Egypt was the exact opposite . . . they built civilizations and found great cities with splendid architecture but the culture of shepherds was repulsive to them. But even till today, shepherds do not fit the city culture. Shepherds were amongst the first to know of the birth of Christ, as they were led to the manager where He lay. Christ is referred to as the good shepherd. Christians are likened to sheep not wolves . . . sheep who hear and recognize the call of their master.

The work of the shepherd is boring, tedious and messy. Leading sheep to waters and protecting them from wolves and lions or bears can be risky? But David, the man after God's heart started as a shepherd, and it was amongst sheep that he was prepared for the palace. The same with Moses . . . unlike Solomon - who was a builder of cities that people came from afar to see. The ways of shepherds do not agree with city dwellers just as serving God and mammon cannot both be done. Doing one makes you and enemy to the other. The culture of the kingdom of God is abomination to that of earthly civilizations and vice versa is also true. Invariably we must choose.

Joseph - the good shepherd, may have told them to disguise their occupation to be accepted in Egypt and freely mingle with the Egyptians . . . this may have its benefits - but it would have been a choice that would have led to the destruction of their Hebrew culture which God wanted preserved. What choice are you making? Do you see the gulf of difference between the present culture of today and the ways of the kingdom? Every culture and civilization has its supervising principality . . . thus we are told we wrestle not against flesh and blood but spiritual entities that control earthly kings and worldviews.

It is a good sign when there is a tension between your kingdom habits and how the world cultivates its success. Do not be surprised at the enmity that seems to thrive between the culture of the kingdom of God and the culture of postmodern civilization. Again, the question is "who is on the Lord's side, who will serve the King?" The work of serving the King is to find lost sheep and bring them back home. The God of civilization is humanism.

Song

Who is on the Lord's side? Who will serve the King? Who will be His helpers, other lives to bring?
Who will leave the world's side? Who will face the foe? Who is on the Lord's side? Who for Him will go?
By Thy call of mercy, by Thy grace divine, We are on the Lord's side—Savior, we are Thine!

Not for weight of glory, nor for crown and palm, Enter we the army, raise the warrior psalm;
But for love that claimeth lives for whom He died: He whom Jesus nameth must be on His side.
By Thy love constraining, by Thy grace divine, We are on the Lord's side—Savior, we are Thine!

Prayer: Lord, Help me to see that serving you will cause some rejection. Comfort me. Amen

JULY 23

Divine Guidance

Bible Text: Genesis 47:1

Gen 47:1 Then Joseph came and told Pharaoh, and said, My father and my brethren, and their flocks, and their herds, and all that they have, are come out of the land of Canaan; and, behold, they are in the land of Goshen.

Joseph undertook to be a guide to ensure the preservation of his brethren - and particularly their culture. You also need a guide, the Great Counselor to help you navigate through your Christian walk, now that you have known the Lord. Do not take a step without checking well from him, what you should or not do. Let the Holy Spirit introduce you into situations. Leaning to your understanding in Egypt is dangerous. Already your ways are taboo to the culture in which you will now dwell. You may not appreciate the irritation you will cause although you mean well. You will need to be kept by Jehovah. Even your substance must be committed to Christ and your entirely family. All must be submitted to God and yielded unto Him completely. Do not attempt to face Pharaoh alone, the outcome could be unpredictable.

We must learn to live by prayer. Prayer is our means of seeking a strategy from the Holy Spirit. Do not enter into a contract without checking? Do not do a deal without checking? Let the Spirit of Christ guide you every step of the way until you reach your goal - Heaven. Do not take for granted that in Goshen, the place of being called out, the place of separation - you are safe. You still need to be baptized by the Holy Spirit and led appropriately. The plan of the Holy Spirit is to keep you in the world but separated from the evil in the world - somehow. This is no easy task - as the world culture is very compelling, forceful and all embracing. The worldview of modernism is very intelligent and logical. As soon as you are immersed through education, media etc. your mind is washed in another flood of a different nature. The seas of the world are tempestuous and full of rapids and hidden rocks . . .

Joh 17:9 I pray for them: I pray not for the world, but for them which thou hast given me; for they are thine. 10 And all mine are thine, and thine are mine; and I am glorified in them. 11 And now I am no more in the world, but these are in the world, and I come to thee. Holy Father, keep through thine own name those whom thou hast given me, that they may be one, as we are. 12 While I was with them in the world, I kept them in thy name: those that thou gavest me I have kept, and none of them is lost, but the son of perdition; that the scripture might be fulfilled. 13 And now come I to thee; and these things I speak in the world, that they might have my joy fulfilled in themselves. 14 I have given them thy word; and the world hath hated them, because they are not of the world, even as I am not of the world. 15 I pray not that thou shouldest take them out of the world, but that thou shouldest keep them from the evil. 16 They are not of the world, even as I am not of the world. 17 Sanctify them through thy truth: thy word is truth.

Christ keeps us from the evil that is in Egypt, giving us the word - the truth . . . to sanctify us through the truth that the world does not know. We are sanctified and kept not by a monastery-type isolation, but by knowing the word of God well. We are guided not by following gurus but mastery of the scriptures. How much of scriptures do you know? How many verses have been intuitively committed to your memory? How many Biblical thoughts have been stored in the crevices of your mind. You cannot be full of scripture and also full of worldliness . . . one must saturate your thoughts or the other will. Make a fresh commitment to study the word of God - day and night.

Song

Lead us, Heavenly Father, lead us - o'er the world's tempestuous sea;
guard us, guide us, keep us, feed us, for we have no help but thee;
yet possessing every blessing, if our God our Father be.

Prayer: Lord, Help me to be separate. Amen

JULY 24

Caution in Egypt

Bible Text: Genesis 47:2

Gen 47:2 And he took some of his brethren, even five men, and presented them unto Pharaoh.

Joseph did not overwhelm Pharaoh with the entire household, but slowly and cautiously progressed a strategy. Egypt is a place of caution. The Pilgrim cannot be impatient and must wait for divine signals - watching for timing and ensuring that the words he uses are the right ones given to him. Indeed, Joseph was influential, but he was still very cautious in confronting the culture of Egypt with the Hebrew race.

God has called you and He will guide you, but you must be exercised in patience and caution. You must learn to wait. An open door is not necessarily a go sign and certainly not a flag to stampede the situation. Tread cautiously in Egypt, for there are many traps.

Psa 106:15 And he gave them their request; but sent leanness into their soul.

Many have mistaken, the granting of requests to mean the pleasure of God. God is not known to be pushed and rushed into situations, mainly driven by lust for specific conclusions and answers . . . and the best way to teach the impatient is often to grant his request and sending a leanness as well to teach a lesson, that God is not our servant, but we are His. God does not exist for our pleasure, but we exist for His. We should not be slothful - but at the same time we should not be careless and filled with presumptions. Our obedience requires discernment on the appropriate strategy. True there are things that must be done with boldness and haste and like Esther we must go fasted but confidently before Ahaseurus . . . but note that this was confirmed by Mordecai. It is wise to receive Godly confirmation and counsel from several witnesses if your spirit advises a general caution. Learn patience . . . it is one of the most noble of virtues.

Song

Order my steps with your word
Let me follow only as I've heard
Teach me to wait as I obey my Lord
Keep me from presumption as I loosen my sword.

Order my steps with your word
Egypt has traps laid . . . and poisons to abort
Watch my lips and help my zeal
Never for a moment to stray from your will.

Order my steps with your word
The doors are open - but why is my Lord
advising caution and urging restraint
as angels precede and make safe the narrow pathways.

Prayer: Lord, Help my zeal . . . order my steps . . . when the doors are open unto me. Amen

JULY 25

Pharaoh's Interview

Bible Text: Genesis 47:3

Gen 47:3 And Pharaoh said unto his brethren, What is your occupation? And they said unto Pharaoh, Thy servants are shepherds, both we, and also our fathers.

Pharaoh seeks to know how the brethren of Joseph will fit into Egypt. What role can they play? He asks a question, a question that is common at job interviews. What can you do, what is your skill, what is your occupation. And they replied we are keepers of sheep.

A man without a skill is useless to the kingdom of God and to the enemy. Laziness, idleness and slothfulness will often produce dabblers with no known specialization. Even in the church, do you see them . . . how some wander with no means of livelihood and no occupation . . . with no interest to learn a skill or trade. Experts in nothing.

It is good to apprehend the call of God upon your life with an effort to build skills . . . indeed many skills. Paul was a lawyer, but knew how to make tents. Today, the hardworking man can self-learn so many competences to be useful in the Kingdom. Programming skills, internet skills, administration, electrical technology and more still. God will preserve us often through honest means of livelihood - even if it seems demeaning to others . . . such as cleaning and sanitation services. Even Pharaoh is not interested to have parasites in Egypt. Everyone must contribute to society - especially saints.

The people of God are busy, diligent and industrious. Meditate on this devotional. There is a skill that God will use to serve the society to which you are sent. Do you have an occupation that will be useful to the environment God has placed you? Can you begin to learn something . . . take a course. As they say, sharpen the saw.

The brothers of Joseph offered their service, and did not expect that they would be harbored to merely consume the fat of the land. They would make legitimate contributions to build the societies God has planted them in. May we be delivered from idleness and the penchant to contribute nothing to our societies . . . as saints we still have social responsibilities. Let God choose an occupation for you, but you must do the hard work.

Song

Since, Lord, thou dost defend, us with thy Spirit,
We know we at the end shall life inherit.
Then fancies flee away!
I'll fear not what men say,
I'll labor night and day to be a Pilgrim.

Prayer: Lord, teach me to labor - night and day. In my community, fulfilling my civic and social responsibilities and also in the kingdom of God in much prayer, fasting and obedience. Amen

JULY 26

Sojourn in Egypt

Bible Text: Genesis 47:4

Gen 47:4 They said moreover unto Pharaoh, For to sojourn in the land are we come; for thy servants have no pasture for their flocks; for the famine is sore in the land of Canaan: now therefore, we pray thee, let thy servants dwell in the land of Goshen

From the onset, the family of Joseph declared they would be in Egypt only for a temporary period, a sojourn while the five years of famine ravaged the lands. They only requested only for a temporary dwelling in Egypt. Of course, we know they eventually stayed longer than they initially stated ... we do not know if the brothers tricked Pharaoh in that they had no intention of going back ... at least not in their life time. It would not have been surprising, as trickery used to be a part of their style. It was more likely that they were so welcome that they decided to stay.

Do we not equally sing that we are pilgrims, yet we are in a time when most doubt that a Heavenly home still exists for us to return to. Indeed our lives on earth are like a tiny needle in a huge haystack -Heaven ... yet we dwell more on that tiny needle. We are lost in the trappings of Egypt and no more see ourselves as pilgrims or sojourners.

The understanding that today's Pharaoh has is that true Christians are Pilgrims. But Satan, the world and the flesh collaborate first to welcome the Pilgrim, make them ever so comfortable and at ease and gradually enslave them into lusts, passions and ambitions until they forget their home - Canaan. Does this plot work ... Do ask the brethren and their family after five years in Goshen if they wanted to return to Canaan ... after tasting the luscious grapes. They will laugh and wonder if you are serious. Indeed, the remaining five years of famine caused them to migrate to Egypt, but what is it that keeps them in Egypt.

In this devotional, I would want you to focus on the word *sojourn*. It means a temporary stopover, a rest, a break ... it is never used to suggest a permanent home. It is used to imply a trip to a place for a period - usually brief. On earth, are you a sojourner or are you a permanent resident. What is the nature of your visa? Is it visiting or does it say permanent resident? Your attitudes, activities and priorities and investments are a reflection on your official status on the earth. Do you see people with temporary visit visas (staying perhaps only for summer) competing with permanent residents for business and opportunities? The tenure of your visa is only known to God ... does this reality fill you with joy nor do you wish like many temporary residents in Britain pray that you will be given a permanent citizenship ... will you marry a non-believer for a permanent resident status. Things can be difficult for the sojourner and tribulations can be many - but his thoughts of home will comfort him. May God help us.

Song

Elect from every nation, Yet one oe'r all the earth,
Her charter of salvation - one Lord, one faith, one birth,
One holy name she blesses partakes one holy food,
And to one hope she presses, with every grace endued.

Mid toil and tribulation, and tumult of her war,
She waits the consummation of peace for evermore.
Till with the vision glorious Her longing eyes are blest,
And the great Church victorious shall be the Church at rest.

Prayer: Lord, remind me always of my true home, awaiting my return. Let me never forget that I am only a Pilgrim for you. Let the purpose of my sojourn be accomplished. Amen

JULY 27

Connected to Christ (Part I)

Bible Text: Genesis 47:5-6

Gen 47:5 And Pharaoh spake unto Joseph, saying, Thy father and thy brethren are come unto thee: 6 The land of Egypt is before thee; in the best of the land make thy father and brethren to dwell; in the land of Goshen let them dwell: and if thou knowest any men of activity among them, then make them rulers over my cattle.

Our connections matter. Who have you been connected to? Notice that the best of the land is given to Joseph and set before him and not to his brothers. But the brothers have come to Joseph. It is the connection to Joseph that makes it possible for the best of the land to be offered. This is not a minor detail. Our connections to Christ as we surrender to him bring us into favor. Similarly, our disconnection will cost dearly in terms of access to our help. Our dependence on God and reliance on him fully is our point of access to the resources we need.

Imagine, the brothers beginning to initiate their own plans outside dependence on Joseph. What a wasted unnecessary effort that would have been. In Christ, all resources have been laid down - for our sustenance and to finance our assignments. But we have severed the connections because of sin and self. To get back on track . . . find a way to be with Christ afresh . . . to rededicate your life afresh . . . to love Him afresh. Learn to love Him more. If sin has caused a disconnection, then repent, never to go back. Soon you will discover that the land of Egypt is before Him and not before you. Also, He is encouraged to make those connected to Him, dwell in peace in Goshen. Christ knows the location of safety - it is the place of dwelling in Him . . . He makes us dwell in green pastures, leads us beside the still waters . . . He restores our soul. What a delight to be connected to Him? What a privilege to be joint-heirs with Him to whom all has been bequeathed?

Song

The Lord's my Shepherd, I'll not want.
He makes me down to lie
In pastures green; He leadeth me
The quiet waters by.

My soul He doth restore again;
And me to walk doth make
Within the paths of righteousness,
Even for His own Name's sake.

Prayer: Lord, let me forever be connected to you. Do not permit me to do whatever will lead to a disconnection.
Amen

JULY 28

Connected to Christ (Part II)

Bible Text: Genesis 47:5-6

Gen 47:5 And Pharaoh spake unto Joseph, saying, Thy father and thy brethren are come unto thee: 6 The land of Egypt is before thee; in the best of the land make thy father and brethren to dwell; in the land of Goshen let them dwell: and if thou knowest any men of activity among them, then make them rulers over my cattle.

Another reason why connections matter is because the one with whom we are connected knows us well. Joseph was told to find men of activity known to him to be made rulers. There are brothers and there are brothers of activity. There are activities known to other men and there are activities known to Christ.

The lazy have no portion in ruling or in enjoying the prosperity of God. The one Christ knows as indolent will be provided for, but will not be entrusted to rule over resources and people. Can it be said that Christ knows you as a man of diligence? Or will it be said that you are a man of words, a man of dreams, a man of proposals, a man of criticisms . . . indeed there are many men . . . but a man known to Christ as a man of action is rare. These will rule.

It is also true that many will say they did so many miracles and exploits in His name, but Jesus will say I never knew you - depart from me, you workers of evil. Being known to Christ as a man of activity is not always referring of exploits seen by men . . . but more so works that will count at the end. So much singing, doing, serving and teaching is not seen by God - because hearts are not pure before God. God cannot reward these activities.

Ultimately, the raptured saints will rule with Christ in the period called the millennium. In eternity we will be elevated in a honor and glory that cannot be described. Our destiny is to reign and rule with Christ. Reflect on this devotional . . . and your connections to Christ. Reflect on this . . . how can Christ expand your coast and put more in your hands - even for the heathen, if He does not know your activity or worse He perceives your work to be from an evil heart.

Song

Yea, though I walk in death's dark vale,
Yet will I fear no ill;
For Thou art with me; and Thy rod
And staff my comfort still.

My table Thou hast furnishèd
In presence of my foes;
My head Thou dost with oil anoint,
And my cup overflows.

Goodness and mercy all my life
Shall surely follow me;
And in God's house forevermore
My dwelling place shall be.

Prayer: Lord, let me forever be connected to you. Do not permit to do whatever will lead to a disconnection. Amen

JULY 29

A Blessing to others

Bible Text: Genesis 47:7

Gen 47:7 And Joseph brought in Jacob his father, and set him before Pharaoh: and Jacob blessed Pharaoh

May I always be a source of blessing to others and not pain. May even my enemies recognize that I am a fountain of blessing over-pouring with goodness that impacts the environment not just for myself but for all that associate with me. Jacob was a blessing to Pharaoh. How can I be a blessing even to my enemies? Meditate on this. I believe Christians praying in a community become such a huge blessing in that neighborhood. Will your absence be felt if you relocate or are you perceived as a nuisance.

Another example of this was David who once was found in the camp of Achish - the Philistine King . . . even in that scenario, David was a blessing and the King was sorry to see him go.

1Sa 29:6 Then Achish called David, and said unto him, Surely, as the LORD liveth, thou hast been upright, and thy going out and thy coming in with me in the host is good in my sight: for I have not found evil in thee since the day of thy coming unto me unto this day: nevertheless the lords favour thee not

Do you know as Christians you carry so much favor that your presence alone can magnetize goodness and healing into situations. An evangelist on holiday once visited a shop and as he browsed the books on the stand, he met a man who had been ill for a while who did not know him as an evangelist but just exchanged greetings and shook his hand. But as he shook his hand, the sick man became well instantly. Have you ever been in situations where non-Christians have felt the positive impact of your presence? If not, then do examine your life again. This is what it means to be salt and light. To be a blessing and an illumination to darkness . . . to restore savor to lack of taste and to be an answer to begging questions.

Worse is if you have become part of the problem, always murmuring and criticizing . . . making things worse. Jacob blessed the heathen King. Lord, make me a blessing even to those that hate me.

Song

Great is thy faithfulness, O God my Father;
there is no shadow of turning with thee;
thou changest not, thy compassions, they fail not;
as thou hast been thou forever will be.

Great is thy faithfulness! Great is thy faithfulness!
Morning by morning new mercies I see;
all I have needed thy hand hath provided;
great is thy faithfulness, Lord, unto me!

Summer and winter and springtime and harvest,
sun, moon and stars in their courses above
join with all nature in manifold witness
to thy great faithfulness, mercy and love. Refrain

Pardon for sin and a peace that endureth
thy own dear presence to cheer and to guide;
strength for today and bright hope for tomorrow,
blessings all mine, with ten thousand beside! Refrain

Prayer: Lord, make me a blessing to all that come in contact with me. Amen

JULY 30

Days of Pilgrimage

Bible Text: Genesis 47:9-10

Gen 47:9 And Jacob said unto Pharaoh, The days of the years of my pilgrimage are an hundred and thirty years: few and evil have the days of the years of my life been, and have not attained unto the days of the years of the life of my fathers in the days of their pilgrimage. Gen 47:10 And Jacob blessed Pharaoh, and went out from before Pharaoh.

Our days on earth are few and evil. How true. If only we can understand this great truth, we will place far less emphasis on them and consider more our eternal future. We will see ourselves as pilgrims and not settlers. We will recognize our true home ... our Heavenly home. 130 years is not a short period from an earthly perspective, but when we consider the eternal future ahead of us ... all our times on earth become truly insignificant. Yet our sojourn is not to be wasted, for it determines how our eternity will be. We will be termed as slothful if our work is not done and we are yet to be able to receive God's well done.

Indeed it is a blessing to be able to know that there is still a lot yet to be done from God's assessment. Many overestimate their accomplishments and a few are deluded that they have done much good. Jacob says evil and few have the days of my life been, as he proceeds to be a blessing to Pharaoh. May we ever lean on the mercies of God to receive help to complete our work be it amongst the heathen or in the body of Christ. Many Christians may not see clearly that God has given them assignments not just in the Church, but in the secular arena as well.

Also remember that this is a pilgrimage, that there will one day be a journey home, a reporting back to the father ... a presentation of accomplishments. How will it be for you on that great appointed day? Will you be empty handed? When God asks ... did you bless X and Y ... how will you answer?

Reflect on your life as a pilgrim and the people and situations you have been sent to bless - and whether you did so. Sadly we focus too much on ourselves and how it was for us and the personal progress we want to make ... but I discern God created us and sent us .... more for others ... to be blessing to them while we may endure our own process of being perfected for our roles in touching the lives of others. I remember so many hymn writers ... many who lived many painful lives but all are blessed by the evergreen poetry they left behind. Take your focus off yourself ... seek grace to be salt and light for others.

Song

I know there is another fellowship in Heaven 4ce.

Prayer: Lord, help my selfishness ... help me to be an instrument of blessing to others. Amen

JULY 31

Selfless Service

Bible Text: Genesis 47:11-12

Gen 47:11 And Joseph placed his father and his brethren, and gave them a possession in the land of Egypt, in the best of the land, in the land of Rameses, as Pharaoh had commanded. Gen 47:12 And Joseph nourished his father, and his brethren, and all his father's household, with bread, according to their families.

Joseph began to play the role for which he was preserved. He gave possessions to His family. We do not read much about Joseph accumulating possessions for himself. Instead, we see a selfless person more careful to see the brothers that ill-treated him in the past well taken care of. Joseph is without any bitterness as he becomes a great blessing to his family. Only the best was given to them.

I researched to see what Joseph had for himself, but found no references on personal accumulations. He must have taken what was given him, but in all humility, he does not ask Pharaoh for any personal favors for himself. Someone once said that selfishness is at the root of all sin, while love covers all misdeeds. The actions of Joseph overflowed with love and forgiveness. Joseph is an example that shows we can truly forgive completely and live as blessings to those who have deeply hurt us in the past. The text also shows that God has been known to arrange for nourishments and provision in the least likely places.

Joseph was not selfish or bitter. He had gone through several painful experiences, but he had diverted energy that could have been wasted on bitter thoughts to service. There is the greater joy of serving and blessing those who had treated you badly. Discover that joy. But this was exactly what Jesus also did. It was painful and not easy to die for those who were spitting and deriding Him. May we follow the footsteps of Jesus.

Song

Sweetly, Lord, have we heard Thee calling,
Come, follow Me!
And we see where Thy footprints falling
Lead us to Thee.

Footprints of Jesus, that make the pathway glow;
We will follow the steps of Jesus where'er they go.

Tho' they lead o'er the cold, dark mountains,
Seeking His sheep;
Or along by Siloam's fountains,
Helping the weak:

If they lead thro' the temple holy,
Preaching the Word;
Or in homes of the poor and lowly,
Serving the Lord:

Then at last, when on high He sees us,
Our journey done,
We will rest where the steps of Jesus
End at His throne.

Prayer: Lord, lead us to follow your foot prints. Amen

AUGUST 1

Jesus - the Nourisher

Bible Text: Genesis 47:11-12

Gen 47:11 And Joseph placed his father and his brethren, and gave them a possession in the land of Egypt, in the best of the land, in the land of Rameses, as Pharaoh had commanded. Gen 47:12 And Joseph nourished his father, and his brethren, and all his father's household, with bread, according to their families.

There are important details in this story. First we see that it is Joseph that places, that gives them a possession, that nourishes the family according to what was commanded. Jesus is indeed a great provider. He nourishes like no one can . . . but His work of provision is neither random nor indiscriminate. Jesus knows His own. He knows His family. He recognizes His brother. He knows His household. It may take a while, but eventually, He will provide for His own. We sometimes feel we can continue to enjoy being a wolf but in sheep's clothing - we can carry titles and say the words but in our hearts we are the same, unchanged and deceptive. We pretend that we have forgiven, we act as though we know God and can even claim that God has blessed when He has not. Indeed, men may bless but when God blesses He does not make mistakes . . . He is not fooled. Jesus like Joseph can distinguish between His own and the others He must provide for. There is a general providence but there is also a special care.

If you are not being nourished by His word. If you have not encountered Him as the great provider. If you have not seen His best, we should ask ourselves first . . . are we truly His? But then you will say that there are people who are not rich and appear to have needs but belong to God. Indeed, but they must know the nourishment of the soul, the spiritual positioning that is the best of God - above principalities and powers . . . they must have tasted the bread of Heaven - the satisfaction that comes from the living word of God. This may not always translate to visible substance in situations when God knows in His infinite wisdom, He will not be glorified. God has a better plan, always. Meditate on the truth that Jesus nourishes. He keeps His own. He comes through to help - sometimes at the last minute and is ever faithful. But He can separate between deceivers and His - when others are confused - He is not. Those that are His will obey His commandments. Those that are His will love His laws. Those that are His will honor Him and will flee from sin. Those that are His are His friends they are His household. These are not those who spend only a few minutes in His presence and can't wait to get on to something else. These are not those who love God only in His words but do not sense a kinship . . . a blood relationship. Have you seen the way a close family behave - the love and oneness that exists between true brothers and sisters? Be assured - Jesus will nourish all that are His.

Song

Be not dismayed whate'er betide, God will take care of you;
beneath his wings of love abide, God will take care of you.

God will take care of you, through every day, o'er all the way;
he will take care of you, God will take care of you.

Through days of toil when heart doth fail, God will take care of you;
when dangers fierce your path assail, God will take care of you.

All you may need he will provide, God will take care of you;
nothing you ask will be denied, God will take care of you.

No matter what may be the test, God will take care of you;
lean, weary one, upon his breast, God will take care of you.

Prayer: Lord, Thank you for the blessed assurance of your provision and nourishment. Amen

August 2

Raised to Shine Part 1

Bible Text: Genesis 47:13

Gen 47:13 And there was no bread in all the land; for the famine was very sore, so that the land of Egypt and all the land of Canaan fainted by reason of the famine.

Stars require darkness to shine. Light is not appreciated without darkness. The value and taste of Christianity is concealed when there is no confusion and turmoil. The destiny of Joseph and his family was to be raised to shine and distribute sustenance in a period of lack. The challenges that the world faces . . . the dearth of truth and the strange famines, recessions and crisis in churches, homes, governments are only opportunities for God's children to be raised to shine.

We are not amongst those who murmur and complain or analyze darkness. Instead, we see the rare opportunities to demonstrate a peculiar people . . . called to show forth the glory of God in any circumstances. In Egypt and in Canaan, there is a famine . . . and all faint. In the community and even in the congregations - there is a dearth . . . there is a fainting. But there is also a peculiar people shining - raised to glow at the worst of times. It is the worst of times that prove our true identity. It is the worst of civilization and the corruptions of the culture that prove the power of God. It is the lack, the famine of joys that helps the chosen to locate the salvation of God.

You have been raised to shine in the darkness, to glow in the confusion, to bring clarity to blurred vision . . . to bring order in a rebellious culture. Do not be like the others who only question the issues, instead be part of the answer, the solution that people are seeking. They come to you because there is something you carry that they need - it is Christ that you carry that makes you different - sought out and desired.

Arise and shine - do not be surprised at the darkness - instead simply glow and enjoy the difference that carrying Christ makes. The Bible says Isaac sowed in the time of a terrible famine . . . but the people of God want to gather . . . No . . . this is time to sow in the life of others, sow in the kingdom . . . sow to bless someone. Soon you will receive like never before.

Gen_26:12 Then Isaac sowed in that land, and received in the same year an hundredfold: and the LORD blessed him.

Song

Sowing in the morning, sowing seeds of kindness, Sowing in the noontide and the dewy eve;
Waiting for the harvest, and the time of reaping, We shall come rejoicing, bringing in the sheaves.

Refrain
Bringing in the sheaves, bringing in the sheaves,
We shall come rejoicing, bringing in the sheaves,
Bringing in the sheaves, bringing in the sheaves,
We shall come rejoicing, bringing in the sheaves,

Sowing in the sunshine, sowing in the shadows,Fearing neither clouds nor winter's chilling breeze;
By and by the harvest, and the labor ended, We shall come rejoicing, bringing in the sheaves.

Going forth with weeping, sowing for the Master, Though the loss sustained our spirit often grieves;
When our weeping's over, He will bid us welcome, We shall come rejoicing, bringing in the sheaves.

Prayer: Lord, You have raised me up for the times of famines. Help me to sow my life . . . shining in the worst of famines. Amen

214

AUGUST 3
Raised to Shine (Part 11)

Bible Text: Genesis 47:13

Gen 47:13 And there was no bread in all the land; for the famine was very sore, so that the land of Egypt and all the land of Canaan fainted by reason of the famine.

Famine is a type of darkness and we have been called to shine. But how do we shine. We do not shine at the expense of others or by pulling others down. Rather we are like the stars in the sky, we shine and allow others to shine as well. We are not bullies nor do we compel others to notice us. Instead we simply glow and the darkness must recognize our light.

Php 2:12 Wherefore, my beloved, as ye have always obeyed, not as in my presence only, but now much more in my absence, work out your own salvation with fear and trembling. 13 For it is God which worketh in you both to will and to do of his good pleasure. 14 Do all things without murmurings and disputings: 2:15 That ye may be blameless and harmless, the sons of God, without rebuke, in the midst of a crooked and perverse nation, among whom ye shine as lights in the world;

Other things mentioned by Paul on how Christians are to shine include 1. Our obedience to God is higher and even more in the absence of supervision and any recognition. 2. We are hardworking to guard our salvation and being cautious not to sacrifice our faith in exchange for lucre or medals. 3. We do all things without murmurings and disputing. 4. We live lives that are blameless and harmless to others . . . we can be trusted in the midst of crookedness and perverseness.

Are we shining in the famine or complaining? Have we done as Paul advises so that we shine as lights in the world? Reflect on these things and remember we are born in Christ to shine. Jesus is the ultimate light of the world . . . we can also learn of Him and of how He shines.

Song

The whole world was lost in the darkness of sin;
The Light of the world is Jesus!
Like sunshine at noonday His glory shone in;
The Light of the world is Jesus!

No darkness have we who in Jesus abide;
The Light of the world is Jesus!
We walk in the Light when we follow our Guide;
The Light of the world is Jesus!

Ye dwellers in darkness, with sinblinded eyes,
The Light of the world is Jesus!
Go, wash at His bidding, and light will arise;
The Light of the world is Jesus!

No need of the sunlight in Heaven, we're told;
The Light of the world is Jesus!
The Lamb is the Light in the city of gold;
The Light of the world is Jesus!

Prayer: Lord, teach us to shine in the darkness as Christ shines. Amen

AUGUST 4

The Vanity of Riches

Bible Text: Genesis 47:14

Gen 47:14 And Joseph gathered up all the money that was found in the land of Egypt, and in the land of Canaan, for the corn which they bought: and Joseph brought the money into Pharaoh's house.

Even Pharaoh serves ultimately the purpose of God. These are times when all that has been gathered bows to God, honors God either in service, judgment or in worship. God will ultimately do as He pleases - He proves that He reigns over everything . . . even money.

Rev_11:15 And the seventh angel sounded; and there were great voices in Heaven, saying, The kingdoms of this world are become the kingdoms of our Lord, and of his Christ; and he shall reign for ever and ever.

What is the point of gathering against the will and purpose of Him who will control it all - eventually. Many serve mammon as though mammon can challenge the reign of God. The worship of money is vain as Christ controls all the substance of the earth and the kingdoms bow to His purpose now and forever until He chooses to come and judge and burn up the vanity.

It is confusing that Joseph gathers money to Pharaoh . . . but Pharaoh serves God . . . in a sense that all of creation serves God - even Satan, has a purpose that he cannot deviate from. There is a purpose to the gathering and that purpose is known to God. It is a delusion that any plan to make money will hurt God . . . the one who is able to gather everything to His glory - when He so desires. Many seek to make money outside God's ways - through evil and wickedness . . . only to see God gather those funds out of their hands into a process that will honor God - using whoever He wills, including Pharaoh. Another vanity is to think you can retain riches when God commands an outflow. God can cause the entire universe to release all it has gathered to Him - whether gathered righteously or not. But only the righteous will reign with Him. Pharaoh may be a gathering point - but it is Joseph that truly rules.

In summary, make Jesus your business partner. Let Him be the manager and inspiration of all your financial deals . . . get to know Him even on money matters. Begin to see Him reign and rule over your money . . . walk with Him in your finances. Enjoy the benefits - similar to what the brothers of Joseph enjoyed as God rules over all the resources. Did He not say . . . The silver is mine, the gold is mine.

Song

I'd rather have Jesus than silver or gold; I'd rather be His than have riches untold;
I'd rather have Jesus than houses or lands; I'd rather be led by His nail-pierced hand

Refrain: Than to be the king of a vast domain - And be held in sin's dread sway;
I'd rather have Jesus than anything - This world affords today.

I'd rather have Jesus than men's applause; I'd rather be faithful to His dear cause;
I'd rather have Jesus than worldwide fame; I'd rather be true to His holy name

Prayer: Lord, Do not permit money take the place that belongs to you in my heart. Amen

AUGUST 5

The Failure of Money

Bible Text: Genesis 47:15

Gen 47:15 And when money failed in the land of Egypt, and in the land of Canaan, all the Egyptians came unto Joseph, and said, Give us bread: for why should we die in thy presence? for the money faileth.

Money can be useful, but we cannot set our hearts on money for it can and will fail. A few have discovered that money can and will fail but many are yet to understand this truth. Do you see that the children of Israel were immune from this failure, because they relied on their kinship to Joseph and not on the money that they had. The Egyptians had to relate to Joseph based on the money they had . . . it is no wonder that Egyptians must gather as much as they can for they will need it for what God wants to give them - even for free. The brothers of Joseph had no money but had the best simply because they were related to Joseph.

There are two financial dispensations at work. The one that is based on money for survival . . . that is driven by inflation and the harsh economic rules of demand and supply - but which is doomed to failure as we already have occasionally seen in great depressions. The other is based on being in the family - our identity as God's chosen brethren. This dispensation enjoys the best - but for free (only because Joseph has paid the price)

Money fails, but our faith in God never fails. Money fails but our relationship to Christ never fails. Money fails but Joseph's provisions never fails. Mammon wants us to focus on money and serve him instead of God . . . he presents money as a sure insurance and a firm foundation but this is a deception. The truth is that money is a resource that is doomed and to a destiny of ultimate failure. Make it, gather as God enables you - but do not set your heart on it. Be always ready to release it as God demands. It is unfortunate that people do all things—even marry for money and go to such great lengths to obtain it.

Song

Take the world, but give me Jesus, All its joys are but a name;
But His love abideth ever, Through eternal years the same.

Refrain: Oh, the height and depth of mercy! Oh, the length and breadth of love!
Oh, the fullness of redemption, Pledge of endless life above!

Take the world, but give me Jesus, Sweetest comfort of my soul;
With my Savior watching o'er me, I can sing though billows roll.

Take the world, but give me Jesus, Let me view His constant smile;
Then throughout my pilgrim journey - Light will cheer me all the while.

Take the world, but give me Jesus. In His cross my trust shall be,
Till, with clearer, brighter vision, Face to face my Lord I see.

You can never never fail 3ce - Jesus the same forever. (Chorus)
The Rock that never fails, let me hide in you - In You there is power (Chorus)

Prayer: Lord, Let my heart be set on you, my foundation - the Rock, that never fails. Amen

AUGUST 6

The Exchange

Bible Text: Genesis 47:16-17

Gen 47:16 And Joseph said, Give your cattle; and I will give you for your cattle, if money fail. 17 And they brought their cattle unto Joseph: and Joseph gave them bread in exchange for horses, and for the flocks, and for the cattle of the herds, and for the asses: and he fed them with bread for all their cattle for that year.

The value of the word of God in our hearts, on our lips and in our churches cannot be overestimated. One day, the true value of the word of God will be seen. One day, the wisdom of Heaven will have its place above all that the earth cherishes and millions will be given to have it . . . but it will not be enough to pay for it. The men of Egypt have exhausted their funds and now give all their cattle, horses and flocks so they will be fed with bread. Why did they not eat the cattle?

Bread has a significance beyond plain dietary matters. It points to the word of God and the truths that can sustain us. Observe the difference in what the brothers had to do to receive bread and what Egypt did. The Egyptians had to exchange all their cattle, wealth and means of survival so that they could have bread - while the brothers of Joseph simply enjoyed it in Goshen. The purpose of occupations is to glorify God and not to survive. The brothers of Joseph supervised the herds and ruled over the livestock operations but did not require wages for food . . . they received princely rations freely

Today, the world seeks wisdom and sustenance and works hard in many occupations to procure health, peace, provision and luxuries . . . only to discover that when they come to Christ - they see that all these have all been freely given.

Remember Peter who fished all night but caught nothing until directed by Christ . . . and then finding a net-breaking haul . . . but only to come to the shore to find a meal of fish already prepared. The Bible says God has prepared a table before us in the presence of our enemies - meaning all things are ready and freely given while others must strive. This does not mean that God wants His children to be slothful, but He does not want us to depend on our occupation or herds of cattle. Our source is Jesus -who controls all and has promised to give us all things freely - even as He has freely been given as a sacrifice for us. Today, ask yourself what you are working for . . . to survive or to glorify God. Today ask if you are receiving the bread of life, the true bread of Heaven . . . freely given as we trust in the living word - Jesus Christ or are we drifting seeking something else, or desiring other sources of wisdom and survival.

Song

I hunger and I thirst;Jesus, my manna be:
ye living waters, burst - out of the rock for me.

Thou bruised and broken Bread, my life-long wants supply;
as living souls are fed, O feed me, or I die.

Thou true life-giving Vine, let me thy sweetness prove;
renew my life with thine, refresh my soul with love.

Rough paths my feet have trod, since first their course began;
feed me, thou Bread of God; help me, thou Son of Man.

For still the desert lies my thirsting soul before;
O living waters, rise - within me evermore.

Prayer: Lord, I hunger and thirst for your presence - fill my thirst and hungry soul with yourself. Amen

AUGUST 7

Eye on the Sparrow

Bible Text: Genesis 47:18

Gen 47:18 When that year was ended, they came unto him the second year, and said unto him, We will not hide it from my lord, how that our money is spent; my lord also hath our herds of cattle; there is not ought left in the sight of my lord, but our bodies, and our lands:

The plight of Egypt in the time of famine is sad. Egypt has given all they have to Joseph, but that is not enough . . . and the famine is still many years. The substance we have gathered will not be enough for that which we need the most . . . our salvation. All the gold, silver and assets could not pay for the salvation of man. How true it is that all we have gathered and given will still one day prove not enough. The brothers of Joseph did not need to gather anything. They did not need money for food. They were provided for by Joseph.

When we understand the difference . . . we can position our lives . . . are we Christians or are we unrelated to Christ? Those who are Christ's need not gather . . . are not driven by acquisitions nor do they fear for survival. They know that they will be cared for even without spending what they have.

God provides for His own . . . if only we could rest in the great truth that we are His. Indeed our savings, assets and what we have can be useful . . . but they are not always relevant to God's plan of provision. The heathen gather for fear that they will need all their acquisitions only to discover that health, peace and joy are not for sale . . . though we deplete all our accounts searching for them.

Today is a good day to meditate on the following scriptures . . . are you like the brothers of Joseph in Egypt or like the magicians and other Egyptians bewitched and bewitching others . . . but ever worried over their means of survival and currency of exchange . . . Lord, help our faith.

Mat 6:25 Therefore I say unto you, Take no thought for your life, what ye shall eat, or what ye shall drink; nor yet for your body, what ye shall put on. Is not the life more than meat, and the body than raiment? 26 Behold the fowls of the air: for they sow not, neither do they reap, nor gather into barns; yet your Heavenly Father feedeth them. Are ye not much better than they? 27 Which of you by taking thought can add one cubit unto his stature? 28 And why take ye thought for raiment? Consider the lilies of the field, how they grow; they toil not, neither do they spin: 29 And yet I say unto you, That even Solomon in all his glory was not arrayed like one of these. 30 Wherefore, if God so clothe the grass of the field, which to day is, and to morrow is cast into the oven, shall he not much more clothe you, O ye of little faith? 31 Therefore take no thought, saying, What shall we eat? or, What shall we drink? or, Wherewithal shall we be clothed? 32 (For after all these things do the Gentiles seek:) for your Heavenly Father knoweth that ye have need of all these things. 33 But seek ye first the kingdom of God, and his righteousness; and all these things shall be added unto you. 34 Take therefore no thought for the morrow: for the morrow shall take thought for the things of itself. Sufficient unto the day is the evil thereof.

Song

I sing because I'm happy - I sing because I'm free
His eye is on the sparrow - and I know He watches me
His eye is on the sparrow and I know He watches me.

Prayer: Lord, Teach me to trust and lean on your everlasting arms. Amen

AUGUST 8

Buy Us and Our Land

Bible Text: Genesis 47:19

Gen 47:19 Wherefore shall we die before thine eyes, both we and our land? buy us and our land for bread, and we and our land will be servants unto Pharaoh: and give us seed, that we may live, and not die, that the land be not desolate.

Without Christ . . . everything is useless and ultimately worthless. There is a day when all will discover this, but for some it will be too late. There are two categories of people - the brothers of Joseph for which a price has been paid and others who cannot afford their own salvation - even with their own lives and lands. The price of our salvation was not cheap. It cost God the blood of His only begotten son.

This is a day to appreciate the great salvation bought at an expensive price . . . no measure of silver or gold could have paid for the precious salvation of God. It is good to be thankful, but when a great act of help is given to the undeserving, we should be even more appreciative . . . How could we ever thank God enough for His love . . . will any song composed ever suffice to appreciate him? Will any shout of hallelujah convey the greatness of His works and to express the glory that words fail to describe.

Israel should be full of appreciation for Joseph. There will not be another Joseph. There is no other way to salvation, there is no other offering for sin . . . no price that any can ever pay for salvation than has already been paid by Jesus. Who else can pay such a price?

We have seen many men of honor - ready to offer their very own lives for their salvation and the salvation of others . . . but this is vain . . . for no other sacrifice has been appointed. Many have made very noble declarations but every religion that denies the already completed work of Christ is vanity.

Why are you still trying to strike a deal with God when a deal has already been done . . . all that is required is your surrender. Give your life to Jesus today and enjoy the difference. Commit all that is yours to Him and experience His generous arrangements in the Goshen set aside for you. There is no other deal but that which Christ struck at the Cross of Calvary, no other way . . . it does not matter what you offer for salvation . . . it will not be enough. This should spur you to spread the gospel . . . It is a gospel of great grace. So much is freely provided.

Song

He giveth more grace when the burdens grow greater, He sendeth more strength when the labors increase,
To added affliction He addeth His mercy, To multiplied trials, His multiplied peace.

His love has no limit, His grace has no measure, His power no boundary known unto men,
For out of His infinite riches in Jesus, He giveth and giveth and giveth again.

When we have exhausted our store of endurance, When our strength has failed ere the day is half-done,
When we reach the end of our hoarded resources, Our Father's full giving is only begun.

Prayer: Lord, reveal the greatness and extent of your grace. Help me to tell of this abundant grace to others. Amen

AUGUST 9

All is Vanity

Bible Text: Genesis 47:20

Gen 47:20 And Joseph bought all the land of Egypt for Pharaoh; for the Egyptians sold every man his field, because the famine prevailed over them: so the land became Pharaoh's.

What are the things that count with God? Why are possessions so important to some? How must we behave concerning earthly possessions when God can commit them into the land of the enemy? I often wonder, if I could hand over something to my enemy, it tells me that it is really not so important. It is not worth clinging to or it means I have something else far more precious than what has been given. A Christian that has not understood that all that the world offers is vanity and can be released to whoever God wishes ... has not understood that the brothers of Joseph were in a far superior position. the position of being cared for by God. It does not matter where the money and lands are and who owns what ... if we are in the "Goshen" of God - then we have it all.

The land can belong to Pharaoh but it is Joseph the instrument of God that directs and manages all that was in the hand of Pharaoh. Jesus told the disciples to go to the mouth of a fish and found a coin ... He knows where the money is kept, because He directed all the flows. But when asked about taxes, Jesus said give unto Caesar that which belongs to Caesar and to God what belongs to God. What are the things that belong to God ... His own, His children .... our hearts, our soul.

Many are trying to give God money and the things that God has no use for that belong to men, while they give their hearts to mammon as they cheat and scheme to gather more. Ask yourself, will that which I am clinging to help me in eternity? Will it be more useful to me in the far more significant periods ... the eternal dispensation of my existence or will it count in the 100 or so years on earth? The answer to that question will help me see that which we can release freely and that which we cannot afford to lose.

The brothers of Joseph had an identity that guaranteed them the best in Egypt ... everything else was vanity. The Egyptians soon ran out of all their possessions and now needed the mercy that only Joseph could dispense. Do not waste a precious minute. Meditate on these truths and see that a life with a heart not given to Christ is vain even when we have great riches. There will be day at the doorway of eternity that the rich man without Christ will have absolutely nothing and must face a hard judgment. Come to Jesus today.

Surely every man walks in a vain show: surely they are disquieted in vain: he heaps up riches and knows not who shall gather them. And now, Lord, what wait I for? My hope is in You. Deliver me from all my transgressions: make me not the reproach of the foolish." Psalm 39:6-8

Song

What profit all the labor here
There's nothing new for you and me!
Remember not the former things
They are all vanity.

Prayer: Lord, let my heart no more be set on that which is vain. Remembering not the former things. Amen

AUGUST 10

Travails of the Wicked

Bible Text: Genesis 47:21-23

Gen 47:21 And as for the people, he removed them to cities from one end of the borders of Egypt even to the other end thereof. 22 Only the land of the priests bought he not; for the priests had a portion assigned them of Pharaoh, and did eat their portion which Pharaoh gave them: wherefore they sold not their lands. 23 Then Joseph said unto the people, Behold, I have bought you this day and your land for Pharaoh: lo, here is seed for you, and ye shall sow the land.

What can the wicked expect but to sow, to work on a land that is not theirs . . . to be dispossessed of their own property . . .

Ecc_2:26 For God giveth to a man that is good in his sight wisdom, and knowledge, and joy: but to the sinner he giveth travail, to gather and to heap up, that he may give to him that is good before God. This also is vanity and vexation of spirit.

Have you observed the wicked rich, how they fuss, plan, worry and put so many ventures into place, only at the end to see it all as a meaningless travail. The sinner does not know the God of Israel. His ignorance is not an excuse, as he travails for Pharaoh, sows on a land that is not his . . . he has been under the yoke of bondage which he does not recognize. He harvests, but is unsure of how much he will enjoy. His days are full of travail. He is dislocated from his family and sent to farm the land in another area . . . he misses his family and groans under burdensome . . . but there is a famine and he must do all that is required to survive. These are the travails of the wicked . . . and not meant for you. The wicked have been sold to evil . . . to Pharaoh to farm his lands. This is the dispensation of modern commerce.

But you have not been sold to Pharaoh, you are a specially preserved people of God. Do not forget this. You are different. You are chosen. Ponder over these verses to appreciate the difference between the lot of the rest of the world and the chosen family of Israel in these times of famine. The difference is not earned by merit . . . It could not be merit . . . what would you say the brothers of Joseph did to deserve this? It was grace and all favor. To be in the family of God and not the camp of the wicked groaning on the farmlands of Pharaoh, sold to sin and foolishness . . . it's all grace. Observe that the best that the sinner can expect no matter how sugar coated or gold plated it may appear - is travail. There is grace to come out of sin.

Song

Marvelous grace of our loving Lord, Grace that exceeds our sin and our guilt!
Yonder on Calvary's mount outpoured, There where the blood of the Lamb was spilled.

Refrain: Grace, grace, God's grace, Grace that will pardon and cleanse within;
Grace, grace, God's grace, Grace that is greater than all our sin.

Sin and despair, like the sea waves cold, Threaten the soul with infinite loss;
Grace that is greater, yes, grace untold, Points to the refuge, the mighty cross.

Dark is the stain that we cannot hide. What can avail to wash it away?
Look! There is flowing a crimson tide, Brighter than snow you may be today.

Marvelous, infinite, matchless grace, Freely bestowed on all who believe!
You that are longing to see His face, Will you this moment His grace receive?

Prayer: Lord, what an amazing grace, what a marvelous grace that spared my life from the travails and the yoke of mammon. I thank You, Lord. May your grace be always more than sufficient. Amen

AUGUST 11

A Grievous Blessing

Bible Text: Genesis 47:24

Gen 47:24 And it shall come to pass in the increase, that ye shall give the fifth part unto Pharaoh, and four parts shall be your own, for seed of the field, and for your food, and for them of your households, and for food for your little ones.

Joseph orders a tax for Pharaoh of 20%. This is not a tithe, but actually more than the tithe. The taxation laws are permitted by God, ordained by God. It is strange that God ordained a tithe . . . 10% for His own . . . but 20% to Pharaoh. Is it a wonder that He says His yoke is easy and is burden is light? This was in period of serious inflation (failure of money) and dearth (outside the barns of Pharaoh) . . . and to add to their pains . . . farming in a time of famine and difficulty . . . perhaps there were no rains and the harvest was lean . . . Do recall that this was in the seven years of leanness. A higher tax is levied again as though the burdens of leanness were not sufficient.

The systems of the world has learnt a lot from what God has assigned to the children of Egypt. The higher taxes, in times of recession . . . the increase in costs and levies in periods of inflation multiplies the travails of the wicked. The wicked must fend for themselves. they must find seed, feed their household out of 80% of what is left after working hard in a tough terrain. But this is not the lot of the children of Israel. Indeed all are bound to obey the rules of the land - even taxation, but there is another kingdom, another realm of spiritual and physical provision. A place called Goshen. All our increase must glorify God as we obey the rules of the land. Are you in any way cheating on your taxes . . . it is a good time to repent and restitute. Although the Egyptians are fed, they do so only through labor harvesting the fields in times of tough famine. God's best is not to keep us from evil through a grievous process. Like Jabez, God has supernatural provisions that keeps us from evil without grievous yokes. May we be so blessed to give so easily from the excess of God in our care.

1Ch 4:10 Jabez called on the God of Israel, saying, Oh that thou wouldest bless me indeed . . . that thine hand might be with me, and that thou wouldest keep me from evil, that it may not grieve me! And God granted him that which he requested.

Song

Zacchaeus was a tax man who one day climbed a tree,
For he was short in stature and said he could not see.
And yet he had a problem that mattered even more:
He didn't see the suffering his greed had caused the poor

O Lord, you saw Zacchaeus-- so wealthy, yet alone.
You said, "Come down—and hurry! I'm coming to your home."
For you broke bread with sinners and saw within each one
A person loved and treasured-- God's daughter or God's son.

It wasn't just the treetop that helped Zacchaeus see;
Your love and welcome showed him how different life could be.
He said that he'd start over and work to make things fair;
He'd speak the truth, bring justice, and find new ways to share.

O Christ, you bid us welcome and help us all to see!
May we respond by building a just society.
Then children won't be hungry and all will share your bread.
Then those who now must struggle will live in joy instead

Prayer: Lord, may I not partake in the lot of the wicked. Change my economic positioning. Amen

AUGUST 12

Two Different Dispensations

Bible Text: Genesis 47:27

Gen 47:27 And Israel dwelt in the land of Egypt, in the country of Goshen; and they had possessions therein, and grew, and multiplied exceedingly.

The Bible presents two broad ways when speaking of prospering and the principles of enterprise. Both ways involve diligence particularly in sowing seed which refers to applying an input. The input could be our business ideas, our career efforts, and our investments in skill development, sacrificial giving or even financial investments of our surplus. These two ways are different but we often can confuse one for the other or be found in a mix, not really having left one approach fully while seeking to enter the other.

Egypt, in the Bible, was a luxurious and wealthy empire but for the children of Israel it eventually represented the place of their captivity and bondage where they were enslaved to deliver target productions of bricks. It represents a dispensation of wealth which enslaves the child of God to mammon—a wicked and crafty hard task master. Egypt can appear welcoming, rewarding and fair—but has a natural disposition to kill, steal and destroy when the opportunity presents itself. Canaan is the land of promise, flowing with milk and honey, but occupied by hostile tribes occupying cities with mighty walls, representing strongholds of thought—which must be pulled down. Between Egypt and Canaan is the wilderness experience, a place where the Israelites grumbled and murmured - never understanding the ways of their God, but often seeing His acts of deliverance and miracles of provision. In the wilderness, the Israelites though not in Egypt still think like Egypt but on a journey out of Egypt to the place of promise. Only few of those who left Egypt enter the Promised Land, but a new generation of Israelites enter and become the citizens of the Land of milk and honey—the land of rest.

In Egypt, there is much industry, achievement and several diagnoses and treatments, but no cures. There is always a longing, a thirsting but never a satisfaction. Vanity is available as the pill to soothe us to sleep and keep us going. The more we have, the more we need to have as more goods become essential and our insatiable thirsts run out of control. In the end we rationalize our situations and say things cannot be perfect—when money fails to satisfy and eventually fails completely.

In this text, the children get a foretaste of the provision of rain from Heaven, enjoying what they have not labored for while Egyptians sold their property and exhausted all their hard earned savings even as money completely failed. In the dispensation of Egypt, Money is the currency—but it always eventually fails. For God, our faith and obedience and mercy combine to a different means of exchange. Goshen is a foretaste of Canaan, the promised land which foreshadows God's Heaven. The question to ask here is this. Are you living by faith or on principles of Egypt? You cannot do both.

Song

I have a God who never fails 3ce
Who never fails—who never fails for ever more
Amen. Jesus never fails 3ce
For ever more

Prayer: Lord, teach me your divine wisdom not to labor in vain. Amen

August 13

A Different Blessing

Bible Text: Genesis 47:27

Gen 47:27 And Israel dwelt in the land of Egypt, in the country of Goshen; and they had possessions therein, and grew, and multiplied exceedingly.

Now we see in these verses describing the different arrangements made for Israel. We read in previous verses that Egypt had to sell all their property, and relocated to work on farms in the famine, and to bring a tax to Pharaoh- only to manage the rest. The different arrangement for Israel as they occupied influential positions enabled them to gather possessions, to grow and multiply exceedingly. They were given special rations and provisions in Egypt.

The blessings for Israel even in Egypt exceeded those enjoyed by the Egyptians because of Joseph. Are Christians going to be blessed even in this wicked world? When Christ spoke of the blessings for His followers, he spoke of a hundred fold in this time . . . and in the world to come;

Mar_10:30 But he shall receive an hundredfold now in this time, houses, and brethren, and sisters, and mothers, and children, and lands, with persecutions; and in the world to come eternal life.

Our contact and surrender to Christ, and obedience to Him places us in a unique position of rare blessing to increase even in famine. This is first spiritual but it will be physical as well . . . as houses etc. also increase. Joseph had given all, and he reaped such a huge harvest, more than enough to cater for his brothers forever. Christ sowed his life and all that truly surrender and love Him are in a covenant to prosper even as their soul prospers even eternally. So why do we still have issues as Christians, why do we experience lack? Why do we not have the abundant life and still have to struggle. Why can we not define our situation as prosperous through the poverty of Christ?

Isa 49:15 Can a woman forget her sucking child, that she should not have compassion on the son of her womb? yea, they may forget, yet will I not forget thee. . . . Isa 1:19 If ye be willing and obedient, ye shall eat the good of the land:

Am I willing? Am I obedient? What do these mean? Can it be that many are not willing to eat the good of the land? Can it be that some are obedient? Are we afraid to be blessed . . . many are unwilling invitees to Him who says all is ready. But God makes us willing in His time, and may God help our obedience for there is still a lot of selective obedience. We cannot antagonize God with our actions and expect the same God to bless us. But our God is also sovereign - He does as He pleases and will be magnified and moves when He desires. He raises up and brings down, without answering to any. He has a timetable for everything. We cannot move ahead of His pre-appointed seasons.

Song

And when before the throne I stand in Him complete,
I'll lay my trophies down, All down at Jesus' feet.

Jesus paid it all, All to Him I owe;
Sin had left a crimson stain, He washed it white as snow.

Prayer: Lord, help me to be willing and obedient to you in every regard. Amen

AUGUST 14

The Best is Ahead

Bible Text: Genesis 47:28

Gen 47:28 And Jacob lived in the land of Egypt seventeen years: so the whole age of Jacob was an hundred forty and seven years.

The best is yet to come. Long years awaited Jacob. Not years of sorrow thinking about Joseph in a famine. But years in which all his long abandoned dreams all came true. Years in which he knew that Jehovah truly reigned. Those 17 years were truly remarkable for Jacob. Every day Jacob must have pinched himself to see if he will wake up and discover that all was only a dream. God has saved the best for the last for you - because that is the best time to experience His best. Those years wiped away all the previous years, and caused him to forget if there was ever a time when Joseph was not with him.

Psa 126:1 A Song of degrees. When the LORD turned again the captivity of Zion, we were like them that dream.

The turning of captivity can be done in different ways. The way God turns captivity is likened by David to a dream. Indeed there were times when David in the caves or running from one place to another or when he got to Ziklag only to find he had lost everything. Times when like Jacob, he must have looked up only for death. But God was still at work, and the story was not over. David was still going to rejoice as King.

Be encouraged. You will see your captivity turned and you will be amazed at what God has in store for you - when you have come to the end of your efforts. When you stop limiting God with your good intentions. when you stop imagining that God is waiting for you to do something instead of realizing that you must simply wait on God. Jacob said he was ready for death at the ripe age of one hundred and thirty when he saw Joseph was alive . . . but God still gave him seventeen extra years of joy . . .

Gen_37:2 These are the generations of Jacob. Joseph, being seventeen years old, was feeding the flock with his brethren; and the lad was with the sons of Bilhah, and with the sons of Zilpah, his father's wives: and Joseph brought unto his father their evil report.

It was after Joseph's seventeenth birthday that his troubles started. That number must have brought bad memories for Jacob. But God used 17 more years to wipe away all the pains that came after Joseph turned seventeen. There is someone reading this devotional . . . wait on the Lord. Soon you will testify saying . . . "Am I dreaming?".

Song

God, your blessings overflow! What can we begin to say?
How can we begin to show, All our gratitude this day?
God, we join to worship you, Giving thanks for all you do.

Thank you for the life you give, For each friend and family,
For the land in which we live, For your love that sets us free.
Thank you, God, for daily bread, And for feasts of joy you spread.

Prayer: Lord, teach me to wait on you. Turn again my captivity that I may say "I must be dreaming . . ." Amen

AUGUST 15

Mortality

Bible Text: Genesis 47:29-31

Gen 47:29 And the time drew nigh that Israel must die: and he called his son Joseph, and said unto him, If now I have found grace in thy sight, put, I pray thee, thy hand under my thigh, and deal kindly and truly with me; bury me not, I pray thee, in Egypt:30 But I will lie with my fathers, and thou shalt carry me out of Egypt, and bury me in their buryingplace. And he said, I will do as thou hast said. 31 And he said, Swear unto me. And he sware unto him. And Israel bowed himself upon the bed's head

We are mortals. This means we will one day wrap up our wok here and go home. Although Jacob lived 147 remarkable years, a time eventually came when he knew God was calling him home. It can be glorious when God gives us notice that it is time to join Him in eternity. This should not cause any to fear—for there is a glory ahead that surpasses all we have ever experienced. But only if we did well in the time we spent in earth. There will be an accounting. For Jacob, he knew what he must do at that time. Death can be very organized and beautiful . . . like an arranged drama presentation in different parts . . . Jacob acted his final scenes like a professional.

First he must receive assurance that he would not be buried in Egypt but in the cave of his fathers. Second he must bless Joseph and his children separately and finally he must bless his other sons. Our love for God fills us with an important sense of assignment. Are there things that God wants us to do that has not been done? Are there things that must be done at our dying moments? How do we die well? A man that lives for God will know exactly what to do. A man who has lived for himself is full of fear and a sense of impending judgment at these final moments. There is no fear for Jacob . . . he has seen God complete His plans through him and has no regrets. How will your own end be? Begin the process of a closer walk with God today and enjoy the benefits of a calm transition to His prepared eternity.

Song

More love to Thee, O Christ, more love to Thee! Hear Thou the prayer I make on bended knee.
This is my earnest plea: More love, O Christ, to Thee; More love to Thee, more love to Thee!

Once earthly joy I craved, sought peace and rest; Now Thee alone I seek, give what is best.
This all my prayer shall be: More love, O Christ to Thee; More love to Thee, more love to Thee!

Then shall my latest breath whisper Thy praise; This be the parting cry my heart shall raise;
This still its prayer shall be: More love, O Christ to Thee; More love to Thee, more love to Thee!

Prayer: Lord, let my love for you which translates to obedience - increase even much more in my dying than it was in times of youth and the earlier days. Amen.

AUGUST 16

Bury me not in Egypt

Bible Text: Genesis 47:29-31

Gen 47:29 And the time drew nigh that Israel must die: and he called his son Joseph, and said unto him, If now I have found grace in thy sight, put, I pray thee, thy hand under my thigh, and deal kindly and truly with me; bury me not, I pray thee, in Egypt:30 But I will lie with my fathers, and thou shalt carry me out of Egypt, and bury me in their buryingplace. And he said, I will do as thou hast said. 31 And he said, Swear unto me. And he sware unto him. And Israel bowed himself upon the bed's head

Does it matter where we are buried? It did to Jacob and taught Joseph an important lesson. Our walk with God does not end with our years of life … even when it is time to return to our maker, God also has instructions that He gives. God can use our life just as He can use our death. There are many men of God who heard detail instructions about their death and how they were to die and be buried. There are many things we may not understand now about death that we will understand in the future.

Jacob did not want to be buried in Egypt, where his body may been ritualized in pagan rites or where his corpse will be in the company of demons. God showed Jacob a future day when his body will be resurrected and he will need to be seen on the streets of Jerusalem … at the time of the crucifixion of Christ … by many.

Joh_5:28 Marvel not at this: for the hour is coming, in the which all that are in the graves shall hear his voice … Mat 27:50 Jesus, when he had cried again with a loud voice, yielded up the ghost. 51 And, behold, the veil of the temple was rent in twain from the top to the bottom; and the earth did quake, and the rocks rent; 52 And the graves were opened; and many bodies of the saints which slept arose, 53 And came out of the graves after his resurrection, and went into the holy city, and appeared unto many

The Bible does not mention the name of the saints and whose graves were opened … but we can safely assume that the graves were not the graves of Egypt. Our God reigns in living and in dying. We must obey Him in living but also more in our dying. I have seen Christians giving strange instructions at their death … to be cremated and their ashes poured in the sea or somewhere … as if they had a right to declare how they wanted to die and their bodies treated. Do not be buried as the Egyptians, just as you did not live like them. The Egyptians were buried with earthly possessions and treasures as though they could take them to the afterlife. When the end comes as it will eventually - remain obedient to the voice that has daily guided you every day of your life. Empty you came and empty you must return. God reigns even in death.

Song

More love to Thee, O Christ, more love to Thee! Hear Thou the prayer I make on bended knee.
This is my earnest plea: More love, O Christ, to Thee; More love to Thee, more love to Thee!

Once earthly joy I craved, sought peace and rest; Now Thee alone I seek, give what is best.
This all my prayer shall be: More love, O Christ to Thee; More love to Thee, more love to Thee!

Then shall my latest breath whisper Thy praise; This be the parting cry my heart shall raise;
This still its prayer shall be: More love, O Christ to Thee; More love to Thee, more love to Thee!

Prayer: Lord, let my love for you which translates to obedience - increase even much more in my dying than it was in times of youth and the earlier days. Amen.

AUGUST 17

Blessings of the Father

Bible Text: Genesis 48:1-2

Gen 48:1 And it came to pass after these things, that one told Joseph, Behold, thy father is sick: and he took with him his two sons, Manasseh and Ephraim. 2 And one told Jacob, and said, Behold, thy son Joseph cometh unto thee: and Israel strengthened himself, and sat upon the bed.

Joseph has a deep understanding of the value of being rejoined to his father. This is not just for the communion and love, but there are powerful pronouncements that only a father can make. Jacob is 147 years old but death does not snatch him unprepared. Joseph is also not unprepared . . . God will help us at important dates to be available when we need to be. God will also provide strength in whatever form it is needed so we do not miss our blessings.

Joseph is the first to be alerted on the sickness of his father. It is not impossible that he had ensured that someone is assigned with the task to monitor the condition of his father. Joseph had been close to Jacob in the first seventeen years and while others kept the flock or ran errands . . . Joseph sat with Jacob and learnt the important lessons that will keep him in Egypt, in prison and eventually as prime minister.

One of the things Joseph had learnt was the importance of the blessing of the father. I can imagine how he must have wondered in the years in prison . . . how the blessings - he had so heard about will come to him - now that he was a slave. But, now Joseph is now no longer a slave, but a leader . . . he is no more far from home but united with his father. His father is greatly honored and does not die hungry in a famine, but lives comfortably in Egypt. All so that the blessings that must come to Joseph and his children are passed down.

Do not despise your father - physical or spiritual. Honor your parents. If you have fallen out with them - go and find them so that they may bless you for good. Joseph had been taught to care more for the father's blessing than all the treasures of Egypt. I wonder where his other brothers were at this time. Do you care about the things of God? Our Heavenly Father has so many blessings stored for us in His word? Do you know about them or care about them? Or do you care more for the visible new comforts and riches that you have just come into. Joseph was taught to get his priorities right. This was the moment he had been waiting all his life for.

Song

Come, Thou Fount of every blessing,
Tune my heart to sing Thy grace;
Streams of mercy, never ceasing,
Call for songs of loudest praise.
Teach me some melodious sonnet,
Sung by flaming tongues above.
Praise the mount! I'm fixed upon it,
Mount of Thy redeeming love.

Prayer: Lord, teach me to care for spiritual things. Help me to watch and wait for the blessings that must come by His grace. Show me all the Father's blessings for me. Let none fail. amen

AUGUST 18

Luz

Bible Text: Genesis 48:3

Gen 48:3 And Jacob said unto Joseph, God Almighty appeared unto me at Luz in the land of Canaan, and blessed me.

There was a time when Jacob was fleeing from his angry brother Esau, after he had stolen the blessings that belonged to Esau. At this time of fear and confusion, God came to comfort him in a place called Luz. Here Jacob vowed that God will be his God forever - if only He could always have the assurance of His presence. Also many years later, Jacob is again faced with the misdeeds of his sons after the daughter of Leah, Dinah is defiled. Again Jacob is told to raise an altar at Luz, getting rid of all the strange gods and idols . . . God appears to him after Rebekah's nurse dies and blesses him.

The most important introduction to Joseph is that blessings come from God. We only succeed because God blesses us to be fruitful. God is the source of our comforts when we need them, all blessings that will last for good and not man - although He uses our earthly and spiritual fathers. Joseph is reminded that the reason for his success and miraculous turnaround was the blessing of God that was upon his father, Jacob - even before Joseph was born.

Pro_10:22 The blessing of the LORD, it maketh rich, and he addeth no sorrow with it.

Jacob was overjoyed at this time and could see that he only had to wait for God to realize that the blessing of the Lord is more than sufficient. Jacob was reminding Joseph to depend on God and teach his children to do the same. Jacob was telling Joseph the source of the blessings that he was about to now bless his son and grandsons with.

In spite of the challenges, rashness, guile and deception that trailed Jacob's life, God's blessing in his life still was able to see him through. Jacob also calls God . . . Almighty. God does not need your help to bring His will to pass. All power belongs to Him. He has no shortages requiring our support. He is Almighty, all powerful and all knowing. Joseph needs to be aware of this and beware of the failings of His father. Today, look up afresh to God. Worship Him as the Almighty God. All blessings come from Him who is faithful and powerful to bring all His purposes to pass. This is a good day to worship Him.

Song

Almighty God, Almighty King
You are the Lord of everything
The Highest Praise to you I bring
Almighty God. Almighty King

Prayer: Lord, I worship you today - The Almighty. Amen

AUGUST 19

An Everlasting Possession

Bible Text: Genesis 48:4

Gen 48:4 And said unto me, Behold, I will make thee fruitful, and multiply thee, and I will make of thee a multitude of people; and will give this land to thy seed after thee for an everlasting possession.

God promised Jacob so many things. It is indeed amazing that Jacob is promised not just the temporal but the everlasting. Fruitfulness, growth and expansion are of God ... an expression of His lavish abundance and inimitable excess. Jacob is to be made fruitful and his seed ... whatever comes from his loins is bound in a covenant that will reach even into eternity. The blessings of Abraham reached down to Isaac, to Jacob ... and today all Christians are God's special children ... they partake in what God has promised.

Please do note that it is God that is making promises and not man and the land is a gift and not earned ... and it will be forever not just for today. It is all grace and mercy and someday in eternity, we will all thank God for what He has given us—things we could never earn.

How can a land be an everlasting possession ... if we are not one day going to become everlasting beings in an everlasting body ... blessed in everlasting residences. What a mystery? To be a people of God with an everlasting possession. To be given and have something that will last forever is not easy to understand in a world that can only appreciate what it can see today. Indeed Jacob was blessed with an everlasting possession but for many decades he lived often confused, manipulative and despondent in thinking God has changed his mind. God has not changed His mind concerning you. You will yet rejoice in your eternal heritage.

Remember, your maker is your Husband - in love with you ... who He sees as the apple of His eye. You wonder how this can be you ... Jacob would also spend years wondering too - but this changed nothing. God still loves you.

Song

Thou my everlasting Portion, more than friend or life to me,
All along my pilgrim journey, Savior, let me walk with Thee.

Close to Thee, close to Thee, Close to Thee, close to Thee;
All along my pilgrim journey, Savior, let me walk with Thee.

Not for ease or worldly pleasure, Not for fame my prayer shall be;
Gladly will I toil and suffer, only let me walk with Thee.

Lead me through the vale of shadows, bear me o'er life's fitful sea;
Then the gate of life eternal - may I enter, Lord, with Thee.

Prayer: Lord, Be my everlasting portion ... Amen

AUGUST 20

Finally Blessed

Bible Text: Genesis 48:5-6

Gen 48:5 And now thy two sons, Ephraim and Manasseh, which were born unto thee in the land of Egypt before I came unto thee into Egypt, are mine; as Reuben and Simeon, they shall be mine. 6 And thy issue, which thou begettest after them, shall be thine, and shall be called after the name of their brethren in their inheritance.

Our identity relates to our level. Who we are matters. Whose we are matters even more. Ephraim and Manasseh were grandchildren but have been promoted to receive the direct blessing of children. All the other children that come after Ephraim and Manasseh will be blessed by Joseph and not by Israel.

Who are you? You are blessed. You are the child of God. You have been blessed directly in Christ Jesus. You do not belong to a pastor or to a prophet. The blessings of our earthly and spiritual parents count but the blessings of God count far more.

We are already a blessed people. We have received the blessings as revealed in the word of God. We cannot obtain any other superior blessing and we do well to stop chasing and seeking after blessings that the word of God already says we possess.

Heb_11:21 By faith Jacob, when he was a dying, blessed both the sons of Joseph; and worshipped, leaning upon the top of his staff. Jas_1:12 Blessed is the man that endureth temptation: for when he is tried, he shall receive the crown of life, which the Lord hath promised to them that love him. Jas_1:25 But whoso looketh into the perfect law of liberty, and continueth therein, he being not a forgetful hearer, but a doer of the work, this man shall be blessed in his deed. Rev_1:3 Blessed is he that readeth, and they that hear the words of this prophecy, and keep those things which are written therein: for the time is at hand. Rev_14:13 And I heard a voice from Heaven saying unto me, Write, Blessed are the dead which die in the Lord from henceforth: Yea, saith the Spirit, that they may rest from their labors; and their works do follow them. Rev_16:15 Behold, I come as a thief. Blessed is he that watcheth, and keepeth his garments, lest he walk naked, and they see his shame. Rev_19:9 And he saith unto me, Write, Blessed are they which are called unto the marriage supper of the Lamb. And he saith unto me, These are the true sayings of God. Rev_20:6 Blessed and holy is he that hath part in the first resurrection: on such the second death hath no power, but they shall be priests of God and of Christ, and shall reign with him a thousand years. Rev_22:7 Behold, I come quickly: blessed is he that keepeth the sayings of the prophecy of this book. Rev_22:14 Blessed are they that do his commandments, that they may have right to the tree of life, and may enter in through the gates into the city.

Thank God - I am blessed in Christ Jesus.

Song.

I'm so glad I belong to Jesus. I belong to Jesus. I belong to my God 2ce (Chorus)

Prayer: Lord, may it never be said that my life and indeed anything in me - rejected your everlasting blessings.

AUGUST 21

Do not despise little things

Bible Text: Genesis 48:7

Gen 48:7 And as for me, when I came from Padan, Rachel died by me in the land of Canaan in the way, when yet there was but a little way to come unto Ephrath: and I buried her there in the way of Ephrath; the same is Bethlehem.

Very often we despise things because they are little. Little beginnings are not appreciated, little places are sometimes disdained and when we are seeking open doors - a little way can be missed altogether. Rachel was buried in the way of Ephrath, at a time of littleness in a place that is now known as Bethlehem. But Bethlehem will be forever remembered as the chosen birthplace of the king of Kings.

Mic_5:2 But thou, Bethlehem Ephratah, though thou be little among the thousands of Judah, yet out of thee shall he come forth unto me that is to be ruler in Israel; whose goings forth have been from of old, from everlasting.

We are often misguided to search for prominence and seek attention, when our place in destiny is meant to be small and unnoticed . . . until God transforms a little seed into a giant tree. Out of Bethlehem, where Rachel is buried at a time when there was but a little way, emerges the ruler of the entire universe - Jesus.

Today, is there anything awesome God is doing in your life? It will more likely be found flickering in a seemingly insignificant corner. Do not despise it. Do not give in to the mockery targeted at the little. The best of God always seemed to start small. Learn from the tongue - so little a member yet so great in its importance. Or a little leaven that eventually leavens the whole lump. But the importance of smallness and the little way . . . the way of humility . . . this is the only way we can receive the kingdom of God.

Luk_18:17 Verily I say unto you, Whosoever shall not receive the kingdom of God as a little child shall in no wise enter therein

When asked to make a choice, Lot chose the well watered cities of Sodom . . . not knowing these were marked out for destruction . . . while Abraham remained in the small tent on harsh terrains . . . Abraham became the father of a blessed people . . . while Lot fell into mischief and many troubles. Do not despise the God of little beginnings, the God in the little way . . . who is close to the humble, the meek and poor in spirit. God has not forgotten you - though the way you see may be little.

Song

God will make a way - Where there seems to be no way
He works in ways we cannot see - He will make a way for me
He will be my guide - Hold me closely to His side
With love and strength - For each new day
He will make a way - He will make a way

By a roadway in the wilderness - He'll lead me
And rivers in the desert will I see - Heaven and earth will fade
But His Word will still remain
He will do something new today

Prayer: Lord, teach me to see and appreciate the little way you have made, and to follow it. Amen

AUGUST 22

Who are these?

Bible Text: Genesis 48:8-9

Gen 48:8 And Israel beheld Joseph's sons, and said, Who are these? 9 And Joseph said unto his father, They are my sons, whom God hath given me in this place. And he said, Bring them, I pray thee, unto me, and I will bless them.

This devotional reminds us of our responsibility as parents. We do not allow our children to grow up in a default mode assuming they will somehow emerge as children of God. First, we must identify them and speak in faith that they are children of God, given by God to shine for God - with a destiny to be blessed of God. Our children are not mistakes - no matter the circumstance of their delivery - nor are they in any way inferior even though we see certain challenges.

The sin of abortion . . . destroying in the womb what God has given is not just murder - but worse ; a grievous rejection of that which God has given as a blessing to mankind. You child is not a wayward urchin. Do not call your son or daughter a vagabond - instead identify him as the gift of God, a good thing - a blessed thing - a wonderful thing. Then you must bring your children to God, by dedicating them and offering them to Him constantly in the place of prayers. Children must be brought to God by teaching them the ways of God and deliberately presenting them to be blessed by His word and truths.

Many drop their children with nannies and bring their children to the TV and cartoon networks or whatever seems convenient. Others have no time to bring their children to God and watch as they are brought to other gods by peers until they end up on the streets. Reclaim your children for God. Begin by calling them the sons and daughters of God - the gifts of God . . . bring them on your knees first to God. Ask God to forgive you for negligence in your role as a parent. Your son or daughter is a good and perfect gift. Confess this truth and let Satan be proven a liar concerning your children.

Jas 1:17 Every good gift and every perfect gift is from above, and cometh down from the Father of lights, with whom is no variableness, neither shadow of turning.

Song

For I am fearfully and wonderfully made.
For I am fearfully and wonderfully made.
God made me specially; yes, very carefully,
For I am fearfully and wonderfully made!

When God made the fish, He said and it was so.
When God made the birds, He said and it was so.
But when it came to making man,
He formed him with His hands,
For I am fearfully and wonderfully made!

Prayer: Lord, teach me to see my children as wonderfully made gifts from above - good and perfect. Amen

August 23

Fruit of Deceit

Bible Text: Genesis 48:10

Gen 48:10 Now the eyes of Israel were dim for age, so that he could not see. And he brought them near unto him; and he kissed them, and embraced them.

Israel was old and could not see. What an unfortunate state? Did we not read of Moses who the Bible tells us was strong in his old age ... Israel like his father, Isaac had weak senses in his old age - Jacob took advantage of this weakness. He reaped the fruit of his deceit. But Moses was different.

Deu 34:7 And Moses was an hundred and twenty years old when he died: his eye was not dim, nor his natural force abated.

Be careful, the seed you sow - especially to the weak and infirmed. Be careful how you treat the aged. God will never be mocked ... we will always reap our seeds. But this also means acts of kindness to the elderly, care for strangers and love to the unlovable will also have its own future harvest. What kind of seed are sowing now? A good seed? What kind of harvest are we reaping now?

I will not worry about past seeds - only ask for God's mercy and fear Him whose mercy reaches to the very Heavens in its inexhaustible capacity but begin to sow kindness, forgiveness, love, charity, gifts .... begin to help the vulnerable, never taking advantage of the helpless. Find those in the community that all have abandoned and begin to show them love. Leave the rest in the hands of God.

Our old age can be glorious- we do not need to end our years in weakness. Our natural forces need not be abated ... we will be strong in our old age. Our youth can be renewed like an eagles ... The best seed is waiting on God ... this is the sowing of our rights to God ... surrendering all to Him. I believe this is what Moses sowed - he could have been a great prince of Egypt but sowed that dream and became the leader of God's people to lead them out of Egypt ... a tough task that cost him much. But though he did not enter the promised land ... he reaped in old age a vigor and vitality that Isaac and Jacob never knew. Moses waited on God all through his life, living for God to be used by Him - starting a challenging ministry at 70 when many will be seeking a quiet retirement ... Moses waited - even to the very end.

Isa_40:31 But they that wait upon the LORD shall renew their strength; they shall mount up with wings as eagles; they shall run, and not be weary; and they shall walk, and not faint.

Song

I will wait on you - Almighty God - In the beauty of your holiness
I will worship you - Almighty God. In the beauty of your holiness

Prayer: Lord, teach me to wait upon you ... have mercy on me that my latter years be even more glorious than my younger days. Amen

AUGUST 24

Blessed beyond our Prayers

Bible Text: Genesis 48:11

Gen 48:11 And Israel said unto Joseph, I had not thought to see thy face: and, lo, God hath shewed me also thy seed

God promises to give us in excess of what we ask or think - beyond all our imaginations and exceeding our thoughts and expectations. God is not limited to what we ask nor do our thoughts hold him to ransom. He will give us the heathen for an inheritance and will cause souls to come into His kingdom beyond all our expectations and thoughts. Indeed, sin will cut us short of the glory we could have had - but there is also a favor and mercy that goes beyond all we could ever deserve and reveals even things we could never search for or seek. It is good to pray, but best to praise God who does beyond our dreams and exceeds all the boundaries of our intercession. God is our exceeding great reward.

Gen_15:1 After these things the word of the LORD came unto Abram in a vision, saying, Fear not, Abram: I am thy shield, and thy exceeding great reward.

The word exceeding is a good word to study. It means to go beyond in quantity, degree, rate, etc. It means to exceed the limit, to go above boundaries and exceed one's understanding. It means to surpass in every way . . . to be superior and to excel. This is who our God is. We can have great thoughts of what He can do - but always be cautioned to know He will always do in excess of all our thoughts. He can give beyond our desires and is not limited by what we can imagine in our limited understanding. In riches, He can bless exceedingly . . . he has no reason to hold back from His abundant stores. Still we see in this text, that Jacob was blessed to see Joseph, not because of Jacob - but so that God's will is done, God exceeds our thoughts and prayers to prosper His plans and not to satisfy our lusts for gain. Perhaps we should spend more time to praise Him for His exceeding greatness that is beyond in all its ramifications.

Song

How sweet the Name of Jesus sounds - In a believer's ear!
It soothes his sorrows, heals his wounds, And drives away his fear.

It makes the wounded spirit whole, And calms the troubled breast;
'Tis manna to the hungry soul, And to the weary, rest.

Dear Name, the Rock on which I build, My Shield and Hiding Place,
My never failing treasury, filled - With boundless stores of grace!

By Thee my prayers acceptance gain, Although with sin defiled;
Satan accuses me in vain, And I am owned a child.

Jesus! my Shepherd, Husband, Friend, O Prophet, Priest and King,
My Lord, my Life, my Way, my End, Accept the praise I bring.

Weak is the effort of my heart, And cold my warmest thought;
But when I see Thee as Thou art, I'll praise Thee as I ought.

Till then I would Thy love proclaim - With every fleeting breath,
And may the music of Thy Name - Refresh my soul in death!

Prayer: Lord, I praise you - for there is no God like you that exceeds our thoughts and even our prayers. Amen.

AUGUST 25

The Final Say

Bible Text: Genesis 48:12

Gen 48:12 And Joseph brought them out from between his knees, and he bowed himself with his face to the earth. 13 And Joseph took them both, Ephraim in his right hand toward Israel's left hand, and Manasseh in his left hand toward Israel's right hand, and brought them near unto him. 14 And Israel stretched out his right hand, and laid it upon Ephraim's head, who was the younger, and his left hand upon Manasseh's head, guiding his hands wittingly; for Manasseh was the firstborn.

There is a song that says Jehovah has the final say. God has a way of doing whatsoever He pleases and defeating all the intentions of men - whether well-meaning or not. God is supreme and does not need our theology and sense of right or wrong. These are for us and not for God. God knows how it must end and decrees as it must be. We cannot dispute His arrangement. Joseph knows that Israel cannot see and so moves the firstborn Manasseh towards Israel's right hand . . . the blessing of the right hand is superior and differs in many regards.

God moves the hand of Israel deliberately . . . wittingly . . . upon Ephraim. Ephraim means God has made us fruitful . . . Manasseh means God has caused us to forget the evils and pains of the past. Indeed both names are important, and both tribes have been adopted by Israel as his sons. But Ephraim is chosen for a special elevation above his elder brother.

What do we learn from this? We see that God lifts up as He chooses. God gives with no recourse to the expectations and preferences of men. He will raise the last and make first if He so wishes. God does as He pleases and not as we want it to be. Let God be who He says He is. Let Him be God. Let Him be above all . . . even our understanding of what He wants to do.

Song.

Above all powers
Above all kings
Above all nature
And all created things
Above all wisdom
And all the ways of man
You were here
Before the world began

Above all kingdoms
Above all thrones
Above all wonders
The world has ever known
Above all wealth
And treasures of the earth
There's no way to measure
What You're worth

Prayer: Lord, teach me to let you have your way. Amen

AUGUST 26

Introducing the Blessing

Bible Text: Genesis 48:15-16

Gen 48:15 And he blessed Joseph, and said, God, before whom my fathers Abraham and Isaac did walk, the God which fed me all my life long unto this day, 16 The Angel which redeemed me from all evil, bless the lads; and let my name be named on them, and the name of my fathers Abraham and Isaac; and let them grow into a multitude in the midst of the earth.

Our testimonies prepare us to be instruments of blessing for others. Israel has suffered much, but in all these he sees the unseen hand that has always been upon his life. Israel has had experiences that enables him to identify the source of the blessing that must also bless his sons. Jacob saw much evil but also saw the God who redeems from evil. Evil can serve a purpose to help us locate the real God. Jacob has located God and can call on this God to bless Joseph and his children.

Be careful who is laying his hands upon you and yours. You need to know the testimony of the father who is blessing, because in that testimony is the God who is the source. Jacob introduces the blessing by identifying the God who blesses and who He is and what He has done in the past. Jacob has not forgotten his past encounters with God - not for pain but to call upon Him who has blessed him and given many promises - who is the same source that will use Jacob to bless others.

The name that is named on us is important. Have evil and demonic names been named on us. We can reject those names - even change them. Fruitfulness and growth in the midst of lack and difficulty is the portion of all of God's children. These are common to all of God's blessed children. Fruitfulness and growth is first spiritual . . . it will subsequently be physical to the glory of God . . . but the end will be glorious for God has promised us . . .

1Co_2:9 But as it is written, Eye hath not seen, nor ear heard, neither have entered into the heart of man, the things which God hath prepared for them that love him.

Song

Abraham's blessings are mine
Abraham's blessings are mine
I am blessed in the morning
Blessed in the morning - blessed in the evening
Abraham's blessings are mine

Prayer: Lord, let your glorious name and right hand of blessing be ever upon me. Amen

AUGUST 27

Displeasure of Men

Bible Text: Genesis 48:17

Gen 48:17 And when Joseph saw that his father laid his right hand upon the head of Ephraim, it displeased him: and he held up his father's hand, to remove it from Ephraim's head unto Manasseh's head.

There are times we see the well-meaning intentions of men which do not align with the will of God. God is displeased when we do not permit Him to have His way - but more often men are displeased when God rules. Men have their own rules and expectations and have their own thoughts . . . often meaning well. But the rules of men and their plans may not be the intention of God. When men are displeased with the plans of God, they are quick to take actions and protest in the place of prayer.

This devotional reminds us that the ways of God and the ways of man are very different. The ways of men - even the best of men are like a small fire made with wood and fuel . . . but the ways of God are like the stars we see burning afar with an unimaginable glow from distances that are unfathomable. His ways are not our ways.

Isa_55:9 For as the Heavens are higher than the earth, so are my ways higher than your ways, and my thoughts than your thoughts.

There are times we must simply humbly bow to the ways of God and leave Him to reveal His plans in His own good time. We can be still even when we do not understand what God is doing . . . and when we think we know what God wants, we will often find ourselves suddenly at a loss. Reflect on this and meditate on this truth. Who are you pleasing? Men - even good, generous and wise men - like Joseph or are you pleasing God. If men who you respect are displeased by your actions, go back to check with God. If God is pleased, if our actions are from the leadings of the Holy Spirit and do not conflict with the written Word. Then be at peace.

Ask God to reveal His ways to you. Is there a matter before you, a decision to be made. Wait on God till you have heard His direction on the matter. Then trust and obey.

Song.

Can you be obedient - To the Lord of all,
Though the earth should totter, Though the heav'ns should fall?
Face e'en a disaster - With a faith-filled heart,
Knowing naught can harm him - Who with Christ will start?
Can you be obedient - To the Lord you serve,
Never even flinch, friend, Never even swerve;
Though your next step onward - Seem to lead to death?
Can you then obey Him - Without bated breath?

Prayer: Lord, let help my obedience. Amen

August 28

Wrong Corrections

Bible Text: Genesis 48:18

Gen 48:18 And Joseph said unto his father, Not so, my father: for this is the firstborn; put thy right hand upon his head.

This devotional is not to encourage rebellion or disobedience - but it is possible that the innovation you are proposing is wrong - not of God. How can you be correcting your spiritual father or leader? It is true that you appear to have observed the mistakes of a blind man and have said nothing but now you must correct the elder on an important matter. You are convinced that you have a clearer sight and keener senses? Often when we notice failing physical senses, we conclude the spiritual is also in decline. But not necessarily. Your leader may be aging, but his spiritual insight may still be razor sharp. Indeed Joseph had observed the blindness and it was obvious that Jacob who was in need of a guide to be led around will need help in blessing correctly. Joseph concludes that here was a man who was ready to plunge into error. Joseph proceeded like any other would - moving decisively and meaning well to correct Jacob - but this was a wrong correction.

Often times youth will observe the faltering steps and the shaky steps of elders and come quickly to the conclusion that God has ceased to work through His authority in a situation. Remember that physical aspects are often very different from spiritual . . . and being able to drive home unaided or push aggressively on a matter is extremely different from spiritual accuracy.

Joseph was young, strong - the star in Egypt - the Prime Minister of a great nation - but he was very wrong spiritually and had perhaps the right heart but his father had a discernment that was for the far future - a dimension completely unseen to the young Joseph.

It is great to be young and full of new initiative - but remember not to be quick in dismissing leadership and the perspective of fathers - we need them to see into dimensions too far for us to possibly understand . . . we will need fathers in touch with God to unravel mysteries that are beyond human insights. Joseph was young - but wrong. Do not be quick to despise the elders and do value the role of fathers - spiritual and physical - who God has preserved to correct our zeal. Fathers have gone through much that we do not know and have been shown far more than we can possibly discern. Jacob had paid a heavy cost in his life to eventually understand that God does not need help - even that of the virile, intelligent and honest Joseph. Ponder over this - when next you are tempted to deride the counsel of those who have gone before us - in ministry. The wisdom of past fathers is priceless. May our fathers not be like Eli . . . who gave control to vagabonds.

Song

Master, let me walk with thee in lowly paths of service free;
tell me thy secret; help me bear the strain of toil, the fret of care.

Help me the slow of heart to move by some clear, winning word of love;
teach me the wayward feet to stay, and guide them in the homeward way.

Teach me thy patience; still with thee in closer, dearer company,
in work that keeps faith sweet and strong, in trust that triumphs over wrong;

Prayer: Lord, open my eyes O Lord. Spare me from presumption. Amen

AUGUST 29

God knows.

Bible Text: Genesis 48:19

Gen 48:19 And his father refused, and said, I know it, my son, I know it: he also shall become a people, and he also shall be great: but truly his younger brother shall be greater than he, and his seed shall become a multitude of nations.

Have you ever been in a situation when God refuses to grant you your request. When you are certain of the validity of your prayers . . . and God says No . . . I have a better plan. It would have been wonderful if God gave very detailed explanations . . . but I wonder how complex this would be and if our human faculties can process the complete interpretations that stretches beyond generations in the past and future. Why does God hate Esau? Why are fallen angels not helped to repent? Why can everyone not end up in Heaven?

The answer is that God knows all. He is omniscient and we are not created to be. It is good to seek knowledge of God, but often better to just worship Him for who He is . . . God Almighty. Joseph's wishes are refused and Joseph must remain perplexed as to God's purpose or reasons for this. Many scholars have debated the agenda of God in this verse. Suffice it to say that "God knows" . . . there is no detail that misses the knowledge of Him who knows our thought from afar off. God knows what we will think in the next decade talk less of our actions.

In this we also see the abundance in God. The greatness of one does not disturb the shining of another. We can be great not at the expense of the greatness of another. The elder brothers greatness will be short of the younger Ephraim . . . but God does not tell all about the situation. The great tribe of Ephraim is later filled with pride and joined to idolatry. The wisdom of God is deep and can be perplexing . . . His ways can be like an ocean with indiscoverable depths.

For this same reason, be assured that though you do not understand the way out of your situation, God has a billion levers that are well beyond your comprehension. You may be disappointed at being refused your desires . . . consider it a great mercy extended to you - when you are not permitted to have your way. Take solace in the truth that this limitless God is the one that helps, comforts and keeps you.

Song

Ask the Savior to help you,
Comfort, strengthen, and keep you;
He is willing to aid you,
He will carry you through.

Prayer: Lord, not my will but thine always. Amen

AUGUST 30

A New Standard.

Bible Text: Genesis 48:20

Gen 48:20 And he blessed them that day, saying, In thee shall Israel bless, saying, God make thee as Ephraim and as Manasseh: and he set Ephraim before Manasseh

God can erase past records and create new standards. God was about to set a new record and a new standard for the word "blessed". People had been blessed before but none was said to become so evident that it will be a standard for nations. I pray for you today, that God will use your life to set a new standard for good. When the word joy is mentioned, everyone will refer to you. When the word peace is described they will speak of your case. When they speak of prosperity, they will speak of your prosperity. God uses His own as standards for good. We know of the wisdom of Solomon . . . Solomon became a standard for wisdom. When it comes to mercy . . . we know of the sure mercies of David. David was a standard for mercy. God will single you out for such exceptional good - it will be used as standard in prayers and in blessing others.

God sets and also un-sets. His decisions are described as indisputably confirmed. It may take a while to see this, but His Word is forever settled. His counsel is immoveable and unchangeable. There are many things that God has prearranged in a sequence that pleases Him and we cannot do anything about it. This is a great day to thank God for His perfect arrangements in the order that pleases Him. God also orders our steps with His word. He directs our paths on a preset trajectory.

God also sets new standards in the negative sense . . . for sorrow and regret. Lord, may our case be set for good - in your perfect and abundant mercy.

Song

Out in the highways and byways of life,
many are weary and sad;
are weary and sad
Carry the sunshine where darkness is rife
making the sorrowing glad.

Refrain:
Make me a blessing,
Make me a blessing,
Out of my life
out of my life
May Jesus shine;
Make me a blessing, O savior, I pray,
I pray Thee, my Savior,
Make me a blessing to someone today.

Prayer: Lord, let me be remembered always for good and not evil. Amen

AUGUST 31

The Land of our Fathers.

Bible Text: Genesis 48:21

Gen 48:21 And Israel said unto Joseph, Behold, I die: but God shall be with you, and bring you again unto the land of your fathers.

Joseph has achieved a lot and has been brought through much and risen to the top in Egypt. But He will still need God to sustain Him and eventually bring him out of Egypt with the rest of the tribes of Israel. Indeed if God is for us who can be against us. It does not matter whatever rises against Joseph, the presence of God in his life will address it. Joseph understands this prayer but does not know that the Red Sea will be parted by God working through Moses to completely fulfill this promise.

Many times, we do not know or even understand the extent of God's blessings and what God means and how He will work to fulfill His word for us. There is a land of our fathers - Heaven and God must be with us through our pilgrimage on earth and bring us to the eternal city. Again it is the work of God and the promise of God. It will be fulfilled in your life. God knows He must bring us to the land of our fathers and so He must keep us from many things. He must say No when our flesh says yes. He must lead, guide and answer all our prayers knowing we have been promised an eternal city.

God does not promise or offer Joseph anything in Egypt in spite of Joseph's authority - as beautiful and luxurious it must have appeared to these desert tribesmen. God ignores all the marble in the palaces, the delicious meals, enchanting music and elegant fashions and speaks of another land. Although we have much authority here and we shine in Egypt, it is worth always remembering that God has not promised us Egypt. At this most important moment for Joseph, he is reminded that there is another land - the land of his fathers. There is a land where we will one day meet with Abraham, Isaac and Israel . . . By His grace I will also see you there.

We came from eternity and we will return again there - by the special mercy and grace of God.

Song

When the battle shall be done,
And the victory be won
Conflict past, conflict past;
In our happy home above,
We'll receive a crown of love,
At the last, at the last.

Prayer: Lord, may your presence be with me and may you bring me again home to your eternal accommodations.
Amen

SEPTEMBER 1

Above Thy Brethren

Bible Text: Genesis 48:22

Gen 48:22 Moreover I have given to thee one portion above thy brethren, which I took out of the hand of the Amorite with my sword and with my bow.

Psa 45:7 Thou lovest righteousness, and hatest wickedness: therefore God, thy God, hath anointed thee with the oil of gladness above thy fellows.

The Psalmist prophesies of Christ, the Holy and anointed Son of God - who has been anointed above his fellows. There are reasons given - the love of righteousness and hatred for wickedness. In a similar way Joseph is given a superior portion. Much is said about grace but God is also a God of merit as well as the God of grace. What God rewards is however different . . . the indicators that God measures are vastly different. Two measurements are mentioned in this text. Joseph loved righteousness and that bore the fruit of love, peace, long suffering and forgiveness. Joseph walked with God and loved the ways of God. The righteousness of God shone in the life of Joseph who went through great troubles but was never found to murmur or complain. Joseph hated wickedness and so did not compromise his character in the house of Potiphar. He would not betray Potiphar . . . he hated disloyalty and would go to jail for it . . . we do not hear him even defending himself or murmuring—not even once. He took it all—not seeking to grasp anything for himself even when He was right.

Be assured that God is a rewarder. He does not assign the portions randomly. From the wicked and idle servant talents will be taken and given to he who invests his talents. Joseph had several gifts and he did not bury them . . . he had visions and dreams, he interpreted dreams, he could discern God and possessed the wisdom for administration. But all these gifts were used to the glory of God.

Heb_11:6 But without faith it is impossible to please him: for he that cometh to God must believe that he is, and that he is a rewarder of them that diligently seek him. . . . Mat_25:28 Take therefore the talent from him, and give it unto him which hath ten talents

The wicked - who bury the promises and gifts of God - their talents differ in their portion to the righteous saint working diligently . . . applying every talent from Heaven even as he is given more. Can you expect a superior portion from God? Is your service remarkable? Do not be idle.

Song

In works of labour, or of skill,
I would be busy too;
For Satan finds some mischief still
For idle hands to do.

Prayer: Lord, help me to be fruitful and diligent in the gifts entrusted with me as you guide me to love righteousness and hate wickedness. Amen

September 2

Gather Yourselves

Bible Text: Genesis 49:1

Gen 49:1 And Jacob called unto his sons, and said, Gather yourselves together, that I may tell you that which shall befall you in the last days. 2 Gather yourselves together, and hear, ye sons of Jacob; and hearken unto Israel your father.

Jacob did not have to call Joseph to be blessed. We read in chapter 48 that Joseph heard his father was sick and came perhaps he suspected the end was coming - and he took his sons along or he was a constant visitor of his aging father. Either way - there is a bond of love and wanting to be with him in the end. We do not know the location of the brothers or the things that concerned them - but they were perhaps unaware of the father's blessing or were not so interested. They may have still suffered under a shadow of guilt and fear . . . thinking after their father passed on, Joseph will unleash a plan of revenge.

God has a word for them. He speaks to them as a group . . . preferring them to all be present at the same time. It was also a comfort to Jacob perhaps to see them all together . . . now united to hear from God. Jacob was the priest of the home - a true father in both spiritual and physical terms. Jacob kept his communion with God as the priest of the house till the very end. He did not delegate this assignment to any. He could speak for God and accurately too.

Can I speak for God concerning my children? Will my children gather knowing God has a message for them from their father? Indeed, this was also a final opportunity for the brothers of Joseph to make amends . . . perhaps they will individually and collectively repent and mourn before God - like King Hezekiah did when told by the prophet to prepare for death . . . how will you react when God speaks as you gather to Him ? Will you resign yourself to fate or will you plead for His mercy. Your children will not respond to you if you have been an irresponsible father. Play the role of a parent. Ask God for wisdom to lead your home.

Isa_38:1 In those days was Hezekiah sick unto death. And Isaiah the prophet the son of Amoz came unto him, and said unto him, Thus saith the LORD, Set thine house in order: for thou shalt die, and not live. 2 Then Hezekiah turned his face toward the wall, and prayed unto the LORD, 3 And said, Remember now, O LORD, I beseech thee, how I have walked before thee in truth and with a perfect heart, and have done that which is good in thy sight. And Hezekiah wept sore. . . . 5 Go, and say to Hezekiah, Thus saith the LORD, the God of David thy father, I have heard thy prayer, I have seen thy tears: behold, I will add unto thy days fifteen years.

Song

Master, speak! Though least and lowest, Let me not unheard depart;
Master, speak! For O, Thou knowest - All the yearning of my heart,
Knowest all its truest need: Speak! and make me blest indeed.

Master, speak! and make me ready, When Thy voice is truly heard,
With obedience glad and steady - Still to follow every word.
I am listening, Lord, for Thee: Master, speak! O, speak to me!

Prayer: Lord, Speak to me . . . I need a word now to prepare for the last days. Amen

SEPTEMBER 3

Reuben - the Unstable (Part 1)

Bible Text: Genesis 49:3-4

Gen 49:3 Reuben, thou art my firstborn, my might, and the beginning of my strength, the excellency of dignity, and the excellency of power: 4 Unstable as water, thou shalt not excel; because thou wentest up to thy father's bed; then defiledst thou it: he went up to my couch

Reuben is introduced as a man with great potential. He was the first born and that conferred to him several advantages automatically in the culture of Israel. Reuben was strong and described as possessing the excellency of power. He seems to be a man that started well, and in possession of many admirable qualities. He is already on the way to the top and described as already a man of excellence. So what is the problem.

The present may appear good but the future of Reuben is scarred because of the irrepressible law of consequence. The Bible warns us to consider our ways, our moral ways. Everything has a consequence. The curse and the blessing do not come causeless. Tozer said once "everything we do has a dual importance. It is important for what it is in itself and it is important for what it causes to be." Often times there appears to be no consequence, but at these times it may be best to pray that we bear the pains of our consequence early when we can bear the burdens and not so much later like Reuben when at old age, the sorrow is unbearable. It is strange that Reuben is not chastened by Jacob and little mention of any consequence is recorded concerning the evil that Reuben did. Tozer goes on to add in "The Dangers of a Shallow Faith" that it is therefore important to consider our choices. Everything we see is as a result of our choices. What we are today is as a result of choices we made yesterday. Reuben made bad choices. A person's choices distinguish him as either wise or foolish. The wise man knows he must give account of the deeds done in the body, but the fool does not. A fool is not a man of mental deficiencies but one who acts without regard for consequences. We must choose well and choose life knowing that grace and consequences exist.

Song

Conquering now and still to conquer, rideth a King in His might;
Leading the host of all the faithful into the midst of the fight;
See them with courage advancing, clad in their brilliant array,
Shouting the Name of their Leader, hear them exultingly say:

Refrain:
Not to the strong is the battle, not to the swift is the race,
Yet to the true and the faithful vict'ry is promised through grace.

Conquering now and still to conquer, who is this wonderful King?
Whence are the armies which He leadeth, while of His glory they sing?
He is our Lord and Redeemer, Savior and Monarch divine;
They are the stars that forever bright in His kingdom shall shine.

Prayer: Lord, have mercy on me . . . give me the grace to make the right choices daily. Amen.

September 4

Reuben - the Unstable (Part II)

Bible Text: Genesis 49:3-4

Gen 49:3 Reuben, thou art my firstborn, my might, and the beginning of my strength, the excellency of dignity, and the excellency of power: 4 Unstable as water, thou shalt not excel; because thou wentest up to thy father's bed; then defiledst thou it: he went up to my couch

Jacob suddenly changes his tone to address some issues that cannot be just swept off. The instability of Reuben who is described as one cursed to be ever unstable because he would not exercise self-control not to defile his father's bed. Instability is a great curse. Water assumes any shape it finds itself. It will be cylindrical in a cylindrical vessel and be conical in a conical vessel. Have you seen Christians that blend with any situation . . . they adapt and flow in all scenarios and can be whatever they need to be for the situation - but they never excel. They will never stand out for anything . . . They are too weak to shine.

Often times we carry the consequences of past choices in the form of serious character limitations that bind us to mediocrity. We imagine we do not excel because we are not trying enough - but really we cannot be used of God as a divine star because our destiny is polluted. God cannot use an unstable person for he can receive nothing of the Lord. Not even the forgiveness - so urgently needed.

Jas 1:6 But let him ask in faith, nothing wavering. For he that wavereth is like a wave of the sea driven with the wind and tossed. 7 For let not that man think that he shall receive any thing of the Lord. 8 A double minded man is unstable in all his way.

What does it mean not to excel? It means not to shine. It means to always be under a cloud of mediocrity and be far less than God has ordained us to be. What can we do? First we can repent and begin to make the right choices. Second we can go to God for mercy and help. Third, *Gal 3:13 Christ hath redeemed us from the curse of the law, being made a curse for us: for it is written, Cursed is every one that hangeth on a tree:*

Christ has redeemed us from the curse of the law, being made a curse for us. Seek the grace that is sufficient to walk in the freedom God has ordained. If God must ask us to bear our consequences - though forgiven . . . help us not to be bitter, but to sow new seeds of love and forgiveness that will eventually reap mercy and healing of all our scars. You will not miss your crown. There is eternal hope.

Song

The consecrated cross I'll bear Till death shall set me free?
And then go home my crown to wear for there's a crown for me

Prayer: Lord, as I sow forgiveness for others, help me to reap a total and complete forgiveness. Amen

SEPTEMBER 5

Simeon and Levi : Instruments of Cruelty (Part I)

Bible Text: Genesis 49:5-7

Gen 49:5 Simeon and Levi are brethren; instruments of cruelty are in their habitations. 6 O my soul, come not thou into their secret; unto their assembly, mine honour, be not thou united: for in their anger they slew a man, and in their selfwill they digged down a wall. 7 Cursed be their anger, for it was fierce; and their wrath, for it was cruel: I will divide them in Jacob, and scatter them in Israel.

Simeon and Levi came from a good home. They are brothers and must have shared many things. They were a pair that could have been united to do great things for God. They were close as brothers usually are - but they also had a sister called Dinah, who was defiled by Shechem the son of Hamor - the Hivite.

This infuriated them and caused them to execute a plot of violent murderous revenge. They were ruled by their violent passions . . . to be ruled by your passions is to be highly reactive and uncontrollable. How can God trust the power to work out a great destiny if this power will one day be misused. It is a great virtue to learn to be patient, quiet and be deliberate . . . never reacting to anything . . . most certainly never walking in revenge. We must take time to reflect over issues and discover that what has happened in the past must be released to God. Indeed, there may be pains we bear for acts of perceived injustice but consider Christ that dwells in us likened as a lamb going to be slaughtered who had all power to resist but refused to say a word of defense as he was led to the cross to be killed for our sins.

There are injustices we must bear without reacting in anger. This reflects the nature of the sheep of the pasture of Christ. Justice must be left in the hands of the righteous judge who knows details beyond what you can ever rationalize in your mind. Leave revenge to God, instead praying to release issues and also for those who hurt and curse us. As we release the baggage of past hurts we are strengthened to move forward into higher levels with God.

Song

Soft as the voice of an angel, Breathing a lesson unheard,
Hope with a gentle persuasion whispers her comforting word:
Wait till the darkness is over, wait till the tempest is done,
Hope for the sunshine tomorrow, after the shower is gone.

If, in the dusk of the twilight, dim be the region afar,
Will not the deepening darkness brighten the glimmering star?
Then when the night is upon us, why should the heart sink away?
When the dark midnight is over, watch for the breaking of day.

Hope, as an anchor so steadfast, rends the dark veil for the soul,
Whither the Master has entered, robbing the grave of its goal.
Come then, O come, glad fruition, come to my sad weary heart;
Come, O Thou blest hope of glory, never, O never depart.

Whispering hope, oh how welcome thy voice,
Making my heart in its sorrow rejoice.

Prayer: Lord, Jesus . . . meek and mild and my hope of glory - never depart from me. Amen

SEPTEMBER 6

Simeon and Levi : Instruments of Cruelty (Part II)

Bible Text: Genesis 49:5-7

Gen 49:5 Simeon and Levi are brethren; instruments of cruelty are in their habitations. 6 O my soul, come not thou into their secret; unto their assembly, mine honor, be not thou united: for in their anger they slew a man, and in their self-will they digged down a wall. 7 Cursed be their anger, for it was fierce; and their wrath, for it was cruel: I will divide them in Jacob, and scatter them in Israel.

Simeon and Levi are not cursed, but their anger is cursed. Like the citizens who sought to build a Tower at Babel, they must not be allowed to remain together to avoid worse consequences of their uncontrollable passions. They will be scattered, divided and so weak. A divided house is a doomed place where nothing will work well. Do you not see that your anger must be curbed and you must bring your passions under control or else you will have to suffer needlessly. The anger of Simeon and Levi was not the common anger that lasts for brief moments but it was a fierce anger degenerating into cruel wrath. Cruelty is often not far from unabated anger. It is not as noisy but a quiet anger that plots a deep and painful act of revenge . . . and refuses help and support to those in need because of past hurts. May God help us. We discover later that the tribe of Levi is rescued from this terrible predicament when in the time of Moses they alone united and stood out for the Lord amongst the other tribes. They became a special tribe of priests - their destiny was changed by an act of singular exceptional courage for God.

Exo 32:26 Then Moses stood in the gate of the camp, and said, Who is on the LORD'S side? let him come unto me. And all the sons of Levi gathered themselves together unto him. . . . Num 3:6 Bring the tribe of Levi near, and present them before Aaron the priest, that they may minister unto him.

We learn in this devotional that actions have consequences that go far into the future. We also see that God can wipe out the negative consequences and replace them with fresh good consequences for unusual exceptional choices at critical moments. May we be found standing up for Jesus in the present times when faith in God is under virulent attack. May God give us grace to end well.

Song

Stand up, stand up for Jesus, ye soldiers of the cross; Lift high His royal banner, it must not suffer loss.
From victory unto victory His army shall He lead,Till every foe is vanquished, and Christ is Lord indeed.

Stand up, stand up for Jesus, the solemn watchword hear; If while ye sleep He suffers, away with shame and fear;
Where'er ye meet with evil, within you or without, Charge for the God of battles, and put the foe to rout.

Stand up, stand up for Jesus, the trumpet call obey; Forth to the mighty conflict, in this His glorious day.
Ye that are brave now serve Him against unnumbered foes; Let courage rise with danger, and strength to strength oppose.

Stand up, stand up for Jesus, stand in His strength alone; The arm of flesh will fail you, ye dare not trust your own.
Put on the Gospel armor, each piece put on with prayer; There duty calls or danger, be never wanting there.

Stand up, stand up for Jesus, each soldier to his post, Close up the broken column, and shout through all the host:
Make good the loss so heavy, in those that still remain, And prove to all around you that death itself is gain.

Stand up, stand up for Jesus, the strife will not be long;This day the noise of battle, the next the victor's song.
To those who vanquish evil a crown of life shall be; They with the King of Glory shall reign eternally.

Prayer: Lord, Help me to stand up for you . . . and be numbered among your special army. Amen

SEPTEMBER 7

Judah - The Conqueror

Bible Text: Genesis 49:8

Gen 49:8 Judah, thou art he whom thy brethren shall praise: thy hand shall be in the neck of thine enemies; thy father's children shall bow down before thee.

Quite unexpectedly Judah is singled out as he whom others will praise. His name means praise and Judah will stand out ahead of all the other tribes. Every knee bows to the Lion of Judah. Jesus - the Lion of Judah . . . that all tribes will praise. What a glorious prediction. Quite an unexpected choice that mirrors the awesome grace of God - given Tamar's "story". This is one of the early predictions of Christ and the work He will do. Judah is presented as an aggressive undefeatable conqueror - The Lord of Hosts Himself. This Tribe will be glorious in battle. The image of a warrior's hand gripping the neck of His enemies is a picture of military conquest and sure victory. It would be a strong and courageous tribe.

When Jesus - the Lord of Hosts fights His battles - we are sure to see sure victory. The strategy of turning over the battle to Him presents our enemies as His enemies. Our cause is a kingdom cause because we are His children. It is vain to fight your battles, when the Lion of Judah . . . the undefeatable conqueror who supervises the mighty hosts of the Heavens wants to grab the neck of His enemies in our homes, businesses and situations. It is not that our hands will be on the neck of our enemies but the hand of Judah.

Turn over the battle to the Lord of Hosts. Be still to see His salvation and conquest manifest in that situation. More importantly be sure you are not one of the enemies of Judah.

Song

At the Name of Jesus, every knee shall bow, Every tongue confess Him King of glory now;
'Tis the Father's pleasure we should call Him Lord, Who from the beginning was the mighty Word.

Mighty and mysterious in the highest height, God from everlasting, very light of light:
In the Father's bosom with the spirit blest, Love, in love eternal, rest, in perfect rest.

At His voice creation sprang at once to sight, All the angel faces, all the hosts of light,
Thrones and dominations, stars upon their way, All the Heavenly orders, in their great array.

Humbled for a season, to receive a name - From the lips of sinners unto whom He came,
Faithfully He bore it, spotless to the last, Brought it back victorious when from death He passed.

Bore it up triumphant with its human light, Through all ranks of creatures, to the central height,
To the throne of Godhead, to the Father's breast; Filled it with the glory of that perfect rest.

Name Him, brothers, name Him, with love strong as death - But with awe and wonder, and with bated breath!
He is God the Savior, He is Christ the Lord, Ever to be worshipped, trusted and adored.

In your hearts enthrone Him; there let Him subdue - All that is not holy, all that is not true;
Crown Him as your Captain in temptation's hour; Let His will enfold you in its light and power.

Brothers, this Lord Jesus shall return again, With His Father's glory, with His angel train;
For all wreaths of empire meet upon His brow, And our hearts confess Him King of glory now.

Prayer: Lion of Judah. Fight my battles. Let your enemies in my life be all defeated and conquered. Amen

September 8
Lion of Judah

Bible Text: Genesis 49:9

Gen 49:9 Judah is a lion's whelp: from the prey, my son, thou art gone up: he stooped down, he couched as a lion, and as an old lion; who shall rouse him up?

The Lion of Judah is our Lord Jesus Christ. The picture of the strong young tearing the prey apart and going up to His rest undisturbed by any is an image of both royalty, power and indisputable reign over all. Judah will be formidable to his enemies. Even when the Lion sleeps refusing to respond to apparent threats around Him, there is none that can push Him to act.

Christ in us is compared not to a lion raging but to a calm King enjoying the satisfaction of his great power and unmatchable success. Satan is described as a raging lion seeking whom to devour ... but the king of Kings is couched quietly knowing everything bows to Him whenever and wherever.

The lesson here is that we His children can be still and assured that we are safe in His bosom. We are safe as the sheep of His pasture. The fact that His enemies appear permitted for a while to rage and roar in evil is no indication that they can continue to do so when He commands silence. It is the greatness, power and strength in Christ that permits Him to rest undisturbed till the determined time. Indeed, none have the ability to prod Him to make haste or to stop Him when He pounces on His prey. All we can do is to praise Him and worship Him. To thank Him and remain His friend ... always close to Him. The enemy is not crazy ... he waits for us to wander into sin before he can devour any of His own. No demon will risk the defense of the Lion of Judah. None. Therefore remain in Christ.

Song

Safe in the arms of Jesus, safe on His gentle breast,
There by His love o'ershaded, sweetly my soul shall rest.
Hark! 'tis the voice of angels, borne in a song to me.
Over the fields of glory, over the jasper sea.

Safe in the arms of Jesus, safe on His gentle breast
There by His love o'ershaded, sweetly my soul shall rest.
Safe in the arms of Jesus, safe from corroding care,
Safe from the world's temptations, sin cannot harm me there.
Free from the blight of sorrow, free from my doubts and fears;
Only a few more trials, only a few more tears!

Jesus, my heart's dear Refuge, Jesus has died for me;
Firm on the Rock of Ages, ever my trust shall be.
Here let me wait with patience, wait till the night is over;
Wait till I see the morning break on the golden shore.

Prayer: Lion of Judah. Let me not wander from your sight. Keep me safe forever. Amen

SEPTEMBER 9

Prince of Peace

Bible Text: Genesis 49:10

Gen 49:10 The sceptre shall not depart from Judah, nor a lawgiver from between his feet, until Shiloh come; and unto him shall the gathering of the people be.

The sceptre speaks of the throne. King David was from the tribe of Judah fulfilling this prophesy and Christ was also from this tribe, the Holy one unto whom the gathering of the people will forever be. The Kingship of Christ is everlasting. We are, also in Him, kings . . . a royal priesthood, a Holy nation and our Lord is the King of kings.

Jacob saw through the eyes of God the many things that the brothers could perhaps never understand. When we walk closely with God. God shows us what He intends to do and gives prophetic insight to assure us on our journey. When Shiloh comes - referring to Christ then all must bow to Him. Strong's Concordance translates the Hebrew word Shiyloh as "tranquil" or peace. Undoubtedly, this refers to the Messiah soon to come. He is called, "The Prince of Peace." Another expression of "Shiloh," is found in the expression: "How beautiful upon the mountains are the feet of him that brings good tidings, that publishes peace." He promises to " . . . extend peace to her like a river . . ." and "great shall be the peace of your children." Are you weary or troubled, Christ in you is the Prince of Peace. His word publishes peace and His promise to us is that great shall be our peace. Receive His peace afresh today. Shiloh has come - gather unto Him. Cease from fretting.

Song
When peace, like a river, attendeth my way,
when sorrows like sea billows roll;
whatever my lot, thou hast taught me to say,
It is well, it is well with my soul.

Refrain: It is well with my soul, it is well, it is well with my soul.

Though Satan should buffet, though trials should come,
let this blest assurance control,
that Christ has regarded my helpless estate,
and hath shed his own blood for my soul.

My sin, oh, the bliss of this glorious thought!
My sin, not in part but the whole,
is nailed to the cross, and I bear it no more,
praise the Lord, praise the Lord, O my soul!

And, Lord, haste the day when my faith shall be sight,
the clouds be rolled back as a scroll;
the trump shall resound, and the Lord shall descend,
even so, it is well with my soul.

Prayer: Shiloh. As I come to you, let my peace be great. Amen

September 10

Wine and Milk

Bible Text: Genesis 49:11

Gen 49:11 Binding his foal unto the vine, and his ass's colt unto the choice vine; he washed his garments in wine, and his clothes in the blood of grapes: 12 His eyes shall be red with wine, and his teeth white with milk.

Isa 55:1 Ho, every one that thirsteth, come ye to the waters, and he that hath no money; come ye, buy, and eat; yea, come, buy wine and milk without money and without price.

Judah continues to symbolize Christ and what He would stand for. In Him is wine and milk which has already been paid for. His wine and milk is available to those that have no money, yet those with great fortunes cannot afford to buy it. Christ brings salvation that has been paid with His own blood - a priceless but potent fluid to cleanse us from all our sins . . . bringing us clean before God.

Jacob foresees the cross, the saints washed by the blood of Jesus - crushed like grapes for us. Jacob foresees a time of nourishing and refreshing of the soul by the milk of the word. He foresees a time of joy that the world does not give and cannot take away. Christ is the true Vine; wine being the symbol of His blood shed at Calvary for sinners. Wine and milk are also pictures of prospering of the soul, the blessings of the gospel foretold for all that thirsteth - invited to come to the living waters - the Holy Spirit given to comfort us. Wine is also a symbol of the Holy Spirit which fills us to an overflowing enabling us to speak in other tongues -walking in a fresh power and anointing.

In the text, we see that God already foreknew all that Christ would be and do and the tribe of Judah was pre-chosen just as the blessings of the chosen - those that belong to Christ are foreshadowed in the cleansing blood of Jesus, the Holy Spirit, the joy of the Lord, the anointing and peace of God and the milk of the word of God that nourishes the new believer. Be encouraged as saints, that God has indeed made a complete provision through Christ - of the Tribe of Judah. Salvation, cleansing, sustenance, joy, direction and power . . . all in Him.

Song

Rock of Ages, cleft for me,
Let me hide myself in Thee;
Let the water and the blood,
From Thy wounded side which flowed,
Be of sin the double cure;
Save from wrath and make me pure.

Nothing in my hand I bring,
Simply to the cross I cling;
Naked, come to Thee for dress;
Helpless look to Thee for grace;
Foul, I to the fountain fly;
Wash me, Savior, or I die.

Prayer: Christ, O Christ . . . wash me, Savior, or I die. Amen

Zebulun

Bible Text: Genesis 49:13

Gen 49:13 Zebulun shall dwell at the haven of the sea; and he shall be for an haven of ships; and his border shall be unto Zidon.

Jos 19:10 And the third lot came up for the children of Zebulun according to their families: and the border of their inheritance was unto Sarid: 11 And their border went up toward the sea, and Maralah, and reached to Dabbasheth, and reached to the river that is before Jokneam;

Jacob accurately predicted that Zebulun will be noted for being mariners, merchants and traders of the sea, with borders towards the seas. This was an event that eventually came to pass, generations after Jacob and his children. Many of the blessings and promises pronounced over your life will be things that will happen over a hundred years after you are dead. God dwells in eternity, speaks in eternity and is an eternal God. This means yesterday, today and tomorrow . . . a thousand years ago . . . a thousand years to come . . . all these are like a second before God. He has perfect memory and foresight with no lack of clarity whatsoever. Mankind on the other hand are impatient, they are anxious concerning a tomorrow they do not know and have already forgotten the lessons of last week.

If only we can just remain still and learn to trust God to do what He has promised at the time. Zebulun are a family enjoying the hospitality of Egypt - perhaps thinking there is no more - but Jacob sees far . . . he sees beyond the exodus outside Egypt, way beyond the wanderings in the wilderness . . . Jacob sees beyond the conquest of Jericho . . . He sees the apportioning that Joshua did concerning Zebulum.

Someone reading is already blessed. Someone reading is a trading giant . . . used by God in Industry and Commerce. Leading in Banking and Manufacturing. A manager of conglomerates . . . and it will all be the doing of the Lord. Only do not forget Him who makes you to prosper. Do not forget that it was the doing of the Lord. It is perhaps likely that many had forgotten the blessings of Jacob concerning Zebulun, as Joshua apportioned land to them . . . May we not forget the promises of God and teach our children to remind their children . . . there is a home in eternity . . . there is an eternal inheritance. We have responsibilities to honor God in our evangelism, giving and thanksgiving as He prospers His purposes in our time. You are blessed. Blessings are waiting to come to pass in your generation. Hallelujah.

Song

In His time, In His Time
He makes all things beautiful in His time.
Lord please show me every day
As your teaching me Your way
That You do just what You say

In Your time.
In Your time, In Your Time
You make all things beautiful in Your time.
Lord my life to You I bring
May each song I have to sing
Be to you a lovely thing
In Your time.

Prayer: Father, May all your glorious promises concerning - come to pass - In your time. Amen.

September 12

A Strong Ass

Bible Text: Genesis 49:14

Gen 49:14 Issachar is a strong ass couching down between two burdens: 15 And he saw that rest was good, and the land that it was pleasant; and bowed his shoulder to bear, and became a servant unto tribute.

God needs burden bearers. There are many burdens that must be borne for the Kingdom. Financial burdens, prayer burdens ... burdens to serve the loveless and the hopeless. Burdens to give expecting little in a hard demanding land. God needs burden bearers who will go where none want to go and remain in thankless positions. A few are like Issachar ... blessed to be strong in service and carrying the loads and weights that must be carried. They are slowed because of the burdens they bear but they are special before God. They couch between two burdens when most will not even carry one.

Why do they carry? Because they see there is a rest - that is worth serving for. The rest of the hard working farmer is sweet. The sleep of the one who has labored all day is deep and undisturbed. Issachar sees that the rest was good and the land is pleasant ... and they bow again to bear more burdens.

May we be motivated by the eternal rest ahead to serve. May we think of Heaven and may the thoughts of its goodness motivate to do more, give more, sacrifice more and help more. Scriptures tell us that Issachar was blessed to be strong and unusually industrious and reliable. Inclined naturally to labor when others declined. Zebulun was called upon for rents and taxes ... financially blessed ... a wealthy tribe founded on a work ethic of diligence and sacrifice. Perhaps you have been blessed to be like Issachar to give, carry double burdens and thrive in sacrificing for others. Do not despise this unusual grace that you have. One day in Heaven ... you will truly say "the rest is good ... the rest is good ... the rest is good"

Song

Would you live for Jesus, and be always pure and good?
Would you walk with Him within the narrow road?
Would you have Him bear your burden, carry all your load?
Let Him have His way with thee.

His power can make you what you ought to be;
His blood can cleanse your heart and make you free;
His love can fill your soul, and you will see
'Twas best for Him to have His way with thee.

Would you have Him make you free, and follow at His call?
Would you know the peace that comes by giving all?
Would you have Him save you, so that you can never fall?
Let Him have His way with thee.

Would you in His kingdom find a place of constant rest?
Would you prove Him true in providential test?
Would you in His service labor always at your best?
Let Him have His way with thee.

Prayer: Father, May I live for Jesus - also, to find and testify always ... the rest is good ... the rest is good. Amen

SEPTEMBER 13

The Subtle Judge

Bible Text: Genesis 49:16

Gen 49:16 Dan shall judge his people, as one of the tribes of Israel. 17 Dan shall be a serpent by the way, an adder in the path, that biteth the horse heels, so that his rider shall fall backward.

Dan was the son of a concubine . . . but blessed amongst the tribes of Israel. You origin will not disqualify you. Dan is needed in the family of God and must play his role. There are many ways to bring down the enemies of God. There are bold fighters that pounce on their enemies like Judah the Lion. But there are some enemies who will not be brought down by direct means. They will need those like Dan, adders who know how and when to bite the heels of their horses . . . so that they fall to their end.

Dan is both subtle and knows the law of God. Cunning to advance the interest of the Kingdom through intelligent arguments but also by brutal warfare. Being a judge and a subtle attacker provide an interesting blend of skills to push the agenda of God and resist the oppression of the culture.

There are many laws today that are not Godly . . . advanced by atheists pretending to care more for the people offering a peace that is not there. These enemies of all that is Godly cannot always be brought down directly and God will use shrewd processes to still have His way. There are many evil riders in society, leadership and the cultures . . . that must be made to fall backward without anyone touching them. Saints like Dan are needed . . . to complement the more open courage and fierceness of the lion in Judah. Dan is wise. He is like a lawyer who argues his case well and floors his opponent with superior legal logic but also anointed in spiritual warfare.

Song

I dare not be defeated with Calvary in view,
Where Jesus conquered Satan, where all His foes He slew;
Come, Lord, and give the vision - to nerve me for the fight,
Make me an overcomer - clothed with Thy Spirit's might.

A victor, a victor! Because of Calvary.
Make me an overcomer,   A conqu'ror, a conqu'ror, Lord, in Thee.

I dare not be defeated - Since Christ, my conquering King
Has called me to the battle - Which He did surely win.
Come, Lord, and give me courage, Thy conquering Spirit give,
Make me an overcomer, In power within me live.

I dare not be defeated, When Jesus leads me on
To press through hellish regions - To share with Him His Throne;
Come, Lord, and give Thy soldier - The power to wield the sword,
Make me an overcomer - Through Thine inerrant Word.

I dare not be defeated, Just at the set of sun,
When Jesus waits to whisper, "Well done, beloved, well done";
Come, Lord, bend from the Glory, On me Thy Spirit cast,
Make me an overcomer, A victor to the last.

Prayer: Father, Make me undefeatable in Spiritual Warfare. Amen

SEPTEMBER 14

Thy Salvation - O Lord

Bible Text: Genesis 49:18

Gen 49:18 I have waited for thy salvation, O LORD

Jacob is interrupted in this most important duty by his thoughts and he voices these thoughts - so important that they are recorded. I believe these are perhaps the most important messages that summarize an entire life. In the end Jacob could say "I have waited". Jacob was a deeply spiritual man - in spite of many issues and weak spots . . . in the end he spoke for God like no one ever could in his generation. He was God's voice and priest on the earth. He did not lose any of his children - God kept them in His own special way . . . preserved them from death by hunger in a famine and brought him to a wealthy place.

Jacob started with many schemes and plans . . . many ambitious thoughts and agenda . . . but he ended well. He saw the salvation of the Lord in everything that happened to him. It was all the salvation of the Lord and he had learnt to wait to see it. For Jacob had discovered that when God is saving us we cannot always know it . . . often we think he is destroying or hurting us. Everything . . . from the barrenness of Rachel, the favoritism that Joseph enjoyed leading to his unfortunate adventures . . . imprisonment in Egypt of his son. It was all God saving the chosen tribe from starvation and preserving them in Egypt until the foretold time of the Exodus. In the end . . . the waiting of Jacob was rewarded. He saw that salvation and it all made sense to him. He sees all his children gathered around him - perhaps for the last time . . . He gasps . . . I have waited for thy salvation. He cannot believe his eyes and the evidence of the fruit of waiting on God.

There are many promised sources of salvation . . . the salvation of God works differently in ways that are not our ways. Wait for it - It is already at work in your life, only you do not see it . . . you cannot see it. You must wait on the Lord. Soon . . . you will rejoice to discover that none of your children are lost.

Song

Only Jesus can save my brother Only Jesus can save Hallelujah

There is no other way my brother Only Jesus can save Hallelujah

Money cannot save my brother Only Jesus can save Hallelujah

Friends cannot save my brother Only Joseph can save Hallelujah

Prayer: Father, Teach me to wait for thy salvation and your salvation alone. Amen

SEPTEMBER 15

An Overcomer at last

Bible Text: Genesis 49:19

Gen 49:19 Gad, a troop shall overcome him: but he shall overcome at the last

Be strong and encouraged. The story is not over for you. Gad was told that a troop - a major defeat would befall him. The Gadites were men of war but it is their persistence that make them stand out. The Moabites and the Ammonites were formidable foes with many troops and armed fighters . . . and Gad was overcome in many skirmishes . . . but they were eventually completely subdued - Gad playing a major role in their defeat.

An elder once said, it does not matter how the battle goes . . . what matter is who is standing in the end. I want to encourage someone reading . . . do not confuse the process with your destiny. In the process, like Gad, there are many troops defeating you, but you are learning from every defeat. Your destiny is to overcome at last. In the end in Christ you win.

Spiritually you may be down, fallen, defeated and overcome by so many things you cannot begin to explain but I want to let you know that you shall overcome at last. You will sing "At last - I win".

Remember the tribe of Gad and do not give up . . . instead prepare again for battle. Soon . . . you will say ". . . at last"

Song

Get up and fight . . . Receive strength from God
You are an overcomer - you are born to shine
Destined to win. Win at last.

Arise and fight . . . Believe His word
The Blood conquers - you are born to shine
Destined to win. Win at last.

Be unstoppable . . . always getting up again.
Be unconquerable . . . . always returning to the ring . . .

Troops overcame Gad but in the end he overcame
Arise, Get up and Fight. At last - your victory.

Just Trust and Obey
For there is no other way
To be happy in Jesus
But to trust and Obey

Prayer: Father, Lift me up once more . . . for now I overcome. Amen

September 16

Wealth, Food and Royal Dainties

Bible Text: Genesis 49:20

Gen 49:20 Out of Asher his bread shall be fat, and he shall yield royal dainties.

Asher is foretold to be a wealthy tribe. Well nourished . . . described as "fat" . . . a symbol of overflowing substance . . . exporting beautiful things and dainties sought by royalty. This tribe will be known not just for agriculture but its royal contributions. The diligent and uncommonly talented will stand before Kings. Asher is a diligent and disciplined tribe. Not a tribe spoilt by opportunity . . . renowned for a rare excellence sought for in the palaces of the world.

Friends, excellence does not come easily. Only the outstanding will be admitted into the palaces. Fatness and laziness are unrelated. The bread basket of Israel are a tribe who will serve the best and will have great wealth and riches. God is not against the wealth of His diligent sons. Someone reading is going to excel in large scale agriculture . . . exporting grains for the best quality ingredients that will be desired in the ovens of royal palaces.

Asher is the younger brother of Gad; these two being the sons of Zilpah, the handmaid of Leah. God promotes the handmaid that served well . . . her sons are raised up amongst the tribes - even excelling in substance. Asher is said to mean "blessing" . . . again God lifts up the lowly . . . For someone reading "All generations shall call you blessed". You will blessed both spiritually and materially. Your substance will be said to be "fat" . . . and Kings will seek you out - for your excellence. Despite your background, you will shine in Christ like a thousand stars . . . Labor for excellence.

Song

Lord the Light or Your Love is shining,
In the midst of the darkness shining,
Jesus light of the world shine upon us,
Set us free by the truth You now bring us,
Shine on me. Shine on me.

Shine Jesus shine
Fill this land with the Father's glory
Blaze, Spirit blaze,
Set our hearts on fire
Flow, river flow
Flood the nations with grace and mercy
Send forth Your word
Lord and let there be light.

As we gaze on Your kindly brightness.
So our faces display Your likeness.
Ever changing from glory to glory,
Mirrored here may our lives tell Your story.
Shine on me. Shine on me.

Prayer: Father, May the Daystar shine through all my endeavors. Amen

SEPTEMBER 17

Goodly words

Bible Text: Genesis 49:21

Gen 49:21 Naphtali is a hind let loose: he giveth goodly words.

Naphtali means wrestling implying a destiny with struggles but which prevails. The disposition of the hind can be swift, loving and gentle, zealous or even trembling in danger but more importantly this hind is let loose . . . enjoys liberty. For a name that suggests conflict, Naphtali is the tribe that enters into a true joy that comes from freedom to serve and worship God unhindered. The contribution of Naphtali are his words . . . good, seasoned and uplifting.

A man with goodly words is a rare gift of God. Words can be very powerful and the fruit of comforting words goes far in ways we underestimate. The one who gives goodly words is the encourager, telling us, we can still make it . . . we can make Heaven . . . God has not abandoned us . . . we can receive healing. Goodly words are not flattering words - and the goodly must often be laced with bitter herbs to find that unique satisfying taste. Goodly words that are just sugary are like a rich chocolate cake with far too much sweeteners, fruits and currants . . . we soon feel bloated and uncomfortable . . . chastening is goodly because we are helped forward by our pilgrim journey as a result of hearing words of correction. Disputing and arguing is a waste of time . . . it is a reaction to that which is vain. Even if you won all your arguments - how does that move you forward.

Naphtali is a poet, an author . . . a composer of hymns . . . whose words have come from a hard wrestling with life and eventual God-given breakthrough in spite of daunting odds. I discover that the most encouraging and inspiring words in the Hymns came from saints that rose through difficult struggles and suffered much.

Do not be afraid to express the creativity that is in you. Only remember to be kind.

Song

Sing them over again to me, wonderful words of life,
Let me more of their beauty see, wonderful words of life;
Words of life and beauty teach me faith and duty.

Beautiful words, wonderful words, wonderful words of life,
Beautiful words, wonderful words, wonderful words of life.

Christ, the blessèd One, gives to all wonderful words of life;
Sinner, list to the loving call, wonderful words of life;
All so freely given, wooing us to Heaven.

Sweetly echo the Gospel call, wonderful words of life;
Offer pardon and peace to all, wonderful words of life;
Jesus, only Savior, sanctify us forever.

Prayer: Father, May I be like Naphtali . . . a man of goodly words. Amen

SEPTEMBER 18

A Fruitful Bough

Bible Text: Genesis 49:22

Gen 49:22 Joseph is a fruitful bough, even a fruitful bough by a well; whose branches run over the wall:

Joseph is unusually gifted in administration, interpretation of dreams, discerning God ... but Jacob has no words to waste on his gifts. It is the fruit of Joseph that is praised. It takes longer to bear fruit - the fruits of the spirit will often require the seed of the word to go deep and be well rooted in us before we can be truly patient, genuinely loving and long suffering. But Joseph is lavish in spiritual fruit. He does not plant gardens for himself or erect a memorial nor are we that told he built palaces. Instead, he had a heart to forgive that was so generously demonstrated. There were no arguments or disputes ... only a peaceful reconciliation with his family.

Gal 5:22 But the fruit of the Spirit is love, joy, peace, longsuffering, gentleness, goodness, faith, 23 Meekness, temperance: against such there is no law.

Eph_5:9 (For the fruit of the Spirit is in all goodness and righteousness and truth;)

Joseph was not just gifted and fruitful ... but also a man of influence and the positive impact of his life could be seen all around him. His contributions for good could be seen all over Egypt. Goodness seemed to overflow out of his life ... impacting nations that needed bread, who came to Egypt. He was famous ... yet so humble. What a testimony. A man who went through a process in which most would have cursed God or murmured bitterly. He ended up being what God wanted him to be, in spite of being thrown into the cesspool of Egypt ... as a hungry slave. If Joseph could be fruitful for God - no doubt intensively prepared and taught in the early days by Jacob while others were in the field. The seed that was planted by God in him bore a huge harvest ... that he is called a fruitful bough. The question you should ask yourself - will I be termed a fruitful bough or just gifted?

Song

Love divine, all loves excelling,
Joy of Heaven to earth come down;
Fix in us thy humble dwelling;
All thy faithful mercies crown!
Jesus, Thou art all compassion,
Pure unbounded love Thou art;
Visit us with Thy salvation;
Enter every trembling heart.

Breathe, O breathe Thy loving Spirit,
Into every troubled breast!
Let us all in Thee inherit;
Let us find that second rest.
Take away our bent to sinning;
Alpha and Omega be;
End of faith, as its Beginning,
Set our hearts at liberty.

Prayer: Father, Help me to be fruitful. Amen

261

SEPTEMBER 19

A Target of the Archers

Bible Text: Genesis 49:23

Gen 49:23 The archers have sorely grieved him, and shot at him, and hated him:

Every promise and bearer of that promise is countered by a different agenda and archers bearing arrows. Perhaps Joseph was not wise to disclose the dreams he had. But if he had not disclosed the dreams they would not have come true. God works with what we call our mistakes and errors and is not unmindful of the activity of the archers. The archers bring grief . . . they aim and shoot bullets and can destroy . . . the archers are behind the hatred of Joseph - finding allies in his brothers.

Have you been sorely grieved? Has every promotion propelled you to a place of being shot at with fresh arrows . . . have you encountered the archers . . . spiritual devils assigned to monitor and truncate destiny. Have you been greeted by a strange hatred that has forced you into an unbearable isolation? Think not that your experience is unique for many of your fathers have been brought to ruin by their incessant onslaughts. But you have survived. You are still alive only because God has helped you. How could you ever have survived the bullets of the unseen hosts of darkness . . . if God had not been on your side.

Another character well familiar with the archers is David. They became his everyday company - living with them not knowing which aspect of his life would be attacked next. David survived the arrows and hatred of his brothers, Goliath, Saul, Ahithophel, and Absalom. He overcame the spiritual arrows of lust, greed, sorrow, depression, accusation and isolation. He was sorely grieved and put all his faith in God --- producing the most beautiful verses of poetry that continue to inspire and encourage others in the Psalms.

Be encouraged. Encourage yourself. Celebrate your life. It only means God is still on your side and He that began a good thing and sustained you till today will keep you till you accomplish your goals.

Psa 57:2 I will cry unto God most high; unto God that performeth all things for me. 3 He shall send from Heaven, and save me from the reproach of him that would swallow me up. Selah. God shall send forth his mercy and his truth. 4: My soul is among lions: and I lie even among them that are set on fire, even the sons of men, whose teeth are spears and arrows, and their tongue a sharp sword. 5 Be thou exalted, O God, above the Heavens; let thy glory be above all the earth. 6 They have prepared a net for my steps; my soul is bowed down: they have digged a pit before me, into the midst whereof they are fallen themselves. Selah. 7 My heart is fixed, O God, my heart is fixed: I will sing and give praise.

Song

Why so downcast O my soul - put your hope in God,
Put your hope in God · Put your hope in God

Why so downcast O my soul - put your hope in God,
And bless the Lord - Oh my soul.

Prayer: Lord, Save my soul from the wicked archers surrounding me. Amen

SEPTEMBER 20

Strengthened by God

Bible Text: Genesis 49:24

Gen 49:24 But his bow abode in strength, and the arms of his hands were made strong by the hands of the mighty God of Jacob; (from thence is the shepherd, the stone of Israel:)

May your own bow abide in the strength of the Almighty. It is one thing to be strong and it is something else to abide in the strength of God. It is one thing to be made strong by knowledge, support of men, funds and political positioning - it is another to be made strong by the Almighty God. When God makes you strong, you become undefeatable. Nothing can be more plain and simple. Nothing can defeat you - whether internal, external . . . subtle or direct. You will win eventually . . . when you fall it will only be to rise up to a higher level.

The faith of Joseph did not fail until he came out a conqueror. He was strengthened with wisdom, courage, and patience, which are better than all weapons of battle. He maintained his integrity and bore all his burdens . . . refusing to be drowned by the tumultuous floods. But it was God. His grace was more than sufficient and his strength is made perfect in our weakness.

Joseph was like a shepherd and a stone to his brothers. A shadow of Christ, the shepherd of our soul and the stone the builders rejected that became the chief cornerstone . . . a sure pillar to carry our destiny. Christ our Savior was hated, despised . . . the man of sorrow . . . acquainted with grief . . . but still advanced to be the shepherd and stone of Israel. The lesson here is that you can fight your battles with your strength - you have already failed before you started. Similarly, how can you fail if God is fighting for you - impossible. He who has helped us till now will help us in the future. Do not risk annoying Him or losing His favor on your life. Seek to always remain in Him - no matter what and you will always know His victory.

Song

What a fellowship, what a joy divine,
Leaning on the everlasting arms;
What a blessedness, what a peace is mine,
Leaning on the everlasting arms.

Leaning, leaning, safe and secure from all alarms;
Leaning, leaning, leaning on the everlasting arms.

O how sweet to walk in this pilgrim way,
Leaning on the everlasting arms;
O how bright the path grows from day to day,
Leaning on the everlasting arms.

What have I to dread, what have I to fear,
Leaning on the everlasting arms;
I have blessed peace with my Lord so near,
Leaning on the everlasting arms.

Prayer: Lord, keep me leaning on the everlasting arms. Amen

SEPTEMBER 21

Categories of Blessings

Bible Text: Genesis 49:25

Gen 49:25 Even by the God of thy father, who shall help thee; and by the Almighty, who shall bless thee with blessings of Heaven above, blessings of the deep that lieth under, blessings of the breasts, and of the womb:

Joseph is encompassed with divine help and blessings of different kinds. Joshua came from the tribe of Joseph . . . the chief commander in the wars of Canaan - helped by God as the walls of Jericho fell down flat . . . and as victories followed victories. Jacob blesses Joseph - pronouncing the blessings of Heaven above - the good things that come from the physical Heaven - rain, good weather and favorable winds. The blessings of the deep that lieth under refer to all the mineral wealth, fruitful fields and the cooperation of the earth to favor Joseph. The blessings of the breasts and of the womb . . . refer to safe delivery and nursing of infants . . . none will still be barren, none will be still born . . . nor will any infant die at the early stages of nursing and nurturing . . . this refers to fruitfulness and expansions and a prolific unusual fertility. May all these blessings be also yours in the name of Jesus. The Almighty shall bless you with all manner of blessings. May you be singled out for all categories of blessings like the tribe of Joseph.

Joseph has become a blessing not just to Egypt, but to all that will born through him - his many descendants will enjoy a rare grace to flourish that will cause others to stare in amazement. All of creation was commanded to favor the descendants of Joseph and so it was. To be blessed by all categories of blessings is an incredible favor that has far reaching effects to generations even yet unborn.

Song

I need Thee every hour, most gracious Lord;
No tender voice like Thine can peace afford.

I need Thee, O I need Thee; Every hour I need Thee;
O bless me now, my Savior, I come to Thee.

I need Thee every hour, stay Thou nearby;
Temptations lose their power when Thou art nigh.

I need Thee every hour, in joy or pain;
Come quickly and abide, or life is in vain.

I need Thee every hour; teach me Thy will;
And Thy rich promises in me fulfill.

I need Thee every hour, most Holy One;
O make me Thine indeed, Thou blessèd Son.

Prayer: O Lord, Bless me indeed - O Lord bless me like you blessed Joseph. Amen

September 22

Prevailing Blessings

Bible Text: Genesis 49:26

Gen 49:26 The blessings of thy father have prevailed above the blessings of my progenitors unto the utmost bound of the everlasting hills: they shall be on the head of Joseph, and on the crown of the head of him that was separate from his brethren

The blessings of the ancestors of Jacob seemed somewhat limited. We do not understand why both Jacob and Esau could not be equally blessed or why of all the children of Abraham . . . only Isaac seems remarkable. It seems there was a limit or barrier of some sort . . . a boundary - one that Jacob prevailed over. Jacob blessed all his children lavishly . . . passing the blessings of growth to all such that after his death, there was an incredible multiplication. The seventy that came into Egypt became rapidly a great nation. The Bible says there were 600,000 fighting men among the Israelites, a figure which excluded the entire tribe of the Levites. Scholars say that this would correspond to at least two and a half million people, including women, children, the elderly and infirm. The Israelites were so prolific in birth that the Egyptians were alarmed.

Joseph was separated from his brothers and this served in future to mark him out for unusual blessing. In a similar way, our sanctification is our ticket to a different crown of glory. We are told "Be ye separate" . . . "be not unequally yoked" . . . denying us much that we may have wanted to partake in but this also marks our heads for a different basket of divine blessings. How can God single us out to be uniquely blessed if we live like children of darkness. We are chosen, called out to show forth the virtues of Him who has called us out of darkness. We are called out to be blessed and to show forth a different lifestyle that causes us to be peculiar. Even from the beginning, it would seem that the extent of our separation for God has been the measure to which we can expect our blessings to be outpoured. Joseph was pulled out of everything he knew and cherished for God's purpose - even from his own blood brothers - but it was not in vain.

Song

I am Thine, O Lord, I have heard Thy voice,
And it told Thy love to me;
But I long to rise in the arms of faith
And be closer drawn to Thee.

Draw me nearer, nearer blessèd Lord,
To the cross where Thou hast died.
Draw me nearer, nearer, nearer blessèd Lord,
To Thy precious, bleeding side.

Consecrate me now to Thy service, Lord,
By the power of grace divine;
Let my soul look up with a steadfast hope,
And my will be lost in Thine.

O the pure delight of a single hour
That before Thy throne I spend,
When I kneel in prayer, and with Thee, my God
I commune as friend with friend!

Prayer: O Lord, Draw me nearer to you . . . bid me come up higher. Amen.

SEPTEMBER 23

The Wolf can Change

Bible Text: Genesis 49:27

Gen 49:27 Benjamin shall ravin as a wolf: in the morning he shall devour the prey, and at night he shall divide the spoil.

The tone of blessings suddenly changes as Jacob must speak to Benjamin. Jacob is not guided by affection but by God - the Spirit of Prophecy. He is not as tender with Benjamin who is clearly one of his favorite children. He describes this tribe as a war like strong and daring tribe that devours the prey and plunders the spoil which is divided. They are feared by the enemies of God - but their lack of tenderness will sometimes place them as allies of darkness. The image of a wolf is always negative especially in the New Testament but this blessing also may mean they change for the better. Wolves do not share spoil . . . but at night . . . when others rest, the tribe becomes an instrument of charity.

The Apostle Paul is often singled out from this tribe as an example of a fulfillment of this prophecy. In his early years he went about persecuting Christians. But in his old age, he was a preacher, wrote letters that blessed many and was poured out for thousands . . . even by his writings to this very day. Benjamin has different temperaments.

Do not give up on any. There may be many "Benjamins" in our midst - favored but spoilt souls who start very badly acting in a fiercely destructive manner who God will use in future years to share the gospel of peace. Do not write anyone off. Do not give up on yourself in being used by God. His ways are not our ways. The miracle of late night transformation is the story of Benjamin . . . the last that becomes the best . . . the least likely that becomes the most gentle . . . the destroyer that becomes the helper . . . the friend of the enemy that is transformed to God's ally.

Let the unique blessing of Benjamin give you hope for that brother, friend or soul you see raving as a dangerous wolf . . . keep praying and wait patiently for the night. The night also represents a time when none can work . . . old age, or a difficult circumstance. Sometimes brethren are transformed by night seasons in their life to much better vessels and instruments . . . yielded to the patient hands of the master potter. Do not give up on any situation whatsoever. The wolf is only an act . . . soon Benjamin emerges.

Song

Jesus - you are changing me,
By your Spirit - you are making me like you;
Jesus - you are transforming me
May your loveliness be seen in all I do.

You are the potter and I am the clay,
Help me to be willing to let you have your way.
Jesus - You are changing me
As I let you reign supreme within my heart.

Prayer: O Lord, Remember the Benjamins - touch their hearts even now . . . change the heart of stone to that of flesh.

September 24

Your Blessings

Bible Text: Genesis 49:28

Gen 49:28 All these are the twelve tribes of Israel: and this is it that their father spake unto them, and blessed them; every one according to his blessing he blessed them

Everyone is blessed according to his blessing. Blessings had been decided by God and Jacob merely was instrumental to speak that which each already had been decided. The blessings are not general statements that could have been picked up by any. The blessings of Judah could not be given to Naphtali. When were the blessings original owned . . . It was already known before the foundations of time that Christ will be borne in the tribe of Judah. Judah did not earn this blessing. Again, it was all grace at work. God has already determined to bless us with our own blessings. But again, the blessings need to be spoken by a father who is honored. Hence we are told to honor parents. God has given fathers accuracy in the spirit to match blessings with heads. Joseph could not bless himself. All the food and care in Egypt was not enough to multiply the Israelites so much as to alarm Egypt. It required the specific blessings of the father uniquely revealed to Jacob. It takes a true spiritual father and not anyone to bless us with our own blessings. Jacob may be old and blind but he was still needed for a most important task that only he could accomplish. Only Jacob could know of the archers . . . only Jacob could remember Reuben's indiscretions . . . only Jacob had the revelation of the coming Lion of Judah.

What is the lesson? Honor your father - physical and spiritual. Do not be anxious to get rid of them when they are old and their steps are faltering . . . for you will need their spiritual insight someday. They will see what you can never see and more importantly what others do not see . . . concerning you.

This is why the devil hates fathers and destroys fathers and fatherhood . . . making homes fatherless and turning churches into clubs without spiritual fathers . . . the devil knows that a blessed people are invincible and the blessing of the father is not just powerful but spiritually accurate. Blessings are not random good words that any can pronounce.

Song

Dear Lord and Father of mankind,
Forgive our foolish ways!
Re-clothe us in our rightful mind,
In purer lives thy service find,
In deeper reverence praise.

O Sabbath rest by Galilee!
O calm of hills above,
Where Jesus knelt to share with thee
The silence of eternity,
Interpreted by love!

Drop thy still dews of quietness,
Till all our strivings cease;
Take from our souls the strain and stress,
And let our ordered lives confess
The beauty of thy peace.

Prayer: O Lord, The Father of all mankind - thank you for blessing me. Thank you for my physical and spiritual Father. Bless them O Lord. Amen.

SEPTEMBER 25

The Gathering to come

Bible Text: Genesis 49:29

Gen 49:29 And he charged them, and said unto them, I am to be gathered unto my people: bury me with my fathers in the cave that is in the field of Ephron the Hittite,

Jacob was dying but still speaking that there is more coming. He now speaks concerning his own future having explained what would happen to his children. He does not say I am dying just bury me somewhere. He says there is a day that me and my fathers will be gathered and there is a location from which this can happen and it is not Egypt.

Many think how we are buried does not matter. It mattered to Jacob that he was with his fathers. He knew that there was a day of gathering. Many Bible scholars will say that this happened at the death of Christ when the graves of the saints were opened and the saints were seen resurrected.

Today, many saints need to be reminded that the dead in Christ shall rise first when Christ comes at the future event called the rapture. Jacob says very little about Egypt apart from his reminder that they will be brought out. There is no attraction for Egypt to Jacob whatsoever. He looks forward to this gathering and identifies where he needs to be buried. Jacob is not influenced by Egypt in his last words.

As you meditate, reflect on what adjustments or instructions need to be given before you leave the physical world . . . it may not be the location of your burial . . . it may be the way and manner of burial . . . it may be people you need to forgive . . . we should be more concerned with eternity . . . it may be prayers we need to pray for loved ones . . . our dying moments are not to be wasted with trivialities. One may not have the opportunity to make those adjustments and so the time to make vital corrections is now.

1Co_15:52 In a moment, in the twinkling of an eye, at the last trump: for the trumpet shall sound, and the dead shall be raised incorruptible, and we shall be changed.

The Bible says the rapture of the saints will be sudden . . . in the twinkling of an eye. Be ready therefore to be gathered now. Our preparations for gathering depends on the gathering that is to come. For us the gathering is at the rapture . . . coming without like a "thief in the night". The time to do anything for the kingdom is NOW. The time to make any adjustment or urgent arrangements for the gathering is NOW.

1Co 15:51 Behold, I shew you a mystery; We shall not all sleep, but we shall all be changed, 52 In a moment, in the twinkling of an eye, at the last trump: for the trumpet shall sound, and the dead shall be raised incorruptible, and we shall be changed. 53 For this corruptible must put on incorruption, and this mortal must put on immortality. 54 So when this corruptible shall have put on incorruption, and this mortal shall have put on immortality, then shall be brought to pass the saying that is written, Death is swallowed up in victory. 55 O death, where is thy sting? O grave, where is thy victory?

Song

Will you be ready when the Lord shall come
I will be ready - I will be ready - I will be ready when the Lord shall come
I will be ready - I will be ready - I will be ready when the Lord shall come.

Prayer: O Lord, Help my readiness for the coming of the Lord. Amen.

SEPTEMBER 26

The Cave

Bible Text: Genesis 49:30

Gen 49:30 In the cave that is in the field of Machpelah, which is before Mamre, in the land of Canaan, which Abraham bought with the field of Ephron the Hittite for a possession of a burying place.

Jacob is buried in a cave though he lived in a culture where pyramids are erected and people buried with earthly treasures. The ways of God and the ways of the culture differ even in death. Quiet humility that typified Israel disdains the pyramids of Egypt and memorial statues and instead a poverty in spirit is the hall mark of the early fathers.

The cave is also a picture of a place of rest in the field of Machpelah. Now the cave is concealed by a mosque; this was formerly a church, built by the Crusaders between 1167 and 1187. But we know that in the time of Christ, the graves opened and the patriarchs came out of this cave . . . and were briefly seen. Abraham who was given a vision of great lands died possessing only this field . . . and was still accomplished.

The cave and this field of rest pictures Heaven and eternity . . . the ultimate promised place which we cannot enter but through death or bodily transformation at the rapture. Comparing Heaven and Egypt is like comparing in the physical - pyramids with caves. The doors to God's eternity are the humble and simple life for which earthly possessions count for nothing. Many of the saints do not have great memorials erected and we may have forgotten them because they made no effort to immortalize their names . . . but God has His roll of honor in the humble caves of eternity. May God reveal what it truly means to be humble. His humility is the door to His eternity. Jacob lived and died as a pilgrim. Many erected pyramids to eternalize their memory . . . only to be rejected from God's eternity.

Song

He who would valiant be 'gainst all disaster,
Let him in constancy follow the Master.
There's no discouragement shall make him once relent
His first avowed intent to be a pilgrim.

Who so beset him round with dismal stories
Do but themselves confound - his strength the more is.
No foes shall stay his might; though he with giants fight,
He will make good his right to be a pilgrim.

Since, Lord, Thou dost defend us with Thy Spirit,
We know we at the end, shall life inherit.
Then fancies flee away! I'll fear not what men say,
I'll labor night and day to be a pilgrim.

Prayer: O Lord, Help me not to be trapped in the lies of the heathen culture that surround me. Amen.

September 27

Rise again from Burial

Bible Text: Genesis 49:31

Gen 49:31 There they buried Abraham and Sarah his wife; there they buried Isaac and Rebekah his wife; and there I buried Leah.

All that was buried in the cave in the field of Machpelah will one day rise up. Jacob knew this . . . it was a guarded family secret . . . passed on by his fathers to him. The family of faith will still meet again after death. Teach your children and grandchildren that there is a day by the grace of God when all that are saved will meet with other Christian ancestors. All these ancestors were buried but there is a day in eternity when they will gather together. The cave - was a place of burial . . . but pictures to us that there is a place of rest where we will all be. Saints are not to fear death. Saints should also be familiar with the saints that have gone . . . their teachings - promises and the prophecies and blessings they pronounced. What is buried will come back again to life. One day we shall see Abraham, Sarah, Isaac, Rebekah and Leah.

What men buried - God will one day bring back to life. This refers also to dreams, joys, aspirations and destinies. God can bring back again . . . that which men have buried and forgotten. All that is buried by men, circumstances and time by the special grace of God comes back again to life. The early fathers continued to bury their dead knowing there is a day that they will be gathered and rise again to a place unseen.

Heb_11:8 By faith Abraham, when he was called to go out into a place which he should after receive for an inheritance, obeyed; and he went out, not knowing whither he went. . . . 9 By faith he sojourned in the land of promise, as in a strange country, dwelling in tabernacles with Isaac and Jacob, the heirs with him of the same promise: Heb_11:13 These all died in faith, not having received the promises, but having seen them afar off, and were persuaded of them, and embraced them, and confessed that they were strangers and pilgrims on the earth.

Song

Go ahead, drive the nails in My hands Laugh at me where you stand
Go ahead, and say it isn't Me The day will come when you will see

'Cause I'll rise again . . . Ain't no power on earth can tie me down!
Yes, I'll rise again . . . Death can't keep Me in the ground

Go ahead, mock My name - My love for you is still the same
Go ahead, and bury Me - But very soon, I will be free!

Go ahead and say I'm dead and gone But you will see that you were wrong
Go ahead, try to hide the Son But all will see that I'm the One!

'Cause I'll come again! Ain't no power on earth can keep Me back!
Yes, I'll come again Come to take My people back

Prayer: O Lord, Help me to keep seeing the promised rest. Help my faith. Amen.

SEPTEMBER 28

Purchase of God

Bible Text: Genesis 49:32

Gen 49:32 The purchase of the field and of the cave that is therein was from the children of Heth.

Gen 23:15 My lord, hearken unto me: the land is worth four hundred shekels of silver; what is that betwixt me and thee? bury therefore thy dead. 16 And Abraham hearkened unto Ephron; and Abraham weighed to Ephron the silver, which he had named in the audience of the sons of Heth, four hundred shekels of silver, current money with the merchant. 17 And the field of Ephron, which was in Machpelah, which was before Mamre, the field, and the cave which was therein, and all the trees that were in the field, that were in all the borders round about, were made sure

Abraham was offered to buy this field for any price he wanted although the actual price was 400 shekels. Abraham insisted on paying the full price. The rest - the salvation we have in Christ was purchased . . . the price was to be the blood of an unblemished lamb, the kinsman Redeemer . . . the blood of Christ.

On the cross, Christ said it is finished. The price for the rest of the saints, the promised land that Abraham saw . . . the Heaven of the redeemed - has now been fully paid as the blood of Christ was shed at Calvary.

Jacob rested in the fields that he did not pay for . . . someone else - father Abraham had paid for the field. Christ has paid the price for our salvation and he did not negotiate the price. He paid in full. Rest in that truth. It is all paid for.

Song

I hear the Savior say, "Thy strength indeed is small;
Child of weakness, watch and pray, Find in Me thine all in all."

Jesus paid it all, All to Him I owe;
Sin had left a crimson stain, He washed it white as snow.

For nothing good have I - Whereby Thy grace to claim;
I'll wash my garments white - In the blood of Calv'ry's Lamb.

And now complete in Him, My robe, His righteousness,
Close sheltered 'neath His side, I am divinely blest.

Lord, now indeed I find - Thy pow'r, and Thine alone,
Can change the leper's spots - And melt the heart of stone.

When from my dying bed - My ransomed soul shall rise,
"Jesus died my soul to save," - Shall rend the vaulted skies.

And when before the throne I stand in Him complete,
I'll lay my trophies down, All down at Jesus' feet.

Prayer: O Lord, Lead me into your purchased rest. Amen.

SEPTEMBER 29

The Final Moments

Bible Text: Genesis 49:33

Gen 49:33 And when Jacob had made an end of commanding his sons, he gathered up his feet into the bed, and yielded up the ghost, and was gathered unto his people.

The staging of the final moments of Jacob are very vividly detailed in this verse. First - he made an end of commanding his sons ... he did not advice his sons or give them elegant options. He commanded as Abraham and Isaac commanded their sons. We must learn to speak the will of God to our sons as commandments which must be hearkened to. We are in a culture which deemphasizes fathers and idolizes children. Children are given options and encouraged to do as they wish instead of obeying the commandments of their fathers ... this is great error that displeases God.

Second, he made final physical preparations of gathering his feet and released his spirit. It was not taken from him unwillingly. His work was done and it was time to go. He gathered his body and yielded the ghost. Finally, he was gathered unto his people. The pilgrim crosses into another phase. It does not say he perished or that all ended for him ... instead the Bible records that he was gathered to his people, the family of God waiting for him. The saints who have gone before and angels of God in eternity are waiting for you. You will not miss this ultimate gathering.

Song

Someday the silver cord will break,
And I no more as now shall sing;
But oh, the joy when I shall wake
Within the palace of the King!

And I shall see Him face to face,
And tell the story—Saved by grace;
And I shall see Him face to face,
And tell the story—Saved by grace.

Someday my earthly house will fall.
I cannot tell how soon 'twill be;
But this I know—my All in All
Has now a place in Heav'n for me.

Someday, when fades the golden sun
Beneath the rosy tinted west,
My blessèd Lord will say, "Well done!"
And I shall enter into rest.

Some day: till then I'll watch and wait,
My lamp all trimmed and burning bright,
That when my Savior opens the gate,
My soul to Him may take its flight.

Prayer: Lord, may the day come when I shall be gathered unto your people in eternity. Amen

September 30

The Love of God

Bible Text: Genesis 50:1

Gen 50:1 And Joseph fell upon his father's face, and wept upon him, and kissed him.

There was an uncommon love between Joseph and his father. It was not faked, it was a love so real and palpable that the brothers of Joseph in his early years envied him. Joseph was pained when separated from his father and thrown into a different culture and not because he remembered the coat of many colors . . . Joseph never asked what happened to the coat . . . but his father was always on his mind. Joseph had lived many years in luxury as a senior official - but the attachment between him and his father remained strong till death. There is no greater pain for the saint than that of separation with God. Those in love cannot bear separation.

Luke 11:42 But woe unto you, Pharisees! for ye tithe mint and rue and all manner of herbs, and pass over judgment and the love of God: these ought ye to have done, and not to leave the other undone.

The Pharisees tithed and obeyed in many ways but passed over the love of God. It is possible to be in the church doing many things and not love God. The love of God is so strong . . . *Rom_8:39 Nor height, nor depth, nor any other creature, shall be able to separate us from the love of God, which is in Christ Jesus our Lord.*

How can we know if we truly love God? *2Co 5:14 For the love of Christ constraineth us; because we thus judge, that if one died for all, then were all dead:*

There are many decisions we could have taken in one direction, but we decide differently because we love God. The love of God makes us different - constraining us in a willing consecration even in the most private moments. We fear to engage in hidden and private sins more than the open ones because we love the God who sees all. We care about what God thinks and how he sees us. The question today could be "do you love God ?" and how does that constrain you . . . Joseph was very attached to his father and was mentored by a very deeply spiritual man who knew and loved God so deeply. Joseph loved his father deeply . . . loving even more the God that his father loved more than anything else. We see the evidence of this in the constraints that he placed on his life. That love survived the depths of prison and the heights of the office of prime minister . . . constraining him to live a God-fearing life.

Song

The love of God is greater far - Than tongue or pen can ever tell.
It goes beyond the highest star - And reaches to the lowest hell.
The guilty pair, bowed down with care, God gave His Son to win;
His erring child He reconciled - And pardoned from his sin.

O love of God, how rich and pure! How measureless and strong!
It shall forevermore endure - The saints' and angels' song.

When hoary time shall pass away, and earthly thrones and kingdoms fall;
When men who here refuse to pray, on rocks and hills and mountains call;
God's love, so sure, shall still endure, all measureless and strong;
Redeeming grace to Adam's race— The saints' and angels' song.

Prayer: Lord, O for grace to love you even more. Amen.

OCTOBER 1

Commitment

Bible Text: Genesis 50:5 -6

Gen 50: 5 My father made me swear, saying, Lo, I die: in my grave which I have digged for me in the land of Canaan, there shalt thou bury me. Now therefore let me go up, I pray thee, and bury my father, and I will come again. 6 And Pharaoh said, Go up, and bury thy father, according as he made thee swear.

There are things we have to put behind us ... for there is work to be done. Dwelling in the past is a sad error. It is good to mourn, but we must learn to move forward. Joseph said I will come again. This is a lesson in commitment. Christians must be people of commitment. Indeed Egypt was not the promised land but Joseph had commitments to serve in Egypt. Many make mistakes to think they cannot serve God by serving in secular roles. Even in Egypt, there is a role that God wants us to play but we do not look to the cultures and ways of God. The immorality of Egypt and the witchcraft notwithstanding Joseph was to be a blessing to Egypt. What promises have you made? ... and have you fulfilled that promise ... Commitment is very important to God. Have you done all that you will say that you will do? When you said you will come again ... did you come again? Disloyalty is extremely obnoxious to God ... no matter the guise in which it is presented. Many made promises to God and men but only seek to use God and manipulate men ... they ended up like Gehazi. May God helps us. Be careful to fulfill your commitments. The love of God should not be an excuse to abandon contractual responsibilities and be disloyal to your word. Pharaoh released Joseph for a while but knowing he will return to do that which he has promised. Joseph was committed to his destiny in Egypt. Be a man or woman of integrity.

Song

It may not be on the mountain's height, or over the stormy sea;
It may not be at the battle's front my Lord will have need of me;
But if by a still, small voice He calls to paths I do not know,
I'll answer, dear Lord, with my hand in Yours,
I'll go where You want me to go.

I'll go where You want me to go, dear Lord,
O'er mountain, or plain, or sea;
I'll say what You want me to say, dear Lord,
I'll be what You want me to be.

Perhaps today there are loving words which Jesus would have me speak;
There may be now, in the paths of sin, some wand'rer whom I should seek.
O Savior, if You will be my Guide, though dark and rugged the way,
My voice shall echo the message sweet,
I'll say what You want me to say.

There's surely somewhere a lowly place in earth's harvest fields so wide,
Where I may labor through life's short day for Jesus, the Crucified.
So, trusting my all unto Your care, I know You always love me!
I'll do Your will with a heart sincere,
I'll be what You want me to be.

Prayer: Lord, Help me to be committed ... give me strength to finish that which you have helped me to start.
Amen

October 2

Vain Followers

Bible Text: Genesis 50:7

Gen 50:7 And Joseph went up to bury his father: and with him went up all the servants of Pharaoh, the elders of his house, and all the elders of the land of Egypt,

Serving God is not about leading multitudes. It matters that we know God and love Him. People follow men for different reasons. We do not know exactly why many from Egypt followed Joseph . . . I suspect it was from the respect and admiration for Joseph or perhaps a duty in respect of the office he carried. But they did not know the God of Joseph, nor did they understand why Joseph had to travel so far out of Egypt only to bury his father. Going up out of Egypt is not always a deliverance . . . this time it was a temporary trip in the escort of many Egyptians. Perhaps the Egyptians escorted Joseph with the agenda of ensuring that he came back to Egypt. What is the agenda of the many who follow you? Any following of a man of God that does not reveal the God of that man to the followers is a vain following no matter how many they are.

First, they followed Joseph out of Egypt - escorting the brothers of Joseph and others only to attend a burial. This is very different from the Exodus out of Egypt. Notice there was no conflict with Pharaoh . . . it was peaceful and quiet - there was no confrontation with Egypt and its culture and no need for the plagues. But it was a vain following like many followings. Is your assembly in your church a crowd of servants of Pharaoh, mixed with elders of Israel and elders of Egypt? It may be a well-intended following but they do not know God. As you meditate on this devotional, remember that coming out of Egypt is not just a physical exit but must be accompanied with a spiritual liberation requiring conflict, confrontation with the status quo and the mighty hand of God. How do we explain the crowd that follows you? Where are they going and who do they serve? You will know if you have a vain following from the warfare. If there is no warfare, be assured that none have been delivered. Captives are not released so easily.

God knew there was still going to be a coming out of Egypt generations later that would be completely different.

Song

Ascribe greatness to our God the rock
His work is perfect and all His ways are just.
Ascribe greatness to our God the rock
His work is perfect and all His ways are just.

He is a God of faithfuness without injustice
Good and perfect is He
He is a God of faithfulness without injustice
Good and perfect is He.

Prayer: Lord, Help me to know you and serve you as God the rock, the God of faithfulness without injustice, the good and perfect God—incomparable to all the false gods of Egypt. Amen

OCTOBER 3

Great but Incomplete

Bible Text: Genesis 50:8

Gen 50:8 And all the house of Joseph, and his brethren, and his father's house: only their little ones, and their flocks, and their herds, they left in the land of Goshen. 9 And there went up with him both chariots and horsemen: and it was a very great company.

What is a great company? I already said this trip was accompanied with the elders of Egypt and the servant of Pharaoh but now we have more details of what they took with them and what they did not take with them. What does this mean? We know that they would return to Egypt because they left behind their little ones and flocks.

One knows a revival that will last and one that will not. Observe the youth and the teachings on wealth and how people give. When our young ones and substance are in the clutches of Babylon, we can be assured that . . . this revival will return to Egypt. When our young ones are leading and active in serving God and our substance is truly given to God, we can be sure of the stability of the revival and the work of God. This was described as a great company because of their chariots and horsemen but it was an incomplete company without the little ones and their herds to be sacrificed for worship. Where are the little ones . . . where are your herds? Ponder this day on the location of your young ones . . . that is where you will eventually return. May our young ones join us in praising God.

Song

Children of Jerusalem - Sang the praise of Jesus' Name:
Children, too, of modern days - Join to sing the Savior's praise.

Hark, hark, hark! While infant voices sing,
Hark, hark, hark! While infant voices sing
Loud hosannas, loud hosannas, Loud hosannas to our King.

We are taught to love the Lord, We are taught to read His Word;
We are taught the way to Heav'n: Praise for all to God be giv'n.

Parents, teachers, old and young, All unite to swell the song;
Higher and yet higher rise, 'Til hosannas fill the skies.

Prayer: Lord, Do not permit our children and young ones to be left in Egypt. Help us - O Lord. Amen

October 4

The Threshing floor of Atad

Bible Text: Genesis 50:10

Gen 50:10 And they came to the threshingfloor of Atad, which is beyond Jordan, and there they mourned with a great and very sore lamentation: and he made a mourning for his father seven days.

There is an interesting relationship between worship and the "threshing floor". This verse is the first mention of the threshing floor in the Bible. We are told Joseph and his brothers mourned the death of their father, Israel. Why mourn at a "threshing floor"? I believe the reason becomes more apparent as we see its significance in Old Testament typology. It was at the "threshing floor", that Uzzah was struck dead for taking hold of the Ark of the Covenant (II Sam. 6:6-7). The Temple was built at the threshing floor David had purchased from Ornan the Jebusite (I Chron. 22:1). Ruth came to Boaz at the "threshing floor" (Ruth 3:6-14). Boaz represents Christ (our kinsman redeemer) and Ruth, the Bride of Christ.

At the center of the threshing floor, one finds two large flat stones, one resting on the top of the other. They were "fitted and joined" together. The top stone was known as the "female" and the bottom stone the "male". The "grinding of grain" was a depiction of the act of marriage (Job 31:10). The act of marriage is a physical depiction of the "spiritual communion" God desires between Himself and Man. When God's covenant people stray from Him and worship other gods, God calls it "adultery" or "playing the harlot" (Ezek. 23:37, Hosea 4:12). Notice what God says to Israel in Hosea 9:1, "You have loved harlots earnings on every threshing floor".

The "threshing floor" speaks to us about a place of encounter with God, a place of worship. Worship for us is to be a time of "threshing", when God separates the "wheat' from the "chaff" in our lives. When we enter into worship, we are stepping onto God's "threshing floor" where He deals with those things which need to be "winnowed" out of our lives. Joseph and his brothers mourned at the threshing floor. I do not think they just mourned for the loss of their father in very ripe old age . . . but for their wickedness and evil ways even as God exposed their terrible deeds and evil motivations to them. May we receive grace to mourn for the things of God not in our life and seek repentance rather than just the blessings we lost. May we worship at the threshing floor . . . meaning we also come, as we worship, to the realization of what needs to be winnowed out of our lives. May we meet God at the threshing floor . . . and mournfully rediscover our need for fresh consecration.

Mat 5:4 Blessed are they that mourn: for they shall be comforted.

I pray that I will begin to see worship from the perspective of the "threshing floor".

Song

Purify my heart - Let it be as gold as precious silver.
Purify my heart - Let it be as gold - pure gold
Refiners fire - my heart's one desire is to be holy - set apart for you Lord.
I choose to be holy. Set apart for you my master - ready to do your will.

Prayer: Lord, Bring me to the threshing floor where the rubbish in my life can be revealed and separated. Amen

OCTOBER 5

Abelmizraim

Bible Text: Genesis 50:11

Gen 50:11 And when the inhabitants of the land, the Canaanites, saw the mourning in the floor of Atad, they said, This is a grievous mourning to the Egyptians: wherefore the name of it was called Abelmizraim, which is beyond Jordan.

Abelmizraim means "this is a grievous mourning to the Egyptians". When Egypt observe the mourning they were somewhat perturbed or at best surprised if not aggrieved by it. The world does not understand why the Lord Jesus would say "Blessed are they who mourn . . . ." Why should God's children mourn . . . for a man that has lived to such a mature age. The world will urge us not to mourn, but instead to laugh and be happy . . . essentially . . . just live for pleasure. Any further sorrowing or grave soberness when Egypt has offered the best of Goshen is not quite what Egypt expected. Why should the brethren mourn when the best of Egypt is at their beck and call? The call to repent, to fast . . . to mourn for sin when the world tells us we are doing well is a call that irritates the world. The message of the world is enjoy . . . but your best life is certainly not now !

Luke 6 [25] Woe unto you that are full! for ye shall hunger. Woe unto you that laugh now! for ye shall mourn and weep. The Bible is full of pictures that lets us see He saves the best for the last. His Eternity in Heaven is His best. His way is to serve the best wine last . . . the way of the antichrist is the exact opposite. Eternal damnation is the worst of all worst case scenarios . . . and it is saved also for the last. Christians are told especially in the end-times to endure . . . and that it will be worth the wait. The antichrist says there is nothing to wait for so don't miss out on the joys of the moment at the expense of your soul. Christ suffered and was acquainted with grief . . . initially . . . before His glorification.

Egypt is still going to mourn many generations later when it is plagued and its soldiers drowned in the sea. Then Israel will truly laugh and dance. It will be worth the wait. Wait on God. God has saved the best for the last. Rejoice that there is a tomorrow that is assured. Those who wait for God to complete His processes in their lives and bring His victory at the right time will laugh last. Many in the world who are grieved at the soberness of the saints will one day mourn unstoppably . . . when the saints find eternal bliss as tears are finally wiped away. Remember . . . Israel laughed last. You will laugh last.

Song

Alas! and did my Savior bleed - And did my Sovereign die?
Would He devote that sacred head - For such a worm as I?
Thy body slain, sweet Jesus, Thine—And bathed in its own blood—
While the firm mark of wrath divine, His Soul in anguish stood.

Was it for crimes that I had done - He groaned upon the tree?
Amazing pity! grace unknown! And love beyond degree!
Well might the sun in darkness hide - And shut his glories in,
When Christ, the mighty Maker died, For man the creature's sin.

Thus might I hide my blushing face - While His dear cross appears,
Dissolve my heart in thankfulness, - And melt my eyes to tears.
But drops of grief can ne'er repay - The debt of love I owe:
Here, Lord, I give my self away - 'Tis all that I can do.

Prayer: Lord, teach me to wait and set my eyes on the glory that is ahead. Amen

October 6

Sons of Greatness

Bible Text: Genesis 50:12

Gen 50:12 And his sons did unto him according as he commanded them:

Teaching our children to obey parents is important. The commanding of sons and daughters by parents was also commended in the days of Abraham. God places a lot of premium to this issue. Our greatness is linked to how we raise our children. The worldview of today weakens the role of the parent and the government is emerging as a replacement to protect and guide the child. This seems to be the modern thing but needs a closer look. God is Great and so can be trusted to teach us about greatness.

Gen 18:18 Seeing that Abraham shall surely become a great and mighty nation, and all the nations of the earth shall be blessed in him? 19 For I know him, that he will command his children and his household after him, and they shall keep the way of the LORD, to do justice and judgment; that the LORD may bring upon Abraham that which he hath spoken of him

If you are a parent, you do have a responsibility to know God and the way of the Lord. Jacob commanded according to the way of the Lord. Do not experiment with your children. As you know the way of the Lord, you can then provide guidance that is compelling and not vague. Abraham founded a clan of greatness though him or his sons were not perfect. God said he was sure they would be a great and mighty nation. This is because children and household are commanded and instructed according to the way of the Lord. We owe a lot to our parents. Thank God for your parents or an elderly guardian God has placed in your life. Seek more grace to be obedient to them. Pray for them.

Another reason why you need to know God is to be able to put your children on the right path in all things. Commanding our children does not mean we are "overbearing" . . . we select the important events requiring guidance - expecting obedience. This is also a picture of God commanding us and of an obedience that must be complete . . . with His help and grace.

Isa 1:19 If ye be willing and obedient, ye shall eat the good of the land:

Song

Can you be obedient to the Lord of all,
Though the earth should totter, though the heav'ns should fall?
Face e'en a disaster with a faith-filled heart,
Knowing naught can harm him - Who with Christ will start?
Can you be obedient to the Lord you serve,
Never even flinch, friend, never even swerve;
Though your next step onward - seem to lead to death?
Can you then obey Him without bated breath?

Prayer: Lord, I want to obey you fully and completely. Help me. Amen

OCTOBER 7

His sons carried him

Bible Text: Genesis 50:13

Gen 50:13 For his sons carried him into the land of Canaan, and buried him in the cave of the field of Machpelah, which Abraham bought with the field for a possession of a burying place of Ephron the Hittite, before Mamre.

When your time is done . . . my prayer is that your sons will carry you and not the other way round. God will protect your children to supervise this final duty not to be executed in your absence. There are burdens and roles that cannot be carried by any. Duties that God wants executed by saints and not by the heathen.

For example, the ark was supposed to be borne by priests in the time of David. David decided a more convenient approach and thought to use oxen instead. When the cart stumbled, Uzzah put his hand to steady the ark . . . and he was struck dead. We are created to give God pleasure and the creator is entitled to define how the created should do things. David's innovation did not go down well with God. The sons of Jacob were preserved so they would obey their father and pass on the ways of God to their children. The priests were to carry the burden of bearing the ark. In the new covenant, we are priests and expected to bear the presence of God and this has its implications. Following God involves a yoke of obedience - which the Bible says is easy . . . but there are responsibilities and things God asks us to do that should not be delegated to "Oxen" . . . Is there any burden that God has asked you to carry . . . preaching the gospel to members of your family who do not know the Lord, calling on a sick neighbor no one visits . . . etc.

Can God trust me to carry the many things for which He has preserved my life? For example we must put on our armor ourselves . . . no one can carry for us the armor to win the personal battles we must fight. We must pray fervently.

Song
Soldiers of Christ, arise,
And put your armor on,
Strong in the strength which God supplies,
Through His eternal Son;
Strong in the Lord of Hosts,
And in His mighty pow'r,
Who in the strength of Jesus trusts
Is more than conqueror.

Pray, without ceasing pray,
Your Captain gives the word;
His summons cheerfully obey,
And call upon the Lord:
To God your every want
In instant prayer display;
Pray always; pray, and never faint;
Pray, without ceasing pray.

Prayer: Lord, Help me not to choose the flowery beds of ease. Let me not be overcome by the spirit of ease. Amen

OCTOBER 8

God's Ambassador

Bible Text: Genesis 50:14

Gen 50:14 And Joseph returned into Egypt, he, and his brethren, and all that went up with him to bury his father, after he had buried his father.

The trip to the land of Canaan escorted by chariots and elders of Egypt must end with return to Egypt. Jacob had told Joseph that a time was coming when they would all be brought out Egypt. Joseph knew he was returning - but one day . . . he must also be brought back to the land of Canaan. The timing was in the hands of God not in the hands of Joseph. Joseph had a job to do. He obeyed God in returning but knew his bones cannot be left in Egypt. He is God's ambassador reporting for duty - or at best a pilgrim but will he never be buried an Egyptian.

An ambassador is a diplomatic official of the highest rank, sent by one sovereign or state to another as it resident representative. He represents God on a temporary assignment. Pharaoh thinks Joseph is protected by him and is his appointee. Joseph knows God has appointed him and that God will protect him - not any man . . . not even Pharaoh. His prime role is to defend the ways of God and ensure the interests of Israel are always protected. Pharaoh may or may not know this - but he needs Joseph. As your reflect on life, ponder over the truth that you are God's ambassador. God is your employer . . . your rewarder and you carry His authority. Let this encourage you. But it is God that must not be offended and not Pharaoh. Do not postpone answering to the call to being God's ambassador.

Song

Beneath the cross of Jesus I fain would take my stand,
The shadow of a mighty rock within a weary land;
A home within the wilderness, a rest upon the way,
From the burning of the noontide heat, and the burden of the day.

O safe and happy shelter, O refuge tried and sweet,
O trysting place where Heaven's love and Heaven's justice meet!
As to the holy patriarch that wondrous dream was given,
So seems my Savior's cross to me, a ladder up to Heaven.

There lies beneath its shadow but on the further side
The darkness of an awful grave that gapes both deep and wide
And there between us stands the cross two arms outstretched to save
A watchman set to guard the way from that eternal grave.

Upon that cross of Jesus mine eye at times can see
The very dying form of One Who suffered there for me;
And from my stricken heart with tears two wonders I confess;
The wonders of redeeming love and my unworthiness.

Prayer: Lord, Let me never forget my true identity, rewarder and employer and the cross. Amen

OCTOBER 9

Forgiven

Bible Text: Genesis 50:15

Gen 50:15 And when Joseph's brethren saw that their father was dead, they said, Joseph will peradventure hate us, and will certainly requite us all the evil which we did unto him.

Fear is a highly destructive emotion. It distorts clear thinking and finds an ally in guilt and uncertainty. The death of Jacob creates an instant vacuum of leadership . . . and fears suddenly surface. Leadership is important in all situations. The Pastor must be a leader and not a club manager . . . the father must be a leader and not a quiet coach . . . businesses and nations need leadership. Leaders can be imperfect and may God spare us from evil leadership . . . but absence of leadership in any situation gives a green light to chaos. Jacob was hardly buried and imaginations begin to run riot. Guilt and fears arise and it seems certain that Joseph will revenge now that Jacob was buried. It is difficult to understand forgiveness more because it is a divine gift . . . Joseph was enabled by the spirit of God to release hurts that were so deep. The brothers of Joseph did not understand how or why Joseph should forgive.

As you meditate on this text. Reflect on the truth that forgiveness is not a natural reaction. Most people control their actions well but are only compelled to postpone demonstration of revenge until the opportunity presents itself in a more convenient form that covers their real agenda of revenge. For Joseph that opportunity has now come. Joseph, as a leader, could easily organize processes and events that will inflict pain on his brothers at the same time pretending innocence. This is a common abuse of office.

"Are you a leader" . . . is there a leadership vacuum in your situation? do you lead in your home as the father? What kind of leader are you? Are you full of tricks masking your inability to forgive and thirst for revenge? Ask God to search you and to give you the gift from Heaven to truly forgive others. How do you take decisions when there seems to be none to challenge or hold you to account . . . remember that God holds you accountable. God forgives and the blood of Jesus cleanses us . . . do not allow past guilt to trap you into fears. God's grace that brought you safe thus far will surely lead you home

Song

Amazing Grace, how sweet the sound,
That saved a wretch like me.
I once was lost but now am found,
Was blind, but now I see.

T'was Grace that taught my heart to fear.
And Grace, my fears relieved.
How precious did that Grace appear
The hour I first believed.

Through many dangers, toils and snares
I have already come;
'Tis Grace that brought me safe thus far
and Grace will lead me home.

Prayer: Lord help me to receive your forgiveness and more grace to forgive others. Amen

October 10

Fear, Lies and Tears

Bible Text: Genesis 50:16

Gen 50:16 And they sent a messenger unto Joseph, saying, Thy father did command before he died, saying, 17 So shall ye say unto Joseph, Forgive, I pray thee now, the trespass of thy brethren, and their sin; for they did unto thee evil: and now, we pray thee, forgive the trespass of the servants of the God of thy father. And Joseph wept when they spake unto him.

The fearful brothers send a message to Joseph hiding under a lie ... a command to forgive by Jacob. Joseph knew it was a lie. He had spent many private moments with Jacob and not once was this issue raised by his father. Joseph wept. Why? Here was someone who had given his entire life for them. It is painful to Joseph that his brothers could not understand the love he had for them. Joseph was their friend who was given for them ... yet they still doubted him. If God could give us His only begotten son for our salvation, why do we still find it difficult to receive the love of God. Why do we think God will not forgive us - when he said Christ has paid it all. Two cannot pay for the same offence. Jesus paid. We are free. Joseph also paid ... his brothers can receive that salvation. It is sad that we still distrust the love and generosity of God after all God has done ... giving us His Son.

Why do we come with lies, vows we cannot keep - to cover our fears ... why can we not be frank and come as we are heavy laden with fear and doubts ... just simply surrendering to Christ who understands our weak frame. We want things to be complicated. The real issue was the perceived absence of the strong leadership of Jacob and the emerging fears. As you reflect on this devotional - consider that the God of Jacob is in control ... and even all strong men can die, fall or leave ... Jesus remains the same ... yesterday, today and forever. Come clean to Jesus who says ... He will forgive. *Mat_11:28 Come unto me, all ye that labor and are heavy laden, and I will give you rest*

Song

Just as I am, without one plea, But that Thy blood was shed for me,
And that Thou bidst me come to Thee, O Lamb of God, I come, I come.

Just as I am, and waiting not - To rid my soul of one dark blot,
To Thee whose blood can cleanse each spot, O Lamb of God, I come, I come.

Just as I am, though tossed about - With many a conflict, many a doubt,
Fightings and fears within, without, O Lamb of God, I come, I come.

Just as I am, poor, wretched, blind; Sight, riches, healing of the mind,
Yea, all I need in Thee to find, O Lamb of God, I come, I come.

Just as I am, Thou wilt receive, Wilt welcome, pardon, cleanse, relieve;
Because Thy promise I believe, O Lamb of God, I come, I come.

Just as I am, Thy love unknown hath broken every barrier down;
Now, to be Thine, yea, Thine alone, O Lamb of God, I come, I come.

Just as I am, of that free love the breadth, length, depth, and height to prove,
Here for a season, then above, O Lamb of God, I come, I come!

Prayer: Lord I come to you laden with fears. Let me see your redeeming love afresh. Amen

OCTOBER 11

Worship God

Bible Text: Genesis 50:18

Gen 50:18 And his brethren also went and fell down before his face; and they said, Behold, we be thy servants.

In the previous verse, we see the brothers sending a messenger to Joseph. Joseph weeps realizing that his brothers do not trust him thinking he did all because of his father. But Joseph was given for them. As if realizing his wrong, they now come to him, falling down . . . saying they are his servants.

Jesus wants you to come directly to Him. Worship is always the right response. When did you spend an hour worshipping him last. Instead of coming with long confessions and admission why don't you just go to Him and worship Him. Worship ascribes all worth to the object of our worship . . . communicating that he is worthy to be served, worthy to be praised . . . worthy of adoration. You cannot worship by proxy. The choir or music leader cannot worship for you . . . you must come yourself. If Joseph - a man . . . was greeted with his brothers falling before his face . . . what then should be our posture or manner as we worship the King of kings. Surely, if the angels cover their faces and feet with their wings when they worship - we should show a little more respect.

Song

Praise, my soul, the King of Heaven;
To His feet thy tribute bring.
Ransomed, healed, restored, forgiven,
Evermore His praises sing:
Alleluia! Alleluia!
Praise the everlasting King.

Praise Him for His grace and favor
To our fathers in distress.
Praise Him still the same as ever,
Slow to chide, and swift to bless.
Alleluia! Alleluia!
Glorious in His faithfulness.

Fatherlike He tends and spares us;
Well our feeble frame He knows.
In His hands He gently bears us,
Rescues us from all our foes.
Alleluia! Alleluia!
Widely yet His mercy flows.

Angels, help us to adore Him;
Ye behold Him face to face;
Sun and moon, bow down before Him,
Dwellers all in time and space.
Alleluia! Alleluia!
Praise with us the God of grace

Prayer: Lord, I worship you and will worship you forever -the God of Grace

OCTOBER 12

Am I in the place of God?

Bible Text: Genesis 50:19

Gen 50:19 And Joseph said unto them, Fear not: for am I in the place of God?

Joseph points them to God. We should point those who want to worship us to God. Touching the glory that belongs to God is risky. There are those who did this and only lived to regret it. The brothers of Joseph expecting Joseph to revenge bow before him . . . in a plea for mercy. Joseph does not permit this. He knows it was all God at work. It is God and God alone that should be worshipped and never men. Indeed, men and women may hurt us. Be quick to forgive . . . seek grace to put the hurts behind you and move forward. Do not permit them to come to worship you or encourage them into long processes of making amends. Doing this makes you their God.

Herod was once so admired for his oratory that the people shouted . . . the voice of god !!!

Act 12:21 And upon a set day Herod, arrayed in royal apparel, sat upon his throne, and made an oration unto them. 22 And the people gave a shout, saying, It is the voice of a god, and not of a man. 23 And immediately the angel of the Lord smote him, because he gave not God the glory: and he was eaten of worms, and gave up the ghost.

Herod did not have time to react to the oratory . . . he was immediately struck down. Even angels will refuse the worship of men . . . as they will not dare share in God's glory. In what way are you seeking glory that belongs to God. God will promote us in His time. Be still and stay far from God's glory.

Song

God and God alone,
created all these things we call our own;
from the mighty to the small,
the glory in them all
is God's and God's alone.

God and God alone
reveals the truth to all we call unknown.
And the best and worst of man,
won't change the Master's plan,
it's God's and God's alone.

God and God alone
is here to take the universe's throne.
Let everything that lives,
reserve it's truest praise
for God and God alone.
God and God alone

will be the joy of our eternal home.
He will be your one desire,
our hearts will never tire,
with God and God alone.

Prayer: Lord, do not permit me to stray near the glory that is yours and yours alone. Amen

OCTOBER 13

God is good

Bible Text: Genesis 50:20

Gen 50:20 But as for you, ye thought evil against me; but God meant it unto good, to bring to pass, as it is this day, to save much people alive.

God is good. Even when men think evil and think they prosper in it . . . God is still good and works through it. This can be hard to understand. How can such a negative development have any good to it? Why does evil seem to thrive and yet Joseph says God meant it unto good. The child of God is safe from evil—what men mean for evil, if God chooses to permit it—is turned to good. Joseph was an instrument to save much people alive. God needed the brothers and their arrows to push Joseph into his destiny.

It would have never occurred to Joseph that his destiny was in Egypt. God had told Abraham and Isaac not to go down to Egypt—a symbol of evil. But to save many alive, Joseph needed to be brought into Egypt. The way to achieve this was for his brothers to sell him into slavery after hating and despising him for years. Jacob loved Joseph specially and spent more time teaching him and preparing him on the ways of God as others went to look after the flock. Joseph did not know what he was being specially loved for. He did not know he would be isolated in the pits of an Egyptian prison for years. But it was Joseph and not anyone else who says it was all good. God is good . . . whatever you are going through.

Song

God is good all the time
He put a song of praise in this heart of mine
God is good all the time
Through the darkest night, His light will shine
God is good, God is good all the time

If you're walking through the valley
And there are shadows all around
Do not fear, He will guide you
He will keep you safe and sound
'Cause He's promised to never leave you
Nor forsake you and His Word is true

We were sinners - so unworthy
Still for us He chose to die
Filled us with His Holy Spirit
Now we can stand and testify
That His love is everlasting
And His mercies - they will never end

Lord I may not understand
All the plans He has for me
My life is in your hands
And through the eyes of Him I can clearly see

Prayer: Lord, keep me in your goodness—though I may not understand all you are doing. Amen.

October 14

Child of Destiny

Bible Text: Genesis 50:21

Gen 50:21 Now therefore fear ye not: I will nourish you, and your little ones. And he comforted them, and spake kindly unto them.

Joseph pledges to nourish his brothers and their family in the famine. This was his destiny. There is a beautiful destiny and purpose to your life. Soon you will see it. All your upbringing, trials, victories and defeats will suddenly clarify a master plan that God arranged. Your destiny will banish fears of loss because it will position you to preserve his covenant people. You are a child of destiny—only you do not see it . . . look again. Joseph now knew what his life was designed for and why he suffered all that he had gone through.

Do you know your destiny? Reflect on the following questions? Where is your present location? What are the crisis points of your life and what did these crisis points achieve? What were the most painful experiences you had ever had? What are you always drawn to? Where have you been celebrated? What are your gifts? What upsets you the most? Is there something you know . . . some insight that your past experiences and current revelation of God's word—that will be a great help for others? Is there a good, you feel in your heart, God is calling you into? As you find answers and reflect on these, God will help you to see your unique destiny. There is a kingdom agenda waiting for your "fear not" . . . waiting to be nourished by you.

Joseph spoke kindly. When the bitterness is past, and your words are kind and worries have all abated . . . no one challenges you anymore . . . then you will know that you have found your own wealthy place.

Song

Though the world may promise me more,
I'm just made to be filled with the Lord.
Nor it's life worth living a day,
For the things that will soon pass away.
Doesn't matter how rich or successful I'd be,
Or how many pleasures be offered to me.
There's nothing that compares to my destiny—
To be thoroughly filled with the Lord.

Now although I'm still kind of small,
And the future is in front of me.
In my heart I've heard the Lord's call,
Just to follow Him absolutely.
Though the path may be holding
Much joy or much pain,
What matters is that more of Him I would gain,
Regardless what happens,
I never would change.
'Cause I'm made to be filled with the Lord.
Yes, I'm made to be filled with the Lord.

Prayer: Lord, help me to fulfill my purpose . . . the reason for my existence. Amen

OCTOBER 15

The Best Saved for the Last

Bible Text: Genesis 50:22

Gen 50:22 And Joseph dwelt in Egypt, he, and his father's house: and Joseph lived an hundred and ten years.

Joseph was loved and cherished by Jacob for seventeen years after which he was taken to Egypt. Joseph suffered bitter trials for thirteen years until he was 30 when he became in charge of Egypt's grain preservation. After seven years of plenty and famine began, Joseph is joined to his family. For eighty years Joseph dwelt in Egypt in peace as a ruling officer of Egypt. The best wine is always brought out later.

Remember the wedding at Cana . . .

Joh 2:9 When the ruler of the feast had tasted the water that was made wine, and knew not whence it was: (but the servants which drew the water knew;) the governor of the feast called the bridegroom, 10 And saith unto him, Every man at the beginning doth set forth good wine; and when men have well drunk, then that which is worse: but thou hast kept the good wine until now.

Every man will do their best and be exhausted . . . the devil offers vanity and then it becomes clear there is only grief at the end (ask most Hollywood icons) . . . Esau thrives and is rich, while Jacob is still running for fear. All these tell us that God saves the best for the latter years. His Heaven is the future . . . but now we must suffer many things, bear many things and grow in obedience . . . becoming progressively better. The best of God is eternal . . . a second will cause us to forget all our trials . . . Joseph forgot the thirteen years of disgrace, shame and imprisonment. I do not know your story . . . but God will wipe all your tears away. It will soon be clear to you—that He saves His best for the latter years. Just keep holding on.

Song

Hold on, Hold on
The best wine comes at the end.
Hold on, Hold on
You will soon rejoice again.
Hold on, Hold on
He wipes away your tears.
Hold on, Hold on
Wait for the latter years.

Hold on, Hold on
The best is yet to come
Hold on, Hold on
to God and God alone.
Hold on, Hold on
Though the trials endures
Hold on, Hold on
Heaven has all cures

Prayer: Lord, help me keep holding on to you—no matter what. Amen

October 16

Fruitful and United

Bible Text: Genesis 50:23

Gen 50:23 And Joseph saw Ephraim's children of the third generation: the children also of Machir the son of Manasseh were brought up upon Joseph's knees.

Joseph saw Ephraim's and Manasseh's grand-children. Already his clan was unusually fruitful as was prophesied. Within eighty years—three generations were born from the loins of Joseph. The blessings of waiting on God manifest in an unusual fruitfulness. It is a great blessing to be able to impact the lives of future generations . . . it is a great joy when you see your seed bringing forth much fruit and the young ones are brought upon your knees. I pray that your home will be united even as three generations will gather together in communion and fellowship. There are many homes that scatter in different directions in only one generation. Some have left home to settle in strange lands . . . some are never to be seen again. I pray by the special grace of God that your sons and daughters scattered in faraway locations will reunite in joyful communion. I pray that you will place your great grandchildren on your knees and bless them as your father blessed you. I pray that situations that scatter homes and alienate parents from their children will not arise in your family.

Isa_43:6 I will say to the north, Give up; and to the south, Keep not back: bring my sons from far, and my daughters from the ends of the earth;.

It is one thing to be fruitful—It is another to be united and of the same mind as your children and grandchildren in knowing and loving God. These are special graces. Joseph not only lived long, he was fruitful and his children were fruitful . . . and they were brought to his knees. God will cause your final years to be full of such joys.

Song

The Lord's my Shepherd, I'll not want.
He makes me down to lie
In pastures green; He leadeth me
The quiet waters by.

My soul He doth restore again;
And me to walk doth make
Within the paths of righteousness,
Even for His own Name's sake.

Yea, though I walk in death's dark vale,
Yet will I fear no ill:
For Thou art with me; and Thy rod
And staff my comfort still.

My table Thou hast furnishèd
In presence of my foes;
My head Thou dost with oil anoint,
And my cup overflows.

Prayer: Lord, thank you for fruitfulness and unity. May future generations yet unborn know you as Lord. Amen

OCTOBER 17

I will Bring you Out

Bible Text: Genesis 50:24

Gen 50:24 And Joseph said unto his brethren, I die: and God will surely visit you, and bring you out of this land unto the land which he sware to Abraham, to Isaac, and to Jacob.

The royal ambassador is about to be recalled. Joseph knows his sojourn in Egypt is about to be over. He now speaks to his brethren telling them the most important things they must know. Indeed Egypt is beautiful, all seems to be going well and there is no reason to leave and God has blessed them in Goshen . . . but Goshen is not home. God will visit them and bring them out. God knows that the future and orders our steps . . . Israel must never be so taken in by Egypt's hospitality to forget to worship and honor the true God.

Many times God says things that may seem unnecessary or irrelevant. There was no motivation to leave Egypt and the desert tribesmen had tasted what it was like to live in marble villas . . . but God had something better. There are times we do not appreciate that God has something better for us. But He does and he promises to bring us into it. God sees your situations and knows that although you have been blessed . . . there is still a greater promise beyond your imaginations that He wants to bring us into.

1Co_2:9 But as it is written, Eye hath not seen, nor ear heard, neither have entered into the heart of man, the things which God hath prepared for them that love him.

God has prepared a place beyond our sensual appreciation if we will love him and not cling to Egypt. The most important message of Joseph was to remind his brothers that there is a place God is bringing them to. Today, many hear little about Heaven. Many do not consider what it means to love God . . . they have been hypnotized by the grandeur of Egypt and all its treasures and offerings.

Reflect on your Heavenly home. Consider that God has blessed you—but He must still bring you out to a far better place—your promised home.

Song

O what a wonderful, wonderful day - day I will never forget;
After I'd wandered in darkness away, Jesus my Savior I met.
O what a tender, compassionate friend - He met the need of my heart;
Shadows dispelling, With joy I am telling, He made all the darkness depart.

Heaven came down and glory filled my soul, When at the cross the Savior made me whole;
My sins were washed away - And my night was turned to day -Heaven came down and glory filled my soul!

Born of the Spirit with life from above into God's fam'ly divine,
Justified fully thru Calvary's love, O what a standing is mine!
And the transaction so quickly was made when as a sinner I came,
Took of the offer of grace He did proffer - He saved me, O praise His dear name!

Now I've a hope that will surely endure after the passing of time;
I have a future in Heaven for sure, there in those mansions sublime.
And it's because of that wonderful day when at the cross I believed;
Riches eternal and blessings supernal from His precious hand I received.

Prayer: Lord, bring me to the promised home in Heaven. Amen

OCTOBER 18

Day of Visitation

Bible Text: Genesis 50:25

Gen 50:25 And Joseph took an oath of the children of Israel, saying, God will surely visit you, and ye shall carry up my bones from hence.

There is no doubt in the mind of Joseph that God will do what Jacob had said He would. Joseph was absolutely convinced on the word of God. Such faith is commendable. Are you certain God will accomplish what he has said He would in your life. Have no doubt—God is surely faithful. But men have to be bound in an oath . . . Joseph takes an oath of the children of Israel to carry his bones out of Egypt to Canaan when the visitation happens. This oath is passed from generation to generation until it is fulfilled in the generation of Moses. There is a day of visitation. This is not like any other day and it will surely come. But when is this day going to be? This day was a terrible day for Egypt . . . a day when Egypt was judged and its armies drowned . . . but it was also a day of great joy and victory for Egypt. Abraham also had a vision concerning this day . . . predicting how long it would take—400 years of affliction must pass . . . and the iniquity of the Amorites must be full.

Gen 15:12 And when the sun was going down, a deep sleep fell upon Abram; and, lo, an horror of great darkness fell upon him. 13 And he said unto Abram, Know of a surety that thy seed shall be a stranger in a land that is not theirs, and shall serve them; and they shall afflict them four hundred years; 14 And also that nation, whom they shall serve, will I judge: and afterward shall they come out with great substance. 15 And thou shalt go to thy fathers in peace; thou shalt be buried in a good old age. 16 But in the fourth generation they shall come hither again: for the iniquity of the Amorites is not yet full.

1Pe_2:12 Having your conversation honest among the Gentiles: that, whereas they speak against you as evildoers, they may by your good works, which they shall behold, glorify God in the day of visitation

When is the future day of visitation? It is a day when God will be glorified. It is a day when evildoers will realize they made a grave error . . . It is a day when the cup of evil will have been full, but also a day when good works will be seen and honest conversation wins. As you reflect on this passage . . . consider which group you belong to. The evil doing "Amorites", speaking against children of God or honest sons and daughters whose good works seem not to be appreciated. Will you be like Egypt who got a terrible surprise or like the children of Israel who received by grace a great deliverance. We are in a time when many say there is no Heaven, no hell . . . no judgment while the Bible has pictures from the book of Genesis that warn that there is a day of visitation . . . a day that will be very ugly for wicked souls . . . and a day of joy unspeakable. Make the choice as to what that day will mean for you and adjust your life by repentance and ethical corrections. I pray the day of visitation will be a good day for you. What is your decision? On the day of visitation, it was terrible for Egypt.

Song

I have decided to follow Jesus—I have decided to follow Jesus—I have decided to follow Jesus
No turning back—no turning back.
If no one joins me still I will follow—If no one joins me still I will follow—if no one joins me still I will follow
No turning back—no turning back

The cross before me, the world behind me—The cross before, the world behind me—The cross before me, the world behind me
No turning back—no turning back

Prayer: Lord, help my firm decision never to turn back from being yours and yours alone. Amen

OCTOBER 19

Embalmed

Bible Text: Genesis 50:26

Gen 50:26 So Joseph died, being an hundred and ten years old: and they embalmed him, and he was put in a coffin in Egypt.

It does not matter where life and circumstances have put you. You will still be brought out. It might be years later, your situation may have become like dried and flaky bones . . . you will still be brought out. They put Christ in the grave and found a huge stone to make it impossible for him to come out . . . but the Holy Spirit is unstoppable. Not even by death. The dried bones of joseph would still one day be carried through the Dead Sea . . . after a mighty victory over all of Pharaoh's resistance.

I want the reader to reflect on how God can overcome extremely unlikely odds to still achieve his purpose. Death, embalmment and Egypt cooperated to keep Joseph down . . . but one day He was brought up. It does not matter how many generations would pass . . . and that it would be about 400 years later . . . Time cannot stop the promises of God. It is never too late.

Be encouraged if hopes seem dead and buried . . . for Lazarus, his body had already started stinking . . . for Jesus it was after three days . . . for Joseph—it was generations after. Egypt will never be your home for there is no rest in Egypt—symbolizing worldliness. But there is a place of rest. God enjoys demonstrating His power over everything the world will call impossible . . . whatever the world has closed its file on . . . God will open up . . . in His appointed time. A day was coming when that coffin would be disturbed . . . and a day was coming when Joseph will come out. Death is not the end for the end for the pilgrim . . . instead it is the beginning of a glorious transition. Your trouble is not the end. It seems over but it is really a new beginning in disguise.

Song

It's not over. I'm coming out
Nothing can stop me . . . not even the grave
The bones may dry up . . . people may forget
But it's not over . . . the Spirit is moving
Soon the Red Sea must part
To remind all that nothing - absolutely nothing
Can stop what the Lord brings out.
Not even a coffin or centuries in a sealed grave
Will stop my rising again.
It's only a new beginning waiting to start.

Prayer: Lord Jesus, in you mercy . . . let your love keep and guide me through the final journey back home.

October 20

A New Beginning

Bible Text: Exodus 1:1

Exo 1:1 Now these are the names of the children of Israel, which came into Egypt; every man and his household came with Jacob. Reuben, Simeon, Levi, and Judah, Issachar, Zebulun, and Benjamin, 4 Dan, and Naphtali, Gad, and Asher. 5 And all the souls that came out of the loins of Jacob were seventy souls: for Joseph was in Egypt already. 6 And Joseph died, and all his brethren, and all that generation. 7 And the children of Israel were fruitful, and increased abundantly, and multiplied, and waxed exceeding mighty; and the land was filled with them.

Beginnings tend to be deceptive. They could like the end has come . . . beginnings sometimes resemble endings and we need to look closer to see fresh starts when I senses observe only sad closures. The book of Exodus starts with an account of the number that entered Egypt. God is concerned about details, the Bible says even the strands of hair is numbered to God. God does not miss any detail. The entire generation of 70 souls died.

Deu_1:11 (The LORD God of your fathers make you a thousand times so many more as ye are, and bless you, as he hath promised you!)

The Lord can multiply that which is placed obediently in His hand. The Children of Israel multiplied and they became renowned and influential. I believe God can take that ministry, that vision . . . that business concept . . . whatever seems to be starting in death is about to suddenly explode in fantastic multiplication and growth. Just remain in His purpose . . . do not stray from where He has positioned you. Take your eyes off the corpse of Joseph and look to His God. What looks like the end is really a blessed new beginning. A nation cannot be a nation if the citizens are few. The nation of Israel is incubated (not in Canaan) . . . becomes a people in the least likely place . . . in Egypt. God wants you to know that He is unlimited by location . . . only your disobedience frustrates your destiny. Be still in Him. Soon all that pertains to you will be a thousand times more.

Song

Our God, our help in ages past, Our hope for years to come,
Our shelter from the stormy blast, And our eternal home.

Under the shadow of Thy throne - Thy saints have dwelt secure;
Sufficient is Thine arm alone, And our defense is sure.

Before the hills in order stood, Or earth received her frame,
From everlasting Thou art God, To endless years the same.

Thy Word commands our flesh to dust, "Return, ye sons of men:"
All nations rose from earth at first, And turn to earth again.

A thousand ages in Thy sight - Are like an evening gone;
Short as the watch that ends the night - Before the rising sun.

Prayer: Lord Jesus, be our security, our help and shield in all situations. Amen

OCTOBER 21

Contrary Winds

Bible Text: Exodus 1:8

Exo 1:8 Now there arose up a new king over Egypt, which knew not Joseph.

Troubles can also come in different new forms. Past victories can be suddenly made irrelevant, the situation can change but God cannot change. Our friends and supporters can change but God cannot change. Our benefactors can change but God remains the same. We cannot place our trust and hopes on mortal flesh.

Jer_17:5 Thus saith the LORD; Cursed be the man that trusteth in man, and maketh flesh his arm, and whose heart departeth from the LORD

Our hope cannot be in man. There is no man that we can rest our hopes on. Men even the best are mortal and things can change after their death. Joseph was a good man who did everything possible to ensure everything was in place to favor generations after him . . . but he died like all men must die. Situations can suddenly change for the better or for the worse. We are not told the children of Israel sinned . . . it seems good winds and ill winds blow on all. The difference is that we have an anchor that keeps the soul steadfast and sure while the billows roll . . . fastened. A different wind was about to blow . . . it was going to be a contrary wind . . . but again this ill wind would usher in an awesome deliverance that had been predicted four hundred years ago. Have you seen a sign that things are not what you expected? Be not dismayed . . . wait on God . . . and see His awesome greatest deliverance disguised as the beginning of sorrows.

Song

Will your anchor hold in the storms of life,
When the clouds unfold their wings of strife?
When the strong tides lift and the cables strain,
Will your anchor drift, or firm remain?

We have an anchor that keeps the soul
Steadfast and sure while the billows roll,
Fastened to the Rock which cannot move,
Grounded firm and deep in the Savior's love.

It is safely moored, 'twill the storm withstand,
For 'tis well secured by the Savior's hand;
And the cables, passed from His heart to mine,
Can defy that blast, thro' strength divine.

It will surely hold in the Straits of Fear—
When the breakers have told that the reef is near;
Though the tempest rave and the wild winds blow,
Not an angry wave shall our bark o'erflow.

It will firmly hold in the Floods of Death—-
When the waters cold chill our latest breath,
On the rising tide it can never fail,

While our hopes abide within the Veil.

Prayer: Lord Jesus, keep me anchored to you at all times. Amen

October 22

Enemy Observations

Bible Text: Exodus 1:9

Exo 1:9 And he said unto his people, Behold, the people of the children of Israel are more and mightier than we:

This was an awesome testimony . . . but it was also a dangerous one. It is good to be envied . . . but it can be dangerous. Being successful, talented and prominent can attract observations that will soon be suffocated with envy. God must hide us sometimes and not bring us out too quickly until He is ready to work even through the envy of men to promote us. God caused the children of Israel to overtake the Egyptians because he knew this was the way to trigger a phase of persecution that will lead to a mighty deliverance that will end with the armies of Egypt drowned.

Prosperity and blessings cannot be hidden from men . . . In Christ we are more than conquerors . . . but as you conquer soon you will begin to hear the comments of men setting you up. Pharaoh needed the support of his people to oppress the Israelites. Every success needs help. Hide and commit all your successes in Him and pray that God prospers His purpose and not ours. It is highly dangerous to assume control once successful. This is very much like entering a dragon's den defended only with a pen knife.

David after his success over Goliath soon found himself the target of the reigning monarch. It suddenly became hot . . . but God saw David through. Be strong. He will also see you through . . . go to your knees.

Let God be your hiding place.

Song

In the warfare that is raging
For the truth and for the right,
When the conflict fierce is raging
With the powers of the night,
God needs people brave and true;
May He then depend on you?

Refrain

May the Lord depend on you?
Loyalty is but His due;
Say, O spirit brave and true,
That He may depend on you!

See, they come on sable pinions,
Come in strong Satanic might,
Powers come and dark dominions
From the regions of the night.
God requires the brave and true;
May He then depend on you?

Prayer: Lord Jesus, Hide me always in the shadow of your wings . . . fill my heart with songs of deliverance. Amen

OCTOBER 23

The Devil's Wisdom

Bible Text: Exodus 1:10-11

Exo 1:10 Come on, let us deal wisely with them; lest they multiply, and it come to pass, that, when there falleth out any war, they join also unto our enemies, and fight against us, and so get them up out of the land. 11 Therefore they did set over them taskmasters to afflict them with their burdens. And they built for Pharaoh treasure cities, Pithom and Raamses.

It is worth studying the wisdom of Egypt to stop the multiplication of Israel. The fear of Pharaoh was that they could form an alliance with enemies of Egypt to drive them out. Pharaoh decided to afflict them with burdens and appoint task masters to keep them discouraged, weak and exhausted. A people who are discouraged, burdened and tired—bound under wicked task masters will eventually be hindered in productivity and fruitfulness. The enemy uses the same approach today . . . and has different task masters on his employment . . . Some even sneak into the church. These task masters place burdens on the people of God to keep them discouraged, barren and eventually unproductive. These "mega ministries", "multinationals" etc. are the modern day cities of Pharaoh. The wisdom of its captains targets the arrest of true spiritual growth . . . exhausting membership in ceaseless activity.

Ponder over this and be watchful. The wisdom of Pharaoh is to set them on assignments to build "treasure cities" . . . Being prayerful and sober, knowing the will of God and guarding our hearts helps us to resist the wisdom of hell. You will prevail over the devil's wisdom.

Song

Strange and mysterious is my life,
What opposites I feel within!
A stable peace, a constant strife,
The rule of grace, the pow'r of sin:
Too often I am captive led,
Yet daily triumph in my Head.

I prize the privilege of prayer,
But o! what backwardness to pray!
Though on the Lord I cast my care,
I feel its burden every day:
I seek his will in all I do,
Yet find my own is working too.

I call the promises my own,
And prize them more than mines of gold;
Yet though their sweetness I have known,
They leave me unimpressed and cold
One hour upon the truth I feed,
The next I know not what I read.

Prayer: Lord Jesus, Help me to be watchful and to pray . . . finding God's will in all situations. Amen

October 24
Unstoppable Growth

Bible Text: Exodus 1:12

Exo 1:12 But the more they afflicted them, the more they multiplied and grew. And they were grieved because of the children of Israel.

Affliction did not stop the children of Israel. Instead, it made them even more productive. Only God's people increase and become stronger even with more affliction. The blessings of Jacob have produced an unstoppable race.

Affliction can be helpful. Have you not noticed the fruits of the spirit manifesting more . . . you have learnt patience, love and meekness not in the class room but in ovens of affliction. It is a supreme proof to recognize true children of God . . . they blossom in afflictions. But affliction is also to be borne only for a short while.

Egypt we read was also grieved because of the children of Israel. Though the Israelites were unstoppable in growth - the hatred and envy of Egypt was equally unstoppable. It also grew. Is it not interesting to see grace and wickedness growing side by side? Sometimes we have a mixture of those growing and those grieving . . . often only God can separate the wheat from tares. You are a child of God destined to grow . . . and manifesting the fruits of the Holy Spirit is the sign of this growth. Affliction and pain may be the trigger to greater joy. God truly works in mysterious ways.

Song

He giveth more grace as our burdens grow greater,
He sendeth more strength as our labors increase;
To added afflictions He addeth His mercy,
To multiplied trials He multiplies peace.

When we have exhausted our store of endurance,
When our strength has failed ere the day is half done,
When we reach the end of our hoarded resources
Our Father's full giving is only begun.

Fear not that thy need shall exceed His provision,
Our God ever yearns His resources to share;
Lean hard on the arm everlasting, availing;
The Father both thee and thy load will upbear.

His love has no limits, His grace has no measure,
His power no boundary known unto men;
For out of His infinite riches in Jesus
He giveth, and giveth, and giveth again

Prayer: Lord Jesus, Multiply peace, grace, love, patience and kindness in my life. Amen

OCTOBER 25

Crisis and Deliverance

Bible Text: Exodus 1:12

Exo 1:13 And the Egyptians made the children of Israel to serve with rigor: 14 And they made their lives bitter with hard bondage, in morter, and in brick, and in all manner of service in the field: all their service, wherein they made them serve, was with rigor . . . 16 And he said, When ye do the office of a midwife to the Hebrew women, and see them upon the stools; if it be a son, then ye shall kill him: but if it be a daughter, then she shall live.

A new beginning soon develops into what looks like a serious crisis. Joseph is in the grave . . . dead and forgotten. They multiply only to be bitterly envied . . . causing them to be afflicted. But God caused them to grow—even as affliction graduated into bitter and hard bondage and eventually murder of the sons. This is now crisis. But God strengthened the midwives to preserve the sons . . . but these were very difficult times . . . the children of Israel began to groan under the wicked bondage of Egypt.

But God heard their cries. Years later God sent Moses . . . prepared him, processed him and guided him to lead the children of Israel in a mighty deliverance out of Egypt. It seems for things to get better they must initially get worse and descend to crisis levels. For the Hebrews, death began to threaten all their sons. But deliverance was also near. I do not know how low you have gone and if things have suddenly gone from bad to worse. Death is now threatening as health problems and depression converge to attack your life. Christ is the deliverer. Sometimes things really go very bad before God steps in . . . He has already planned an awesome deliverance but the cup of the Amorites must be full. Wait on God. Soon Christ the Lord of Hosts will manifest a victory that will shock you. The cup of enemies of God in your life will soon fill up with their evils . . . God is about to say . . . enough. You are about to sing a song of victory. Things went very bad because the time to come out had come. The period close to delivery of a baby can be more painful as the unborn baby kicks. The pain and fears are at their peak at the verge of delivery. The announcement to murder the sons of Egypt coincided with the birth of Moses. The generation that will carry out the bones of Joseph are about to be born in a time when all male Hebrew babies are to be killed. The victories of God are awesome . . . wait for it.

Song

Victory, victory Hallelujah Hallelujah Hallelujah
Victory, victory Hallelujah
Jesus conquered the devil completely
He has given us victory I will lift Him higher Jehovah
I will lift Him higher.
He has given us victory I will lift Him higher Jehovah
I will lift Him higher.
Victory, victory Hallelujah Hallelujah Hallelujah
Victory, victory Hallelujah
Jesus conquered the devil completely

He can never never fail
He can never never fail
He can never never fail
Jesus the same for ever

Prayer: Lord Jesus, Show me your awesome unfailing victories again and again. Amen

October 26

Moses and Joseph

Bible Text: Exodus 13:19

Exo 13:19 And Moses took the bones of Joseph with him: for he had straitly sworn the children of Israel, saying, God will surely visit you; and ye shall carry up my bones away hence with you.

Eighty years pass. Moses having spent 40 years in Egypt and 40 years in the wilderness is prepared as God's servant for the deliverance of the children of Israel . . . as Abraham, Jacob and Joseph had said would happen. Eventually God's mighty hand forces Pharaoh to release the children of Israel from the bondage of Egypt. Moses does not leave Egypt without carrying the bones of Joseph. The Red Sea parts before the bones of Joseph and Joseph's body is carried out of Egypt.

Do you know that God reciprocated this important kindness in the life of Moses by carrying the body of Moses. The Bible tells us God buried Moses. This important seed produced its harvest.

Deu 34:5 So Moses the servant of the LORD died there in the land of Moab, according to the word of the LORD. 6 And he buried him in a valley in the land of Moab, over against Bethpeor: but no man knoweth of his sepulchre unto this day.

Do you know that there are many acts of kindness that appear useless, worthless and meaningless but count very much with God. Moses treasured the promises and ways of God and because he loved God. He knew he must obey Joseph's commandment to have his body taken out of Egypt. When we seek instant gratification we miss great opportunities to serve God. When we take personal pains concerning divine instructions unnoticed and unrewarded by men . . . God registers it and does not forget. God does not forget unusual service of obedience . . . especially in a time when men will not appreciate strict obedience to divine commandments. God was so deeply committed to Joseph . . . even to his dried embalmed bones . . . the harvest of Joseph's rare commitment to God.

God visited the children of Israel even though hundreds of years passed. All the prophecies of God concerning your life will be completely fulfilled. But ponder . . . what kind of harvest is waiting for me? Amen.

Song

We reap what we sow . . . as we scatter the seed
On the ground of obedience of love
What men reward—God has already paid
But seeds of sacrifice that go unsung
Are seeds for GOD himself to nurture
What harvest is waiting for me—when the trumpet eventually sounds.

We reap what we sow . . . as we scatter the seed
The word of God looking for hearts
When men praise us—God has already paid
But the word that causes repentance and many lonely nights
Is the word GOD himself will nurture.
What harvest is waiting for me—when the trumpet eventually sounds

Prayer: Lord Jesus, Help me to sow good seeds only. Amen

OCTOBER 27

Favored to Fight

Bible Text: Numbers 1:1-16

Num 1:1 And the LORD spake unto Moses in the wilderness of Sinai, in the tabernacle of the congregation, on the first day of the second month, in the second year after they were come out of the land of Egypt, saying,2 Take ye the sum of all the congregation of the children of Israel, after their families, by the house of their fathers, with the number of their names, every male by their polls; 3 From twenty years old and upward, all that are able to go forth to war in Israel: thou and Aaron shall number them by their armies . . . 5 And these are the names of the men that shall stand with you: of the tribe of Reuben; Elizur the son of Shedeur. . . . Of Simeon; Shelumiel the son of Zurishaddai. 7 Of Judah; Nahshon the son of Amminadab. Of Issachar; Nethaneel the son of Zuar.9 Of Zebulun; Eliab the son of Helon. 10 Of the children of Joseph: of Ephraim; Elishama the son of Ammihud: of Manasseh; Gamaliel the son of Pedahzur. . . . 16 These were the renowned of the congregation, princes of the tribes of their fathers, heads of thousands in Israel.

Joseph emerged as the favorite of God—his two children elevated to be represented not as children of Joseph but as children of Jacob. This meant Joseph had a double portion. But this is not just to inherit lands but it is first to contribute frontline fighters to lead Israel in Battle. Of the senior warriors, the princes of war that followed Moses . . . able to go forth to war . . . the leaders of armies, Joseph provided twice what the others contributed.

Those favored by God will be made to face more foes and put in more dangerous assignments for Him. These are like Job, David, Daniel, John the disciple and Jesus. They will be at the forefront of satanic conflicts and will be called upon to give and do much more than the others. This is a privilege many saints will find difficult to understand. The tribe of Joseph are expected to contribute twice in war. Indeed they were also renowned but they were expected to be fighters. They will be on their guard . . . waiting for Moses to call upon them anytime. Can God count on you as His favorite to fight the tougher battles, face the demons that take longer to defeat and open new ground for him? Can He count on you to be faithful in tougher persecutions, to be consistent in more difficult trials. This is the lot of the favored. More is expected in times of warfare from them.

Observe also the qualities of fighters . . . not inexperienced, able to go forth to war, male (representing strength) . . . fit for war . . . none with bodily weakness, blindness, lameness or with diseases were considered. The Church is the known as the church militant. The favorites of God tend to be the prayer warriors who will pray much longer while others are permitted relative ease. If you study Numbers 1, you will observe that the descendants of Joseph were amongst the highest in representation at battle. Judah also had a high representation of warriors. These were unusually favored and blessed tribes.

Song

Onward, Christian soldiers, marching as to war,
With the cross of Jesus going on before.
Christ, the royal Master, leads against the foe;
Forward into battle see His banners go!

Onward, Christian soldiers, marching as to war,
With the cross of Jesus going on before.

At the sign of triumph Satan's host doth flee;
On then, Christian soldiers, on to victory!
Hell's foundations quiver at the shout of praise;
Brothers lift your voices, loud your anthems raise.

Prayer: Lord Jesus, strengthen me to stand and fight for you—when others will fail you. Amen

OCTOBER 28

Unusual Workers

Bible Text: Numbers 13:1-11

Num 13:1 And the LORD spake unto Moses, saying, 2 Send thou men, that they may search the land of Canaan, which I give unto the children of Israel: of every tribe of their fathers shall ye send a man, everyone a ruler among them. 3 And Moses by the commandment of the LORD sent them from the wilderness of Paran: all those men were heads of the children of Israel. 4 And these were their names: of the tribe of Reuben, Shammua the son of Zaccur. 5 Of the tribe of Simeon, Shaphat the son of Hori.6 Of the tribe of Judah, Caleb the son of Jephunneh. 7 Of the tribe of Issachar, Igal the son of Joseph. 8 Of the tribe of Ephraim, Oshea the son of Nun. 9 Of the tribe of Benjamin, Palti the son of Raphu. 10 Of the tribe of Zebulun, Gaddiel the son of Sodi. 11 Of the tribe of Joseph, namely, of the tribe of Manasseh, Gaddi the son of Su.

Again we see when Moses required loyal workers to go and spy the land . . . Joseph had two workers . . . Joshua from the tribe of Ephraim and Gaddi from the tribe of Manasseh. Note that Caleb was from the tribe of Judah. The blessings on Joseph and Judah continue to cause these tribes to stand out. God's favored will be unusual workers . . . faithful workers. A blessed and favored worker is unusually faithful. You recall that Joshua and Caleb stood out . . . the favor on the children of Joseph brings them to honor in leadership many generations after Joseph had died.

Do not imagine that Joseph's reward ended in Egypt . . . many generations after it was Joshua of the tribe of Ephraim who brought them into the promised land and not Moses. The blessing of Jacob to bring the younger Ephraim ahead of Manasseh again manifests. God's reward for faithful service can reach into many generations in future. God can also punish far into generations unborn. Surely, it pays to be faithful. Do you know many faithful and unusual workers are fruits of faithful ancestors who were unusually blessed and who pleased God at levels most did not care for?

To be favored as Joseph was implies greater demands of faithfulness and a greater grace to fulfill leadership responsibilities and be successful.

Song

I will not doubt, I will not fear;
God's love and strength are always near
His promised gift helps me to find
An inner strength and peace of mind.

I give the Father willingly my trust,
My prayers, humility.
His Spirit guides His love assures
That fear departs when faith endures.

Prayer: Lord Jesus, help me to stand out as a worker of unusual faithfulness. Amen

OCTOBER 29

Remarkable Increase

Bible Text: Numbers 26:34

Num 26:34 These are the families of Manasseh, and those that were numbered of them, fifty and two thousand and seven hundred.

Why is this text significant? You will recall at Mount Sinai God ordered that the soldiers be numbered. After the plague brought upon by whoredoms with daughters of Moab and 24,000 perished, God requested another census. When you compare the numbers you will observe interesting patterns. The numbers of each tribe in total had decreased by 1,820 fewer but seven tribes increased. Judah increased by 1,900, Issachar by 9,900, Zebulun by 3,100, Manasseh increased unusually by 20,500, Benjamin by 10,200, Dan by 1,700 and Asher by 11,900. Reuben had decreased by 2,770, Simeon decreased by 37,100, Gad by 5,150, Ephraim by 8,000 and Napthali by 8,000. Again we see the tribe of Joseph excelling this time through Manasseh.

It may be inferred that Simeon . . . called instruments of cruelty by Jacob and cursed to be scattered . . . is beginning to suffer the negative effects of actions. Manasseh is becoming more and more prominent . . . rapidly increasing more than the others. The blessing for Joseph's faithfulness manifests in unusual increase many generations in the future.

Are you tempted to cheat, or just take it easy on the mission field . . . or relax. Do not. The blessings of the future even unto generations unborn include a remarkable increase in all that concerns you and generations in your future. How can I make it clearer that God blesses into generations unborn for loyalty and faithfulness. Be an icon of faithfulness. You can make a good decision that will affect the destiny of your descendants . . . . now. When they speak of you, they will say . . . Look, see how he has increased!

Song

Deeper, deeper in the love of Jesus
Daily let me go;
Higher, higher in the school of wisdom,
More of grace to know.

O deeper yet, I pray,
And higher every day,
And wiser, blessèd Lord,
In Thy precious, holy Word.

Deeper, deeper, blessèd Holy Spirit,
Take me deeper still,
Till my life is wholly lost in Jesus,
And His perfect will.

Deeper, deeper! though it cost hard trials,
Deeper let me go!
Rooted in the holy love of Jesus,
Let me fruitful grow.

Prayer: Lord Jesus, let my spiritual growth be evident to all. Amen

OCTOBER 30

Daughters of Zelophehad

Bible Text: Numbers 27:1-7

Num 27:1 Then came the daughters of Zelophehad, the son of Hepher, the son of Gilead, the son of Machir, the son of Manasseh, of the families of Manasseh the son of Joseph: and these are the names of his daughters; Mahlah, Noah, and Hoglah, and Milcah, and Tirzah. 2 And they stood before Moses, and before Eleazar the priest, and before the princes and all the congregation, by the door of the tabernacle of the congregation, saying, 3 Our father died in the wilderness, and he was not in the company of them that gathered themselves together against the LORD in the company of Korah; but died in his own sin, and had no sons. 4 Why should the name of our father be done away from among his family, because he hath no son? Give unto us therefore a possession among the brethren of our father. 5 And Moses brought their cause before the LORD. 6 And the LORD spake unto Moses, saying, 7 The daughters of Zelophehad speak right: thou shalt surely give them a possession of an inheritance among their father's brethren; and thou shalt cause the inheritance of their father to pass unto them.

The daughters of Zelophehad made a special case because their father had no sons and they were about to lose their inheritance. They would not be the first to be in this situation . . . but they would be favored. They were also women with exceptional character and integrity. They came from the families of Manasseh, the son of Joseph. They spoke boldly and declared they were not of the company of rebels but had been faithful. A special case was made for them and the rules were changed. The Lord personally intervened and created a new rule to favor these daughters of the tribe of Manasseh.

God can change the rules just to favor you. God can make you a notable exception. Again consider the virtues of integrity and the importance of faithfulness of generations before them. Joseph unusually was picked out to suffer . . . .his female descendants were singled out to be favored. Rules were changed for their favor.

The blessings of faithfulness are immeasurable. God can create a new rule for an entire nation just to see that you are favored. Remain faithful even when others do not notice. The things God will do for you and your descendants—no one will believe it or be able to do it. Concerning your family, It will be said God changed the rules to favor you. His grace towards generations yet unborn in your loins will be truly remarkable. Generations will call you blessed. Concerning you and yours they will say your case is different. Like Esther came before the King uninvited ready to die . . . you will not die . . . but the rule will not just be changed, it will be completely suspended . . . all because of you. Praise the King of kings.

Song

All hail the power of Jesus' Name! Let angels prostrate fall;
Bring forth the royal diadem, and crown Him Lord of all.
Bring forth the royal diadem, and crown Him Lord of all.

Let highborn seraphs tune the lyre, and as they tune it, fall
Before His face Who tunes their choir, and crown Him Lord of all.
Before His face Who tunes their choir, and crown Him Lord of all.

Crown Him, ye morning stars of light, who fixed this floating ball;
Now hail the strength of Israel's might, and crown Him Lord of all.
Now hail the strength of Israel's might, and crown Him Lord of all.

Prayer: Lord Jesus, the all-powerful Lord of all . . . let my case meet with your exceptional favor. Amen

OCTOBER 31

Favored for early Rewards

Bible Text: Numbers 32:33

Num 32:33 And Moses gave unto them, even to the children of Gad, and to the children of Reuben, and unto half the tribe of Manasseh the son of Joseph, the kingdom of Sihon king of the Amorites, and the kingdom of Og king of Bashan, the land, with the cities thereof in the coasts, even the cities of the country round about.

The Reubenites and the Gadites made a proposal concerning some of the lands already conquered before they crossed the promised land. This seemed like a greed or coveting of prime real estate that had caught the eyes of the Reubenites (cursed not to excel) and the Gadites. They later agree to fight to conquer the promised land but laying claim to these lands. Moses agreed to give them with conditions but he also allocates part of the land to half the tribe of Manasseh. Again it is not clear why the tribe of Joseph is chosen for this early reward especially when they did not ask for it. Moses settles the matter with Eleazar and with Joshua to be done as he instructs. It may be that the land was too extensive for just two tribes or because the war-like Manassite clan, was being rewarded for courage, and outstanding bravery ahead of all the others. Moses was displeased because the Reubenites and Gadites were focused on the reward and not on God or his promised land which still seemed in the future. Already God had said the tribe of Reuben will not excel . . . the mediocre cannot wait on God. They always want it all now . . . they cannot be delayed.

The exceptional bravery and faithfulness of the tribe of Manasseh is singled out for early rewards they did not solicit for. There is someone reading this devotional who is wondering . . . when will I be rewarded? The Lord says soon . . . you will be singled out for an inheritance you did not expect or ask for. God is a rewarder. The diligent, the faithful, the consecrated, the obedient will eat nit just the fruit of the land but will be surprised with honors they did not lobby for. Again the tribe of Joseph excel amongst other tribes and favored inexplicably with an early award of extensive lands. Hold on. Do the work. Fight the good fight. Leave the rest to God. Be still. The Lord is on thy side.

Song

Be still, my soul: the Lord is on thy side.
Bear patiently the cross of grief or pain.
Leave to thy God to order and provide;
In every change, He faithful will remain.
Be still, my soul: thy best, thy Heavenly Friend
Through thorny ways leads to a joyful end.

Be still, my soul: thy God doth undertake
To guide the future, as He has the past.
Thy hope, thy confidence let nothing shake;
All now mysterious shall be bright at last.
Be still, my soul: the waves and winds still know
His voice Who ruled them while He dwelt below.

Be still, my soul: when dearest friends depart,
And all is darkened in the vale of tears,
Then shalt thou better know His love, His heart,
Who comes to soothe thy sorrow and thy fears.
Be still, my soul: thy Jesus can repay
From His own fullness all He takes away.

Prayer: Lord Jesus, let my eyes be on you and not on the reward. Amen

NOVEMBER 1

Princes of Faith

Bible Text: Numbers 34:23

Num_34:23 The prince of the children of Joseph, for the tribe of the children of Manasseh, Hanniel the son of Ephod 24 And the prince of the tribe of the children of Ephraim, Kemuel the son of Shiphtan.

God himself appointed princes to divide the land. The tribe of Joseph provides two princes again double the others. Even as they fought double, they will have double influence in sharing the territories conquered. Moses is guided by the Holy Spirit to choose the tribes but always recognizing the double portion of Joseph.

Christ is the Prince of peace. Our Lord is the King of kings . . . as His children we are also princes. In Christ we are led by the Holy Spirit to minister the graces of the kingdom to others. Peace comes to those we minister to . . . they can learn and know of Christ as we teach our righteousness and there is a joy that the world cannot give. These princes are men of high integrity and diligence. They are fair and can be trusted to hear God and obey whatever they are instructed to do.

I pray that God can entrust me with His special gifts and graces. Note that the children of Israel have not entered the land yet but they already know they will win and so they already appoint the princes ahead of victory. In their minds, they have already won. Such faith moves God who moves the impossible. In your mind what is your conclusion. Your actions will reveal what you believe.

We must learn to live by faith and not by sight. Consider the boldness and faith that makes appointments well ahead of the conquest of territories. In your situation, what is the evidence that you live by faith? Begin to make more decisions out of faith in God's victory. Begin to see the end—victory—even before the battle has begun. Know for a certainty that you will enter the promises of God because He will help you as He has before. May we be called Princes of faith by God's mercy. You are not only blessed but you will apportion blessings to others.

Song

From Heaven above to earth I come,
To bear good news to every home;
Glad tidings of great joy I bring,
Whereof I now will say and sing.

'Tis Christ our God, who far on high
Had heard your sad and bitter cry;
Himself will your Salvation be,
Himself from sin will make you free.

He brings those blessings long ago
Prepared by God for all below;
That in His Heavenly kingdom blest
You may with us forever rest.

Prayer: Lord Jesus, we believe we have your eternal rest—give us more faith to move the mountains. Amen

NOVEMBER 2

Chosen to be a Blessing

Bible Text: Deut 21:11

Deu 27:11 And Moses charged the people the same day, saying, 12 These shall stand upon mount Gerizim to bless the people, when ye are come over Jordan; Simeon, and Levi, and Judah, and Issachar, and Joseph, and Benjamin: 13 And these shall stand upon mount Ebal to curse; Reuben, Gad, and Asher, and Zebulun, Dan, and Naphtali.

Moses was close to the end of his days. An important aspect of the life of the Israelites was to hear the law . . . understanding that God blesses us when we obey Him and there are curses that will come if we disobey. The tribes were to gather around different mountains and different tribes would declare blessings and different the curses. The house of Joseph were amongst those to declare the blessing with the house of Judah. This is further symbolic of the ancestry of Joseph who was not just blessed but a blessing to the entire tribe.

May God make you not just a blessing but an instrument to teach people the importance of hearing and obeying the truths of God. Others will have the role of reminding you that God abhors disobedience and there are curses for the disobedient. Have you heard people say God cannot do this or cannot do or that miracles are for the bible days . . . preaching often to a people who already refuse to hear talk less of obeying the laws and commandments. There are many examples of rebellion and disobedience that teach us that curses are harvested from rebellion. These are like those on Mount Ebal.

Indeed the disobedient are cursed . . . but the tribe of Joseph amongst others are chosen to bless. Christ is of the house of Judah, another tribe chosen to bless. Indeed Christ spoke hard words and said woe to the Pharisees . . . but His life was a blessing to those who surrendered to Him and a curse to those who didn't.

You are chosen to be a blessing to others, to be an instrument God will use to increase others in the knowledge of Him and encourage others to obey Him fully. To remind others that God is a God who opens His good treasure . . . making us the head. In the parable of the talents . . . the lazy one who buried His talent declared that God is a wicked master. I see that our lives can preach the goodness and blessings of God teaching and encouraging others to model their lives to do the same—like the life of Joseph . . . or our lives can model what happens when we God's laws are disregarded. Joseph modeled the unfathomable possibilities available when God is pleased with us. As you read this devotional, be committed to make your life a letter that teaches that God blesses the obedient. Tell God you do not want to be a parable to warn others of the wrath that comes when we refuse to hearken to and obey God's laws. What kind of preacher are you? What is your life preaching to others?

Song

Lead me Lord I will follow
Lead me Lord—I will;
You have called me—I will answer,
Lead me Lord—I will Go.

Prayer: Lord Jesus, let my life teach that you bless those who are obedient to you. Amen

NOVEMBER 3

Mercy for Reuben

Bible Text: Deut 33:6

Deu 33:6 Let Reuben live, and not die; and let not his men be few.

Moses pronounced blessings on the tribes of Israel. These were different from those of Jacob many years before, but they point to a God of mercy. Many generations have passed and much has happened since then. As the children of Israel get ready to enter the promised land and Moses about to die, he blesses the people he has led for forty years.

Reuben is blessed with forgiveness. Reuben shall be permitted to live and to also grow like the others. This is a blessing to strengthen a tribe previously plagued with a shorter lifespan and few men . . . perhaps a lower fertility than other tribes. Moses speaks a blessing to heal this situation. God is a God of mercy. God gives us a new chance every day to start afresh. His anger is for a moment but his mercy endures.

There is a reader somewhere who imagines he is cursed and carrying burdens that has paralyzed spiritual growth . . . living under a constant fear of death. As you read, I pray a second touch will come to you like Moses came to the Reubenites . . . but this time God's mercy will lift past weights and you will be free to live a fulfilled life and to expand in every realm of life. Receive the blessings of God that do not add any sorrow. But fear God. Do not go back to your vomit—the misdeeds that earned God's wrath in the first place.

I pray that as you look up to Jesus, you will live, you will grow in the Lord. You will not fail and will not be put to shame. Spiritual immaturity and greed—signs of refusing to grow spiritually, will no more weigh you down. Like an eagle you will begin to fly. You will expand in all sides and barrenness will no more be mentioned concerning you. Remain forever blessed.

Song

Your mercy flows like a river wide
Healing comes from your hand
Suffering children are safe in your arms
There is none like you.

There is none like you
No one else can touch my heart like you do
I could search through all eternity long and find
There is none like you.

Prayer: Lord Jesus, In your great mercy help us to repent and let healing come to all your suffering children.

NOVEMBER 4

Released to Thrive

Bible Text: Deut 33:6

Deu 33:6 Let Reuben live, and not die; and let not his men be few.

There are many cases in scripture of people that have been cursed—who found themselves in situations where circumstances must limit their growth always. Just as they are about to make progress in an important area they fall. Just when pregnancies and new deliveries are about to happen they abort the embryo. Gradually they are dying . . . slowly out of discouragement, depression and a cancerous pain that screams from within.

Reuben represents that kind of situation. But God is merciful. Indeed, a father figure representing God speaks to reverse situations like this. Prophesy over your children for good. It may be that curses have been pronounced by ancestors before your birth and you do not know. You can speak the opposite to your sons and daughters. Perhaps there is a hereditary sickness or it seems the women are barren or that there are no men in the household. Gather your children and pray over them. Begin to declare . . . Let (put their names) live and not die . . . and let the men in the house of (put your name) not be few. Do not wait for death to knock on your door as you pronounce these important spiritual reversals in the name higher than any other name. In the name of Jesus.

God had mercy on Reuben. When the tribes are mentioned in the book of Revelation, Reuben is not missing. Reuben was favored, forgiven and helped again by God. This is a good day to declare concerning all your children . . . let them live and let them thrive and be many times more than they are at present. Cancel every other negative declaration over their lives. And so shall it be. In Jesus name.

Song

It shall be permanent
It shall be permanent
What the Lord Has done for us
It shall be permanent. Amen

Prayer: Lord Jesus, In your great mercy let there be a permanent change from limitation to unlimited expansion in all that concerns me and my family. Let sorrow and grief be driven far from our habitations.

November 5

Helped by God

Bible Text: Deut 33:7

Deut 33:7 And this is the blessing of Judah: and he said, Hear, LORD, the voice of Judah, and bring him unto his people: let his hands be sufficient for him; and be thou an help to him from his enemies.

Judah is blessed again. Moses now pronounces that Judah will never be short of assistance. There will always be hands, helpers for him. When enemies come against him, God will come to him as Divine Help.

This will also be your blessing. You will not be short of resources in any form to do the work of God. You will always find the support to be what God has ordained you to be. It does not matter, the type of enemies . . . old or new . . . internal or external . . . familiar or unfamiliar, seen or invisible, big or small . . . every enemy that you face today will bow to the help of God in your life. It will be said concerning all that you laid your hands upon that God is sufficient . . . and God is able. You will not lack for bread, finances, graces and vital strength on a daily, monthly or yearly basis. As challenges expand so will your resources greatly expand. Your enemies will say "it is God that helped him". You will say "If it had not been for the Lord, how would I have survived . . ." The peace of God will envelope you. You will not be tormented with worries about supply for tomorrow. Like Moses pronounced a second round of blessings to take this tribe even higher. You will go even higher to achieve the elevation and promotion God has already ordained for you. It will be said that you are unstoppable—because God helped you. Like pouring rain showers, help will drench your habitations . . . like floods, help will overflow its banks to carry away all your burdens . . . like a great shield, help will still all the arrows aimed at you.

Jesus, when He walked the earth, testified that there were always angels ready to defend Him and help Him, even as He asked Peter to put back His sword when Christ was about to be arrested. God will make the help of men irrelevant.

Song

I will lift up my eyes unto the hills
From whence cometh my help
My help cometh from the Lord. The Lord who made Heaven and earth
He said. He will not suffer your foot. Your foot to be moved.
The Lord that keepeth thee
He will not slumber nor sleep
For the Lord is my keeper.
The Lord is my shade upon the right hand
Upon the right hand
For the sun shall not smite thee by day or the moon by night
He shall preserve your soul—even for ever more.
My Help . . . my help . . . . My help
All of my help cometh from the Lord.

Prayer: Lord Jesus, Help me and be my Help and song. Amen

NOVEMBER 6

Levi—No more scattered

Bible Text: Deut 33:8

Deu 33:8 And of Levi he said, Let thy Thummim and thy Urim be with thy holy one, whom thou didst prove at Massah, and with whom thou didst strive at the waters of Meribah; 9 Who said unto his father and to his mother, I have not seen him; neither did he acknowledge his brethren, nor knew his own children: for they have observed thy word, and kept thy covenant. 10 They shall teach Jacob thy judgments, and Israel thy law: they shall put incense before thee, and whole burnt sacrifice upon thine altar. 11 Bless, LORD, his substance, and accept the work of his hands: smite through the loins of them that rise against him, and of them that hate him, that they rise not again

Levi was scolded by Jacob for his anger . . . a curse that manifested even in the life of Moses from that same tribe. But God now changes the curse to be scattered because of Levi's unusual loyalty when Moses needed his support. Levi will now be a priest, a teacher of the law. The blessing of the priest of God is placed upon the tribe of Levi. He is no more to be a scattered instrument of anger and cruelty . . . but now a meek priest of God.

I pray for someone reading this devotional. Mercy will consider your works and change your harvest from bad to good. Christ is our eternal high Priest. Christ will help you as a servant of God to be upright and have the understanding to please God. You will love, know and teach the word of God and warn convincingly of His judgments. Your sacrifices of worship will find acceptance before God. The work of your hands will be blessed and accepted. Your substance will be blessed, protected and not diminished. As the waters of the ocean will not dry out, your resources will never fail.

When the enemy attacks you with your past—God will answer for you. All those for any reason that rise against you and that hate will be smitten completely in their loins . . . never to rise again. You will not defend yourself. Instead God will be your great defense. In your ministry, you will not fail. You will succeed where others were brought down. I decree like Levi, you will never more be scattered. Strength and unity shall be your portion. In Jesus name. Amen

Song

Be not dismayed whate'er betide, God will take care of you;
Beneath His wings of love abide, God will take care of you.

God will take care of you, Through every day, over all the way;
He will take care of you, God will take care of you.

Through days of toil when heart doth fail, God will take care of you;
When dangers fierce your path assail, God will take care of you.

All you may need He will provide, God will take care of you;
Nothing you ask will be denied, God will take care of you.

No matter what may be the test, God will take care of you;
Lean, weary one, upon His breast, God will take care of you.

Prayer: Lord Jesus, let it be said that you took good care of me. Amen.

NOVEMBER 7

Covered by God

Bible Text: Deut 33:12

Deu 33:12 And of Benjamin he said, The beloved of the LORD shall dwell in safety by him; and the LORD shall cover him all the day long, and he shall dwell between his shoulders.

Benjamin is called the beloved of the Lord. I pray that this is how God sees you. As a special son who must be protected and kept safe—no matter the circumstance. Moses blesses Benjamin with divine safety. Who can reach through the umbrella of God to hurt his beloved. Who can take what God has covered between his shoulders. If God has called you beloved, who can call you desolate?

Dear reader . . . I pray for you and it will be said—God kept you safe and not men. No evil will be able to reach you anymore for you will be closely kept under God's cover. Spiritually you will be covered. Mentally you will covered. Physically, you will be covered. Financially you will be covered. God Himself will be your insurance against every evil wind. Where things fall apart, you will be standing high. Where others fail you will be going even higher. Where storms pull down lives, yours will be standing tall. Where the earth opens to swallow everything on its path, its mouth will shut before you. The blood of Jesus will cover you from the power and lure of sin, you will be covered from the tongue of men and the arrows of your enemies. You will be safe from the counsel of evil men. You will be hidden from confusion and discord. No wonder . . . you shall be called the beloved of God. So shall it be in Jesus name. Have faith in Jesus. Believe in Him and His cover and be saved.

Song

Working will not save me; Purest deeds that I can do,
Holiest thoughts and feelings too, Cannot form my soul anew;
Working will not save me.

Jesus wept and died for me; Jesus suffered on the tree;
Jesus waits to make me free, He alone can save me.

Weeping will not save me; Though my face were bathed in tears,
That could not allay my fears, Could not wash the sins of years;
Weeping will not save me.

Waiting will not save me; Helpless, guilty, lost I lie,
In my ear is mercy's cry; If I wait I can but die:
Waiting will not save me.

Praying will not save me; All the prayers that I could say
Could not wash my sins away, All I owe could never pay:
Praying will not save me.

Faith in Christ will save me; Let me trust Thy gracious Son,
Trust the work that He has done, To His arms, Lord, help me run;
Faith in Christ will save me.

Prayer: Lord Jesus, increase my faith in you—that I may be saved. Amen.

NOVEMBER 8

Remembered again

Bible Text: Deut 33:13-15

Deu 33:13 And of Joseph he said, Blessed of the LORD be his land, for the precious things of Heaven, for the dew, and for the deep that coucheth beneath, 14 And for the precious fruits brought forth by the sun, and for the precious things put forth by the moon, 15 And for the chief things of the ancient mountains, and for the precious things of the lasting hills, 16 And for the precious things of the earth and fulness thereof, and for the good will of him that dwelt in the bush: let the blessing come upon the head of Joseph, and upon the top of the head of him that was separated from his brethren.

About four hundred or so years later . . . Joseph is still remembered for good. His descendants are blessed again. How can I fail to encourage you to do the good that God helps you to do . . . for the reward cannot be quantified or remotely estimated. Both Manasseh and Ephraim are said to be the blessed of the Lord. Whatever the tribes of Joseph touch is blessed. I pray that this will be your blessings in Christ Jesus.

The land that you stand upon and land that you possess shall be blessed. The precious things of Heaven will cooperate to bless you. The wealth of the deep, the precious fruits and things of the sun and moon will all align in agreement to bless you. Even the ancient mountains and the lasting hills will bring forth for you. All the precious things of the earth and even those that hide in the bush will work in your favor. Because you suffered a consecration—painful separation from your brethren - for the purpose of God, all the goodness of God will come upon your head. Even many generations after—you will still be remembered for good. So shall it be for you, In Jesus Name. Your labors of faith are remembered. Mercy remembers you. But it was consecration—a separation for God's purpose that qualified Joseph to be so singled out to be blessed.

Song

Jesus the Truth, the Life, the Way,
Unworthy though I be,
I trust since thou hast bid me pray
Thou wilt remember me.

When tempest tossed with care, my breast
Is like the troubled sea,
Sweet peace shall hush the storm to rest
If Thou remember me.

My former friends regard me not
Since I have followed Thee,
But let me be by them forgot
So Thou remember me.

When I was bound and chained in sin
Thy mercy set me free.
And each day since, a proof has been
Thou dost remember me.

I hope though now my time of death
Unable to foresee
To say, when yielding up my breath
Now Lord, remember me

Prayer: Lord Jesus, Remember me for good . . . even now I pray for grace and mercy. Amen.

NOVEMBER 9

The Elevation of Ephraim

Bible Text: Deut 33:17

Deu 33:17 His glory is like the firstling of his bullock, and his horns are like the horns of unicorns: with them he shall push the people together to the ends of the earth: and they are the ten thousands of Ephraim, and they are the thousands of Manasseh.

Manasseh and Ephraim are to be a glorious team. Strong, bold, unstoppable . . . a force God will use to advance the Kingdom even to the ends of the earth. But Ephraim will be more in number . . . they will be increased over their elder brother. It is God that raises one up over another. We cannot explain why Ephraim is persistently elevated over his elder one even from the time of Jacob—it was to be so . . . and Joseph did not understand it. Still both tribes were blessed. There are two issues here as you read this devotional—we must remember that it is God that elevates—it is vain to feel superior when it was never our doing in the first place. It is more sad to be grieved at the elevation of your brother. This is the second issue.

The reason for the expansion is to serve God and to move the purposes of God forward. For this purpose God requires thousands of Manasseh and ten thousand of Ephraim. The purpose of God's differential elevation is to be of greater use to God. To be able to serve him more and help others even more.

The older brother must not be bitter and the younger must not be puffed up. May God help us in all our situations . . . keeping us focused on Him as we serve with different gifts and under different callings.

Let there be no bitterness in service and may we all find humility to bring all that God has equipped us with into his vineyard for His glory.

Song

Of all the gifts Thy love bestows,
Thou Giver of all good,
Not Heaven itself a richer knows
Than the Redeemer's blood.

Faith too that trusts the blood through grace
From that same love we gain;
Else, sweetly as it suits our case,
The gift had been in vain.

We praise Thee, and would praise Thee more;
To Thee our all we owe;
The precious Savior, and the power
That makes Him precious too

Prayer: Lord Jesus, Giver of all good - thank you for your gifts, blessings and love. Teach me to give thanks and not envy others. Amen.

November 10

Different but Blessed

Bible Text: Deut 33:18

Deu 33:18 And of Zebulun he said, Rejoice, Zebulun, in thy going out; and, Issachar, in thy tents. 19 They shall call the people unto the mountain; there they shall offer sacrifices of righteousness: for they shall suck of the abundance of the seas, and of treasures hid in the sand.

Zebulun and Issachar are sons of Jacob by Leah and are of very different temperaments. One is outgoing, travelling to far lands abroad . . . trading and fruitful across oceans . . . known in the sea ports—but Issachar must rejoice in his tents. His business does not require travel. He works in farms, at home in a single locality. Sometimes the work of God is served through different temperaments. There are those who carry the gospel to distant lands . . . spreading the seed - always on the move. And there are those who must remain in one place . . . looking after the seed, helping it . . . protecting it with care and food . . . long after the evangelist is gone. In business, there are those whose business takes them abroad and across oceans and seas and prospering in intercontinental trade. But there are other types of business that is done at home, in only one location . . . some are writers and some are soldiers in distant lands.

We can be so different from the many others around us - but still rejoicing that we know and serve the purpose of God in our own unique way. If the whole body were an eye, where were the hearing? Moses reminds Zebulum and Issachar to rejoice knowing that they will both be prosperous albeit through very different avenues. One will have of the abundance of the seas . . . the other will enjoy the treasures of the sand.

Lord, we thank you for the diversity in the body and different manifestations of His grace to serve. You are blessed. Rejoiced in your own unique calling and the wealth given to you by God. Both Zebulun and Issachar will be wealthy. Blessed to prosper in their industry. Find where God has positioned you and prosper.

Song

Though we are many we are one body,
we are one body in Christ 2ce

> *One faith in the one God, One hope in our Lord Jesus Christ, One Father over all*

Though we are many we are one body,
we are one body in Christ 2ce

Prayer: Lord Jesus, teach me to rejoice in the diversity of callings prospering the kingdom by different ways. Amen.

November 11

Enlarged to serve

Bible Text: Deut 33:20

Deu 33:20 And of Gad he said, Blessed be he that enlargeth Gad: he dwelleth as a lion, and teareth the arm with the crown of the head. 21 And he provided the first part for himself, because there, in a portion of the lawgiver, was he seated; and he came with the heads of the people, he executed the justice of the LORD, and his judgments with Israel.

Like Gad. God will enlarge you. God will strengthen you. Gad is blessed to have the strength likened to the Lion. A predator feared by enemies of God—it is said that Jehu who was sent after Jezebel was of this tribe. God needs fierce Lions in His service to deal with certain types of situations quickly and mercilessly. Gad tears the arms of God's foes. But Gad is also a gentle and fair judge—executing justice and judgments with Israel.

Someone reading is uniquely blessed with a rare boldness to challenge evil and administer fierce judgments—but also self-controlled to share portions to others and to obey the laws of God. Someone reading is unusually enlarged but must not forget that it is God that enlarges and not any man. Gad causes Moses to praise God for His blessings of exceptional enlargement bestowed on Gad. Reflect on how God enlarges His own and the great strength in the Church—the Church that waits upon God like a lion. Sometimes underestimated when quiet but never weak and at occasions awesome in fierce victories through prayer. Worship the God that enlarges in the beauty of His holiness.

Song

Worship the Lord in the beauty of holiness,
bow down before him, his glory proclaim;
gold of obedience and incense of lowliness,
bring and adore him the Lord is his Name.

Low at his feet lay thy burden of carefulness,
high on his heart he will bear it for thee;
comfort thy sorrows and answer thy prayerfulness,
guiding thy steps as may best for thee be.

Fear not to enter his courts in the slenderness
of the poor wealth thou wouldst reckon as thine;
truth in its beauty, and love in its tenderness,
these are the offerings to lay on his shrine.

These though we bring them in trembling and fearfulness,
he will accept for the Name that is dear,
mornings of joy give for evenings of tearfulness,
trust for out trembling, and hope for our fear.

Worship the Lord in the beauty of holiness,
bow down before him, his glory proclaim;
gold of obedience and incense of lowliness,
bring and adore him the Lord is his Name.

Prayer: Father, you are the God that enlarges. Enlarge my coast for your glory even as I worship you. Amen.

NOVEMBER 12

Dangerous Dan

Bible Text: Deut 33:22

Deu 33:22 And of Dan he said, Dan is a lion's whelp: he shall leap from Bashan.

Dan is dangerous and deadly to God's enemies. Jacob blessed this tribe with the cunning of a serpent and now Moses bestows the courage, strength and fierceness of a lion on him. What can stop the one who has the head of a serpent and the strength and heart of a lion. Bashan is a mountain noted for its fierce lions, who come down to seize prey on the lower plains.

Dan takes the enemies of God by surprise. They leap with speed and before the prey can escape, God has completed His work. These are men with uncommon speed and accuracy in the work of God. They are the dangerous weapons feared by the enemy. Because of their strength and the damage they can do to the enemy they are often highly sought after in battle. But they can be proud.

Samson who tore lions apart and lifted gates like they were nothing - was of the tribe of Gad. The tribe was typically known for taking the enemies of God by surprise in guerilla warfare combined with overpowering strength. Samson in his pride becomes careless depending less and less on God and more on the strength. He lost the strategy of seeking divine direction on how to overcome the enemy . . . and ended up blinded and buried under the rubble of his victory. May God help us not to miss it—when we are strong not to depend on our strength and never to forget to lean on God, our strength—obeying Him as He explains his elected strategies of victory for each particular battle.

Help us to be like David who will never go to battle without asking God whether to pursue or not. Teach us to be strong and wise at the same time. Let us never forget that as you make us dangerous to your enemies we do not become careless in matters of consecration and hearing God such that our own strength eventually turns against us in destruction. Make us true soldiers of the Cross O Lord. Today, as you battle in spiritual war—you will experience a great victory. Amen

Song

Am I a soldier of the cross, a follower of the Lamb,
And shall I fear to own his cause or blush to speak his name?

Shall I be carried to the skies on flowery beds of ease,
While other fought to win the prize and sail through bloody seas?

Are there no foes for me to face? Must I not stem the flood?
Is this vain world a friend of grace, to help me on to God

Sure, I must fight, if I would reign: Increase my courage, Lord!
I'll bear the toil, endure the pain, Supported by thy word.

Thy saints in all this glorious war, Shall conquer, though they die;
The see the triumph from afar, By faith they bring it night.

When that illustrious day shall rise, And all thy armies shine
In robes of victory through the skies, The glory shall be thine.

Prayer: Father, Let it be said that I was a danger to your enemies O Lord. Amen.

November 13

Satisfied and full

Bible Text: Deut 33:23

Deu 33: 23 And of Naphtali he said, O Naphtali, satisfied with favour, and full with the blessing of the LORD: possess thou the west and the south

Naphtali is a happy tribe. To be applauded and admired for being satisfied, blessed and full is a wonderful thing. This was the portion of Naphtali. Napthali, blessed by Jacob to be a kind tribe with good words for others, now reaps favor and kindness in return. They are happy because they are content to be favored of God. They are happy because they are full with the blessing of the Lord. They are happy because they have possessed a great inheritance from the Lord. I suspect these are pointers on how God causes delight and satisfaction. I pray that you will discover God's favor afresh in your life and be satisfied with what God does. I pray it will be said of you that you are full to the brim with blessing, over-pouring with blessings to others . . . and that you have all that God has meant you to have.

Naphtali does not have the riches that drive dissatisfaction and an unabated thirst for even more. Many are blessed and favored but they do not know it and they only need to see their neighbors riches to be plunged into tensions. May we not search and long for the possessions of others. May God bless us with contentment. Contentment is important for happiness.

Again, this text tells us divine prosperity and peace that the world does not give. It is God's will that we should be satisfied and at peace even as we have possessions and are full with all manner of blessings. How true it is that the blessings of God do not add sorrow . . . but adds contentment, happiness, satisfaction and all round peace. To be full is to be complete . . . to miss nothing . . . to desire for no more riches. The blessed do not need to pray and seek for riches—they seek for God and riches are added to a barn that is already overflowing. Giving to others is easy and generosity is natural for the full has nowhere to store blessings that keep coming. The foolish builds more storage barns . . . but the blessed give more to others, becoming instruments of flow of great wealth to establish the covenant and purposes of God. In the kingdom, we also have spiritual possessions that cannot be bought with money—His righteousness, peace and joy in Christ. May you not lack anything that will bring permanent satisfaction into your heart. Let me be contented with your blessings in my life.

Song

I have seen the Lord's goodness
His mercy and compassion
I have seen the Lord's goodness
Hallelujah praise the Lord
I have seen the Lord's goodness
His mercy and compassion
I have seen the Lord's goodness
Hallelujah, praise the Lord

O Lord you have been so good You are so good to me
O Lord you are excellent in my life everyday
O Lord, you have been so good. You are so good to me
O Lord you are excellent in my life.

Prayer: Father, let me be satisfied with your favor, filled with your goodness and blessed by a glorious inheritance of righteousness, peace and joy in the Holy Ghost. Amen.

NOVEMBER 14

Anointed Richly

Bible Text: Deut 33:24

Deu 33:24 And of Asher he said, Let Asher be blessed with children; let him be acceptable to his brethren, and let him dip his foot in oil. 25 Thy shoes shall be iron and brass; and as thy days, so shall thy strength be.

Isa_10:27 And it shall come to pass in that day, that his burden shall be taken away from off thy shoulder, and his yoke from off thy neck, and the yoke shall be destroyed because of the anointing.

The Bible says the anointing of God causes burdens to be taken off and yokes destroyed. Asher is blessed with children and enjoys the favor, love and good will of neighbors. Asher's secret is revealed in the next phrase which says he has so much oil, he may not only anoint his head, body and legs but even his feet. Everything about Asher destroys the yoke of the enemy. Asher is a spiritual power house. Asher will therefore be so strong ... his shoes will be iron and brass ... the enemy runs from such an open display of power. But Asher will also live to very old age. He will be stronger as he goes older and not the other way round. His strength will never abate. Asher does not slow down with age—rather he becomes more anointed and powerful for God.

There are people seeking retirement ... but not of the tribe of Asher. I pray you will be like Asher ... so richly anointed. Blessed with many children and finding favor with your brethren. I pray that you will be invincible in power, strength and wealth. I pray that as you grow older you will become stronger for God ... ready for greater assignments and exploits. I pray your anointing will so overflow even the dust of the ground in which you tread will be blessed.

Like Asher, you will live to ripe old age. Doing ministry and prospering for God when others have slowly declined ... you will be like a man just starting afresh—anointed and more strong than in your youth.

Song

A charge to keep I have,
A God to glorify;
A never-dying soul to save,
and fit it for the sky.

To serve the present age,
My calling to fulfill,
O, may it all my powers engage
To do my master's will.

Arm me with jealous care,
As in thy sight to live;
And O, they servant, Lord, prepare
A strict account to give.

Prayer: Father, anoint me richly to be used to save souls and keep the charge that I have and that God may be glorified. Amen.

NOVEMBER 15

The Cost of Rebellion

Bible Text: Deut 33:29

Deu 33:29 Happy art thou, O Israel: who is like unto thee, O people saved by the LORD, the shield of thy help, and who is the sword of thy excellency! and thine enemies shall be found liars unto thee; and thou shalt tread upon their high places.

It is strange that Deuteronomy ends with Simeon left out and not blessed.by Moses. In the book of Numbers, you recall there were two instances when there was a census. The results revealed a lot especially the second census of male soldiers after a plague devastated the Israelites after immorality with the Moabites. According to Numbers 1; Simeon was the third largest group with 59,300 only after Judah 74,600 and the tribes of Manasseh and Ephraim combined to 72,200.

Now, let's examine the second census taken approximately 40 years later listed in Numbers 26. Numbers 26:2 confirms that it is again the sum of males "twenty years old an upward . . . all that are able to go to war in Israel," so each census was conducted with the same criteria. Simeon, the third largest tribe in Israel had plummeted to be the smallest of the tribes . . . loosing 37,100 people while Manasseh gains 20,500 people and if you combine with Ephraim, the tribe of Joseph have taken the lead.

In the previous chapter we learn that Phineas, a Levite, executed "a prince in of a chief house among the Simeonites for his audacity in taking a Midianite woman into his tent at a time when God was punishing Israel for such deeds. Indeed, God a plague which killed 24,000 people was stayed by the action of Phineas. The Bible gives no details of the tribes that suffered the most . . . but to account for a drop of 37,100 people makes us suspect that the Simeonites bore the brunt of this plague. Simeon cursed with Levi for being an instrument of cruelty for the vengeance over the rape of Dinah now worsens its situation with immorality with the Midianites. It is suspected that there was a crisis after this incident that led to a mutiny of many men of Simeon . . . only 22,200 can now be counted.

Genesis 49:5-7 prophesies that impulsive wrathfulness leading to violence would characterize both Simeonites and Levites. Now the Levite has executed a Simeonite Prince. God mercifully re-directed the Levites' propensity to violence into becoming a tribe of butchers, killing, cutting up and sacrificing innumerable animals under the system of animal sacrifices established in ancient Israel. Simeon fades out from the army either through a mutiny or a natural

The final result is that Levi is forgiven and blessed by Moses but concerning the tribe of Simeon, Moses is completely silent. While Levi regained an important and blessed role, the Simeonites you could go say go from bad to worse.

Moses ends his blessings by declaring that Israel are a happy people saved by the Lord . . . all their enemies shall be proven to be liars.

Reflect on this devotional. Are you in mutiny against the people of God. Is the correction of God to flee immorality and worldliness too severe for you to bear. Learn from the Simeonites and the blessings they eventually missed.

Song

Holy, Holy, Holy 2 ce Holy is the Lord 2ce.
Mighty, Mighty, Mighty 2ce Mighty is the Lord 2ce.
Faithful, Faithful, Faithful 2ce. Faithful is the Lord 2ce.

Prayer: Father, Lord help me . . . I repent of everything that could cost me my destiny.

NOVEMBER 16

Liars

Bible Text: Deut 33:29

Deu 33:29 Happy art thou, O Israel: who is like unto thee, O people saved by the LORD, the shield of thy help, and who is the sword of thy excellency! and thine enemies shall be found liars unto thee; and thou shalt tread upon their high places.

The enemies of the Lord in the end shall be proven to be liars. Often times, the word of God is distorted by God's enemies. So many false interpretations have hurt the body of Christ. Indeed many are unclear about so many matters on marriage, ministry, parenting, business and other aspects. Someone said . . . you do not know what to believe anymore because there are so many versions of truth. God must intervene.

God must expose His enemies to be liars so that their followers must flee from them. God must expose His enemies to be against him and not for Him so that it can be clear who really is on the Lord's side. So much damage will be done and many will be discouraged if God does not silence the mocking voices and change the testimony of those who say "where is your God?" Many times when ministries prosper, it is assumed they are serving God and indeed many are . . . but the few that are not must be exposed or else many flock to join these congregations and are hurt.

Today some say there is no hell, no rapture and no judgment . . . and God is not wicked to leave anyone unsaved. There are so many heretic teachings and more are being incubated. As you reflect on this devotional, pray that God Himself will intervene to expose the lies of the enemies. Indeed God may elect to wait till the end to separate the wheat from the tares but the damage would have been more extensive.

Lord, have mercy and let your enemies be found to be liars. Expose teachings that are false that the truth may set your children free.

Song

My God is a consuming fire 2ce
Wont you heed the warning—my God is fire 2ce.

Refiners fire our heart's one desire is to be Holy set apart for you Lord.

Prayer: Father, Lord help us . . . By your consuming fire, expose all your enemies as liars. Amen

NOVEMBER 17

Double for your Shame

Bible Text: Joshua 14:4

Jos 14:4 For the children of Joseph were two tribes, Manasseh and Ephraim: therefore they gave no part unto the Levites in the land, save cities to dwell in, with their suburbs for their cattle and for their substance.

The children of Joseph we read were two tribes causing them to exceed others in many respects. But we can also reminder that Joseph had enough troubles for which God recompensed him. The Bible says He gives double for our troubles. God is not unmindful of the challenges we bear for His purpose. It is worth pausing to reflect on the kindness of God. He observes all the burdens and weights we may carry. He knows of all the problems and the shame of being thrown into pit and ending up in the prisons of Egypt.

Job_5:19 He shall deliver thee in six troubles: yea, in seven there shall no evil touch thee.

Isa_61:7 For your shame ye shall have double; and for confusion they shall rejoice in their portion: therefore in their land they shall possess the double: everlasting joy shall be unto them

You are not the victim or the victimized if God is at work in your life. Instead you are being set up for double possessions. You have a reward here on earth and also in eternity. In Christ, you are free from the guilt of sin and also from its power. Like Elisha who received double of the anointing on Elijah, Christ told us the least in the kingdom is greater than John the Baptist who led the prophets. Our walk with God in Christ is a superior walk than that of the early prophets.

The shame of Christ at Calvary was our shame—Christ being our elder brother, the first fruits of them that sleep . . . and we are blessed as saints. We must get rid of the victim mentality . . . forgetting the shame, and instead put on the glory mentality of those who have inherited a double portion of the good things of God. Joseph was not a victim, although it looked very much like it at the time . . . God who dwells in eternity always saw him as a man - targeted for a double inheritance. His brothers saw him as a loser. Potiphar's wife saw him as an uncooperative tool. The fellow prisoners saw him as a convenient helper—a victim who knew nobody. But God always saw Joseph as blessed. Do not be labeled by the shame or by how men elect to see you. Hold on to God. Soon you will celebrate . . . a double rejoicing that will extend into eternity is yours. Double means to rejoice here and now as well as in the world to come. Christ is risen. Get rid of a victim mentality.

Song

Conquerors and overcomers now are we
Through the blood of Jesus we have victory
If the Lord be for us we can never fail
Nothing 'gainst His mighty power can e'er prevail.

Conquerors are we, thr'o the blood of Jesus
God will give us victory, thro' the blood of Jesus
Through the Lamb for sinners slain,
Yet who lives and reigns again,
More than conquerors are we,
More than conquerors are we

Prayer: Father, Lord teach me to praise my way out of the shame into double joy. I declare I am a victor and not a victim. Amen.

NOVEMBER 18

Marred by Blessings

Bible Text: Joshua 16:5-10

Jos 16:5 And the border of the children of Ephraim according to their families was thus: even the border of their inheritance on the east side was Atarothaddar, unto Bethhoron the upper; 6 And the border went out toward the sea to Michmethah on the north side; and the border went about eastward unto Taanathshiloh, and passed by it on the east to Janohah; 7 And it went down from Janohah to Ataroth, and to Naarath, and came to Jericho, and went out at Jordan. 8 The border went out from Tappuah westward unto the river Kanah; and the goings out thereof were at the sea. This is the inheritance of the tribe of the children of Ephraim by their families. 9 And the separate cities for the children of Ephraim were among the inheritance of the children of Manasseh, all the cities with their villages. 10 And they drave not out the Canaanites that dwelt in Gezer: but the Canaanites dwell among the Ephraimites unto this day, and serve under tribute.

The Ephraimites are now ahead in numbers to the elder tribe Manasseh. Joshua the leader is also of this tribe . . . it has become a tribe of much influence. But the Bible tells us they did not drive out the Canaanites as God had commanded them to do. Sadly this begins a trend. This may have been out of carelessness, cowardice, overconfidence or because of lack of faith in the god who promises victory . . . . Moses had warned them and advised them on what would happen if they did not drive out the Canaanites . . . but they did not give heed to Moses. The zeal to honor God was slowly fading. Ephraim was slowly being marred by overconfidence in their blessings and known destiny of greatness over the elder twin tribe.

Num 33:52 Then ye shall drive out all the inhabitants of the land from before you, and destroy all their pictures, and destroy all their molten images, and quite pluck down all their high places: 53 And ye shall dispossess the inhabitants of the land, and dwell therein: for I have given you the land to possess it. 54 And ye shall divide the land by lot for an inheritance among your families: and to the more ye shall give the more inheritance, and to the fewer ye shall give the less inheritance: every man's inheritance shall be in the place where his lot falleth; according to the tribes of your fathers ye shall inherit. 55 But if ye will not drive out the inhabitants of the land from before you; then it shall come to pass, that those which ye let remain of them shall be pricks in your eyes, and thorns in your sides, and shall vex you in the land wherein ye dwell. 56 Moreover it shall come to pass, that I shall do unto you, as I thought to do unto them.

The Ephraimites who should know better now set a very poor example. Perhaps out of greed or laziness. Soon they are defiled by idolatry . . . eventually to fall. It may also be that they tended to relax because of their favored and obviously blessed condition. But God is not partial. He does not make different rules for His favored nor does He countenance disobedience from any. We are often deceived into thinking the blessed of God are free from His laws and obedience to them. The opposite is usually the case. God expects even more from his favored. The tendency to compromise with the word of God tends to be a common temptation for the increased and enlarged. They will deceive themselves to think . . . surely God's mercy will permit this minor indiscretion. But hear the word of God.

Jos 24:20 If ye forsake the LORD, and serve strange gods, then he will turn and do you hurt, and consume you, after that he hath done you good.

The goodness of God is no license to experiment with strange company. This is what Ephraim began to do. It started with not confronting the Canaanites—to destroy all their molten images and high places. These were accommodated. Blessed child of God. What are you accommodating that is against the will of God . . . that you are confusing for grace. Get rid of the offensive relationship and ways. There is time to return.

Song

Holy is the Lord of Host - Holy is the Lord. Merciful and full of compassion—Holy is the Lord (chorus)

Prayer: Father, Help and teach me to fear and obey you and do your will completely. Amen.

NOVEMBER 19

Spreading Cancers

Bible Text: Joshua 17:12

Jos 17:12 Yet the children of Manasseh could not drive out the inhabitants of those cities; but the Canaanites would dwell in that land. 13 Yet it came to pass, when the children of Israel were waxen strong, that they put the Canaanites to tribute; but did not utterly drive them out.

Disobedience tends to be like cancer. Once it starts, it soon begins to spread and can become a new norm. We read that the Ephraimites could not drive out the Canaanites. We soon read in the following chapters that the children of Manasseh were also in a similar situation. They put the Canaanites to tribute—but that was not what the Lord instructed. Disobedience acts like a spreading cancer once unchecked.

Be careful of the familiar things that you observe and accept. Because a certain approach is popular and seems to work does not mean it pleases the Lord. Joshua we are not told corrected the tribe of Ephraim and the way of accommodating the inhabitants of Canaan soon became the norm. It is easier to do nothing. It is easier not to fight or confront that which is wrong. It is easier to simply embrace errors and popular methods. But when we go against the norm, we will soon hear . . . "but the blessed tribe of Ephraim, the leader's tribe are doing it differently . . ." why do you want to do yours differently.

Leaders should be extra careful because they will be copied . . . what the leadership accepts will preach far more than what they teach. Like cancer, the error of compromise to accommodate the Canaanites soon began to spread. Watch out for things others—especially those in leadership do, that do not model Christ. Christ is our model and not any leader. Leaders, like any other men can be weak, tired and too intimidated to face certain issues. You must be ready to stand alone for what you believe in—contend for the faith. Still obey all the same . . . still fight even if you are alone and unaided . . . if the truth of God is your ally then God will fight with you. Like David fought Goliath alone when all the more capable and stronger warriors were in hiding . . . you will not run from battle . . . you will fight and you will win. Manasseh gave up quickly and accommodated what they were meant to drive out. What are you tolerating in your life that God wants you to deal with firmly. Do not delay another minute . . . drive out the Canaanite.

Song

Jehovah is your name 4ce
Mighty warrior; Great in battle
Jehovah is your name.
Mighty warrior; Great in battle
Jehovah is your name.

The name, the name of Jesus. Is greater and higher than all names
It is not an ordinary name. It's a name that's full of power and praise.
At that name all sicknesses bow. Demons tremble at the sound of that name
It is not an ordinary name. It's a name that's full of power and praise.

Prayer: Father, I reject every Canaanite making itself useful to my flesh—I drive them all out . . . I walk out of every evil relationship. Amen.

NOVEMBER 20

Wake me up

Bible Text: Joshua 17:14

Jos 17:14 And the children of Joseph spake unto Joshua, saying, Why hast thou given me but one lot and one portion to inherit, seeing I am a great people, forasmuch as the LORD hath blessed me hitherto? 15 And Joshua answered them, If thou be a great people, then get thee up to the wood country, and cut down for thyself there in the land of the Perizzites and of the giants, if mount Ephraim be too narrow for thee. 16 And the children of Joseph said, The hill is not enough for us: and all the Canaanites that dwell in the land of the valley have chariots of iron, both they who are of Bethshean and her towns, and they who are of the valley of Jezreel. And Joshua spake unto the house of Joseph, even to Ephraim and to Manasseh, saying, Thou art a great people, and hast great power: thou shalt not have one lot only: 18 But the mountain shall be thine; for it is a wood, and thou shalt cut it down: and the outgoings of it shall be thine: for thou shalt drive out the Canaanites, though they have iron chariots, and though they be strong.

How is it that the blessed are so easy to fall prey to pride? The heart is so deceitful. There are times when we seek more souls and labor well for God, but there are times when pride is at work. The children of Joseph challenge their tribesman Joshua on the size of their lot. Joshua is wise and a man of integrity. He has not favored his tribe beyond what God has asked him to do. But the children of Joseph are displeased. Murmuring to leadership is pointless . . . often we are telling God—He does not know what He is doing. In previous verses, we note that the children of Joseph could not drive away the Canaanites in the land given to them—this was to be their immediate focus . . . rather they focus on acquiring more lands. Is it not common when we have not been faithful in a little, we still want to have more. Observe the reply of Joshua. You must fight for more. Joshua tells them they must work for the rest . . . they must cut down the wood and drive out the Canaanites even though they are strong with iron chariots.

God is telling someone. God has given you a small place to make you a fighter. You must rise up and cut down the wood and drive out the Canaanites. You need skills and experience to overcome resistance of all sorts . . . you need to learn patience . . . you need to know how to win and how to lose . . . you need to grow into your greatness.

Amo 6:1 Woe to them that are at ease in Zion, and trust in the mountain of Samaria, which are named chief of the nations, to whom the house of Israel came! 2 Pass ye unto Calneh, and see; and from thence go ye to Hamath the great: then go down to Gath of the Philistines: be they better than these kingdoms? or their border greater than your border? 3 Ye that put far away the evil day, and cause the seat of violence to come near;4 That lie upon beds of ivory, and stretch themselves upon their couches, and eat the lambs out of the flock, and the calves out of the midst of the stall; 5 That chant to the sound of the viol, and invent to themselves instruments of musick, like David; 6 That drink wine in bowls, and anoint themselves with the chief ointments: but they are not grieved for the affliction of Joseph. 7 Therefore now shall they go captive with the first that go captive, and the banquet of them that stretched themselves shall be removed.

It is often not the will of God to make greatness too easy . . . hence we slide into entertainment and vanity. God help us when we cannot be put at any convenience. We can be over pampered. So many have lost the will and urge for spiritual warfare. They do not even know what spiritual warfare is. They are being set up to fail. This will not be our portion. Come out of that dangerous state of ease. Be strong and very courageous to battle on your knees again.

Song

I praise I praise you—Oh Lord 2ce I see what you are doing. One more time . . . I lift my hands in praise of your name. 2ce

Prayer: Father, wake me up. Amen

NOVEMBER 21

Final Rest Part I

Bible Text: Joshua 24:32

Jos_24:32 And the bones of Joseph, which the children of Israel brought up out of Egypt, buried they in Shechem, in a parcel of ground which Jacob bought of the sons of Hamor the father of Shechem for an hundred pieces of silver: and it became the inheritance of the children of Joseph.

The bones of Joseph were to see no rest until the children of Israel arrived and rested at the land of promise. There is a difference between death and rest, between sleeping and rest, between peace and rest. Rest does not just mean quietness . . . because there is a quietness that can be disguised trouble. Rest refers to a final state of quiet bliss.

Rev_21:4 And God shall wipe away all tears from their eyes; and there shall be no more death, neither sorrow, nor crying, neither shall there be any more pain: for the former things are passed away.

The key thing in God's rest is not that there is no pain, but there is no more pain . . . meaning pain is banished forever. Sorrow is banished forever . . . tears are banished forever and all former things will never again be brought up again. All the saints wait for this rest and until we all come up on the appointed day, this rest will still be a place that we see ahead and wait for. The bones of Joseph waited hundreds of years to enter this rest—which is a shadow of the divine rest that we are all awaiting.

Note that Joseph knew about the rest, he made preparations towards it—gave instructions that puzzled others concerning it. He spoke of that rest as though he were absolutely certain it would happen. Joseph believed that he would find that rest centuries later in a land he did not see . . . likewise we can believe in the eternal rest it foreshadows.

Christ spoke of the eternal rest—when he said . . . *John 14:2 In my Father's house are many mansions: if it were not so, I would have told you. I go to prepare a place for you.*

Christ also paid the full price for the rest. Christ is God and we can believe him. Today, many saints are no more sure about Heaven. If they are not sure, how can they make any arrangements to be there? The old saints spoke of Heaven as if it were a place they were so certain they would one day go. Today's culture makes jest of Heaven . . . even many saints are uncertain and some preachers doubt. The devil knows that doubters will not make arrangements. If Joseph doubted Jacob, many years after - he would have not have given instructions to be carried out. His doubts would have told him, this was pointless. Be sure there is an eternity worth making plans for.

Song

It's a highway to Heaven. None can walk up there - But the pure in heart
It's a highway to Heaven. I am walking up the King's Highway.

Prayer: Father, put my feet on the journey to Heaven—the King's Highway. Amen.

NOVEMBER 22

Final Rest Part II

Bible Text: Joshua 24:32

Jos_24:32 And the bones of Joseph, which the children of Israel brought up out of Egypt, buried they in Shechem, in a parcel of ground which Jacob bought of the sons of Hamor the father of Shechem for an hundred pieces of silver: and it became the inheritance of the children of Joseph.

The faith that see God's final rest is not cheap. The rest of God is not randomly offered to any. A study of the word will help us to understand—as well as the shadow of Heaven provided for us in the journeys of Joseph. Eternity is for fighters—for he that overcometh. Overcoming sin, the enemy, the world, the flesh are not accidental achievements. Those who have done it will know by their battles and the victory in Christ. We also know those that will not be there.

Rev 21: 4 And God shall wipe away all tears from their eyes; and there shall be no more death, neither sorrow, nor crying, neither shall there be any more pain: for the former things are passed away. 5 And he that sat upon the throne said, Behold, I make all things new. And he said unto me, Write: for these words are true and faithful. 6 And he said unto me, It is done. I am Alpha and Omega, the beginning and the end. I will give unto him that is athirst of the fountain of the water of life freely. 7 He that overcometh shall inherit all things; and I will be his God, and he shall be my son. 8 But the fearful, and unbelieving, and the abominable, and murderers, and whoremongers, and sorcerers, and idolaters, and all liars, shall have their part in the lake which burneth with fire and brimstone: which is the second death.

Liars, whoremongers, the abominable and the unbelieving will not be there. Those who doubt the existence will soon lose the motivation to overcome and will justify their defeats. Those who cease from the fight of faith do so because they do not see the rest ahead. Those who look for rest here and value the earthy rest will do everything to obtain it and will soon forget about the reality of God's eternal best. Be extremely cautious of forgetting eternity . . . are you making preparations to be there. If you are not—it may mean you will not be there. Ponder over these words. Joseph made it (not because he suffered a lot or that he was the favorite of Jacob, but because he made careful preparations towards the place of his final rest. Are you preparing yourself?

Song

Some glad morning when this life is o'er, I'll fly away;
To a home on God's celestial shore, I'll fly away (I'll fly away).

I'll fly away, Oh Glory - I'll fly away; (in the morning)
When I die, Hallelujah, by and by, I'll fly away (I'll fly away).

When the shadows of this life have gone, I'll fly away;
Like a bird from prison bars has flown, I'll fly away (I'll fly away)

I'll fly away, Oh Glory - I'll fly away; (in the morning)
When I die, Hallelujah, by and by, I'll fly away (I'll fly away).

Just a few more weary days and then, I'll fly away;
To a land where joy shall never end, I'll fly away (I'll fly away)

Prayer: Father, show me how to prepare for the place of your final rest reserved for all your children. Amen

NOVEMBER 23

Unbelief

Bible Text: Judges 1:27-34

Jdg 1:27 Neither did Manasseh drive out the inhabitants of Bethshean and her towns, nor Taanach and her towns, nor the inhabitants of Dor and her towns, nor the inhabitants of Ibleam and her towns, nor the inhabitants of Megiddo and her towns: but the Canaanites would dwell in that land. 28 And it came to pass, when Israel was strong, that they put the Canaanites to tribute, and did not utterly drive them out. 29 Neither did Ephraim drive out the Canaanites that dwelt in Gezer; but the Canaanites dwelt in Gezer among them. 30 Neither did Zebulun drive out the inhabitants of Kitron, nor the inhabitants of Nahalol; but the Canaanites dwelt among them, and became tributaries. 31 Neither did Asher drive out the inhabitants of Accho, nor the inhabitants of Zidon, nor of Ahlab, nor of Achzib, nor of Helbah, nor of Aphik, nor of Rehob: 32 But the Asherites dwelt among the Canaanites, the inhabitants of the land: for they did not drive them out. 33 Neither did Naphtali drive out the inhabitants of Bethshemesh, nor the inhabitants of Bethanath; but he dwelt among the Canaanites, the inhabitants of the land: nevertheless the inhabitants of Bethshemesh and of Bethanath became tributaries unto them. 34 And the Amorites forced the children of Dan into the mountain: for they would not suffer them to come down to the valley: 35 But the Amorites would dwell in mount Heres in Aijalon, and in Shaalbim: yet the hand of the house of Joseph prevailed, so that they became tributaries

A new normal way gradually evolves. Laziness and cowardice gives birth to compromise. Covetousness and greed help the new culture of disobedience. Nothing is new. The enemy of our soul uses the same tactics. The Canaanites have chariots of iron and are difficult to drive out. The land is a good land, rich, fertile and flowing with milk and honey and idolatry—but the Canaanites are not easy to drive out. So what do the children of Israel do.

Many believers start well, with a lot of promise and zeal, but are soon hindered as Satan floods them with temptations, lusts, brings guilt and anguish to pollute their consciences until they give up to some sort of accommodation of Satan. God does not want us to have any accommodation with the enemy in any form, therefore we are wise to keep fighting until as promised every failure is brought under our feet. Saul fell because of this weakness of accommodation of that which God instructed to be destroyed and this ruined him ultimately.

Hold on to the promises of God and keep fighting evil—internally, externally . . . in your home, nation, church . . . everywhere it shows up . . . do not permit evil to serve you . . . making evil your tributaries is a dangerous strategy. The house of Joseph applied this strategy of using the Canaanites as servants when they prevailed upon the Amorites, but this was not the instruction of God. It is unbelief that disallowed the children of Israel from entering the promised land . . . it is unbelief that stops them from conquering the Canaanites. They have forgotten that they entered the promised land not because they were strong but because God fought for them . . . . the walls of Jericho did not fall because the children of Israel were strong but because their God was. Unbelief is the chief of failings and the arrows of doubt are Satan's chief weapons.

Song

Have faith in God
Have faith in God
Have faith in God
For deliverance have faith in God.

Prayer: Father, Help my unbelief. Amen

NOVEMBER 24

Jeroboam—Opportunity abused Part 1

Bible Text: 1Kings 11:28

1Ki 11:28 And the man Jeroboam was a mighty man of valour: and Solomon seeing the young man that he was industrious, he made him ruler over all the charge of the house of Joseph.

The tribe of Ephraim produces a future King. The Bible introduces Jeroboam as a mighty man of valor A man that was industrious who was initially given charge of the house of Joseph in the time of Solomon. He is introduced as the enemy of the King. God had ordained that Solomon's legacy would be split because he did not keep the commandments and statutes of God. God said He will give part of this kingdom to his servant. That man was Jeroboam.

Jeroboam started well. He was hardworking, and from the prestigious tribe of Ephraim, next in honor to the tribe of Judah. He must have been spotted to be reliable, brave and with integrity. Diligence promoted Jeroboam but diligence is not enough. Character must make him end well. Jeroboam had a weak point—he loved power more than God. This was not initially evident . . . it is often wiser to promote someone who is godly . . . a man after God's heart. Men or women who love power can appear hardworking—they look like they can be trusted with major assignments. Indeed they can start very well, but soon love of power above God will cause them to do strange things and enter into all sorts of evil alliances for power.

A good track record is not enough—we must keep searching our hearts to expose hidden cracks that we may find corrections before the enemy finds us useful to work as his instruments against God's will. An early promotion to a very senior position can be a sign of greater potential . . . but a man that has not been prepared enough as Joseph was in the dungeon of Egypt is soon spoilt by power.

Jeroboam was told by the Prophet Ahijah that he would have the throne someday . . . but he was told the reason for the opportunity . . . only because Solomon had failed. Good sense would have taught Jeroboam to ponder over why Solomon failed and avoid a similar fate . . . but an ambitious man does not think this way . . . all he saw was an opportunity for a throne he did not deserve.

Ponder over this text. Has an opportunity suddenly opened before you ? Ask God to give you grace not to abuse it. Ask God to search your heart.

Song

Can you be obedient
To the Lord of all,
Though the earth should totter,
Though the heav'ns should fall?
Face e'en a disaster
With a faith-filled heart,
Knowing naught can harm him
Who with Christ will start?

Prayer: Father, search my heart and prove me . . . expose the cracks that could destroy me in future. Heal these cracks. Amen

Jeroboam—Opportunity abused Part II

Bible Text: 1Kings 11:28

1Ki 11:28 And the man Jeroboam was a mighty man of valor: and Solomon seeing the young man that he was industrious, he made him ruler over all the charge of the house of Joseph.

In Part I we saw the beginnings of Jeroboam the leader of the tribe of Joseph. Hardworking and industrious he was but the prophet who prophesied he would be King also encouraged him to hearken to all the commandments of God as did . . . keeping his statutes and commandments.

1Ki 11:38 And it shall be, if thou wilt hearken unto all that I command thee, and wilt walk in my ways, and do that is right in my sight, to keep my statutes and my commandments, as David my servant did; that I will be with thee, and build thee a sure house, as I built for David, and will give Israel unto thee.

David was not perfect. But he loved the Lord and kept his statutes and commandments. The corollary to this encouragement was that if Jeroboam did as Solomon did . . . he would also end badly. Jeroboam soon flees to Egypt to avoid being killed by Solomon. But Jeroboam was a very bad ruler who refuses to heed the warning . . . he is now obsessed with the power that has been promised to him and diligently begins to plot his eventual ascension.

Not once do we see any interest to worship God or to serve Him. Jeroboam does not seek the face of the Lord. He waits until after Solomon's death, the people of Israel rebelled against the house of David and invited him to be king. The tribe of Ephraim has produced a king in a split kingdom. Jeroboam takes advantage of this evil division ordained by God to retain power at all costs. Jeroboam built Shechem into a beautiful capital and dwelt therein. He now proceeds with his evil plans.

I pray none reading this devotional will end up like this wicked Ephraimite. I pray when opportunities come to you, you will remember God. I pray you will seek His face and meditate over his commandments—day and night and seek to please him. I pray you will not be deceived by early successes and a track record of diligence. Be a man after God's heart. May you be like David who thirsted for God. Men who thirst for power instead of God are easily corrupted.

Song

As the deer, panteth for the waters so my soul longeth after thee
You alone are my heart desire and I long to worship thee
You alone are my strength and shield
To you alone may my spirit yield
You alone are my heart's desire and I long to worship you.

You're my friend and you are my brother even though you are a King
I love you more than any other—so much more than anything
You alone are my strength and shield
To you alone may my spirit yield
You alone are my heart's desire and I long to worship you.

Prayer: Father, let my priority not be power but to worship you. Amen

NOVEMBER 26

Jeroboam—Opportunity abused Part III

Bible Text: 1Kings 11:28

1Kings 11:28 And the man Jeroboam was a mighty man of valor: and Solomon seeing the young man that he was industrious, he made him ruler over all the charge of the house of Joseph.

In Parts I & II we saw the beginnings of Jeroboam the leader of the tribe of Joseph. Now that he had part of the split kingdom, he quickly devised a plan to consolidate his throne. Many clever maneuvers of men are driven by seeking power and maintaining the authority they want over men.

1Ki 12:26 And Jeroboam said in his heart, Now shall the kingdom return to the house of David: 27 If this people go up to do sacrifice in the house of the LORD at Jerusalem, then shall the heart of this people turn again unto their lord, even unto Rehoboam king of Judah, and they shall kill me, and go again to Rehoboam king of Judah. 28 Whereupon the king took counsel, and made two calves of gold, and said unto them, It is too much for you to go up to Jerusalem: behold thy gods, O Israel, which brought thee up out of the land of Egypt. 29 And he set the one in Bethel, and the other put he in Dan. 30 And this thing became a sin: for the people went to worship before the one, even unto Dan. 31 And he made an house of high places, and made priests of the lowest of the people, which were not of the sons of Levi.

This man was afraid to lose power and so he set up false altars at convenient places so people would not go to Jerusalem and made priests of the lowest of the people, which were not of the sons of Levi. Many still do this ... so many Churches have risen up ... the main strategy of their evangelism is to stop followers from finding the truth ... so they expand rapidly ... spreading junk. Offering show biz, glamour, ease and motivational self-improvement seminars which preserve the flesh and embrace worldliness ... these are done with such zeal ... but this is nothing but wickedness and abuse of power. Jeroboam ends up being the standard in evil Kings, as David was the standard in righteousness. He ended up badly as well as his entire household. It became apparent that he was a choice of God to judge not just Solomon but the wicked people he also ruled. May God have mercy on us. May God help us to see our wrong and expose the wickedness in our hearts. Do not be deceived. God is never mocked. The fruits of the wickedness of men will always be harvested. It did not matter that this was the tribe of Ephraim ... This tribe that was so specially chosen and elevated ... it seems perfected the abuse of God's grace and special love. The fact that God blessed us specially is not enough. May we not be chosen for judgment but chosen only for mercy and glory. If we hearken to God's commandment and love His statutes, our end will be good. How it must pain God that the house of Ephraim descends this low. Be watchful. What are your motives for ministry? It may take decades ... but we surely reap the fruits of wickedness if all we have sown are evil seeds.

Song

Breathe on me, breath of God, Fill me with life anew,
That I may love what Thou dost love, And do what Thou wouldst do.

Breathe on me, breath of God, Until my heart is pure,
Until with Thee I will one will, To do and to endure.

Breathe on me, breath of God, Blend all my soul with Thine,
Until this earthly part of me - Glows with Thy fire divine.

Breathe on me, breath of God, So shall I never die,
But live with Thee the perfect life - Of Thine eternity.

Prayer: Father, let my priority be ever to honor and worship you. Amen

NOVEMBER 27

Jeroboam—Opportunity Abused Part IV

Bible Text: 1Kings 11:28

1Ki 11:28 And the man Jeroboam was a mighty man of valor: and Solomon seeing the young man that he was industrious, he made him ruler over all the charge of the house of Joseph.

In this final section on Jeroboam. I want to focus again on Solomon's reason for choosing Jeroboam to lead the house of Joseph. The Bible says he saw the young man . . . Solomon judged based on his sight that here was a good leader. Judging by sight is deceptive.

Lot judged by sight and chose the rich lands of Sodom. Even Samuel when he looked at the sons of Jesse came to the wrong conclusions. God's choice to bless us—is often not aligned with what our sight portrays. When we have the Holy Spirit we are led by another personality.

Isa 11:1 And there shall come forth a rod out of the stem of Jesse, and a Branch shall grow out of his roots: 2 And the spirit of the LORD shall rest upon him, the spirit of wisdom and understanding, the spirit of counsel and might, the spirit of knowledge and of the fear of the LORD; 3 And shall make him of quick understanding in the fear of the LORD: and he shall not judge after the sight of his eyes, neither reprove after the hearing of his ears: 4 But with righteousness shall he judge the poor, and reprove with equity for the meek of the earth: and he shall smite the earth with the rod of his mouth, and with the breath of his lips shall he slay the wicked.

Do not be quick to come to conclusions or make decisions. Let the Holy Spirit guide you. Your sight will produce answers that will support your carnal foolishness. Instead, wait on God and let God show you what you must do. Pray for mercy because your heart is wicked and your motivations are selfish. Be patient to let God choose for you in the decisions you make. When we see only with our eyes, we are prone to make judgments that may make sense but are not godly. Eventually we see that there are things that God must inspect for us that we do not have the faculties to know. I want to encourage someone about to take a decision based on a perceived situation. Do not lean on your understanding. Go and get a word from the Lord. Do not make a move until you have heard from God. Will you make mistakes in hearing God? Yes. But as you determine in your heart to please God, God will watch over your decisions and help you to hear Him clearly . . . speaking to you in so many diverse ways. But when God knows you prefer to do what your eyes perceive, He will leave you to your devices knowing how it will end—His purpose is still achieved with the sad end of Jeroboam.

Song

Be Thou my Vision, O Lord of my heart; Naught be all else to me, save that Thou art
Thou my best Thought, by day or by night, Waking or sleeping, Thy presence my light.

Be Thou my Wisdom, and Thou my true Word; I ever with Thee and Thou with me, Lord;
Thou my great Father, I Thy true son; Thou in me dwelling, and I with Thee one.

Be Thou my battle Shield, Sword for the fight; Be Thou my Dignity, Thou my Delight;
Thou my soul's Shelter, Thou my high Tower: Raise Thou me Heavenward, O Power of my power.

Riches I heed not, nor man's empty praise, Thou mine Inheritance, now and always:
Thou and Thou only, first in my heart, High King of Heaven, my Treasure Thou art.

Prayer: Father, be my vision . . . now and forever. Amen

NOVEMBER 28

Grace Rules over Birthright

Bible Text: 1Chronicles 5:1-2

1Ch_5:1 Now the sons of Reuben the firstborn of Israel, (for he was the firstborn; but, forasmuch as he defiled his father's bed, his birthright was given unto the sons of Joseph the son of Israel: and the genealogy is not to be reckoned after the birthright. 2 For Judah prevailed above his brethren, and of him came the chief ruler; but the birthright was Joseph's:)

This is a right, privilege or possession to which a person is entitled by birth. The first born is entitled to a double-portion of the inheritance. This right should have been Reuben's just as this right should also have been Esau's. The Bible says Esau was a fornicator and a profane person who sold his birthright for one morsel of meat. Reuben was equally profane to defile the bed of his father. Sin brings down and brings an indelible stain. The advantages of the birthright include power, inheritance and influence. Instead of Reuben getting double of what the other brothers would get. Two tribes from the House of Joseph are raised to each get the same portion as Reuben. The genealogy is set aside and Judah representing praise and grace prevails to reign above the others. Christ did not come by Joseph but by Judah. Did Jacob or Joseph deserve the birthright? Why does God always chose grace rather than rights. Because our best are filthy rags. If Christ is our righteousness and his grace triumphs over all our struggles, we can repent and enjoy the salvation in that grace. The parable of the elder son brings the power of grace over any rights.

Luk 15:11 And he said, A certain man had two sons: 12 And the younger of them said to his father, Father, give me the portion of goods that falleth to me. And he divided unto them his living. 13 And not many days after the younger son gathered all together, and took his journey into a far country, and there wasted his substance with riotous living. 14 And when he had spent all, there arose a mighty famine in that land; and he began to be in want. 15 And he went and joined himself to a citizen of that country; and he sent him into his fields to feed swine. 16 And he would fain have filled his belly with the husks that the swine did eat: and no man gave unto him. 17 And when he came to himself, he said, How many hired servants of my father's have bread enough and to spare, and I perish with hunger! 18 I will arise and go to my father, and will say unto him, Father, I have sinned against Heaven, and before thee, 19 And am no more worthy to be called thy son: make me as one of thy hired servants. 20 And he arose, and came to his father. But when he was yet a great way off, his father saw him, and had compassion, and ran, and fell on his neck, and kissed him. 21 And the son said unto him, Father, I have sinned against Heaven, and in thy sight, and am no more worthy to be called thy son. 22 But the father said to his servants, Bring forth the best robe, and put it on him; and put a ring on his hand, and shoes on his feet: 23 And bring hither the fatted calf, and kill it; and let us eat, and be merry: 24 For this my son was dead, and is alive again; he was lost, and is found. And they began to be merry. 25 Now his elder son was in the field: and as he came and drew nigh to the house, he heard musick and dancing. 26 And he called one of the servants, and asked what these things meant. 27 And he said unto him, Thy brother is come; and thy father hath killed the fatted calf, because he hath received him safe and sound. 28 And he was angry, and would not go in: therefore came his father out, and intreated him. 29 And he answering said to his father, Lo, these many years do I serve thee, neither transgressed I at any time thy commandment: and yet thou never gavest me a kid, that I might make merry with my friends: 30 But as soon as this thy son was come, which hath devoured thy living with harlots, thou hast killed for him the fatted calf. 31 And he said unto him, Son, thou art ever with me, and all that I have is thine.

True repentance is the highest of all actions and true Christianity willingly surrenders all its rights. Indeed grace must triumph over rights. Rejoice in this truth.

Song

Only by grace can we enter. Only by grace can we stand. Not by our human endeavor but by the blood of the lamb Into your presence You call us. You call us to come. Into your presence you draw us. Now by your grace we come

Prayer: Lord, let your grace abound in my life. Amen

NOVEMBER 29

The Arm of the Lord

Bible Text: Psalm 77:15

Psa_77:15 Thou hast with thine arm redeemed thy people, the sons of Jacob and Joseph. Selah.

There are times we cannot be blamed when we see limitations, or observe the failing support of trusted allies or consider the dark hours and the familiar defeats mirrored once again in the situation at hand—only to come to the conclusion that there is no hope. Moses in a similar mode, could not possibly understand how the multitude in the wilderness would be fed . . . even if the seas found a strange route to the desert and vomited all the fish therein. Even if all the cattle were slaughtered and they encountered animals—even more than they could ever expect . . . how could there be enough to feed this multitude? But Moses was now, unlike in early premature attempts to move ahead of God's schedule, a man who sought God . . . not just for his acts. Many times we have looked at our challenges, difficulties or seen the decay in our nations or the dearth of truth in the wilderness of wandering saints . . . and like Moses say "I'm standing here surrounded by 600,000 men on foot and God says, 'I'll give them meat, meat every day for a month.' So where's it coming from? Even if all the flocks and herds were butchered, would that be enough? Even if all the fish in the sea were caught, would that be enough?"

Have you asked . . . where is my help going to come from? Where is the deliverance of our nations going to come from? Jacob, Joseph and his brothers found themselves in this situation. But the arm of the Lord rescued them. God answers Moses . . . *Numbers 11[23] And the LORD said unto Moses, Is the LORD'S hand waxed short? thou shalt see now whether my word shall come to pass unto thee or not . . .*

The Church does not believe God. She trusts in her committees, taskforces . . . her means, her good men . . . her prayer bands and missionaries . . . her new found wealth. The Church does not believe that by a strong hand and by fire there shall be an awesome revival. She trusts in the flock, the crowds, her means . . . her leaders and the strong organization . . . But God does not require this to move—good as they may be. Doubt no more, take no thought of the worsening challenges or the defeats that appear imminent . . . instead consider that it is the Lord's hand that is promised as your tool of deliverance and not yours or your weary allies. God is speaking to someone and He says . . . you will see whether His word will come to pass or not. Believe your God and you shall prosper. The joy of the Lord is our strength. Look again . . . see Him and live. Cursed sin of unbelief . . . be gone from us. It is the gracious, loving, strong and long hand of the Lord that attends to the matters before our nations. Has the sacrifice of Christ and the blood of Jesus lost its efficacy? . . . Why do you distrust Christ with a mock humility that your sins are varied and many? Is He unwilling to forgive? . . . Come to the foot of the cross and lay down all your burdens . . . exchange your waning strength for reliance on His sure hand. Could you dare to trust Him and live again? Take your eyes off the headlines of horror, do not be distracted by the voices that say "how can it be?" . . . God has not promised to deliver us by mortal hands—especially yours.

Song

Abide with me; fast falls the eventide; The darkness deepens; Lord with me abide.
When other helpers fail and comforts flee, Help of the helpless, O abide with me.

Swift to its close ebbs out life's little day; Earth's joys grow dim; its glories pass away;
Change and decay in all around I see; O Thou who changest not, abide with me.

Not a brief glance I beg, a passing word; But as Thou dwell'st with Thy disciples, Lord,
Familiar, condescending, patient, free. Come not to sojourn, but abide with me.

Prayer: Lord, come with your mighty arms to my help. Amen

November 30

Chosen

Bible Text: Psalm 78:67

Psa 78:67 Moreover he refused the tabernacle of Joseph, and chose not the tribe of Ephraim: 68 But chose the tribe of Judah, the mount Zion which he loved.

During the allocation of the land to the various tribes of Israel, all gathered at Shiloh and set up the tent of meeting or tabernacle (Joshua 18:1), which is also called the house of God in Joshua 18:31. Joshua being an Ephraimite, this is also called the tabernacle of Joseph. But what happened to it. Many years later, the Israelites in the time of Eli decided to take the ark of the covenant down to the battle field near the coastal plain. The Philistines defeated the Israelites on that occasion and captured the ark of the covenant. The ark never returned to Shiloh. Eventually, after the Philistines sent it back to the Israelites, David took it to Jerusalem.

Jer 7:12 But go ye now unto my place which was in Shiloh, where I set my name at the first, and see what I did to it for the wickedness of my people Israel.

The ark was taken by David to a place called Kiriath Jearim belonging to the tribe of Judah and later moved by David of the same tribe of Judah to Mount Zion. Christ came as the Lion of Judah. It is good to remember that it is God who chooses and not man. God sees the end from the beginning when He chose us. It is also God who refuses and not man. If you are still in Christ—rejoice you are the choice of God who said ;

Joh_15:16 Ye have not chosen me, but I have chosen you, and ordained you, that ye should go and bring forth fruit, and that your fruit should remain: that whatsoever ye shall ask of the Father in my name, he may give it you.

We are a chosen generation. We are not accidents but chosen and foreknown to be His children in the dispensation of grace. The one who has chosen reveals what He has chosen us for. To go and bring forth fruit. That the fruit may remain and so we may have whatsoever we ask in the name of Jesus. We are not chosen to lack or to be barren. Nor are we chosen to have nothing to show as fruit. God needs us to know that we did not choose God, rather it was the other way round. Similarly, it is God who will refuse and reject us—when we stray from His statutes and ways . . . even long before we think we have abandoned Him. He is God. Eli the priest miscalculated thinking God was still going to fight for Israel even when they were in terrible sin and the temple was being defiled . . . but the glory had long departed. Be careful. Do not fool with God. He has chosen Christ, the truth, the way and the life . . . the Lion of the Tribe of Judah. It is in His name and not in the name of Joseph, Ephraim or any other name that we may ask knowing we shall surely receive. Come to Jesus and live. The Lion of Judah.

Song

Fairest Lord Jesus, Ruler of all nature, O Thou of God and man the Son,
Thee will I cherish, Thee will I honor, Thou, my soul's glory, joy and crown.

Fair are the meadows, fairer still the woodlands, Robed in the blooming garb of spring;
Jesus is fairer, Jesus is purer, Who makes the woeful heart to sing

Prayer: Lord, Lion Of Judah — reign forever in me. Amen

DECEMBER 1

Sing aloud

Bible Text: Psalm 81:1-6

Psa 81:1 Sing aloud unto God our strength: make a joyful noise unto the God of Jacob.2 Take a psalm, and bring hither the timbrel, the pleasant harp with the psaltery. 3 Blow up the trumpet in the new moon, in the time appointed, on our solemn feast day. 4 For this was a statute for Israel, and a law of the God of Jacob. 5 This he ordained in Joseph for a testimony, when he went out through the land of Egypt: where I heard a language that I understood not.

There are many reasons to praise God with all of our strength. To make a joyful noise unto Him. To blow the trumpet in the appointed day. First to praise God is a statute and a law of God. When we praise God, the psalmist remembers what God has done and how Joseph is a testimony to God's greatness and worth above all other Gods.

Our praise declares the glory and greatness of God which are so vividly testified in scripture. God is so great. Even in Egypt where they spoke a strange language and no one knew God or understood anything about Him . . . no one was praying to Him or interceding . . . Still God found in Joseph a son to use to confound all the wisdom of an advanced civilization. God moved mightily and preserved the wicked brothers who did not deserve to be preserved by bringing them into a place where the language was strange to them. God is magnified in all cultures.

Our praise declares what God already is—awesome and mighty. Our praise testifies to awesome things He has done and reminds us of might that is incomparable. But most importantly our praise tells God we love and obey Him. He tells us to praise Him. This is a statute and a law. Those who hearken and obey his laws will be blessed. But again, the psalmist declares the feast days of the Lord are solemn. Praise can be loud and joyful at the appointed time but the gatherings must still retain their solemnness. Come to God with pleasant harps and psaltery, with trumpets . . . make a joyful noise unto the Lord. Remember the life of Joseph as a loud singing unto the Lord . . . songs that declare that when men have said it is over, God is only just beginning . . . songs that express that God has no limits . . . Songs that declare that God does the impossible. Songs that place no boundaries on God's love and his grace and power. Songs that place God's intelligence and strategic methods completely and far above what any human can fathom . . . songs that declare that God controls all kings, Pharaohs, magicians and even in the depths of the darkest undiscovered seas or the deepest forests . . . where the language is strange . . . God is still mighty and moving unhindered to bring his purposes to fruition. True songs of praise focus on God and what He has done and not us or our needs. Today many worship songs are not songs of praise. Instead they put the focus on our problems and issues. Praise Him.

Song

All creatures of our God and King - Lift up your voice and with us sing, Alleluia! Alleluia!
Thou burning sun with golden beam, Thou silver moon with softer gleam! O praise Him! O praise Him! Alleluia! 3ce

Thou rushing wind that art so strong Ye clouds that sail in Heaven along, O praise Him! Alleluia!
Thou rising moon, in praise rejoice, Ye lights of evening, find a voice! Alleluia! 3ce

Thou flowing water, pure and clear, Make music for thy Lord to hear, O praise Him! Alleluia!
Thou fire so masterful and bright, That givest man both warmth and light. Alleluia! 3ce

Dear mother earth, who day by day - Unfoldest blessings on our way, O praise Him! Alleluia!
The flowers and fruits that in thee grow, Let them His glory also show. Alleluia! 3ce

Prayer: Lord, open thou my lips that I might praise you like never before. Amen

December 2

The Sovereignty of God

Bible Text: Psalm 105:16

Psa 105:16 Moreover he called for a famine upon the land: he brake the whole staff of bread. 17 He sent a man before them, even Joseph, who was sold for a servant: 18 Whose feet they hurt with fetters: he was laid in iron: 19 Until the time that his word came: the word of the LORD tried him. 20 The king sent and loosed him; even the ruler of the people, and let him go free. 21 He made him lord of his house, and ruler of all his substance: 22 To bind his princes at his pleasure; and teach his senators wisdom. 23 Israel also came into Egypt; and Jacob sojourned in the land of Ham. 24 And he increased his people greatly; and made them stronger than their enemies. 25 He turned their heart to hate his people, to deal subtilly with his servants.

God is sovereign. He is behind the entire saga. The story of Joseph and his brothers is only a small line in all the scripts He had long written and controls. You mean even the famine in Egypt was God. Yes . . . it was God who sent Joseph to Egypt. It was God who suddenly increased the people of Israel in Egypt causing them to become a great tribe in Egypt. And when it was time for Moses to be born, again it was God who made the Egyptians hate the children of Israel and make their lives terrible. God is indeed sovereign and rules over the affairs of men. He reigns and controls even thoughts and affections. In summary, God knows what He is doing while we do not. We can praise Him, we can seek His face on many things but we cannot hope to understand everything He does and why He does it.

That is why you must trust Him and worship Him. He is the sovereign God. There are no mistakes with Him. Everything is going according to His plan. You are safe in Him. Soon you will declare even to those that sought to hurt you that you can never be a victim or be victimized by men. Because our God is sovereign over all.

Song

Crown Him with many crowns, the Lamb upon His throne. Hark! How the Heavenly anthem drowns all music but its own. Awake, my soul, and sing of Him who died for thee, And hail Him as thy matchless King through all eternity.

Crown Him the virgin's Son, the God incarnate born, Whose arm those crimson trophies won which now His brow adorn; Fruit of the mystic rose, as of that rose the stem; The root whence mercy ever flows, the Babe of Bethlehem.

Crown Him the Son of God, before the worlds began, And ye who tread where He hath trod, crown Him the Son of Man; Who every grief hath known that wrings the human breast, And takes and bears them for His own that all in Him may rest

Crown Him the Lord of life, who triumphed over the grave, And rose victorious in the strife for those He came to save. His glories now we sing, Who died, and rose on high, Who died eternal life to bring, and lives that death may die.

Crown Him the Lord of peace whose power a scepter sways from pole to pole that wars may cease and all be prayer 'n praise. His reign shall know no end, and round His piercèd feet - Fair flowers of paradise extend their fragrance ever sweet.

Crown Him the Lord of love, behold His hands and side, Those wounds, yet visible above, in beauty glorified. No angel in the sky can fully bear that sight, But downward bends his burning eye at mysteries so bright.

Crown Him the Lord of Heaven enthroned in worlds above, Crown Him the King to whom is given the wondrous name of Love. Crown Him with many crowns, as thrones before Him fall; Crown Him, ye kings, with many crowns, for He is King of all.

Crown Him the Lord of lords, who over all doth reign, Who once on earth, the incarnate Word, for ransomed sinners slain, Now lives in realms of light, where saints with angels sing Their songs before Him day and night, their God, Redeemer, King.

Prayer: Lord, Let all declare that you are crowned, Lord of lords forever and ever. Amen

DECEMBER 3

Something New

Bible Text: Psalm 105:16

Psa 105:16 Moreover he called for a famine upon the land: he brake the whole staff of bread. 17 He sent a man before them, even Joseph, who was sold for a servant: 18 Whose feet they hurt with fetters: he was laid in iron: 19 Until the time that his word came: the word of the LORD tried him. 20 The king sent and loosed him; even the ruler of the people, and let him go free. 21 He made him lord of his house, and ruler of all his substance: 22 To bind his princes at his pleasure; and teach his senators wisdom. 23 Israel also came into Egypt; and Jacob sojourned in the land of Ham. 24 And he increased his people greatly; and made them stronger than their enemies. 25 He turned their heart to hate his people, to deal subtilly with his servants.

When it was least expected, Joseph was conceived and born and added on. The name Joseph means add on or increase . . . as I meditated on his life before becoming Egypt's Prime Minister, Joseph seemingly was in a place of decrease and decay, he was in a dungeon. It seemed he lived contrary to the prophetic symbolism of His name. The text also reminds us of the constraint of the feet of Joseph, until the time of release.

Similarly the famine constrained the Patriarch Jacob to Canaan. I often wondered how the place of promise and inheritance, called Canaan now becomes a place of famine. The previous and divine injunction to Jacobs' Father and Grandfather was 'not to go to Egypt.' Egypt in this dispensation has been come a place of providence.

In Egypt Joseph (the DREAM) is alive. When Jacobs's sons brought back word to Jacob that Joseph was alive, it was subtle but it was A NEW THING! it was clearly recorded in Genesis 45 verse 26b that Jacob's heart fainted, be believed them NOT. The heart of the man fainted because; his heart had been broken and sorely disappointed, how many nights of agony, or longing for the return of the DREAM . . . Joseph. Joseph that was a cursor of the future.

In the meantime Joseph had sent wagons and cart loads of provision for the journey of his father and the brothers to Egypt. Goshen was waiting for them . . . A New place The Bible clearly records that in verse 27 *when Jacob saw the carts his heart revived.* There is a place for 'seeing carts!!!' that is both convincing and reassuring. It encourages faith and its revives the heart. It was an invitation to move out from a place of decrease and decay. Its causes us to do cartwheels, no pun intended !!!!!

So Jacob leaves for Egypt but via Beersheba (Genesis 46 verse 1). Beersheba the place of oath, the place of revelation, and the place where God visits again, and reassures Jacob of the 'way of the spirit' is to go to Egypt and the added benediction that Jehovah will make you 'a great nation there'. In Egypt God increased his people greatly (Psalm 105 verse24). He added to them, they multiplied; the prophetic name of Joseph was fulfilled in a most unlikely place and a most unlikely time . . . A New thing

Song

Do something new in my life, something new in my life, something new in my life—today
Do something new in my life, something new in my life, something new in my life—today

Prayer: Lord, Let a new thing begin in my life. Amen

DECEMBER 4

The Stick for Joseph

Bible Text: Eze 37:15

Eze 37:15 The word of the LORD came again unto me, saying, 16 Moreover, thou son of man, take thee one stick, and write upon it, For Judah, and for the children of Israel his companions: then take another stick, and write upon it, For Joseph, the stick of Ephraim, and for all the house of Israel his companions: 17 And join them one to another into one stick; and they shall become one in thine hand.

God does not embrace competition and hostility. Division often leads to strife and bitter regrets. Once we are separated from evil and the world, brethren are to dwell together in unity. Unfortunately this is often not the situation . . . and from the times of the Bible, even the children of God were divided. God predicted that a time was coming when the two kingdoms of Israel and Judah will end their feuding and animosity . . . they will agree in love. Today many still carry sticks of separation and disunity. But there is a blessing that does not fall on marriages, homes, churches, nations until unity is realized.

Psa 133:1 A Song of degrees of David. Behold, how good and how pleasant it is for brethren to dwell together in unity! 2 It is like the precious ointment upon the head, that ran down upon the beard, even Aaron's beard: that went down to the skirts of his garments; 3 As the dew of Hermon, and as the dew that descended upon the mountains of Zion: for there the LORD commanded the blessing, even life for evermore.

United forces are formidable to the enemy. The result of disunity is further portrayed. Ephraim becomes inflamed with envy that drives them to idolatry. Judah becomes a vexation to Ephraim . . . a source of troubles. But see what they achieve when they unite. They are unstoppable in conquest, gaining many spoils and victories causing the enemy to bow before them.

Isa 11:13 The envy also of Ephraim shall depart, and the adversaries of Judah shall be cut off: Ephraim shall not envy Judah, and Judah shall not vex Ephraim. 14 But they shall fly upon the shoulders of the Philistines toward the west; they shall spoil them of the east together: they shall lay their hand upon Edom and Moab; and the children of Ammon shall obey them.

Division in any mode is unwise and has its costs. Whether in ministry, marriage or even in ventures. The divided house is weakened. Aim to build bridges and to unite. God is especially kind to those who work to end cleavages and reunite warring brothers. The worst sections in perdition are reserved for those who fan the embers of envy and vexation amongst brethren. You can decide which role you will choose to play.

Song

Let there be light, Lord God of hosts, Let there be wisdom on the earth;
Let broad humanity have birth, Let there be deeds, instead of boasts.

Within our passioned hearts instill - The calm that endeth strain and strife;
Make us thy ministers of life; Purge us from lusts that curse and kill.

Give us the peace of vision clear - To see our brothers' good our own,
To joy and suffer not alone, The love that casteth out all fear.

Let woe and waste of warfare cease, That useful labor yet may build
Its homes with love and laughter filled; God give thy wayward children peace.

Prayer: Lord, Let us be instruments of unity and oneness amongst brethren and not of discord. Amen

DECEMBER 5
God lifts up His hand

Bible Text: Eze 47:13

Eze 47: 13 Thus saith the Lord GOD; This shall be the border, whereby ye shall inherit the land according to the twelve tribes of Israel: Joseph shall have two portions. 14 And ye shall inherit it, one as well as another: concerning the which I lifted up mine hand to give it unto your fathers: and this land shall fall unto you for inheritance.

God is quoted in several verses to prophesy the double portion that will fall for an inheritance. God is confident an faithful to do what He has promised to do. The verse adds that God lifts up His hand to give it and so it cannot fail to be so. It is important to know that none of God's promises can fail. When he declares something—He lifts up His hand to make it exactly what it must be. Who can resist His hand?

Tit 1:2 In hope of eternal life, which God, that cannot lie, promised before the world began;

The Heavenly Canaan is also promised and will be exactly as God has ordained. The hope of eternal life is a promise of God . . . it is not an afterthought but has always been promised before the world began.

God defines the border and the boundaries. In our walk with God, there are things we can have, and there are things we cannot have. Boundaries imply that there is a limit that God defines. The hand of God also sets boundaries . . . God gives us many things in this world and the next that we do not deserve. But God has His don'ts and places that are not for us . . . there are so called joys that are not for us and there are rivers we are not to swim in. Borders are good for us. God has given us a double portion but within boundaries.

I have seen saints that have it all but have been denied perhaps one little thing or the other. Have we enjoyed the double portion? Why do we long for that which is outside the borders? Many are blind to the double portion and its joys and pine for what God has said is outside the borders. Reflect on this and thank God for what he has given you and said you can have - but thank God for His borders as well. Thank God for the Holy City Heavenly Jerusalem that will one day be ours. God has lifted up His hand—He will see to it that you make it.

Song

Last night I lay a sleeping,
There came a dream so fair,
I stood in old Jerusalem
Beside the temple there.
I heard the children singing,
And ever as they sang,
Methought the voice of angels
From Heav'n in answer rang;
Methought the voice of angels
From Heav'n in answer rang:—
"Jerusalem! Jerusalem!
Lift up your gates and sing,
Hosanna in the highest
Hosanna to your King!"

Prayer: Lord, Lift up your hand concerning all that you have said is mine and let the enemy flee. Amen

DECEMBER 6

Fire in the House

Bible Text: Amo 5:6

Amo_5:6 Seek the LORD, and ye shall live; lest he break out like fire in the house of Joseph, and devour it, and there be none to quench it in Bethel

Amos the Prophet warns that we return to seek the Lord, if we want to live. Seeking means going back to God, it means repentance, it means finding God again. It means going back to his word. It means finding time to pray and going to our knees forgetting the passing hours. The one who needs to begin seeking the Lord is about to die but does not know it. He has been warned severally of impending destruction and the only way out i.e. seeking God. Seeking God may be inconvenient as it means going the farther distance to Jerusalem in Judah . . . a journey that was discouraged by the evil first Ephraimite King of Israel, Jeroboam and replaced with an idol at Bethel. Why do the Ephraimites worship at Bethel instead of Jerusalem. Because it is easier and more convenient and the journey to the Temple of God was farther but also because they were deceived for political reasons to do so.

The evil altar at Bethel was destroyed by a divine fire as predicted by a prophet. God will not continue to tolerate idolatrous deception . . . eventually he must destroy it with a fire that cannot be quenched. This devotional commands us to seek the Lord so we are not destroyed by evil, deception and sin.

God warns us that the liars who deceive saying God understands our sin and tolerates our idolatry cannot stop the fire that breaks out to devour the evil altars and false priests—unemployed vagabonds appointed by Jeroboam. But Amos says it is not late if you are reading this devotional. You can still get it right—seek God . . . seek the Lord and live. It does not say seek a pastor . . . it says seek the Lord.

Deu_4:29 But if from thence thou shalt seek the LORD thy God, thou shalt find him, if thou seek him with all thy heart and with all thy soul. 1Ch_16:10 Glory ye in his holy name: let the heart of them rejoice that seek the LORD. Pro 28:5 Evil men understand not judgment: but they that seek the LORD understand all things.

As you seek the Lord, you will understand all things that pertains to that situation that has puzzled you. God will show the things you need to know. The knowledge and wisdom to live will be yours.

Song

Dear Lord and Father of mankind, forgive our foolish ways;
Reclothe us in our rightful mind, in purer lives thy service find,
In deeper reverence, praise.

In simple trust like theirs who heard, beside the Syrian sea,
The gracious calling of the Lord, let us, like them, without a word,
Rise up and follow Thee.

O Sabbath rest by Galilee, O calm of hills above,
Where Jesus knelt to share with Thee the silence of eternity,
Interpreted by love!

Prayer: Lord, Let my eyes be lifted up to you . . . help me to seek you afresh and live. Amen

December 7

God is Gracious

Bible Text: Amo 5:15

Amo_5:15 Hate the evil, and love the good, and establish judgment in the gate: it may be that the LORD God of hosts will be gracious unto the remnant of Joseph.

Even when God's chosen drift. There is always the remnant that does hold on to God. The blessed house of Joseph is ravaged but there is still a remnant that survives the flood of evil. You are part of that remnant and you are uniquely called to hate the evil, love the good and establish truth and judgment.

There are many who ignore evil and leave others to establish judgment. To hate evil in a society that legalizes it cannot be easy. To establish God's judgment when God says my ways are not your ways—cannot be the popular thing. Most suffer for hating evil and are despised when they seek to establish God's standards in a fallen world. But they will be a remnant who find the grace.

The grace of God is coming to you—to give you another chance to start afresh and rise to where God wants you to be. You are a specially called remnant that will rediscover the forgiveness and mercy that comes with the graciousness of God . . . the sad fate that befell others will not come to you. But you must continue to hate the evil no one wants to confront and love God's laws in a world that prefers to exclude God altogether.

God will send His unstoppable armies to bring refreshment and restoration to His remnant. His remnant will rise again to rejoice and to praise Him . . . worshipping Him in Spirit and in Truth. The remnant are a remaining part when the rest have all gone astray. God is gracious to His remnant.

Song

O Love that wilt not let me go,
I rest my weary soul in thee;
I give thee back the life I owe,
That in thine ocean depths its flow - May richer, fuller be.

O light that followest all my way,
I yield my flickering torch to thee;
My heart restores its borrowed ray,
That in thy sunshine's blaze its day - May brighter, fairer be.

O Joy that seekest me through pain,
I cannot close my heart to thee;
I trace the rainbow through the rain,
And feel the promise is not vain, That morn shall tearless be.

O Cross that liftest up my head,
I dare not ask to fly from thee;
I lay in dust life's glory dead,
And from the ground there blossoms red - Life that shall endless be

Prayer: Lord of Hosts, may I see your graciousness manifest afresh for me. Amen

DECEMBER 8

Hate, Love and Establish

Bible Text: Amo 5:15

Amo_5:15 Hate the evil, and love the good, and establish judgment in the gate: it may be that the LORD God of hosts will be gracious unto the remnant of Joseph.

Three things we are told to do to get back on track. The first is to hate evil and all it stands for. It is not possible to hate something and it will not be evident in our lives. This does not mean we hate evil-doers but evil acts cannot be embraced or tolerated in our homes or where we have influence to disallow it. Many have been misled to think a neutral stance towards evil is good enough. It is not. Being neutral actually means we do not mind as long it does not disturb us. It is rooted in a selfishness.

Second is to love the good. We love the good not because we benefit from it but because it pleases God. It may be very difficult to carry a teenage pregnancy for a single young lady, but we love life and hate murder of the unborn. We prefer to suffer shame and many difficulties even risking our own lives than have the blood of an innocent child on our hands.

Third is to establish fairness. There is too much injustice in the society. The advantaged cheat the less advantaged and manipulate the laws of the land to their favor. Saints are to work to return fairness and truth to law courts.

When we are engaged in any of these, it may be that God will have mercy and extend fresh grace to us to be restored. May God help us.

Song

I regret the hours I have wasted, the pleasures I have tasted that you were never in
And I confess that though your love is in me—it does not always win me when competing with my sin
And I repent making no excuses - I repent no one else to blame
And I return to fall in love with Jesus - I bow down on my knees.
And I return to fall in love with Jesus - I bow down on my knees and I repent.

Prayer: Father, I repent of my love for evil and hatred of your good and my apathy to injustice. Help me to come back to you. Amen

DECEMBER 9

Grieve for Joseph

Bible Text: Amo 6:1

Amo 6:1 Woe to them that are at ease in Zion, and trust in the mountain of Samaria, which are named chief of the nations, to whom the house of Israel came! 2 Pass ye unto Calneh, and see; and from thence go ye to Hamath the great: then go down to Gath of the Philistines: be they better than these kingdoms? or their border greater than your border? 3 Ye that put far away the evil day, and cause the seat of violence to come near; 4 That lie upon beds of ivory, and stretch themselves upon their couches, and eat the lambs out of the flock, and the calves out of the midst of the stall; 5 That chant to the sound of the viol, and invent to themselves instruments of musick, like David; 6 That drink wine in bowls, and anoint themselves with the chief ointments: but they are not grieved for the affliction of Joseph.

Zion is the place of safety in God. But it is not a place for ease. There are many saints especially in more comfortable circumstances . . . perhaps in more economically advantaged nations and cultures who begin to preach the gospel of ease. They write books that encourage to take it easy. These saints forget that there are saints in India, hostile Arab lands . . . saints being killed in prison camps in Korea . . . saints that are being targeted in Pakistan . . . and many next doors going through one affliction or the other. Many saints have backslidden or have falling prey to deception . . . but other saints do not care. They just engage in new selfish expressions of fun.

The gospel that preaches that affliction is synonymous with evil is false . . . as the Bible says many are the afflictions of the righteous . . . but God delivers from them all. Prosperity is part of the gospel but so is affliction. The afflicted must remember the comfortable and pray for them . . . but the comfortable must also intercede for grace and deliverance of the afflicted. In this devotional, the text explains that those who relax in ease and luxury and pleasant courts . . . and who do not feel part of the pains of the persecuted saints—are setting themselves for future destruction. These tend to pray less and less . . . slowly becoming more vulnerable until they are like fattened cattle being prepared for a future slaughter. Spare time, prayers, attention, funds and practical help for brothers and sisters who do not have the comforts we take for granted. A brother in affliction should cause another to be motivated to support in prayer, encouragement and just being there for them. Instead many find themselves judging other saints when they come under afflictions. Beware of Ease in Zion. Amos says Woe . . . meaning cursed are these. Come out of ease.

Song

Lead us, Heavenly Father, lead us
O'er the world's tempestuous sea;
Guard us, guide us, keep us, feed us,
For we have no help but Thee;
Yet possessing every blessing
If our God our Father be.

Savior, breathe forgiveness o'er us;
All our weakness Thou dost know;
Thou didst tread this earth before us,
Thou didst feel its keenest woe;
Lone and dreary, faint and weary,
Through the desert Thou didst go.

Prayer: Lord of Hosts, breathe your forgiveness over us for all our weaknesses, thou dost know. Amen

DECEMBER 10

Divine Flame

Bible Text: Oba 1:18

Oba_1:18 And the house of Jacob shall be a fire, and the house of Joseph a flame, and the house of Esau for stubble, and they shall kindle in them, and devour them; and there shall not be any remaining of the house of Esau; for the LORD hath spoken it.

The imagery of a Fire in describing the refining role of God. Gold cannot be pure until fire has removed the impurities. Fire keeps off flies and demons. The proud and all that do wickedly sometimes need to be shown that the God we serve created the sun and all the stars . . . and they are as stubble only awaiting destruction.

The Church is like a fire . . . its ministers are flames that will not be put out. There are fire extinguishers—wrong relationships, strange marriages and compromising with worldliness. There are smoldering fires about to go out . . . . tired and weakened by prayerlessness and sin . . . but Christ fans the shouldering flames back.

Isa_42:3 A bruised reed shall he not break, and the smoking flax shall he not quench: he shall bring forth judgment unto truth.

Heb_1:7 And of the angels he saith, Who maketh his angels spirits, and his ministers a flame of fire.

God is a consuming fire. Esau is likened to stubble. The fire of God is a holy fire . . . the Holy Spirit is pictured as tongues of fire on the apostles at Pentecost. The fire is maintained by God and will not go out if we remain in Him. There are younger flames that must be protected and there are blazing flames moving fast into enemy territory. What kind of flame are you? Are you growing or is the fire smoking out? Go to God for a fresh touch and for fresh fire. Know that there are extinguishers to be kept at a safe distance. Every extinguisher of divine fire planted to kill the flame of God will be uprooted and burnt away—never to be planted again in your destiny. Keep glowing. Keep burning. Do not let your fire go out.

Song

Holy, holy, holy! Lord God Almighty!
Early in the morning our song shall rise to Thee;
Holy, holy, holy, merciful and mighty!
God in three Persons, blessèd Trinity!

Holy, holy, holy! All the saints adore Thee,
Casting down their golden crowns around the glassy sea;
Cherubim and seraphim falling down before Thee,
Who was, and is, and evermore shall be.

Holy, holy, holy! though the darkness hide Thee,
Though the eye of sinful man Thy glory may not see;
Only Thou art holy; there is none beside Thee,
Perfect in power, in love, and purity.

Prayer: Lord of Hosts, may your Holy Fire burn freely through me. Let demons flee our lives because of the fire of God in us. Amen

DECEMBER 11

Glowing or Destroyed

Bible Text: Oba 1:18

Oba_1:18 And the house of Jacob shall be a fire, and the house of Joseph a flame, and the house of Esau for stubble, and they shall kindle in them, and devour them; and there shall not be any remaining of the house of Esau; for the LORD hath spoken it.

When Shadrach, Meschach and Abednego were sent into the flames, they did not burn. A greater flame of the Holy Spirit completely covered them creating its own conditions that preserved them. They could be seen glowing in the flames. There are flames that burnt the bush that Moses saw that was not consumed. The fire of the Holy Ghost refines the saint and causes them to shine—removing all impurities. But this same flame when exposed to stubble it turns it to ashes.

In the text we read that there shall be nothing remaining of the house of Esau. We already saw in a previous devotion that Esau blossomed very quickly and prospered before Jacob started finding his feet. But gradually over time, Esau became desolate—its renown was burnt off . . . and the ashes blown off. When the Holy Ghost came upon the first Church, remember Peter became bold and glowed in a new leadership role, but Ananias and Sapphira—who lied to the assembly to keep part of the proceeds of sales of their possessions committed to God - were carried out of the meeting . . . dead and to be buried. The flame of revival can be a dangerous fire for those rooted in the ways of Esau. Esau was profane and disdained the promises of God. May we be like Peter - a flame and not like this unfortunate couple who ended up as stubble. Open our eyes to see the path we are on—flame or stubble. Give us grace to make adjustments if need be. Help us to glow in your holy fire. Remove all tendencies to evil still hiding in us.

Song

Let me shine in your holy fire—Reflecting your glory for all to see
Let me glow in your holy fire—a flame ministering deliverance and truth

Let me stand in your holy fire—like the Hebrew boys indestructible;
Let me hear you call in your holy fire—just as Moses did when he saw the burning bush.

Prayer: Lord of Hosts, let me be far from the path of becoming as stubble that will be destroyed. Amen

December 12

Esau to Fade

Bible Text: Oba 1:18

Oba_1:18 And the house of Jacob shall be a fire, and the house of Joseph a flame, and the house of Esau for stubble, and they shall kindle in them, and devour them; and there shall not be any remaining of the house of Esau; for the LORD hath spoken it.

A study of the story of Esau and Jacob show that Esau initially grew and expanded and became so wealthy - such that Jacob feared him. Indeed, it was the entire house of Jacob that initially bowed before Esau. In spite of the prophesy that Esau will serve Jacob. Esau was so rich when they met, that he had no need to receive anything from Jacob.

Gen 33:1 And Jacob lifted up his eyes, and looked, and, behold, Esau came, and with him four hundred men. And he divided the children unto Leah, and unto Rachel, and unto the two handmaids. 2 And he put the handmaids and their children foremost, and Leah and her children after, and Rachel and Joseph hindermost. 3 And he passed over before them, and bowed himself to the ground seven times, until he came near to his brother.

But many years will pass . . . Jacob expands to becoming a noble tribe and Joseph becomes a spreading fire. Edom that came out first is destroyed and ends up desolate . . . *Joe_3:19 Egypt shall be a desolation, and Edom shall be a desolate wilderness, for the violence against the children of Judah, because they have shed innocent blood in their land.*

Why does the stubble come up first? It is easier for stubble to come up first because it is not deeply rooted. A lot that is just stubble shines because of an initial glitter but is really nothing but nonsense that will soon be burnt off. Jacob must wait until he is corrected and trained and properly prepared before his children will be blessed to multiply in Egypt. Esau will glow first with many nations of Edom rising quickly only to become desolate. Do not be deceived by what you see initially. Those without deep roots will typically sprout out earlier than strong trees that will stand forever. That which is stubble is ultimately to be devoured. There will be no remnant of Edom . . . nothing will remain of the house of Esau. Reflect on this . . . pray that God will prepare you for glory and not quickly bring you up only for future destruction.

Song

O God of Bethel, by Whose hand
Thy people still are fed,
Who through this weary pilgrimage
Hast all our fathers led.

Our vows, our prayers, we now present
Before Thy throne of grace;
God of our fathers, be the God
Of their succeeding race.

Through each perplexing path of life
Our wandering footsteps guide;
Give us each day our daily bread,
And raiment fit provide.

Prayer: Lord prepare me to be your sanctuary—pure and holy, tried and true. Amen

DECEMBER 13

Aloofness of Ephraim

Bible Text: Judges 12:1-3

Jdg 12:1 And the men of Ephraim gathered themselves together, and went northward, and said unto Jephthah, Wherefore passedst thou over to fight against the children of Ammon, and didst not call us to go with thee? we will burn thine house upon thee with fire. 2 And Jephthah said unto them, I and my people were at great strife with the children of Ammon; and when I called you, ye delivered me not out of their hands. 3 And when I saw that ye delivered me not, I put my life in my hands, and passed over against the children of Ammon, and the LORD delivered them into my hand: wherefore then are ye come up unto me this day, to fight against me?

Ephraim a blessed and specially chosen tribe slips gradually to an aloofness. They refused to help and support Jephthah who fights without them . . . only to see the Lord's deliverance. Why is Ephraim so aloof? Why has Ephraim become so hard to get along with? Are you the kind of worker that others now find difficult to ask for help? What kind of body language do you communicate in the kingdom . . . are you seen as someone anxious to help or as disinterested in the spiritual battles facing the church.

Some have said, Ephraim although starting well . . . declined gradually from a blessed tribe to an arrogance, laziness and such idolatry which caused God to change His mind. The lesson is that we must never presume on a previous position or past glories or blessings but must continually be striving to please God. What matters is not past prophetic pronouncements made over us but the current state of our devotion, love and service. If we are not walking in love and holiness today, then we cannot expect our historical encounters to make up. It is wise to ask God to search our hearts continually if there be any wickedness slowly growing. It is more prudent to be never overconfident but constantly going to God for help even when others will pronounce us as blessed. Also note that God fights for Jephthah even when Ephraim abandons them. God does not need any man . . . He is the Lord of Hosts.

For many—by the time they turned to God for help, it was too late. If you are reading this devotional . . . it is not late for you to go to your knees to repent of aloofness or any pride hidden under the cover of past glories.

Song

We plough the fields and scatter
The good seed on the land,
But it is fed and watered
By God's almighty hand:
He sends the snow in winter,
The warmth to swell the grain,
The breezes and the sunshine,
And soft, refreshing rain.

All good gifts around us
Are sent from Heaven above;
Then thank the Lord,
O thank the Lord,
For all his love.

Prayer: Lord search me heart and show me my errors . . . do not let any stains be hidden from me. Open my eyes to the folly of my ways. Amen

DECEMBER 14

Ye Delivered Me Not

Bible Text: Judges 12:1-3

Jdg 12:1 And the men of Ephraim gathered themselves together, and went northward, and said unto Jephthah, Wherefore passedst thou over to fight against the children of Ammon, and didst not call us to go with thee? we will burn thine house upon thee with fire. 2 And Jephthah said unto them, I and my people were at great strife with the children of Ammon; and when I called you, ye delivered me not out of their hands. 3 And when I saw that ye delivered me not, I put my life in my hands, and passed over against the children of Ammon, and the LORD delivered them into my hand: wherefore then are ye come up unto me this day, to fight against me?

There are many occasions in which we have sought help from other brethren and were rebuffed. This can be very displeasing to God who positioned others at various stages to help us. Why is it that we are unable to help others and cannot find the time to respond to calls for comfort . . . to join hands in prayers to those who need it.

The men of Ephraim refuse to respond to the call for help from Jepthah and Jepthah looks up to God. How help comes from God not men. Still, God has equipped and blessed us not for selfish consumption but that His covenant may be established. Any threat to the will and purpose of God require us to unite and fight as a holy army. There are singers, prayer warriors, treasurers, ushers etc . . . . everyone can play a part. It is possible that God has blessed you with substance to finance the meetings, to pay for venues and facilities and secure a tent that is adequate. You may not be the preacher or the pastor, but you can help by encouragement and just being there.

Ephraim is already on a downward spiral. Aloofness from God's people and their burdens is a sure sign that we are becoming estranged from the family of God and in urgent need of restoration. God help us to see the burdens we should carry and give us grace to release whatever help we are tempted to withhold.

Song

We will not fail if we fight as one
Each playing his own special part
None withholding help and support
Fighting as God's holy army

We will not fail if we give our all
Not counting the cost
knowing our Lord God gave His life
Fighting as God's holy army

Why are you unmoved by the pains of the saints
Focused on your own trials and nursing your pains
Be not deceived to think you can be at ease
Fighting as God's holy army.

There are times we feel weary and lonely
Confused on the plans for the field
His Spirit revives us as we advance forward
Fighting as God's holy army.

Prayer: Lord teach my hands to fight and to be ready to always do my part in God's army. Amen

DECEMBER 15

Joined to Idols

Bible Text: Hosea 4:17

Hos_4:17 Ephraim is joined to idols: let him alone.

It will be incomplete to study the story of Joseph without considering Ephraim in more detail. Ephraim was the younger of the sons of Joseph, son of Jacob, and Asenath, daughter of Potiphera (priest of the sun god Re of Heliopolis). Ephraim is the ancestor of the Tribe of Ephraim. Before his death, Jacob adopted his grandchildren Ephraim and Manasseh to be equal with his own sons (Genesis 48:5).

When Jacob blessed Joseph's two sons he placed his right hand on the head of the younger boy, Ephraim, and his left hand on the older boy, Manasseh. Joseph was displeased when his father laid his right hand on the younger grandson, rather than the older grandson. But Jacob said that although Manasseh would become the ancestor of a great nation, his younger brother would be the ancestor of an even greater nation. (Genesis 48:19). In the chronicles of the tribes, Ephraim therefore takes precedence over Manasseh in all matters, such as the order of marching, the consecration gifts for the Tabernacle, and the order of the allocation of land. When the Kingdom of Israel divided about 2900 years ago, the northern portion was often referred to by the name of Ephraim. In Revelation 7:1-8, Ephraim is strangely not listed as one of the tribes receiving the Seal of God for 12,000 of its members. The name Ephraim means "fruitful." How does Ephraim end up so badly?

The morale is not to relax on promises and prophesies but remain constantly watchful . . . being careful concerning over confidence. Destinies can be marred if careless.

Your prayer must constantly be "Lord, let my end be good" . . .

Song

We rest on Thee, our Shield and our Defender!
We go not forth alone against the foe;
Strong in Thy strength, safe in Thy keeping tender,
We rest on Thee, and in Thy Name we go.
Strong in Thy strength, safe in Thy keeping tender,
We rest on Thee, and in Thy Name we go.

Yes, in Thy Name, O Captain of salvation!
In Thy dear Name, all other names above;
Jesus our Righteousness, our sure Foundation,
Our Prince of glory and our King of love.
Jesus our Righteousness, our sure Foundation,
Our Prince of glory and our King of love.

We go in faith, our own great weakness feeling,
And needing more each day Thy grace to know:
Yet from our hearts a song of triumph pealing,
"We rest on Thee, and in Thy Name we go."
Yet from our hearts a song of triumph pealing,
"We rest on Thee, and in Thy Name we go."

Prayer: Lord help me to end well. Amen

December 16

Left Alone

Bible Text: Hosea 4:17

Hos_4:17 Ephraim is joined to idols: let him alone.

Ephraim ends up being the standard in unrepentant idolatry. This is likened to a spiritual prostitution . . . compared to whoredom. But why does his happen. Many things lead to idolatry. First is disobedience to God in dealing with sin . . . soon we must be accepted by other gods not as fussy with our errant ways. Another is continued interaction and convenient alliances with cultures that were meant to be destroyed. We often think we can progressively win over evil, but it is evil that often prevails over the spiritually unwatchful. Finally, laziness in spiritual warfare . . . not praying and studying the word will often lead to being brainwashed by a compelling worldview.

But what is so special about Ephraim's idolatry. Is it the length of spiritual prostitution . . . grieving God—day and night for many years ? Is it the rejection of the exalted spiritual positioning that God accorded to Ephraim over Manasseh—and an overconfidence that ends with physical and spiritual whoredom? Or is it the hardness and refusal to hearken to pleas and prophetic warnings? God decides not to bother Ephraim anymore. Let no man reprove him . . . leave him to be given to his own heart's lusts. It is a dangerous sign when we do not hear God warning and chastening us again. When God does not invest in further means to correct us . . . when we have our own defensive answers to all questions seeking to arrest our pride and arrogance? When these happen it may be that God is saying . . . let him alone. It is a very sad conclusion if God eventually says . . . leave him in his sin. This is not grace but the worst of judgments.

God does not continue to correct us when we are hard and prefer to strive with Him. After a while, He must say . . . leave that case alone . . . she will not learn. There are those that will not listen to any sermon and will not respond to any counseling. There is no point trying to change the outcome of certain developments. God may have predetermined a horrible perdition. What is painful is that Ephraim started so well but gradually slipped into pride, slothfulness, unbelief and a progressive hardening and ended badly. Lord, help us to serve you well till the very end.

Song

O Jesus, I have promised to serve Thee to the end;
Be Thou forever near me, my Master and my Friend;
I shall not fear the battle if Thou art by my side,
Nor wander from the pathway if Thou wilt be my Guide.

O let me feel Thee near me! The world is ever near;
I see the sights that dazzle, the tempting sounds I hear;
My foes are ever near me, around me and within;
But Jesus, draw Thou nearer, and shield my soul from sin.

O let me hear Thee speaking in accents clear and still,
Above the storms of passion, the murmurs of self will.
O speak to reassure me, to hasten or control;
O speak, and make me listen, Thou Guardian of my soul.

Prayer: Lord help me to serve you till the very end. Amen

DECEMBER 17

Song of Salvation

Bible Text: Zec 10:6

Zec_10:6 And I will strengthen the house of Judah, and I will save the house of Joseph, and I will bring them again to place them; for I have mercy upon them: and they shall be as though I had not cast them off: for I am the LORD their God, and will hear them.

God does not cast away the entire house of Joseph. God is committed to rescue His remnant. He pledges through the prophet to bring back the house of Joseph . . . to have mercy upon them such that they be as those that were never cast off. God says this will happen again because the Lord strong and mighty is their God. And God hears our cries. God will not permit His own to be completely downcast. God rescues and God saves.

God saves because He is God and as He has promised there is none to stop Him. When God decides to have mercy—who can question or dispute His mercy. The Lord Jesus is sent as our salvation—our hope, our reward. Where Joseph is a shadow, Jesus Christ is the perfection of God's mercy to His children.

This text foretells a time when both Judah and Israel will be strengthened, and rescued from a calamity. Jesus saves. Jesus strengthens. You will not be cast away. There is a mercy the world has never seen before. There is a strength that is beyond all comparison. The prophet Zechariah declares a salvation, that the reader can receive in Christ Jesus. The salvation of God has come. Jesus will hear and answer you. Today. The beauty of God's salvation is such that when it comes it will be as though you had never been cast off before. Rejoice for today your God will hear and answer you. No more will you be cast off. No more will you be desolate. Receive Christ and His salvation afresh.

Song

My Jesus, I love Thee, I know Thou art mine;
For Thee all the follies of sin I resign.
My gracious Redeemer, my Savior art Thou;
If ever I loved Thee, my Jesus, 'tis now.

I love Thee because Thou has first loved me,
And purchased my pardon on Calvary's tree.
I love Thee for wearing the thorns on Thy brow;
If ever I loved Thee, my Jesus, 'tis now.

I'll love Thee in life, I will love Thee in death,
And praise Thee as long as Thou lendest me breath;
And say when the death dew lies cold on my brow,
If ever I loved Thee, my Jesus, 'tis now.

In mansions of glory and endless delight,
I'll ever adore Thee in Heaven so bright;
I'll sing with the glittering crown on my brow;
If ever I loved Thee, my Jesus, 'tis now

Prayer: Lord I surrender my life to you. Hear me and bring me back to you. Amen

December 18

Another Joseph

Bible Text: Mat 1:16

Mat 1:16 And Jacob begat Joseph the husband of Mary, of whom was born Jesus, who is called Christ. . . . Mat 1:18 Now the birth of Jesus Christ was on this wise: When as his mother Mary was espoused to Joseph, before they came together, she was found with child of the Holy Ghost.

Jesus comes from the tribe of Judah and not Joseph as was prophesied. Christ was a child of the Holy Ghost. The father of Jesus is the Holy Ghost. The mother is a virgin—Mary. Joseph will take care of Mary and look after her as his wife in a very difficult circumstance. The Bible says this Joseph was a just man. Can you be trusted with that which is born of the Holy Ghost? The birth of Christ put Joseph in a very difficult situation, which must be borne faithfully.

To be selected, to be trusted with the workings of the Holy Spirit is a great honor bestowed to His own. The Bible says that as many as are led by the Holy Ghost it is these that are the children of God. The Holy Ghost moves in our life and rules our decisions and our lives are shaped based on faith in God.

Did some laugh at Joseph? Was Joseph advised to put Mary out? Would Joseph have been sensible based on the evidence to quietly put Mary away? God does not need us? Jesus could have been born in any circumstance and still be God . . . but Joseph was chosen. For Joseph, it was an opportunity. Joseph was faithful, he was just . . . the work of the Holy Spirit was safe and well kept in the house of Joseph. Joseph will be led by the Holy Ghost . . . protecting Mary and taking the child to Egypt . . . to safety as he was commanded. Joseph was a good and faithful servant . . . in the end, there is a "well done" waiting for Joseph.

Will it be said that you were faithful? What is the work of the Holy Ghost in your hand? How are you taking care of it? In the end? Will God say . . . well done?

Song

O thou who camest from above
the fire celestial to impart,
kindle a flame of sacred love
on the mean altar of my heart.

There let it for thy glory burn
with inextinguishable blaze,
and trembling to its source return
in humble prayer and fervent praise.

Jesus, confirm my heart's desire
to work and speak and think for thee;
still let me guard the holy fire
and still stir up the gift in me.

Still let me prove thy perfect will,
my acts of faith and love repeat,
till death thy endless mercies seal,
and make the sacrifice complete

Prayer: Lord, Help me to be faithful as the Holy Spirit moves in my life, around me and through me. Amen

DECEMBER 19

The Sermon of Stephen

Bible Text: Acts 7:6-18:51-52

Act 7:6 And God spake on this wise, That his seed should sojourn in a strange land; and that they should bring them into bondage, and entreat them evil four hundred years. 7 And the nation to whom they shall be in bondage will I judge, said God: and after that shall they come forth, and serve me in this place. 8 And he gave him the covenant of circumcision: and so Abraham begat Isaac, and circumcised him the eighth day; and Isaac begat Jacob; and Jacob begat the twelve patriarchs. 9 And the patriarchs, moved with envy, sold Joseph into Egypt: but God was with him, 10 And delivered him out of all his afflictions, and gave him favour and wisdom in the sight of Pharaoh king of Egypt; and he made him governor over Egypt and all his house. 11 Now there came a dearth over all the land of Egypt and Chanaan, and great affliction: and our fathers found no sustenance. 12 But when Jacob heard that there was corn in Egypt, he sent out our fathers first. 13 And at the second time Joseph was made known to his brethren; and Joseph's kindred was made known unto Pharaoh. 14 Then sent Joseph, and called his father Jacob to him, and all his kindred, threescore and fifteen souls. 15 So Jacob went down into Egypt, and died, he, and our fathers, :16 And were carried over into Sychem, and laid in the sepulchre that Abraham bought for a sum of money of the sons of Emmor the father of Sychem. 17 But when the time of the promise drew nigh, which God had sworn to Abraham, the people grew and multiplied in Egypt, 18 Till another king arose, which knew not Joseph. . . . Act 7:51 Ye stiffnecked and uncircumcised in heart and ears, ye do always resist the Holy Ghost: as your fathers did, so do ye. 52 Which of the prophets have not your fathers persecuted? and they have slain them which shewed before of the coming of the Just One; of whom ye have been now the betrayers and murderers:

Joseph's life . . . be it with his brothers or in Egypt was the working of the Holy Ghost. But this was a work that was resisted by men. Why did the brothers hate Joseph so . . . Stephen declares that his hearers are stiff necked people whose pedigree is to resist whatever the Holy Ghost is doing. But which of the works of the Holy Ghost could they stop . . . none. In spite of slaying prophets before them and persecuting those that God will use . . . God still is unstoppable . . . The Just One—Jesus Christ could not be stopped by Herod . . . and Him they betrayed and murdered. But God is unstoppable. Even if the flesh can be stopped as Stephen was physically stopped . . . his Spirit was received by God . . . . unstopped.

Unfortunately, people have not changed. The true gospel still cause many men to gnash their teeth in hatred. Be calm. This was the pattern even at the time of the patriarchs . . . the work of the Holy Ghost was always resisted and hated . . . but God still moved in ways they could not fathom or answer to. If the brothers knew other ways of stopping Joseph, they would still have tried it. When Joseph emerged as prime minister in Egypt—all the methods to stop him had been all exhausted.

When God sets you on top, all His enemies will have their hands tied and all their means of stopping you—exhausted.

Song

You are the mighty God—the great I am
Hallelujah Hallelujah
You are the mighty God—the great I am
Hallelujah Hallelujah

Prayer: Lord, Make me Unstoppable. Amen

DECEMBER 20

Faith in God

Bible Text: Heb 11:21

Heb_11:21 *By faith Jacob, when he was a dying, blessed both the sons of Joseph; and worshipped, leaning upon the top of his staff.*

The most important and critical currency of the saint is faith and not dollars or pounds sterling. The enemy really does not need to attack your finances or even your health if he knows that your faith will still stand. Immediately Satan knows your faith will not be moved by loss or gains of that which is material . . . then he leaves that territory and finds something else. It is what we do by faith that is most potent in the kingdom and no what we do by sight.

There is a difference when we bless based on what we can see and do and when we bless based on faith in God. The more unlikely and impossible the situation, the greater the glory and more of faith is required . . . and God's will and unmatchable victories are best seen in scenarios of faith. Faith is important. Faith is a weapon . . . even when it is as small as a mustard seed . . . it will move mountains.

Joshua was told everywhere his feet touches belongs to Him . . . Abraham was told everywhere he could see would belong to Him . . . some received immediately what they believed . . . and others believed as well in the invisible elements of their possessions . . . they believed in Heaven and sought a better resurrection i.e. to be raptured first among the dead before the living. God is pleased by our faith. Whatever happens to you which will increase your faith is a good thing. Pray for more faith. Guard your faith. Protect the faith you have by reading the word, hiding the word in your heart and by doing the works of faith to reinforce your capacity to trust God.

Remember the woman who was called a dog, but who said . . . even dogs can find crumbs to satisfy them. Faith answered when life taunted and mocked her. Jesus said He had never seen such faith. The best genre of faith comes in the winter seasons. When we are unable to stand when things are very tough . . . it means we really had less than little faith that can move mountains. May God help our faith.

Song

Faith of our fathers, living still,
In spite of dungeon, fire and sword;
O how our hearts beat high with joy
Whenever we hear that glorious Word!

Faith of our fathers, holy faith!
We will be true to thee till death.

Faith of our fathers, we will strive
To win all nations unto Thee;
And through the truth that comes from God,
We all shall then be truly free.

Faith of our fathers, we will love
Both friend and foe in all our strife;
And preach Thee, too, as love knows how
By kindly words and virtuous life.

Prayer: Lord, Increase my Faith. Help my Faith. Strengthen my faith. Amen

DECEMBER 21

More Excellent Faith

Bible Text: Heb 11:22

Heb 11:22 By faith Joseph, when he died, made mention of the departing of the children of Israel; and gave commandment concerning his bones.

There are different measures and quality of faith. There is faith like a mustard seed. There is uncommon faith like the faith of the woman who was called a dog. There is faith to bless our children to be what they must be even when the circumstances oppose the blessing. But there is a more excellent faith which sees beyond our physical existence beyond the curtains of death into eternity. Joseph had a faith that saw through centuries of bondage to a deliverance that was far into the future. He saw the promised land and gave a commandment concerning it.

There is a faith that causes us to act as though we are children of eternity. A faith that looks beyond what the world can ever give to another existence in which all tears will be wiped off. A faith that makes mention of a rapture that amuses some great theologians . . . that declares a millennium that seems so far removed from today's realities. Most will ask you to live for today or at least for what you will receive on this earth. But Joseph's faith extended beyond this earthly realm . . . he saw a departing . . . he saw a promised land.

What do you see? Faith to receive for yourself? Faith to bless yourself? Faith to bless your children for the future? Faith beyond your life time? Faith beyond even this side of existence into eternity? Faith that sees the eternal city . . . the invisible city . . . Heavenly Jerusalem . . . a city which hath foundations, whose builder and maker is God?

Heb 11.8 By faith Abraham, when he was called to go out into a place which he should after receive for an inheritance, obeyed; and he went out, not knowing whither he went. 9 By faith he sojourned in the land of promise, as in a strange country, dwelling in tabernacles with Isaac and Jacob, the heirs with him of the same promise: 10 For he looked for a city which hath foundations, whose builder and maker is God.

Seek growth in faith and expansion of faith more than you seek financial wealth.

Song

And once again the scene was changed;
New earth there seemed to be;
I saw the Holy City
Beside the tideless sea;
The light of God was on its streets,
The gates were open wide,
And all who would might enter,
And no one was denied.
No need of moon or stars by night,
Or sun to shine by day;
It was the new Jerusalem
That would not pass away.

Jerusalem! Jerusalem! Sing for the night is o'er!
Hosanna in the highest! Hosanna for evermore!.

Prayer: Lord, expand my faith to see beyond the night . . . to see the Holy City - lighted of God. Amen

DECEMBER 22

Hope for Dry Bones

Bible Text: Heb 11:22

Heb 11:22 By faith Joseph, when he died, made mention of the departing of the children of Israel; and gave commandment concerning his bones.

Joseph does an unusual thing. He gives a commandment to reposition his bones, centuries after his death. He believes that even when these bones are dried and apart, they can and will still live. He does not want to wake up in Egypt or to be revived in the tomb of Pharaohs surrounded by beautiful treasures.

Jacob must have passed on the truth of God's eternity and the revival of the dead to be eternally with Christ. Dry bones can live again and become a mighty army. The dead and dried bones of the saints will be the first to rise to join Christ when the trumpet sounds. Then the living will be raptured. This is what the Bible teaches. But after a period they will return to the earth . . . Christ with ten thousand of His saints as predicted by Enoch to reign and rule with Christ. Ezekiel equally prophesied of dry bones one day becoming an army

Eze 37:3 And he said unto me, Son of man, can these bones live? And I answered, O Lord GOD, thou knowest. 4 Again he said unto me, Prophesy upon these bones, and say unto them, O ye dry bones, hear the word of the LORD. 5 Thus saith the Lord GOD unto these bones; Behold, I will cause breath to enter into you, and ye shall live: 6 And I will lay sinews upon you, and will bring up flesh upon you, and cover you with skin, and put breath in you, and ye shall live; and ye shall know that I am the LORD. 7 So I prophesied as I was commanded: and as I prophesied, there was a noise, and behold a shaking, and the bones came together, bone to his bone. 8 And when I beheld, lo, the sinews and the flesh came up upon them, and the skin covered them above: but there was no breath in them. 9 Then said he unto me, Prophesy unto the wind, prophesy, son of man, and say to the wind, Thus saith the Lord GOD; Come from the four winds, O breath, and breathe upon these slain, that they may live. 10 So I prophesied as he commanded me, and the breath came into them, and they lived, and stood up upon their feet, an exceeding great army.

Joseph knew that God could do the impossible and that even dried bones can live again. Do you act and give commandments as though God can do the impossible? Do you know all the faded rose bushes will next summer bloom again with beautiful flowers. God uses nature to teach us that He causes beauty to replace that which we see as ashes. God is creative to bring the best out of nothing. Who told Joseph to give a commandment concerning his bones? It can only be God. Are there instructions God has given you that you consider ridiculous?

Song

I planted a little rosebush
And tended it with care
Its bud begins to blossom
Its sweet fragrance filled the air.
And winter came and it withered
Its petals drooped and fell to the ground
My heart faints as it faded
Cos I'd forgotten who had made it.

Chorus
Roses will bloom again - just wait and see
Don't mourn what might have been - only God knows how and when Roses will bloom again.

Prayer: Lord, cause life to return to all our dry and dead places. Revive us again. Amen

December 23

Revelation of the End

Bible Text: Rev. 7

Rev 7:1 And after these things I saw four angels standing on the four corners of the earth, holding the four winds of the earth, that the wind should not blow on the earth, nor on the sea, nor on any tree. 2 And I saw another angel ascending from the east, having the seal of the living God: and he cried with a loud voice to the four angels, to whom it was given to hurt the earth and the sea, 3 Saying, Hurt not the earth, neither the sea, nor the trees, till we have sealed the servants of our God in their foreheads. 4 And I heard the number of them which were sealed: and there were sealed an hundred and forty and four thousand of all the tribes of the children of Israel. 5 Of the tribe of Juda were sealed twelve thousand. Of the tribe of Reuben were sealed twelve thousand. Of the tribe of Gad were sealed twelve thousand. 6 Of the tribe of Aser were sealed twelve thousand. Of the tribe of Nepthalim were sealed twelve thousand. Of the tribe of Manasses were sealed twelve thousand. 7 Of the tribe of Simeon were sealed twelve thousand. Of the tribe of Levi were sealed twelve thousand. Of the tribe of Issachar were sealed twelve thousand. 8 Of the tribe of Zabulon were sealed twelve thousand. Of the tribe of Joseph were sealed twelve thousand. Of the tribe of Benjamin were sealed twelve thousand.

What happens in the end is what matters most. It does not count if we did great acts or we suffered though many efforts. The question is that after all these things . . . did we make Heaven? Some will make it and many will not. Most will find it is now too late to do that which they could easily have done which they deferred to another day i.e. repentance. Why do you delay to repent? Are you so certain that your name remains in the book of life? What gives you your confidence when you have many hurts unforgiven and have not reconciled with God on many issues . . . your confession of sin is incomplete and you know that the last few years, you have had no personal devotion with your creator. What gives you your confidence?

But then, your thoughts of the end need not be gloomy if you have the witness of the Holy Spirit that all is well. You are waiting joyfully to be united with your God. You are so excited that the appointed time has come. Soon there will be no more night sand no more pains. On the list of tribes . . . a few are missing. Lord I pray that on that final day, may I not be missing from the gathering of the redeemed.

Song

I am rejoicing my name has been written
I am rejoicing that I am born again
Hallelujah

Prayer: Lord, Help me. Do not let my joys to be turned to shame in the final appointed day of your coming. Amen

December 24

Four Angels

Bible Text: Rev. 7

Rev 7:1 And after these things I saw four angels standing on the four corners of the earth, holding the four winds of the earth, that the wind should not blow on the earth, nor on the sea, nor on any tree. 2 And I saw another angel ascending from the east, having the seal of the living God: and he cried with a loud voice to the four angels, to whom it was given to hurt the earth and the sea, 3 Saying, Hurt not the earth, neither the sea, nor the trees, till we have sealed the servants of our God in their foreheads. 4 And I heard the number of them which were sealed: and there were sealed an hundred and forty and four thousand of all the tribes of the children of Israel. 5 Of the tribe of Juda were sealed twelve thousand. Of the tribe of Reuben were sealed twelve thousand. Of the tribe of Gad were sealed twelve thousand. 6 Of the tribe of Aser were sealed twelve thousand. Of the tribe of Nepthalim were sealed twelve thousand. Of the tribe of Manasses were sealed twelve thousand. 7 Of the tribe of Simeon were sealed twelve thousand. Of the tribe of Levi were sealed twelve thousand. Of the tribe of Issachar were sealed twelve thousand. 8 Of the tribe of Zabulon were sealed twelve thousand. Of the tribe of Joseph were sealed twelve thousand. Of the tribe of Benjamin were sealed twelve thousand.

These four angels feature in the final mention of the tribe of Joseph amongst the sealed in the book of revelation. God uses these angels to restrain four different winds that will not be permitted to blow. The angels of God can hold wind . . . so powerful and so obedient. They stand exactly where they have been instructed—on the four corners of the earth . . . their reach covers the entire globe. But observe that they wait for God . . . existing with all power only to serve the will of God and please God.

The four winds may be doctrines, ideas, evils, thoughts, errors . . . fast spreading ills that cannot be contained by mortal men. God commands that they be restrained so His will is done. I want you to consider this text to understand that the will and purposes of God are not sustained by you or your prayers but by awesome and completely obedient majestic beings . . . supernatural powers that await God's instructions.

When the angles holding the winds are withdrawn and these winds are permitted, we cannot imagine the tribulation and the terrors awaiting inhabitants of the earth. We live and breathe only because God restrains winds against us. We can see another day only because angels permit it to be so. When there are disasters or strange far reaching continental disasters . . . it may be the angels simply releasing their hold only slightly and the result is that nations and millions are devastated . . . even as strange religions and cults devour souls. Thank God that He is in control . . . restraining all that must be stopped from blowing upon the earth, seas and trees until His purpose is accomplished and His will is sealed.

Song

For the beauty of the earth - For the glory of the skies,
For the love which from our birth - Over and around us lies.

Lord of all, to Thee we raise, This our hymn of grateful praise.
For the beauty of each hour, Of the day and of the night,

Hill and vale, and tree and flower, Sun and moon, and stars of light.
For the joy of ear and eye, For the heart and mind's delight,

For the mystic harmony - Linking sense to sound and sight.
For the joy of human love, Brother, sister, parent, child,

Friends on earth and friends above, For all gentle thoughts and mild.

Prayer: Lord, Thank you for your unseen majesty sustaining your will in my life. Amen

December 25

The Seal of the Living God

Bible Text: Rev. 7

Rev 7:1 And after these things I saw four angels standing on the four corners of the earth, holding the four winds of the earth, that the wind should not blow on the earth, nor on the sea, nor on any tree. 2 And I saw another angel ascending from the east, having the seal of the living God: and he cried with a loud voice to the four angels, to whom it was given to hurt the earth and the sea, 3 Saying, Hurt not the earth, neither the sea, nor the trees, till we have sealed the servants of our God in their foreheads. 4 And I heard the number of them which were sealed: and there were sealed an hundred and forty and four thousand of all the tribes of the children of Israel. 5 Of the tribe of Juda were sealed twelve thousand. Of the tribe of Reuben were sealed twelve thousand. Of the tribe of Gad were sealed twelve thousand. 6 Of the tribe of Aser were sealed twelve thousand. Of the tribe of Nepthalim were sealed twelve thousand. Of the tribe of Manasses were sealed twelve thousand. 7 Of the tribe of Simeon were sealed twelve thousand. Of the tribe of Levi were sealed twelve thousand. Of the tribe of Issachar were sealed twelve thousand. 8 Of the tribe of Zabulon were sealed twelve thousand. Of the tribe of Joseph were sealed twelve thousand. Of the tribe of Benjamin were sealed twelve thousand.

The other angel came with the seal of God. Seal means approval. The approval was meant to come before the four winds would be released to hurt the earth, sea or trees. Again, it is all the grace of God . . . because if the winds were not controlled none would stand or be sealed. Who is able to stand or be anything if not for the help of God. The principle of God helping the choicest of saints to stand makes us even more appreciative of the awesome grace and mercy that sustains us.

Reflect on that grace and mercy. Think about the things and events that have been withheld to ensure you become what God wants you to be. Winds of doctrine that have not been permitted to derail your faith as well as winds of sickness and terror that will not be allowed to touch you, until His seal of life has been firmly placed on you.

Job 5:19 He shall deliver thee in six troubles: yea, in seven there shall no evil touch thee. 20 In famine he shall redeem thee from death: and in war from the power of the sword. 21 Thou shalt be hid from the scourge of the tongue: neither shalt thou be afraid of destruction when it cometh. 22 At destruction and famine thou shalt laugh: neither shalt thou be afraid of the beasts of the earth.

Job identifies four winds . . . famine, (war)power of the sword, scourge of the tongue(scandal) and beasts of the earth (evil personalities) . . . these winds have not been permitted to hurt you. Concerning them you will laugh . . . but when you see others bow to them, thank God for your preservation. Do not for a minute think that it was your prayers or your strength that defended you concerning these winds . . . have you considered people living in famine, amongst warring tribes, under fierce accusation and facing demonic beasts? . . . were you in any way better saints than saints in these conditions? No . . . mercy helped you.

I am praying for someone reading this devotional. At destruction and famine, you shall laugh . . . neither shall you be afraid of the beasts that have positioned to devour you. Even in seven troubles, no evil will be permitted to touch you. But give all the glory to the restrainer, the Lord—strong and mighty.

Song

You are worthy O Lord 2ce Invisible God—the miracle worker, you are worthy O Lord
You are mighty O Lord 2ce Invisible God—the miracle worker, you are mighty O Lord
Invisible God—the miracle worker, you are worthy) Lord

Prayer: Lord, make me a sign and a wonder to display your great miraculous preservations. Amen

December 26

The Servants of our God

Bible Text: Rev. 7

Rev 7:1 And after these things I saw four angels standing on the four corners of the earth, holding the four winds of the earth, that the wind should not blow on the earth, nor on the sea, nor on any tree. 2 And I saw another angel ascending from the east, having the seal of the living God: and he cried with a loud voice to the four angels, to whom it was given to hurt the earth and the sea, 3 Saying, Hurt not the earth, neither the sea, nor the trees, till we have sealed the servants of our God in their foreheads. 4 And I heard the number of them which were sealed: and there were sealed an hundred and forty and four thousand of all the tribes of the children of Israel. 5 Of the tribe of Juda were sealed twelve thousand. Of the tribe of Reuben were sealed twelve thousand. Of the tribe of Gad were sealed twelve thousand. 6 Of the tribe of Aser were sealed twelve thousand. Of the tribe of Nepthalim were sealed twelve thousand. Of the tribe of Manasses were sealed twelve thousand. 7 Of the tribe of Simeon were sealed twelve thousand. Of the tribe of Levi were sealed twelve thousand. Of the tribe of Issachar were sealed twelve thousand. 8 Of the tribe of Zabulon were sealed twelve thousand. Of the tribe of Joseph were sealed twelve thousand. Of the tribe of Benjamin were sealed twelve thousand.

Those sealed for eternal life are described as the servants of our God. To serve God is an awesome privilege. There are many gods that are not our God and we can do several things that serve ourselves, our agenda but not the Most High God. What does it mean to serve the most high God. It means to know God, to seek His pleasure and to do His will. It means to live for His pleasure and to use resources for His kingdom agenda. Servants have denied themselves of certain rights and have accepted a humbling that comes with the role but only to please God. They have been chosen for the most arduous tasks, and to go to spread the gospel of Christ where others fail. Servants are denied of normal rewards and must defer the gratification that comes with fair remuneration . . . but knowing that they serve a rewarder of them who diligently serve Him. Why are these described as servants of our God? It is because God demands and values service, but not any kind of service . . . there must be haste, zeal, faithfulness and much endurance . . . many servants will die for their master for the love that they have for them . . . but Jesus already died for us . . . for our salvation.

Still we were saved to serve Him . . . Worship and service is linked. True children of God will serve as no one else can . . . have you ever observed these small family businesses and how the children of the owner look after the interests of the owner. Much better service, giving longer hours beyond what paid employees give and watching over the interest of the business beyond the normal call of duty. May we serve Him like favored children.

Song

I was born to love you . . . to serve you
I was born to know you
I was born to please you . . . to love you
Let me be . . . what I was born to be.

I was born to love you . . . to serve you
I was born to worship you
To yield to and honor you forever
Let me be . . . what I was born to be.

Prayer: Lord, I want to serve you . . . show me how . . . teach me how. Let my service please you. Amen

DECEMBER 27

Rare Overcomers

Bible Text: Rev. 7

Rev 7:1 And after these things I saw four angels standing on the four corners of the earth, holding the four winds of the earth, that the wind should not blow on the earth, nor on the sea, nor on any tree. 2 And I saw another angel ascending from the east, having the seal of the living God: and he cried with a loud voice to the four angels, to whom it was given to hurt the earth and the sea, 3 Saying, Hurt not the earth, neither the sea, nor the trees, till we have sealed the servants of our God in their foreheads. 4 And I heard the number of them which were sealed: and there were sealed an hundred and forty and four thousand of all the tribes of the children of Israel. 5 Of the tribe of Juda were sealed twelve thousand. Of the tribe of Reuben were sealed twelve thousand. Of the tribe of Gad were sealed twelve thousand. 6 Of the tribe of Aser were sealed twelve thousand. Of the tribe of Nepthalim were sealed twelve thousand. Of the tribe of Manasses were sealed twelve thousand. 7 Of the tribe of Simeon were sealed twelve thousand. Of the tribe of Levi were sealed twelve thousand. Of the tribe of Issachar were sealed twelve thousand. 8 Of the tribe of Zabulon were sealed twelve thousand. Of the tribe of Joseph were sealed twelve thousand. Of the tribe of Benjamin were sealed twelve thousand.

The sealed . . . the chosen of God are overcomers because they have been preselected to overcome. God does not release His chosen ones under strong contrary situations without sealing them in safety. By this mark, they are pre-known . . . and seen in the Spirit as different. The mark is on their forehead suggesting that they are known even to principalities that these are the sealed of the Most High God. Even in the worst of trials and temptations, God is already faithful to have made us overcomers ahead of any troubles. The sealed servants are protected in two ways . . . first . . . evil is not permitted until they are sealed and when any evil is permitted to blow, they will overcome . . . not because of anything they can do or not do but because of their identity as God's sealed children and supernatural help linked to the seal of God on their lives.

The lesson is that God sets His chosen apart for safety and mercy even in the worst of times. The other lesson is the concept of a final seal that nothing will be able to unseal. This unusual mercy is reserved for servants . . . this verse pictures a rare grace that is available even in extreme of difficulties . . . so that the servants of God will be permitted to complete their assignments even under the worst of spiritual and physical attacks. Whether the winds are errors, evils or powerful corruptions—they will be delayed until the sealed are well marked out and then the mark of God upon their foreheads send a clear signal to any evil wind that this one is an overcomer . . . no matter what. God's overcomers are unstoppable and helped to defeat every evil wind . . . protected from seeing death until the appointed time.

Song

There is a redeemer, Jesus, God's own Son,
Precious Lamb of God, Messiah, Holy One,

Jesus my redeemer, Name above all names,
Precious Lamb of God, Messiah, Oh, for sinners slain.

Thank you oh my father, For giving us your Son,
And leaving Your Spirit, 'Til the work on Earth is done

Prayer: Lord, Mark me with your seal of life. Amen

DECEMBER 28

The Final List

Bible Text: Rev. 7

Rev 7:1 And after these things I saw four angels standing on the four corners of the earth, holding the four winds of the earth, that the wind should not blow on the earth, nor on the sea, nor on any tree. 2 And I saw another angel ascending from the east, having the seal of the living God: and he cried with a loud voice to the four angels, to whom it was given to hurt the earth and the sea, 3 Saying, Hurt not the earth, neither the sea, nor the trees, till we have sealed the servants of our God in their foreheads. 4 And I heard the number of them which were sealed: and there were sealed an hundred and forty and four thousand of all the tribes of the children of Israel. 5 Of the tribe of Juda were sealed twelve thousand. Of the tribe of Reuben were sealed twelve thousand. Of the tribe of Gad were sealed twelve thousand. 6 Of the tribe of Aser were sealed twelve thousand. Of the tribe of Nepthalim were sealed twelve thousand. Of the tribe of Manasses were sealed twelve thousand. 7 Of the tribe of Simeon were sealed twelve thousand. Of the tribe of Levi were sealed twelve thousand. Of the tribe of Issachar were sealed twelve thousand. 8 Of the tribe of Zabulon were sealed twelve thousand. Of the tribe of Joseph were sealed twelve thousand. Of the tribe of Benjamin were sealed twelve thousand.

In the Bible we often see many lists of the tribes with different significance. This is probably the most important of lists. There is a list by order of birth of the Children of Jacob. Then there is a list with Joseph elevated to a double portion and Simeon excluded as Moses blesses the tribes . . . there are other lists but this final one is said to be the list of the sealed . . . the final chosen. We notice certain tribes omitted.

We also know that names can be blotted from God's Book as Moses was told . . . _

Exo_32:33 And the LORD said unto Moses, Whosoever hath sinned against me, him will I blot out of my book. . . . Rom 9:15 For he saith to Moses, I will have mercy on whom I will have mercy, and I will have compassion on whom I will have compassion. 16 So then it is not of him that willeth, nor of him that runneth, but of God that sheweth mercy.

We may think we have or have not sinned against our fellow men . . . but sin against God may be a completely different matter. Our apologies to men and confessions may have relieved us of certain consequences but to be blotted from the Book of God is surely a more serious issue. Two tribes are not mentioned . . . one is Ephraim and another is Dan. Also the order of the tribes is different . . . Judah is now first. Then we see that there is no difference in the numbers . . . much unlike most other lists where numbers differ greatly according to fruitfulness/physical expansion etc

God seems to be telling us something. First—God will blot whosoever has sinned against him . . . sin will not be trivial issue. Second—God is merciful . . . Reuben is forgiven and restored and so is Simeon . . . but Dan is missing. Third—Ephraim, who emerged as the star in the house of Joseph is omitted . . . teaching us that even stars must be watchful to end well. Fourth—Christ as the Lion of Judah exalts that tribe . . . and the name that is higher than any other name is honored in the final order of the sealed. Whether we see these lists as literal events or a picture or imagery . . . we will all need His mercy to make it to the end . . . to be forgiven we are taught that we must also forgive. May God help us all.

Song

So I'll cherish the old rugged cross,
Till my trophies at last I lay down;
I will cling to the old rugged cross,
And exchange it some day for a crown

Prayer: Lord, Help me to make it to the very end. Let me find mercy at the end . . . chastise me now, correct me now if you must . . . but be merciful to me at the end. Thank you. Amen

DECEMBER 29
Dan's Idolatry

Bible Text: Rev. 7

Rev 7:1 And after these things I saw four angels standing on the four corners of the earth, holding the four winds of the earth, that the wind should not blow on the earth, nor on the sea, nor on any tree. 2 And I saw another angel ascending from the east, having the seal of the living God: and he cried with a loud voice to the four angels, to whom it was given to hurt the earth and the sea, 3 Saying, Hurt not the earth, neither the sea, nor the trees, till we have sealed the servants of our God in their foreheads. 4 And I heard the number of them which were sealed: and there were sealed an hundred and forty and four thousands of all the tribes of the children of Israel. 5 Of the tribe of Juda were sealed twelve thousand. Of the tribe of Reuben were sealed twelve thousand. Of the tribe of Gad were sealed twelve thousand. 6 Of the tribe of Aser were sealed twelve thousand. Of the tribe of Nepthalim were sealed twelve thousand. Of the tribe of Manasses were sealed twelve thousand. 7 Of the tribe of Simeon were sealed twelve thousand. Of the tribe of Levi were sealed twelve thousand. Of the tribe of Issachar were sealed twelve thousand. 8 Of the tribe of Zabulon were sealed twelve thousand. Of the tribe of Joseph were sealed twelve thousand. Of the tribe of Benjamin were sealed twelve thousand.

In Wikipedia concerning Dan it was written. *"In the Book of Judges, in the account of Micah's Idol, describing the tribe of Dan as having used ephod and teraphim in worship, and Samson (a member of the tribe of Dan) being described as failing to adhere to the rules of a Nazarite, classical rabbinical writers concluded that Dan was very much a black sheep; in the Book of Jeremiah, the north of Canaan is associated with darkness and evil, and so rabbinical sources treated Dan as the archetype of wickedness. In the Blessing of Jacob, Dan is described as a serpent, which seems to have been interpreted as connecting Dan to Belial."*

We cannot precisely say why Dan was not mentioned in the final list of the tribes described as servants of God . . . but we see Dan setting up graven images also corrupting many others in the book of Judges.

Jdg 18:20 And the priest's heart was glad, and he took the ephod, and the teraphim, and the graven image, and went in the midst of the people. 21 So they turned and departed, and put the little ones and the cattle and the carriage before them. 22 And when they were a good way from the house of Micah, the men that were in the houses near to Micah's house were gathered together, and overtook the children of Dan. 23 And they cried unto the children of Dan. And they turned their faces, and said unto Micah, What aileth thee, that thou comest with such a company? 24 And he said, Ye have taken away my gods which I made, and the priest, and ye are gone away: and what have I more? and what is this that ye say unto me, What aileth thee? 25 And the children of Dan said unto him, Let not thy voice be heard among us, lest angry fellows run upon thee, and thou lose thy life, with the lives of thy household. 26 And the children of Dan went their way: and when Micah saw that they were too strong for him, he turned and went back unto his house. 27 And they took the things which Micah had made, and the priest which he had, and came unto Laish, unto a people that were at quiet and secure: and they smote them with the edge of the sword, and burnt the city with fire. 28 And there was no deliverer, because it was far from Zidon, and they had no business with any man; and it was in the valley that lieth by Bethrehob. And they built a city, and dwelt therein. 29 And they called the name of the city Dan, after the name of Dan their father, who was born unto Israel: howbeit the name of the city was Laish at the first. 30 And the children of Dan set up the graven image: and Jonathan, the son of Gershom, the son of Manasseh, he and his sons were priests to the tribe of Dan until the day of the captivity of the land. 31 And they set them up Micah's graven image, which he made, all the time that the house of God was in Shiloh.

It seems the ways of idolatry even with their own priests did not begin today. It is a few days after Christmas day—but many will agree that these days it has no resemblance in its observation to the remembrance of the birth of Christ. Instead, it has become an opportunity for all manner of idolatry . . . May God help us

Song

Come and worship. Worship Christ the new born King.

Prayer: Lord, Help me to worship you and you alone. Amen

DECEMBER 30

Dan and Ephraim

Bible Text: Rev. 7

Rev 7:1 And after these things I saw four angels standing on the four corners of the earth, holding the four winds of the earth, that the wind should not blow on the earth, nor on the sea, nor on any tree. 2 And I saw another angel ascending from the east, having the seal of the living God: and he cried with a loud voice to the four angels, to whom it was given to hurt the earth and the sea, 3 Saying, Hurt not the earth, neither the sea, nor the trees, till we have sealed the servants of our God in their foreheads. 4 And I heard the number of them which were sealed: and there were sealed an hundred and forty and four thousand of all the tribes of the children of Israel. 5 Of the tribe of Juda were sealed twelve thousand. Of the tribe of Reuben were sealed twelve thousand. Of the tribe of Gad were sealed twelve thousand. 6 Of the tribe of Aser were sealed twelve thousand. Of the tribe of Nepthalim were sealed twelve thousand. Of the tribe of Manasses were sealed twelve thousand. 7 Of the tribe of Simeon were sealed twelve thousand. Of the tribe of Levi were sealed twelve thousand. Of the tribe of Issachar were sealed twelve thousand. 8 Of the tribe of Zabulon were sealed twelve thousand. Of the tribe of Joseph were sealed twelve thousand. Of the tribe of Benjamin were sealed twelve thousand.

The tribes of Dan and Ephraim are missed out. Jeroboam, the wicked King from the tribe of Ephraim collaborated with Dan in the erection of calves to confuse the people in their worship. This was most successful as many did not go to Jerusalem to worship. This collaboration may also have cost these tribes to be excluded in God's final list of His servants. Amos spoke of this idolatry with Dan.

1Ki 12:28 Whereupon the king took counsel, and made two calves of gold, and said unto them, It is too much for you to go up to Jerusalem: behold thy gods, O Israel, which brought thee up out of the land of Egypt. 29 And he set the one in Bethel, and the other put he in Dan.

Some have said that this list does not mean that Ephraim was excluded from salvation or that Dan was punished. Indeed the tribe of Joseph could be the tribe of Ephraim. But the principle that God blots the names of those who sin against Him was established even from the times of Moses.

Jos_24:19 And Joshua said unto the people, Ye cannot serve the LORD: for he is an holy God; he is a jealous God; he will not forgive your transgressions nor your sins.

It is time to abandon all other gods . . . return to the true jealous God, the only God. Other gods who are not jealous . . . who are indifferent to what you do or do not do are not true. Jehovah will not be worshipped alongside mammon or any other god. I heard some other religions permit other gods and will tolerate wider variety in worship but not this God. He is a jealous God . . . do not expect Him to overlook sin. But you can repent.

Song

Then sings my soul, my Savior Lord to thee
How great thou art . . . how great thou art.
Then sings my soul, my Savior Lord to thee
How great thou art . . . how great thou art.

Prayer: Lord, You hate idolatry. Let me hate idolatry too. Amen

DECEMBER 31

Happy Ending

Bible Text: Rev. 7

Rev 7:1 And after these things I saw four angels standing on the four corners of the earth, holding the four winds of the earth, that the wind should not blow on the earth, nor on the sea, nor on any tree. 2 And I saw another angel ascending from the east, having the seal of the living God: and he cried with a loud voice to the four angels, to whom it was given to hurt the earth and the sea, 3 Saying, Hurt not the earth, neither the sea, nor the trees, till we have sealed the servants of our God in their foreheads. 4 And I heard the number of them which were sealed: and there were sealed an hundred and forty and four thousand of all the tribes of the children of Israel. 5 Of the tribe of Juda were sealed twelve thousand. Of the tribe of Reuben were sealed twelve thousand. Of the tribe of Gad were sealed twelve thousand. 6 Of the tribe of Aser were sealed twelve thousand. Of the tribe of Nepthalim were sealed twelve thousand. Of the tribe of Manasses were sealed twelve thousand. 7 Of the tribe of Simeon were sealed twelve thousand. Of the tribe of Levi were sealed twelve thousand. Of the tribe of Issachar were sealed twelve thousand. 8 Of the tribe of Zabulon were sealed twelve thousand. Of the tribe of Joseph were sealed twelve thousand. Of the tribe of Benjamin were sealed twelve thousand.

Reuben who started by defiling the bed of his father has been redeemed and forgiven. Simeon and Levi are no more scattered. Moses did not bless the tribe of Simeon at his death, but God has restored them back. God is a God of happy endings. Our expected end is a good one. God has no delight that any should perish. We see in many examples that God is good and His mercies endureth forever.

Mercy will undo what justice has said must be done. Mercy will balance out previous inequalities. God says He will have mercy on whom He chooses. We cannot deserve mercy or it will not be mercy. Why is it that some are forgiven and some are not? The true answer is that God is not answerable to any and His final company in eternity is determined by Him. He however told Moses that He will blot out from His book those who sin against Him. As the year ends, do not trivialize sin or mock at its cancerous spread. Sin has the agenda to frustrate you, not now . . . indeed now sin is sweet—but at the most important moment at the gate of eternity.

Song

When the roll I called up yonder
When the roll is called up yonder
When the roll is called up yonder
When the roll is called up yonder
I'll be there.

Prayer: Lord, As the year rolls to an end . . . help me to consider my life afresh . . . and to receive assurance from you that I am still on the path to God's eternal Heaven. Amen

AFTERWORD

Do you sense something is missing in your life? Do you sense that God has not appointed you to be one of the lost? The fulfillment of all your aspirations do not satisfy you because you were created by God for His pleasure. You have tried to fill your life with vain pursuits, acquisitions, new interests and experimented with different lifestyles and religions that only made you feel empty. All you need is a relationship with a person—JESUS.

First, recognize your need for Him, as you see your sins and struggles to finding an ever so elusive peace and joy. Acknowledge your sins and helplessness. Ask Him, to take over your life, as Lord and Savior, by inviting and welcoming Him into your heart. Believe that He is able to save you, as you have received Him in your heart.

John 1[12] But as many as received Him, to them He gave the right to become children of God, to those who believe in His name.

Get a Bible and start to read it. Begin from the Gospels in the New Testament. Ask God to lead you to a good Church, where the truth of the Word of God is preached. Tell everybody else what you have just done and experienced.

It is also possible that you were once an ardent believer and things did not go so well. You are perceived to have failed, but that is not God's assessment of you even though that is how others have labeled you. God is a God of second chances and new beginnings. When He forgives, although in His mercy there may be consequences, He releases us back to our destiny of glory. You can repent and come back to Him today. He will help you start afresh on the path of His truth.

Olabode Ososami
The Redeemed Christian Church of God
House of Victory Parish
59, Itire Rd, Surulere
Lagos, Nigeria
Email: Olabode@ososami.me

Wealth Out of Ashes

Bode Ososami

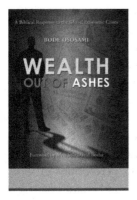

The book is a non-fiction general information Christian book with self help elements. This book seeks to answer questions like "What do you do when everything is melting down and the promises of God seem distant? . . . Is God still relevant in global crises and acute depression? . . . Are there explanations and responses that can put us back on track? It also explains how to see new opportunities in crisis situations.

Wealth out of Ashes was recognized for an award by USA BookNews (2009 National Awards) in the Christian Inspiration Category.

ISBN 978-1-4490-0021-9

Published by Authorhouse 2009

---

www.recessionproofchristianlife.com

The Majesty of God

Bode Ososami

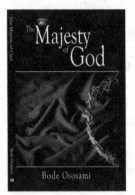

There can be no greater thing than to behold the glory of God in all His majesty. How can mere words extol the indescribable glitter of riches arrayed in a timeless, excellent, great and terrible glory ? The yearning to behold the King of kings who reigns in excellent and glorious majesty is the cry of many. "The Majesty of God" attempts a weak answer to such a plea. This volume, though offering only a vignette of what will unfold gloriously before us when we see Him as He is, still, by the special grace of God, promises a new radiance in the life of all that reflect prayerfully on its meditations. We cannot exceed our perceptions of God and so we need to constantly pray to see and behold His glory and majesty for our personal spiritual growth

ISBN 978-4567-7026-6

Published by Authorhouse 2010

www.recessionproofchristianlife.com

Worship in Spirit and in Truth

Bode Ososami

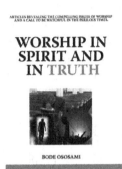

We are in the end-times and the call to watch and pray cannot have too many criers drawing out insights and seeking the face of God to guide and prepare the saints for the perilous times. Our attention must shift to the King of kings. Our focus must return again, truly and completely to Him . . . we must learn to retrace our steps and return to the narrow path of life.

ISBN 978-1-4389-3419-8

Published by Authorhouse 2008

www.recessionproofchristianlife.com

Perfect Fall Wedding

Bode Ososami

"Perfect Fall Wedding" awakens interest on what the Bible is principally about, a marriage. There is a strong sense of something different and need to prepare. We are in end times but cannot predict dates and hours. Harold Camping was wrong in his Oct 21 2011 prediction and many do not believe in Rapture. Read and form your own opinion.

The Jewish Feast of Trumpets, the first of unfulfilled fall feasts, foreshadows a coming royal marriage of the Messiah—ushered by Rapture of the bride. Decades ago, many found the prophecy of "The return of Jesus Christ" rather dour but not anymore. Today there is renewed interest in Bible prophecy, eschatology and readiness for the last days.

ISBN   978-1-4670-0188-5

Published by Authorhouse 2011

www.recessionproofchristianlife.com